I0813930

THE BOOK BY DESIGN

The University of Chicago Press, Chicago 60637

For more information, contact the University of Chicago Press, 1427 E. 60th St., Chicago, IL 60637.
Published 2023
Printed in Italy

32 31 30 29 28 27 26 25 24 23   1 2 3 4 5

ISBN-13: 978-0-226-82409-3 (cloth)
ISBN-13: 978-0-226-82410-9 (e-book)
DOI: https://doi.org/10.7208/chicago/9780226824109.001.0001

Published outside North and South America by the British Library, 2023.

Library of Congress Cataloging-in-Publication Data
Names: Marks, P. J. M., editor. | Parkin, Stephen, editor.
Title: The book by design : the remarkable story of the world's greatest invention / edited by P. J. M. Marks and Stephen Parkin.
Description: Chicago : The University of Chicago Press, 2023. | Includes bibliographical references and index.
Identifiers: LCCN 2023008520 | ISBN 9780226824093 (cloth) | ISBN 9780226824109 (ebook)
Subjects: LCSH: Books—History. | Printing—History.
Classification: LCC Z4 .B6444 2023 | DDC 002.09—dc23/eng/20230329
LC record available at https://lccn.loc.gov/2023008520

Project management by Alison Moss
Design and typesetting by Steve Russell
Photography by Jonathon Vines
Picture research by Sally Nicholls
Print production by Nicola Denny
Publisher: John Lee
Production Editor: Jonny Davidson

Printed and bound in Italy by L.E.G.O. S.p.A.

THE BOOK BY DESIGN

The Remarkable Story of the World's Greatest Invention

Edited by
P. J. M. Marks
&
Stephen Parkin

The University of Chicago Press

CONTENTS

The Contributors
08

Introduction
10

I.
THE LINDISFARNE GOSPELS
by Eleanor Jackson
16

Feature:
ETHIOPIA, AFRICAN SCRIBES AND THE ILLUSTRATED APOCALYPSE
by Eyob Derillo
26

II.
THE DIAMOND SUTRA PRINTED IN 868
by Mélodie Doumy
28

Feature:
THE DEVELOPMENT OF PAPER
by Lucy Vinten
38

III.
THE ARNSTEIN BIBLE
by Kathleen Doyle
40

Feature:
KING HENRY VIII'S COPY OF THE 'GREAT BIBLE'
by Karen Limper-Herz
48

IV.
THE GOLDEN HAGGADAH
by Ilana Tahan
50

V.
THE QUEEN MARY PSALTER
by Kathleen Doyle
60

Feature:
THE HARMONIES OF LITTLE GIDDING
by Felicity Myrone
70

VI.
THE MAINZ PSALTER OF 1457
by Adrian S. Edwards
74

VII.
HYPNEROTOMACHIA POLIPHILI
by Stephen Parkin
84

Feature:
BODONI'S *MANUALE TIPOGRAFICO* AND HIS FOLLOWERS
by Valentina Mirabella
94

VIII.
AKBAR'S *KHAMSAH* OF NIZAMI
by Ursula Sims-Williams
96

IX.
THE SHAKESPEARE FIRST FOLIO OF 1623
by Adrian S. Edwards
106

Feature:
THE TITLE PAGE AND OTHER PARATEXTS
by Stephen Parkin
116

X.
EXCERPTS FROM THE TALE OF GENJI
by Hamish Todd
118

Feature:
A MODERN MESOAMERICAN CODEX
by Mercedes Aguirre
130

XI.
WILLIAM LEIGHTON'S *THE TEARES OR LAMENTACIONS OF A SORROWFULL SOULE*
by James Ritzema and Christopher Scobie
132

Feature:
THE DESIGN OF HUMAN ATLASES
by Sophie Defrance
142

XII.
A DESCRIPTION OF THREE HUNDRED ANIMALS
by Lucy Evans
146

Feature:
MINIATURE BOOKS: THEIR CHARM AND PURPOSE
by Helen Peden and Annalisa Ricciardi
154

XIII.
A QUR'AN FROM ACEH
by Annabel Teh Gallop
158

XIV.
OWEN JONES'S *THE GRAMMAR OF ORNAMENT*
by Edmund M. B. King
168

Feature:
AMERICAN PUBLISHERS' BINDINGS, NINETEENTH CENTURY
by Edmund M. B. King
178

XV.
THE BUDDHA'S LAST BIRTH TALE
by Jana Igunma
180

Feature:
A MATERIAL IDENTITY IN OCEANIA BOOK DESIGN
by Lucy Rowland
190

XVI.
AUDUBON'S *THE BIRDS OF AMERICA*
by Felicity Myrone
192

Feature:
'AN ERROR OF TASTE': SMITHERS, BEARDSLEY AND *THE SAVOY*
by Alex Kither
202

XVII.
THE WORKS OF GEOFFREY CHAUCER
by Helen Peden
204

Feature:
TWENTIETH-CENTURY TYPEFACES
by Philip Parker
214

XVIII.
SADOK SUDEI AND OTHER FUTURIST BOOKS FROM RUSSIA
by Ekaterina Rogatchevskaia
216

Feature:
CARTONERA BOOKS AND PUBLISHERS
by Iris Bachmann and Annalisa Ricciardi
226

XIX.
CENTURY
by Philip Parker
228

Feature:
PENGUIN BOOKS AND THE PAPERBACK REVOLUTION
by Philip Parker
236

XX.
SEA AIR
by Jeremy Jenkins
238

Feature:
WOMEN PUBLISHERS AND DESIGNERS
by Alexandra Pringle
248

XXI.
EDITIONS AT PLAY
by Giulia Carla Rossi
250

Feature:
BOOK DESIGN AS AN AGENT OF CONSERVATION
by Katie McElvanney
258

Epilogue
260

Glossary
262

Notes
265

Further Reading
275

Index
281

Credits
287

QR Codes
288

THE CONTRIBUTORS

P. J. M. Marks is the Curator of Bookbindings at the British Library where she has worked for over thirty-five years. She is the author of the successful *An Anthology of Decorated Papers* (British Library, Thames & Hudson, 2018), *Beautiful Bookbindings* (British Library, 2011) and *The British Library Guide to Bookbinding: History and Techniques* (British Library, 1998) and contributed 'Selected European Decorated Bookbindings in the Arcadian Library' to *The Arcadian Library: Bindings and Provenance* (2014). She developed one of the earliest online databases of bookbindings.

Stephen Parkin is Curator of the British Library's Printed Heritage Collections 1450–1600, and a specialist in early printing in Italy. He has a particular interest in the history of bibliography and collecting and has published in these fields; he also works as a literary translator. He collaborated on the curation of two exhibitions: *Aldo Manuzio: Il Rinascimento di Venezia* at Gallerie dell'Accademia, Venice (2017) and *Leonardo: A Mind in Motion* at the British Library (2019).

Mercedes Aguirre is Lead Curator of Americas Collections at the British Library. She has a research interest in twentieth-century literature and print culture.

Iris Bachmann is Curator of Latin American Published Collections (pre-1850) at the British Library. Her current research interest centres on language practices across the Americas and the Caribbean.

Sophie Defrance is Curator of Romance Collections at the British Library with a research interest in book collectors, livres d'artiste and books as objects.

Eyob Derillo is a reference specialist at the British Library, with a research interest in Ethiopian bookbindings, manuscripts and contemporary literature.

Mélodie Doumy is Curator for Chinese Collections at the British Library, with special responsibility for the Stein Collection and the International Dunhuang Project (IDP).

Kathleen Doyle is the retired Lead Curator of Illuminated Manuscripts. Her recent publications include *The Art of the Bible: Illuminated Manuscripts from the Medieval World*, with Scot McKendrick, reprinted in 2023.

Adrian S. Edwards is a rare books librarian and Head of Printed Heritage Collections at the British Library. His current research interests centre on early Shakespeare editions and the private library of King George III.

Lucy Evans was formerly a Curator with Printed Heritage Collections at the British Library. She is now Special Collections Manager at Senate House Library.

Annabel Teh Gallop is Lead Curator for Southeast Asia at the British Library, with a research interest in the art of the Qur'an in the Indian Ocean world.

Jana Igunma is Henry Ginsburg Curator for Thai, Lao and Cambodian Collections at the British Library, specialising in Southeast Asian materials.

Eleanor Jackson is Curator of Illuminated Manuscripts in the Ancient, Medieval and Early Modern Manuscripts section at the British Library and has a research interest in insular manuscripts.

Jeremy Jenkins is Curator of Emerging Formats, Contemporary British & Irish Published Collections at the British Library. His current research explores twenty-first-century artists' books.

Edmund M. B. King worked at the British Library from 1975 to 2012. He was Head of Newspaper Collections from 1999 to 2012. He has a research interest in Victorian publishers' bindings.

Alex Kither is a rare materials cataloguer at the British Library, with a research interest in fine press printing and publishing in the late nineteenth century.

Karen Limper-Herz is Lead Curator of Incunabula and Sixteenth-Century Printed Books at the British Library, with a research interest in European bookbinding and the history of book collecting in nineteenth-century England.

Katie McElvanney is Curator of Slavonic and East European Collections at the British Library, with particular responsibility for the Ukrainian and Belarusian collections.

Valentina Mirabella is Curator of Romance Collections at the British Library and she specialises in Italian printed collections.

Felicity Myrone is Lead Curator of Western Prints and Drawings. Her current research investigates how the institutional histories of the British Museum, Natural History Museum and British Library have shaped attitudes to prints and drawings.

Philip Parker is a writer, consultant and publisher. He studied history at Trinity Hall, Cambridge. As a publisher, he ran Times books.

Helen Peden is Curator of Printed Heritage Collections at the British Library. She has a research interest in Victorian book illustration, printing techniques and book production.

Alexandra Pringle worked in publishing for forty-five years. The fourth person to join Virago Press in the 1970s, she went on to be Editorial Director at Hamish Hamilton and Editor-in-Chief of Bloomsbury Publishing for over twenty years.

Annalisa Ricciardi is Cataloguer, Americas & Oceania Collections, at the British Library. She specialises in artists' books, fine press and miniature books, and she has research interests in ethics in cataloguing.

James Ritzema was a Collaborative Doctoral Student at the British Library with a research interest in seventeenth-century English sacred music.

Ekaterina Rogatchevskaia is Lead Curator for Slavonic and East European Collections, with research interests in the history of the collections and diaspora and émigré publishing.

Giulia Carla Rossi is Curator for Digital Publications at the British Library, with a research focus on emerging and interactive formats.

Lucy Rowland is Curator of Oceania Published Collections (post-1850) at the British Library. Her research interests include the publishing histories and cultures of Australia, Aotearoa New Zealand and the Pacific Islands.

Christopher Scobie is Lead Curator of Music Manuscripts at the British Library. His research interests include historical experiments in alternative forms of music notation.

Ursula Sims-Williams is Lead Curator of the Persian Collections with a special interest in the arts of the book in the Persianate world.

Ilana Tahan is Lead Curator for Hebrew and Christian Orient Collections. Her current research interests include Hebrew illuminated manuscripts, Hebrew manuscripts produced in Yemen and medieval Jewish craftspeople.

Hamish Todd is Head of East Asian Collections at the British Library, with a research interest in the history of the book in Japan.

Lucy Vinten is an archivist at the British Jesuit Archives, based in Mount Street, London. She cares for the Jesuit Antiquarian Book collection there, a large collection of Jesuit-related books published between the sixteenth and nineteenth centuries.

01.

INTRODUCTION

The Book by Design celebrates the 'book' in all its forms, whether manuscript, printed or digital; scroll or codex; on parchment, paper, palm leaves or cardboard; shaped like a concertina or with moving parts; or of huge or miniature dimensions. It brings together the insight and expertise of the British Library's curatorial teams as well as specialist external authors, and striking new studio photography alongside images from the Library's digitised collections to create a unique survey of the different designs and technologies which have characterised the long and continuing history of this remarkable and enduring invention.

The Book by Design is not intended to be a history of bookmaking, but it does mark major developments and achievements in the production of manuscript and printed books, such as the refinement of page design (or, 'mise-en-page') or the organisation of contents, the use of type and colour printing, the integration of illustrations alongside texts or the introduction of movable parts. A Glossary is provided at the back of the book to explain terms that may not be familiar.

The structure of this book consists of twenty-one essays that run in chronological order. These focus on items in the British Library's collections chosen for their significance in terms of distinctive and successful design – successful in terms of how the form and presentation are aligned with the book's purpose and the requirements of the reader, whether it's the Word of God or a story for children. The 'book' as an artefact is found in all major cultures and spiritual teachings around the world. This is reflected in the selections found in these chapters, which span the last 1,400 years.

01. *Gold leaf decoration, the Queen Mary Psalter. (Royal MS 2 B. vii, f. 68v, detail)*

There are famous books here from many different cultures and periods, such as the Lindisfarne Gospels, Shakespeare's First Folio, the Diamond Sutra, and *The Tale of Genji*, together with less familiar works, but what all have in common is that they are notable achievements of book production.

Interspersed through these chapters are shorter features, seventeen in total, that examine complementary themes, again largely drawing on the British Library's collections. They range from a focus on particular books or categories of books and individual printers to brief overviews of more general topics such as paper or paratexts.

Today, a book's appearance depends largely upon the efforts of a graphic designer, working with an editor and production controller, who is trained in a set of agreed principles and the latest software. This specialist role is a relatively recent occupation, but concern for what a book looks like and how well it fulfils its purpose has been a common and consistent aspect of all book production over the ages. So the question arises: who and what had an impact on earlier practices?

FORMAT AND BINDING

Practical circumstances are a determining factor. The availability of necessary materials, technologies and skills varies according to geography and time period. In both manuscript and printed production successful methods tended to become standardised and associated roles more specialised. This was perhaps particularly the case with the opportunities and challenges posed by the introduction of hand-press printing from the mid-fifteenth century onwards, where a whole range of technical tasks, such as the composition and imposition of the type pages to be printed and the planning of a book's 'format' – 'folio', 'quarto', 'octavo', depending on the number of times the printed sheet of paper had to be folded – quite rapidly became routine ways of organising the work of printing houses. Experimental energies moved into other channels: out-of-the-ordinary productions demanded expensive dedicated set-ups, experienced practitioners and ingenuity. These include miniature and outsized books and publications which employ special techniques such as pop-ups or flaps. John James Audubon had to work out how best to publish his 'American birds' series of 435 extraordinarily large size prints. They were printed on paper measuring a metre in height.

There is a constant interplay between form and ergonomics. An instruction manual, a book to be read aloud, a music score to be played or sung must open easily and the pages should lie flat, achievable via the adoption of particular sewing structures. A large missal used in church liturgies and a poetry book held in the hand or carried around in a pocket reflect quite different needs. Twenty-first-century innovation has resulted in electronic books read on ereaders such as Kindles and other devices; some of the descriptive vocabulary remains attached to the object, for example 'page', but its display is very different, and so too is the reader's relationship with it.

The book artist Susan Allix, whose work *Sea Air* is the subject of one of the chapters, compares the special nature of the physical book with the onscreen alternative: 'What is missing is the tactile experience of materials; the feeling of the pressure of type and plate into paper, the progression of the pages with their folds, cuts or irregularities that make shadows; where inking is positive, letters not quite perfect, small imperfections disguised, and each page an individual that is talking to you.' The digital book, however, does have unique advantages, and its advent is undoubtedly a transformative development in the book as a fixed design in a physical object, so it was important to include it as a concluding chapter in this book through the initiatives of Editions At Play.

A book's binding is part of the tactile experience, but creating a book's cover as an integral part of the design process is a relatively recent aspect of book production.

In the modern age, copies of a printed book are usually sold ready-bound in identical decorative covers to entice customers. In earlier centuries certain categories of bound books were available for purchase 'off the shelf', including prayer books and almanacs, classical texts and books to write *in* (often known as stationery bindings). Other books were sold in a cheap, simple but surprisingly robust format; the folded pages were sewn together in protective wrappers of paper or parchment. The cartoneras represent a modern example of this.

The purchaser could then have a profound impact upon the book's appearance. Some owners preferred to exchange the wrappers for a more substantial and personalised binding (often including their coats of arms or initials) and their choices tell us much. There was a wide variety of textiles, leathers, colours and decorative styles on offer to fit individual tastes and purses. The diarist Samuel Pepys enjoyed collecting examples from different workshops 'for the love of the binding'. And Mr Brownlow comments in Charles Dickens's *Oliver Twist*, 'there are books of which the backs and covers are by far the best parts'.

It is important to note that the original bindings of many early manuscripts and Bibles were replaced – sometimes more than once by consecutive owners – as illustrated by the Victorian binding of the eighth-century Lindisfarne Gospels. Even today,

02. *Monastic scribe. (Yates Thompson 26, f. 2r, detail)*

03. *Paper production from the Chinese encyclopaedia* Tiangong kaiwu, *1637. (15226.b.19, detail)*

04. & 05. *Book binder at the sewing frame and printer's workshop from* Het Menselyk Bedrygf *(*The Book of Trades*) by Jan Luyken, 1694. (12331.dd.1, 61 & 63, details)*

06. *'The engraver' from* The Book of English Trades and Library of the Useful Arts, *1818. (RB.23.a.24349, p. 153)*

07. *Advertisement for a new air brush to be used for lithography and photography, 1885. (Evan.7598)*

03.

04.

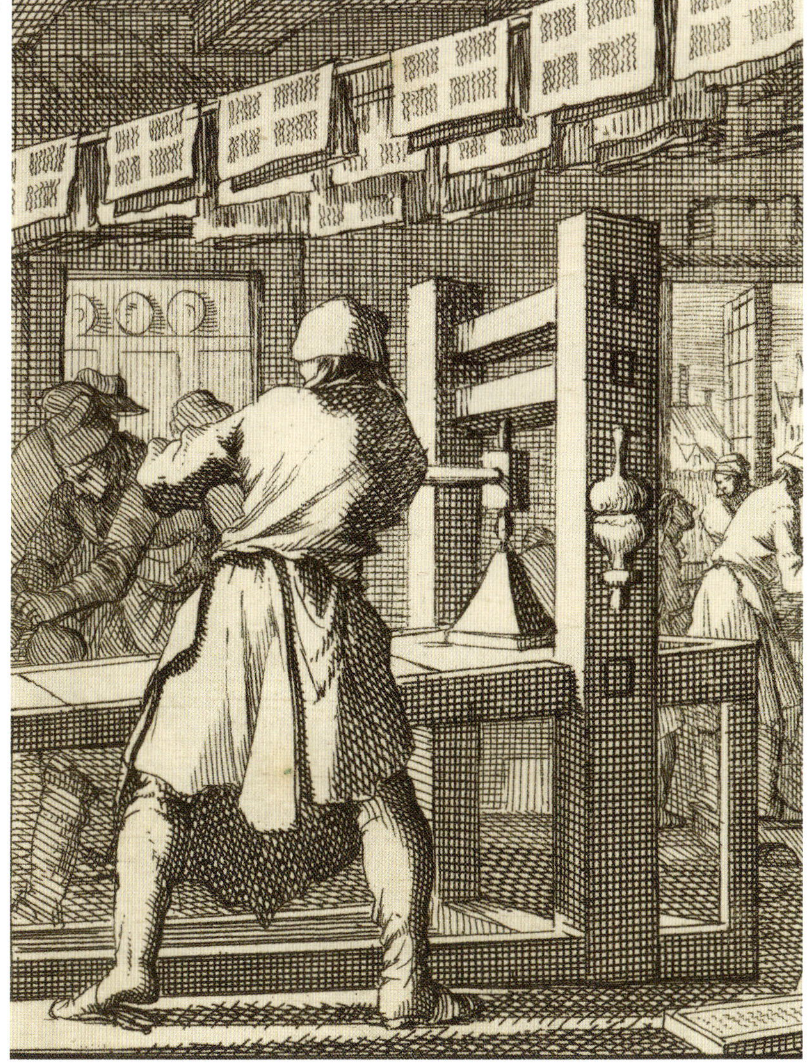

07.

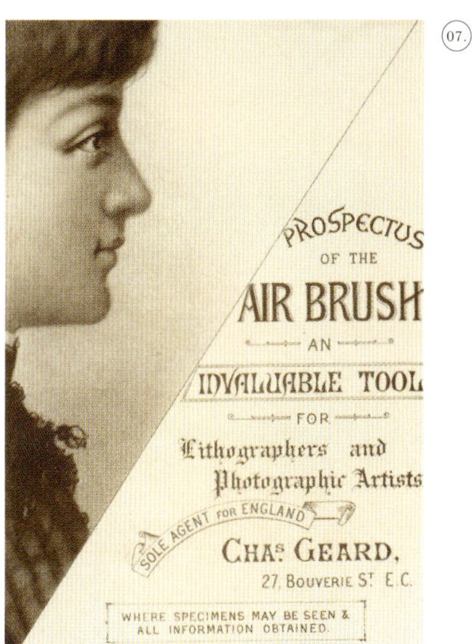
PROSPECTUS
OF THE
AIR BRUSH
AN
INVALUABLE TOOL
FOR
Lithographers and
Photographic Artists
SOLE AGENT FOR ENGLAND
CHAS GEARD,
27. BOUVERIE ST E.C.
WHERE SPECIMENS MAY BE SEEN &
ALL INFORMATION OBTAINED.

08.

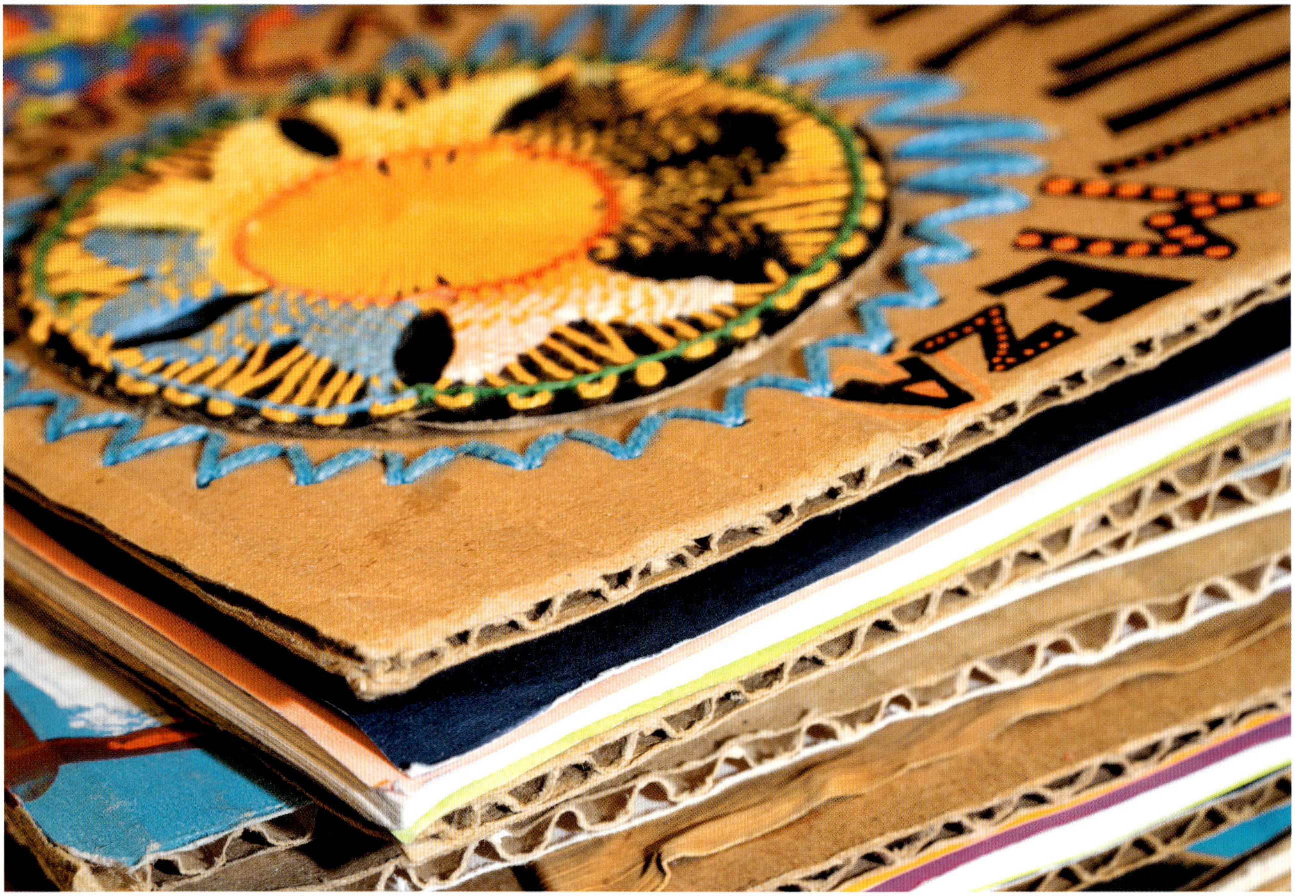

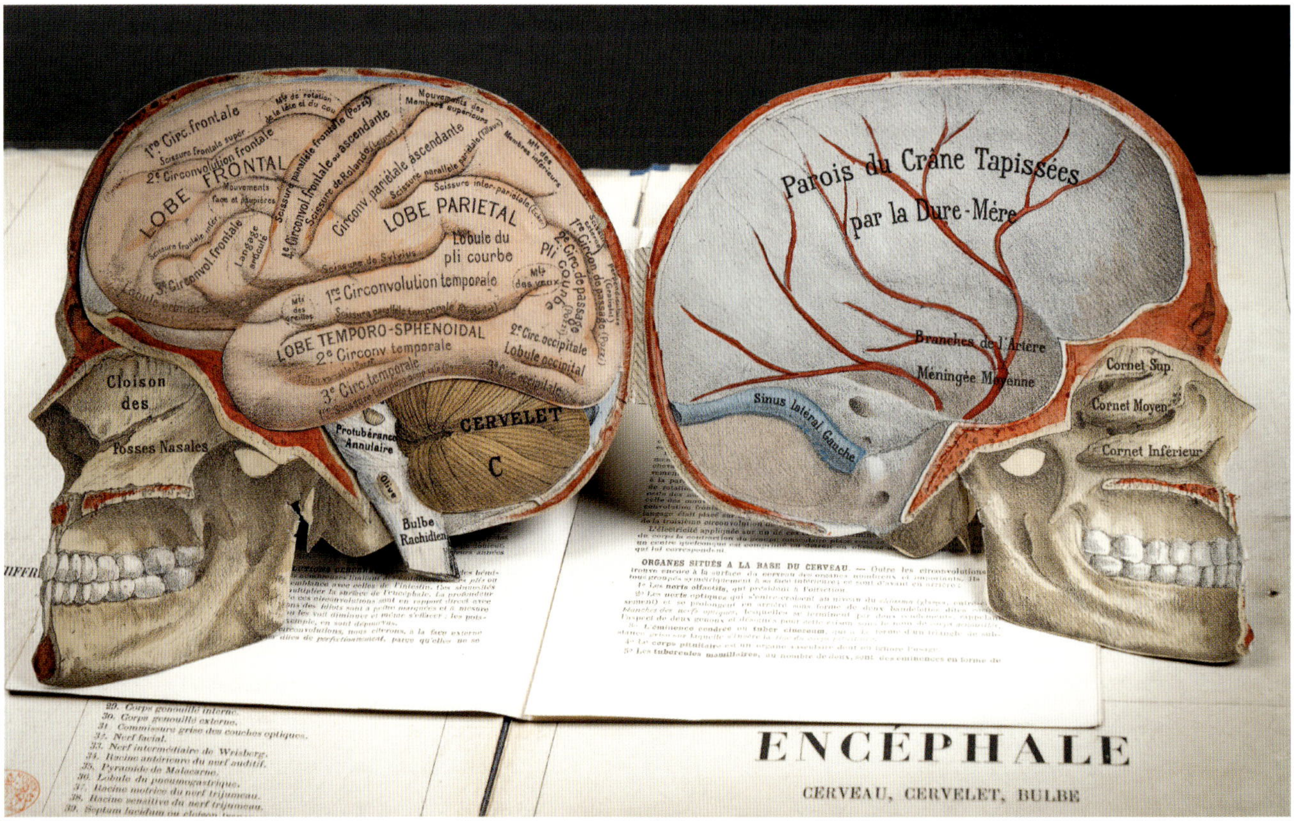
1re Circ. frontale
2e Circonvolution frontale
LOBE FRONTAL
LOBE PARIETAL
Lobule du pli courbe
1re Circonvolution temporale
LOBE TEMPORO-SPHENOIDAL
2e Circonv temporale
3e Circ. temporale
CERVELET
Cloison des Fosses Nasales
Protubérance Annulaire
Bulbe Rachidien
Parois du Crâne Tapissées
par la Dure-Mère
Branches de l'Artère
Méningée Moyenne
Sinus latéral Gauche
Cornet Sup.
Cornet Moyen
Cornet Inférieur
ENCÉPHALE
CERVEAU, CERVELET, BULBE

09.

bibliophiles can choose to have a book rebound at any time, for aesthetic reasons or perhaps because its fragile structure needs attention.

Whatever it looks and feels like, a book must serve its purpose (convey information) and be useable (easy to read).

READABILITY

We probably all have a view of what design is, but a major stimulus is likely to be intent. The creator of a manuscript or book has an ambition for it and anticipates that its finished appearance will represent the *spirit* of their work at the very least. People design books and manuscripts for people but, of course, reader response cannot easily be controlled either at the point of issue or in the future. The Italian novelist and essayist Italo Calvino wrote, 'all books continue in the beyond'.

In the seventeenth century the diarist John Evelyn talked about 'Passions expressible by the art of Designe', but realistically, where the creation of books is concerned, practical and utilitarian considerations have always kept step with, and in the publishing industry increasingly prevailed over, expressive concerns. In Steve Jobs's words: 'Design is not just what it looks like and feels like. Design is how it works.'

Over the centuries books have developed a whole range of tools to facilitate and enhance readability. Punctuation, consecutive page numbers, running titles, clearly marked content divisions such as chapter headings, etc. – the variety is huge – were slow to develop the 'invisibility' such features have today, when readers take them for granted. But the same need to make a book 'work' is also found in the various graphic additions found in manuscripts, including the use of rubrics (written in red ink); drawing and illuminating enlarged capital letters to mark the beginning of new sections; or inserting decorated pages to denote major section breaks, such as between Gospels, and smaller decorative devices at the end of sections, either within the verse or script or alongside in the margins. Artists and illuminators collaborated with scribes and calligraphers to create these divisions as well as illustrating scenes described in the text.

The advent of the printing press with movable type and a proliferating variety of typefaces marked a step change both in the focus on how to make what I. A. Richards called 'a machine for reading' as efficient and effective as possible and in a new concern with marketing books as commercial products and exploiting all aspects of design for that purpose. For example, printers and publishers have increasingly been able to choose from a range of typefaces, alongside other design elements, not only for reasons of legibility but also to establish a commercial identity, to brand an edition or to create a recognisable series style.

Just as Roger Stoddard famously pointed out that 'authors do not write books', so Michele Moylan and Lane Styles observe that 'there is no such thing as a text unmediated by its materiality'. Taken as a whole, across its multiple explorations in both text and image of what makes for distinctive and successful book design, the present volume celebrates the variety of material form and appearance the 'book' as an artefact has assumed over the centuries and throughout the world.

IMAGES

Where possible the precious volumes from the collections have been specially photographed for this book to give a sense of them as bound objects, portraying the condition and texture of their pages and bindings, bringing out the qualities of the inks and applied gold leaf. We are only able to show a limited number of images for each book here, but some of the key volumes in the chapters are fully digitised and their pages can be viewed in their entirety on the British Library's website. For those that can be accessed this way QR codes are provided on the last pages of this book.

08. *The cardboard covers of South American cartoneras.*

09. *Layers of paper flaps are used in Gustave Joseph Witkowski's* Iconoclastic Anatomy: Complementary Atlas of Human Anatomy and Physiology. *(14001.g.15)*

I.

THE LINDISFARNE GOSPELS

The beginnings of book design in England

ELEANOR JACKSON

As with any book, the design of the Lindisfarne Gospels was guided by a mixture of practical requirements and cultural attitudes. Since Gospel Books (copies of the Gospels, the four books of the Bible which tell the life of Christ) were read daily in church and studied regularly by the faithful, the practical requirements included ease of reading. Yet at a time when the entire Bible was rarely produced as a single volume, Gospel Books were the most sacred books that many churches owned. They were revered as the physical Word of God, paraded in processions or displayed on the altar. The design of the Lindisfarne Gospels is also markedly shaped by a desire to express this sacred significance. There is a clear awareness that more than simply transmitting a text, a book can guide its reception in ways that might be thought-provoking, emotional or spiritual. When the book was made around the year 700, this sophisticated use of graphic features, both to improve the ease of reading and to impart beauty and significance, placed the Lindisfarne Gospels at the forefront of book design.

SETTING THE SCENE

To understand how the Lindisfarne Gospels came to look the way it does, we have to go back to the historical circumstances of its production. According to an inscription added in the late tenth century, the manuscript was written by Eadfrith, bishop of Lindisfarne from 698 to 722, 'for God and St Cuthbert and all the holy people who are on the island'. Scholarly analysis supports the view that almost all the original script and decoration was carried out by one highly talented individual, probably over a period of many years. Most scholars accept the evidence of the inscription and conclude that this brilliant scribe-artist was Eadfrith, working on the small tidal island of Lindisfarne off the northeast coast of England. Lindisfarne was home to a monastery, which was founded in 634 by the Irish monk St Aidan (d. 651) as a base for establishing Christianity in the kingdom of Northumbria. A generation later these efforts were bolstered by St Cuthbert (d. 687), bishop of Lindisfarne from 684 to 686, who is known for his work preaching to the remote communities of Northumbria as well as for his feats of asceticism as a hermit.

In the seventh century the kingdom of Northumbria encompassed most of northern England and southern Scotland, literally the lands north of the River Humber. The ruling people of Northumbria were mostly descended from Germanic-speaking settlers who had migrated from the North Sea coast of what is now Denmark, Germany and the Netherlands in the fifth century, bringing with them a pantheon of pagan gods. Their culture was based largely on oral transmission of knowledge. Books were probably more or less unknown to them. But the arrival of Christianity, a religion of the book, stimulated a period of fervent book collection and production in newly founded major religious centres. The result was the creation of many of the finest and most innovative books of their day. It is astonishing to think that in only a few generations, Northumbria went from being virtually illiterate to producing a pinnacle of achievement in book design such as the Lindisfarne Gospels.

01. *The Chi-Rho page, a richly decorated abbreviation of the name of Christ, in the Lindisfarne Gospels. (f. 29r, detail)*

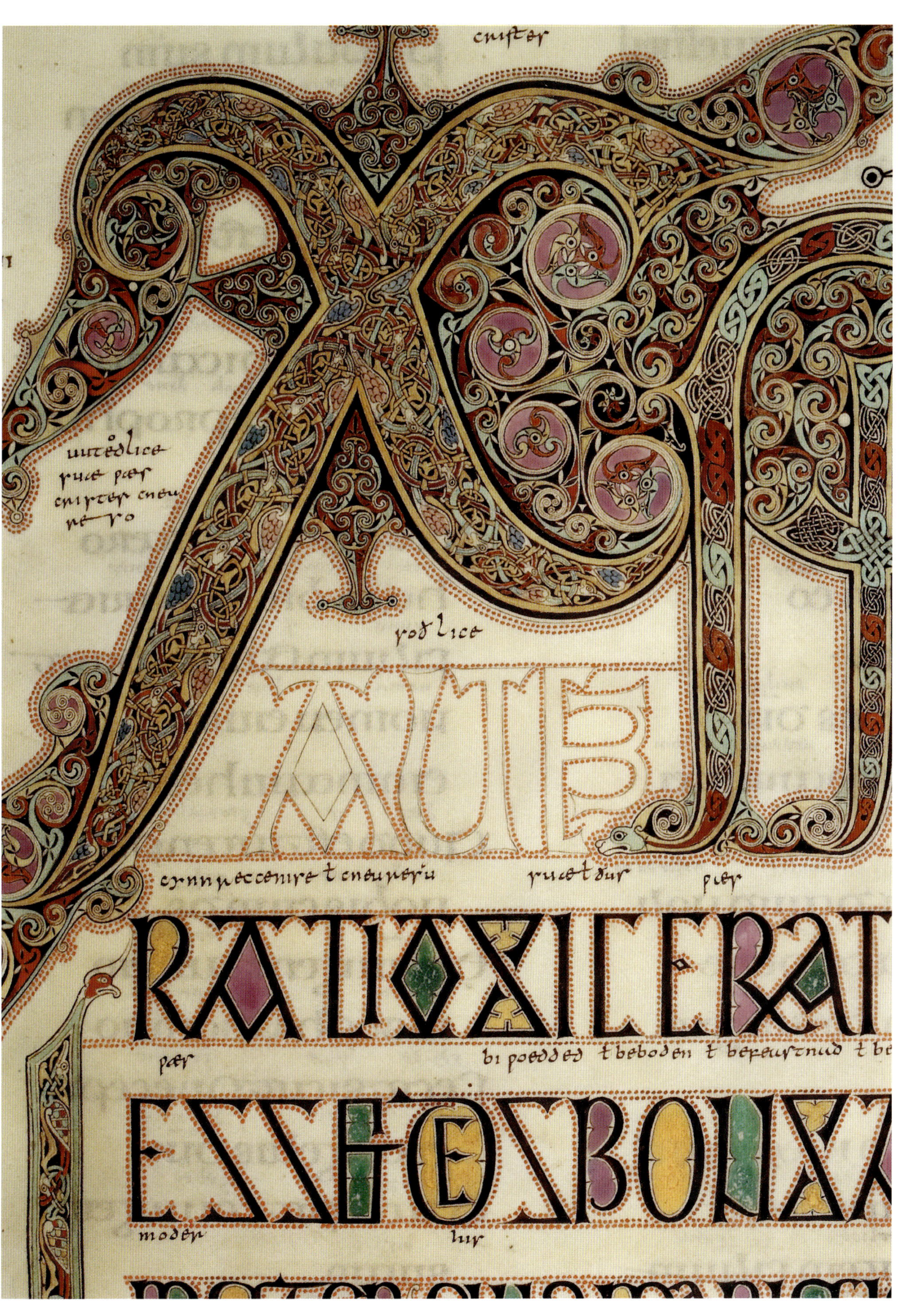

02.

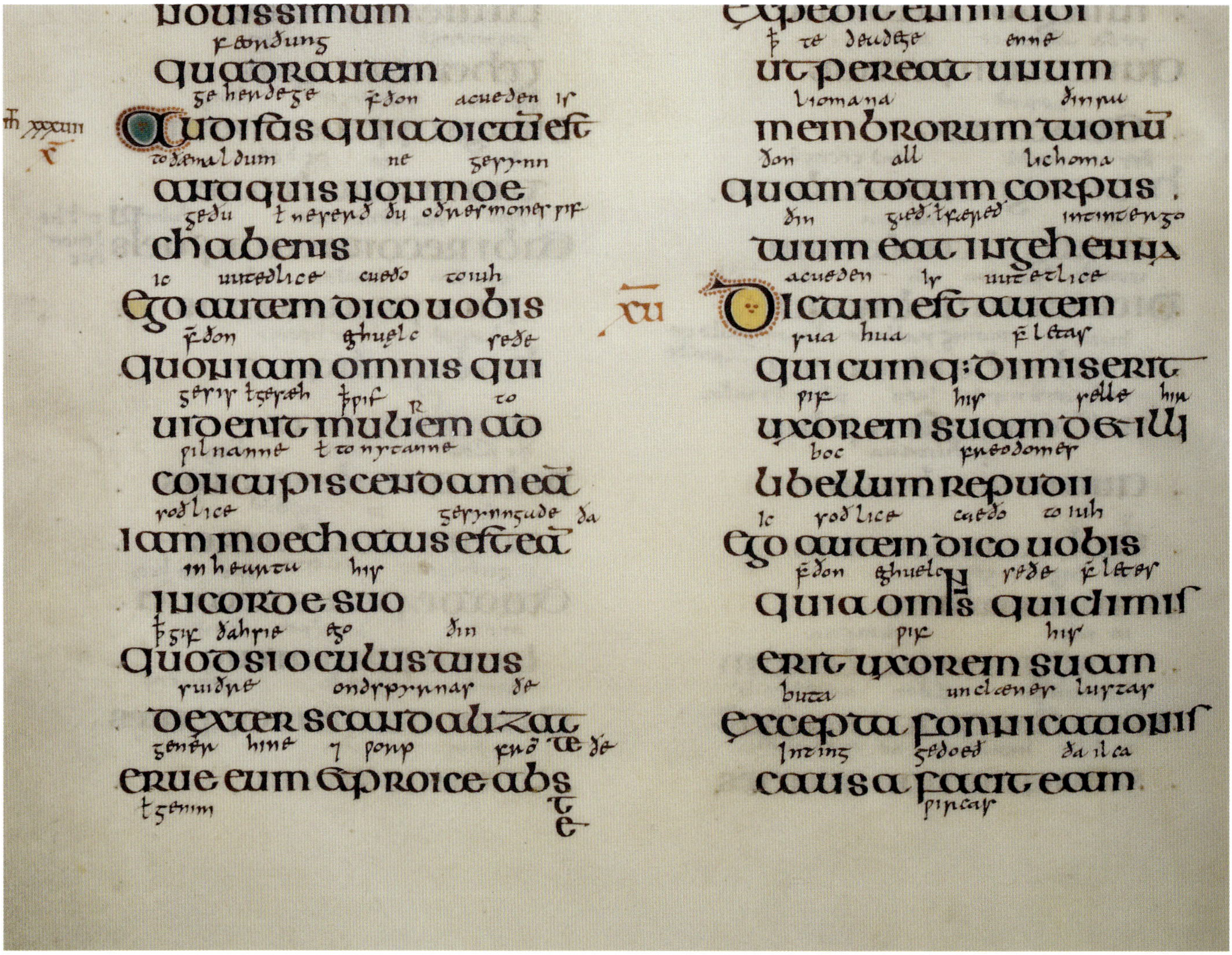

nouissimum
quadrantem
Audistis quia dictum est
antiquis non moe
chaberis
Ego autem dico uobis
quoniam omnis qui
uiderit mulierem ad
concupiscendam eam
iam moechatus est eam
in corde suo
Quod si oculus tuus
dexter scandalizat
erue eum et proice abs
te

expedit enim tibi
ut pereat unum
membrorum tuorum
quam totum corpus
tuum eat in gehennam
Dictum est autem
quicumque dimiserit
uxorem suam det illi
libellum repudii
Ego autem dico uobis
quia omnis qui dimiserit
uxorem suam
excepta fornicationis
causa facit eam

03.

04.

Specification	*Scale*
THE LINDISFARNE GOSPELS Lindisfarne, Northumbria, around the year 700 365 x 275 mm Cotton MS Nero D IV	

BOOKS AND ART IN THE 'GOLDEN AGE'

In fact, it was the unique mixing of cultures which took place in Northumbria that produced the exact conditions for such an achievement. St Aidan and his missionaries brought with them the thriving scribal culture of Ireland, where conversion to Christianity had begun in the time of St Patrick in the fifth century. Due to its relative remoteness from the rest of Christian Europe, book design in Ireland had evolved along different lines to elsewhere. This included the use of distinctive scripts which were probably derived from late antique manuscripts that reached Ireland in the fifth century. Around the seventh century, Irish scribes were the first to develop new graphic conventions which made reading easier, such as word separation. They also developed a new approach to decoration, morphing letters into decorative forms and endowing them with motifs from contemporary Irish metalwork. They were especially known for a decorative style known as Ultimate La Tène due to its origins in the La Tène art of the Celtic Iron Age, consisting of graceful flowing patterns made up of trumpet and spiral shapes often ending in birds' heads. These distinctive characteristics suggest an increased awareness of the visual dimension of writing and its potential for creative expression.

However, books from Ireland were not the only kind known in newly Christianised Northumbria. In 597, Pope Gregory the Great sent a mission from Rome to convert England to Christianity. The missionaries established a base in Canterbury, which developed into a great cosmopolitan centre of learning, attracting students and teachers from as far away as north Africa and the eastern Mediterranean. Inspired by such international contacts, members of the newly founded monasteries of Northumbria were soon turning their attention to Rome and its books. St Wilfrid of Ripon (d. 709/10) travelled to Rome three times. His vigorous advocacy of Roman practice at the Synod of Whitby resulted in Northumbria officially opting to follow the Roman Church in 664. Likewise, Benedict Biscop (d. 690), founder of the twin monasteries of Wearmouth-Jarrow, made five trips to Rome and, in the words of the historian Bede (d. 735), 'brought back an innumerable abundance of books of every kind' (*innumerabilem librorum omnis generis copiam apportavit*).

The late antique books which were brought from Italy to centres such as Canterbury, Ripon and Wearmouth-Jarrow looked very different from the books from Ireland. They employed a stately script known as uncial, made up of broad, rounded capital letters written continuously without spaces to distinguish one word from the next. The main form of punctuation was a system called *per cola et commata*, in which each clause or phrase began on a new line, a practice that was reserved for only the costliest biblical books owing to its extravagant use of parchment. The script had a graceful austerity, with little if any decoration. Some of the grandest examples contained miniatures in a style developed from classical Greek and Roman painting, depicting figures in toga-like costumes, the folds carefully draped to suggest the contours of the body, and employing painterly effects such as shading and highlighting to create a sense of depth. Decoration, when it was included, often consisted of sprigs of delicate foliage or classical architectural elements.

Yet the people of early medieval England also had strong visual traditions of their own. In common with Germanic cultures on the continent, their art was based on stylised animal and bird forms. A favourite motif was animal interlace, in which elongated creatures intertwine to form a dense tangle of elaborate knotwork. They delighted in the effect of

02. *A text page in the Lindisfarne Gospels. (f. 35v, detail)*

03. *The modern binding created for the Lindisfarne Gospels by Messrs Smith, Nicholson and Co., silversmiths of Lincoln's Inn, London, in 1853.*

04. *The Lindisfarne Gospels being prepared for display in the British Library's Anglo-Saxon Kingdoms exhibition in 2018. (© Sam Lane Photography)*

a seeming chaos of pattern which resolves to form a balanced and harmonious composition overall. Their culture is known for its extraordinary accomplishments in metalwork, most famously the finds from the Sutton Hoo ship burial and the Staffordshire Hoard, featuring animal and interlace patterns intricately crafted in gold and garnets. This captivation with finely decorated metalwork is reflected in the descriptions of treasures in the Old English epic poem, *Beowulf.* The mighty sword which the hero Beowulf retrieves from the lake, for example, is described as the 'work of wonder-smiths' (*wundorsmiþa ġeweorc*), its gold hilt 'twisted and ornamented with serpent patterns' (*wreoþenhilt ond wyrmfah*). The poem relates how King Hrothgar examines the wonderful hilt, perceiving stories and meanings in its decoration. This was an art that was made for thoughtful looking.

It was the combination of elements from each of these traditions – Irish, Roman and English – which laid the foundation for the production of the Lindisfarne Gospels. Northumbria's conversion to Christianity brought an influx of people, ideas and books, generating an explosion of artistic and literary production which was characterised by remarkable creativity and cultural synthesis. The Lindisfarne Gospels is one of the creative high points of this exciting moment in history.

DESIGNING THE TEXT

The main text of the Lindisfarne Gospels is written in a particularly fine example of the script known as Insular half-uncial (Image 2). Unlike uncial, Insular half-uncial is a four-line script, meaning that some letters have ascender strokes that rise above the body of the letters and others have descender strokes that go below. Also, in common with other Insular scripts, it features distinctive wedge shapes at the tops of the ascenders. This script originated in Ireland and was adopted and modified in England. The name 'Insular', literally meaning 'of the Isles', is meant to indicate this shared heritage in Ireland and Britain. We can tell by certain rare features that the text of the Lindisfarne Gospels was copied from a manuscript from southern Italy, which would almost certainly have been written in uncial script. This means that Eadfrith had the added task of mentally converting the uncial letterforms of the exemplar into the Insular half-uncial letterforms as he wrote. At the same time, perhaps inspired by the Italian exemplar, he invested the Insular letters with some of the broadness, regularity and rotundity of uncial script. This suggests a careful effort to express the grandeur of late antique writing in a local idiom.

05. *The Evangelist portrait of St Matthew in the Lindisfarne Gospels. (f. 25v)*

The punctuation of the script displays a similarly eclectic approach. The text is arranged *per cola et commata*, the parchment-consuming late-antique system in which each clause or phrase begins on a new line, most likely copied straight from the southern Italian exemplar. Yet Eadfrith also introduced the Irish practice of word separation, inserting a space after each word to distinguish it from the next. Further, he added enlarged letters with coloured infill and an outline of red dots (Image 2) to mark the beginnings of chapters, lections and other small units of text. These features demonstrate a concern to make the text easy to read and navigate, which was perhaps especially important for Irish and English readers for whom Latin was not only a second language but an entirely different sub-family of languages from their Celtic and Germanic mother tongues.

OPENING THE GOSPELS

However, the concern to mark the divisions of the text is taken to extreme lengths in the monumental triad of decorated pages – Evangelist portrait, carpet page and *incipit* page – which open each of the Gospel texts. On the one hand, the use of decoration to mark the opening of the major texts served a practical purpose: in an age before books had page numbers, these eye-catching pages would help the reader to locate the beginning of each text very quickly. On the other, their rich designs

05.

would draw readers in, challenge them to interpret their meanings, and suggest particular ways of perceiving things. In doing so, they shape the act of reading as a spiritual experience. The opening triad of decorated pages to the Gospel of Matthew demonstrates how this might work.

The Gospel begins with a picture of St Matthew, the text's human author. Known as an Evangelist portrait (Image 5), this feature is borrowed from late-antique illuminated Gospel Books and is ultimately based on the classical author portraits which sometimes headed literary and philosophical texts in the ancient world. Such portraits were intended to celebrate the author and to assure the reader of the established authority of the text. In the Lindisfarne Gospels, St Matthew is depicted as a distinguished author of the late antique world. He sits on an elegant painted bench, writing in a book that rests on his lap. The image of the book within the book suggests a link between the original Gospel texts written by the Evangelists and the text of the Lindisfarne Gospels, as though promising authentic transmission from St Matthew's pen to the pages before us. St Matthew wears a classically draped robe in variegated colours, rich green with the folds outlined in red, giving the appearance of shot silk. With his delicate sandals, he is clearly dressed for a balmy Mediterranean climate. His halo signals his holiness and his wide, almond-shaped eyes have a visionary intensity. The figure is labelled in a peculiar mixture of transliterated Greek, '*O Agios*' (Saint), and Latin, '*Mattheus*' (Matthew), inscribed in angular Roman capitals. The attempt at Greek, a language that was little known in eighth-century Northumbria, was probably intended to evoke the sanctity of the original language of the Gospels.

However, other features of the miniature indicate that the Gospel derives its ultimate authority from God. Above the figure of St Matthew is his Evangelist symbol, the winged man, sounding a trumpet and labelled in Latin '*Imago hominis*' (image of the man). The early patristic writers assigned each of the four Evangelists a symbolic creature based on the visions of the four living creatures experienced by Ezekiel and St John in the Bible. The presence of St Matthew's symbol affirms his divinely ordained role within the canon of scripture. To the right, a haloed man holding a book emerges from behind a curtain. His identity has been much debated, with suggestions including God, a representation of the Old Testament, an embodiment of every righteous believer and St Cuthbert. The figure's identity may be left deliberately ambiguous to encourage the reader to ponder the various possible interpretations.

The Evangelist portrait faces a blank page which, on the other side, is entirely devoted to abstract ornament – a feature known as a carpet page. Although their ultimate origins are uncertain, carpet pages are found in some of the finest Insular manuscripts and may have been an Insular innovation. The Matthew carpet page contains a rectangular frame with interlace designs at the corners and mid-points of each side (Image 6). The area within the frame is dominated by a magnificent Latin cross outlined in red, with arms that expand out into chalice shapes. Six small roundels are set into the cross, closely resembling bosses with millefiori glass inlay which were used in fine English and Irish metalwork of the period. The form of the cross is strongly reminiscent of metalwork crosses such as the great gold cross from the Staffordshire Hoard, also featuring expanded arms, a long lower leg and inset jewels, which was probably made to be carried in processions or placed on an altar. With its notional metalwork features, the carpet page evokes the triumphal cross of the Old English poem *Dream of the Rood*, the 'tree of glory' (*wuldres treow*) which is raised up and covered with gold and jewels as a sign of the resurrection.

The entire space inside the frame and the cross teems with finely wrought animal interlace of the kind found on early English metalwork. The area outside the cross is filled with entangled birds and dog-like creatures, their mouths firmly locked around one another's bodies as though engaged in an eternal skirmish. Inside, the cross contains only the dog-like creatures. It is an exciting challenge to mentally disentangle the forms, to work out which distended claw or elongated tail feather belongs to which creature, to trace the extent of a beast from its alert little face, along the twists and turns of its sinuous body, to the tips of its exaggerated claws. Within the dense weave of interlace, there is a captivating play between symmetry and asymmetry. While the general arrangement of beasts appears to be symmetrical along the vertical axis of the page, the order of the interlace is in fact reversed – so where a strand goes underneath on one side, the corresponding strand goes over the top on the other side. In the upper two quadrants the colours are mirrored, but in the lower quadrants and inside the cross the colours are reversed. There are also tiny unique details within the intricate web. For example, just one bird has an open beak and extended tongue, and just one beast has a shoulder joint articulated as a spiral. The impression is of overall harmony belying constant variation, a theme which has been linked to the idea of divine order guiding the vast and complicated universe.

Facing the carpet page is the *incipit* page, a decorated page containing the opening words of the Gospel. Here, the practice of starting a new unit of text with an enlarged letter is taken to fantastical extremes with the initial letters dominating the whole page (Image 7). The decorative treatment of letters is developed to the point that they become a picture, framed and manipulated for visual effect. The first three letters, '*Lib*' (the beginning of the Latin word *liber* meaning 'book') are written as a monogram, their conventional shapes transformed into an ornamental configuration which is almost unreadable. The bodies of the letters are filled with interlace designs, including the dog-like creatures and birds from the carpet page. Billowing spirals and trumpets of Irish Ultimate La Tène decoration erupt from the ends of the letters. The rest of the opening words are written in angular display script, progressively decreasing in size. The whole is surrounded by an interlace frame which seems unable to contain the letters, allowing the '*Lib*' monogram to burst out at the upper and lower left-hand corners, and letting the final line of text escape through a hole at the lower right. With their apparent ability to metamorphose, expand, contract, progress and interact, the letters seem to be living beings, reminiscent of the intricate web of interlaced creatures on the carpet page opposite. More than just signifying sounds which make up words, these letters seem to embody the richness of meaning and spiritual vitality which might be found within the letter of the Gospels.

06 (page 24). *The carpet page of the Gospel of Matthew in the Lindisfarne Gospels. (f. 26v)*

07 (page 25). *The* incipit *page of the Gospel of Matthew in the Lindisfarne Gospels. (f. 27r)*

IMPACT

The introduction of Christian culture from Ireland and Rome to early medieval England supplied all the elements for a new chapter in book design. In the Lindisfarne Gospels, we can see how Eadfrith combined graphic features such as script and punctuation to make the text more reader-friendly, demonstrating a sophisticated awareness of how the visual presentation of a text could affect its reading. Yet he took this concept far beyond the practical requirements of legibility to explore how the visual presentation of a text could also affect its reading in a spiritual sense. Wide-ranging in its cultural references, sophisticated in its composition, dense in its symbolism and evocative in its abstraction, the art of the Lindisfarne Gospels invites readers to enter into a world of meaning and mystery. Under Eadfrith's masterful hand, reading a book is turned into a profound experience through the power of design.

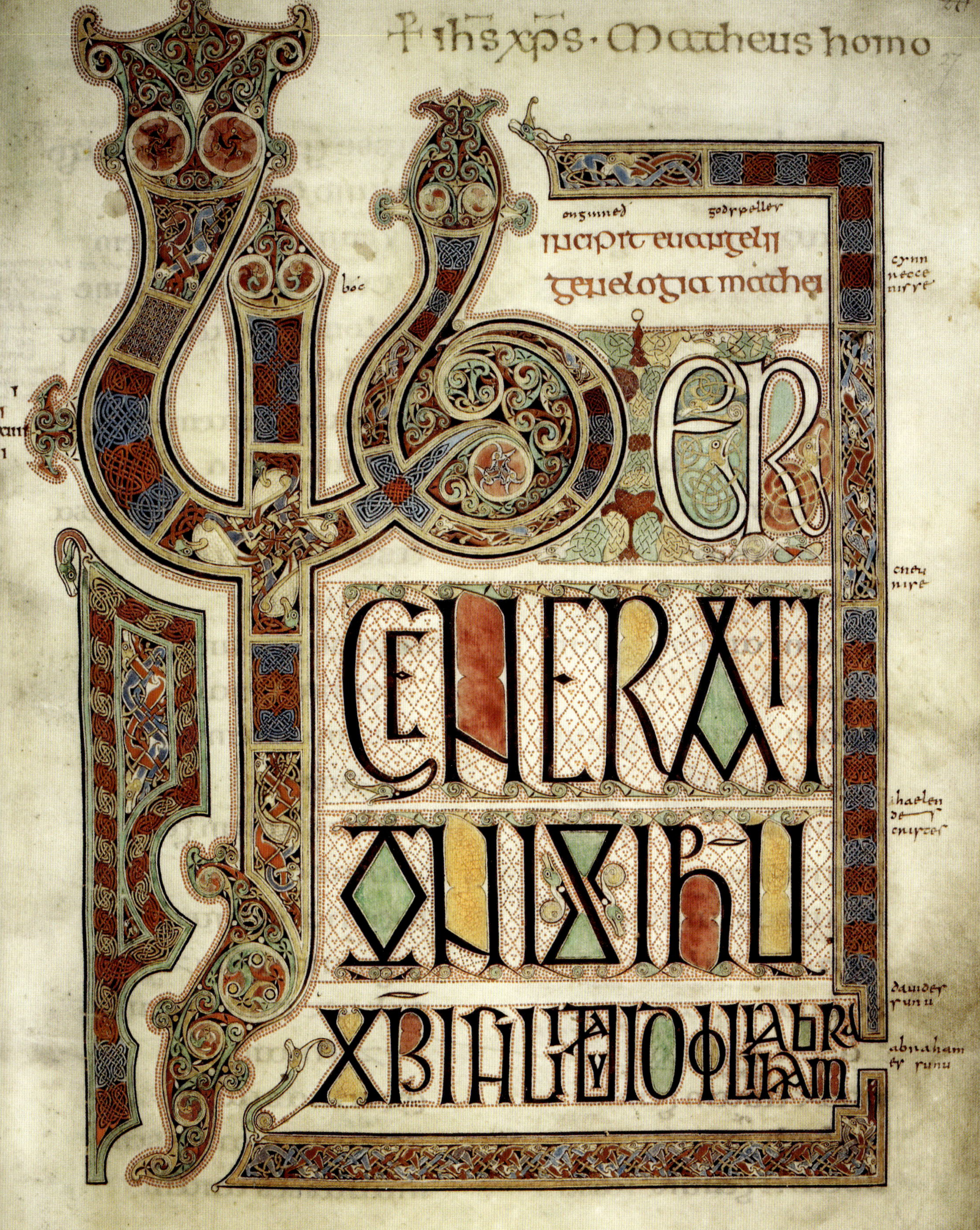

01.

02.

03.

ETHIOPIA, AFRICAN SCRIBES AND THE ILLUSTRATED APOCALYPSE

EYOB DERILLO

Despite being home to the earliest surviving illustrated Christian manuscript, the Garima Gospels c. 390–570 CE, little is known about Ethiopia's long, rich, artistic accomplishments. Western art historians of the early twentieth century were often dismissive, suggesting a proto-colonisation of Ethiopian art and culture which dates back to the 1400s. Today, this view has been challenged.[1]

The bulk, and the largest group of Ethiopian manuscripts incorporated into the British Library's collection, came from the punitive expedition to Ethiopia in 1868. The Magdala collection, resulting from the British expedition sent to Ethiopia in that year, consists of 349 manuscripts from the royal library assembled by King Tewodros II (1855–68).

In Ethiopia, manuscript production was deeply rooted in Christianity. Ethiopia adopted Christianity as its official religion in c. 330 CE, and there has been a tradition of beautifully crafted religious texts ever since. Many Ethiopian Gospel books contain content lost or rejected by other Christian traditions.

The Ethiopian Church produced renowned scholars and theologians, acclaimed artists and copyists. Patronage of the arts by the country's rulers, such as King Iyasu I (1654–1706), peaked in the early seventeenth century. Many exquisitely illustrated manuscripts reflected the vibrant cultural and religious life of the royal court at Gondar. Royal patronage stimulated new iconographic styles and subjects, as exemplified by the various illustrated lives of Ethiopian saints. Unlike Europe, there were no known scriptoria in Ethiopia; the anonymous scribes tended to work alone. Some were inspired by European religious imagery, borrowing well-known visual motifs (for example, those created by the German painter, printmaker and theorist of the German Renaissance Albrecht Dürer (1471–1528) and reworking them into their own theological and artistic style (Image 3). The most likely sources were from books imported by Jesuit missionaries.

Ethiopian manuscripts were written on goat or sheepskin parchment. The pages were marked out for margins, columns and text by faint lines traced with the back of a knife and they closely resemble European medieval manuscripts in layout. Pens were made from reeds, while the inks and pigments came from sources such as carbon, stone, earth and plants.

The bookbinding style of these manuscripts was particular to Ethiopia. The quires (or gatherings) were sewn together using a link stitch and attached to plain wooden boards sewn with the same thread. The covering was leather (probably goatskin) and decorated with geometric shapes impressed via hand tools known as blind tooling. Plain or decorated silk lined the inner boards. An atypical binding incorporating decorated copper gilt panels covers the profusely illustrated *The Acts and Life of St Takla Haymanot* from the eighteenth century (Image 1). It somewhat resembles a Western European 'treasure binding'.

01. The Acts and Life of St Takla Haymanot, *18th century. (Or 728)*

02. *The Revelation of St John, Gondar, 1700–1730. (Or 533, f. 2v)*

03. *The painting shows St John before God and resembles woodcuts by the German artist Albrecht Dürer first published in 1498. (Or 533, f. 3r)*

01.

II.

THE DIAMOND SUTRA PRINTED IN 868

The world's oldest, complete printed book with a date

MÉLODIE DOUMY

Between the fourth and the fourteenth centuries, a large Buddhist cave complex was carved into rock on the edge of the Gobi Desert, in the present-day province of Gansu in northwest China. Known as the Mogao ('Peerless') Caves or Caves of the Thousand Buddhas, this extraordinary site is a 2-kilometre-long cliff face honeycombed with more than 1,000 caves, some of which are richly decorated with Buddhist murals and sculptures. It is located near the oasis-town of Dunhuang that was once a bustling crossroads between the northern and southern branches of the Silk Road, linking China, Central Asia and Europe.

In 1900, a small chamber, located off the corridor of a larger cave, was accidentally discovered during restoration works, revealing a cache of ancient manuscripts, paintings and other artefacts. It had probably been sealed up around the beginning of the eleventh century and contained tens of thousands of manuscripts and printed documents. The majority of these were Buddhist sacred texts or related to Buddhism, but there were also secular texts, including letters, contracts and poems. Among the treasures hidden in the secret repository for almost a millennium was a 5-metre-long scroll, which holds a woodblock printed copy of the Diamond Sutra in Chinese (Image 2).

Like other *sutras*, which are Buddhist scriptures, the Diamond Sutra records one of the sermons delivered by the historical Buddha, Shakyamuni. Amazingly well-preserved through the ages thanks to the dry climate of Dunhuang and its region, this copy of the Diamond Sutra bears a colophon indicating that it was produced in 868 CE. It is the world's earliest complete and reliably dated printed book, and also the oldest illustrated printed book. Its creation precedes Johann Gutenberg's work on movable type printing in Europe by over 500 years, and testifies to the advanced stage of development of the printing industry in ninth-century China.

This copy of the Diamond Sutra was acquired in 1907 by the British-Hungarian explorer Marc Aurel Stein, when he visited Dunhuang during the course of his second Central Asian Expedition (1906–08). Upon hearing about the existence of what has become commonly referred to as the 'Library Cave', Stein contacted its discoverer, Wang Yuanlu, and undertook lengthy negotiations to procure many documents and paintings in exchange for a small payment. These were shipped to England to be divided between the government of India and the British Museum that had funded his mission. The 868 copy of the Diamond Sutra subsequently joined the collections of the British Library after its foundation in 1973.

A SACRED BUDDHIST SCRIPTURE

The Diamond Sutra is known in Sanskrit as the Vajracchedikā Prajñāpāramitā Sūtra, which roughly translates as the 'diamond-cutting perfection of wisdom *sutra*'. It belongs to the Perfection of Wisdom genre of *sutras*, which are the cornerstone of Mahāyāna Buddhism, the branch of Buddhism most common in China, Japan and Korea.[1]

The text helps 'cut through' our perceptions of the world and argues for the illusory nature of phenomena by challenging the common belief that

01. *Detail of the frontispiece showing the historical Buddha, Shakyamuni, and the elderly disciple Subhūti.*

02 (pages 30–31). *The printed scroll of the Diamond Sutra.*

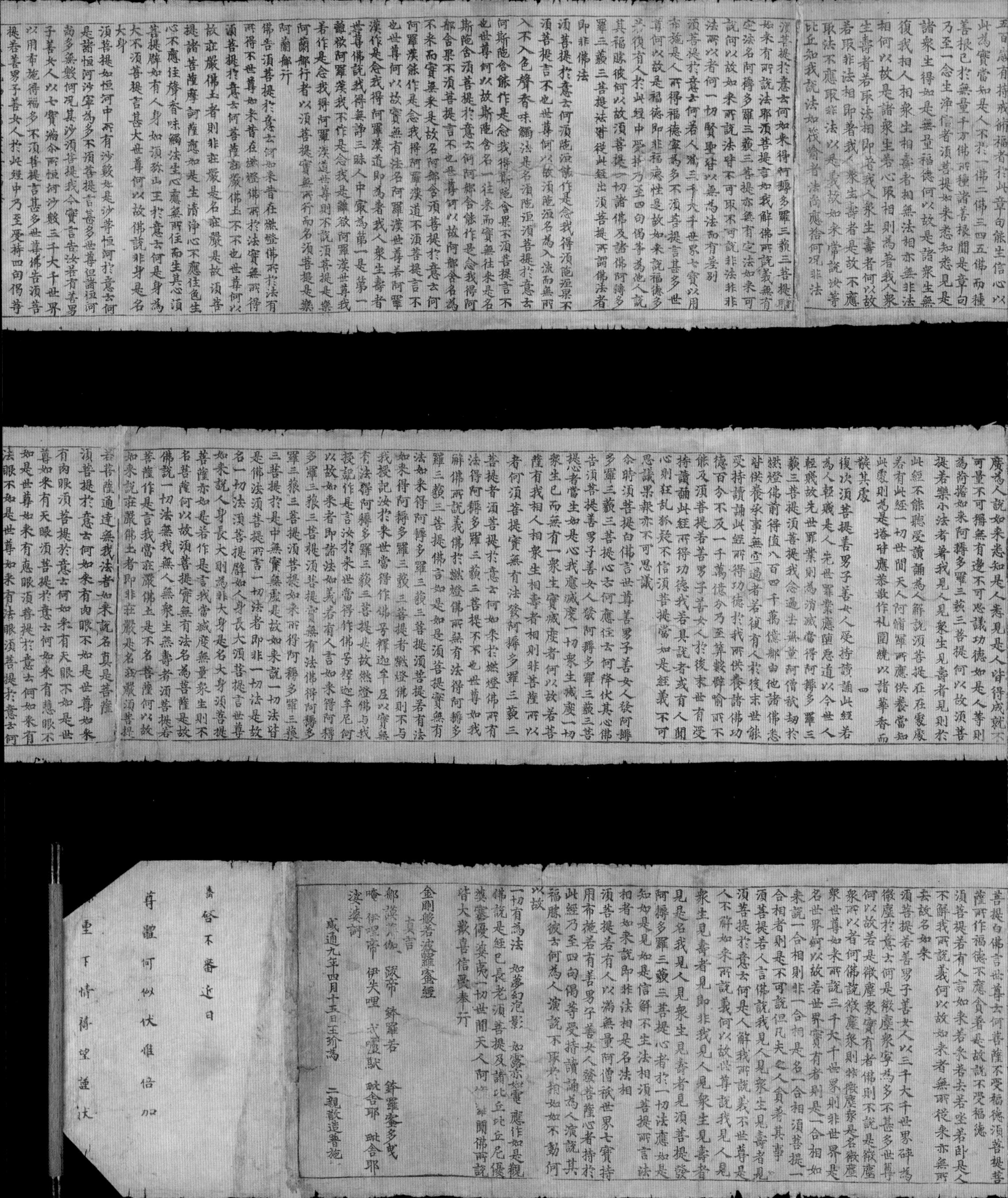

五百歲有持戒脩福者於此章句能生信心以
此為實當知是人不於一佛二佛三四五佛而種
善根已於無量千万佛所種諸善根聞是章句
乃至一念生淨信者須菩提如来悉知悉見是
諸衆生得如是無量福德何以故是諸衆生無
復我相人相衆生相壽者相無法相亦無非法
相何以故是諸衆生若心取相則為著我人衆
生壽者若取法相即著我人衆生壽者何以故
若取非法相即著我人衆生壽者是故不應
取法不應取非法以是義故如来常說汝等
比丘知我說法如筏喻者法尚應捨何况非法
須菩提於意云何如来得阿耨多羅三藐三菩提耶
如来有所說法耶須菩提言如我解佛所說義無有
定法名阿耨多羅三藐三菩提亦無有定法如来可
說何以故如来所說法皆不可取不可說非法非非
法所以者何一切賢聖皆以無為法而有差别
須菩提於意云何若人滿三千大千世界七寶以用
布施是人所得福德寧為多不須菩提言甚多世
尊何以故是福德即非福德性是故如来說福德多
若復有人於此經中受持乃至四句偈等為他人說
其福勝彼何以故須菩提一切諸佛及諸佛阿耨多
羅三藐三菩提法皆從此經出須菩提所謂佛法者
即非佛法
須菩提於意云何須陁洹能作是念我得須陁洹果不
須菩提言不也世尊何以故須陁洹名為入流而無所
入不入色聲香味觸法是名須陁洹須菩提於意云
何斯陁含能作是念我得斯陁含果不須菩提言不
也世尊何以故斯陁含名一往来而實無往来是名
斯陁含須菩提於意云何阿那含能作是念我得阿
那含果不須菩提言不也世尊何以故阿那含名為
不来而實無来是故名阿那含須菩提於意云何
阿羅漢能作是念我得阿羅漢道不須菩提言不
也世尊何以故實無有法名阿羅漢世尊若阿羅
漢作是念我得阿羅漢道即為著我人衆生壽者
世尊佛說我得無諍三昧人中最為第一是第一
離欲阿羅漢我不作是念我是離欲阿羅漢世尊我
若作是念我得阿羅漢道世尊則不說須菩提是樂
阿蘭那行者以須菩提實無所行而名須菩提是樂
阿蘭那行
佛告須菩提於意云何如来昔在然燈佛所於法有
所得不世尊如来在然燈佛所於法實無所得
須菩提於意云何菩薩莊嚴佛土不不也世尊何以
故莊嚴佛土者則非莊嚴是名莊嚴是故須菩
提諸菩薩摩訶薩應如是生清淨心不應住色生
心不應住聲香味觸法生心應無所住而生其心須
菩提譬如有人身如須弥山王於意云何是身為
大不須菩提言甚大世尊何以故佛說非身是名
大身
須菩提如恒河中所有沙數如是沙等恒河於意云何
是諸恒河沙寧為多不須菩提言甚多世尊但諸恒河
尚多無數何况其沙須菩提我今實言告汝若有善男
子善女人以七寶滿尔所恒河沙數三千大千世界
以用布施得福多不須菩提言甚多世尊佛告須菩
提若善男子善女人於此經中乃至受持四句偈等

廣為人說如来悉知是人悉見是人皆得成就不
可量不可稱無有邊不可思議功德如是人等則
為荷擔如来阿耨多羅三藐三菩提何以故須菩
提若樂小法者著我見人見衆生見壽者見則於
此經不能聽受讀誦為人解說須菩提在在處處
若有此經一切世間天人阿脩羅所應供養當知
此處則為是塔皆應恭敬作礼圍繞以諸華香而
散其處
四
復次須菩提善男子善女人受持讀誦此經若
為人輕賤是人先世罪業應墮惡道以今世人
輕賤故先世罪業則為消滅當得阿耨多羅三
藐三菩提須菩提我念過去無量阿僧祇劫於
然燈佛前得值八百四千萬億那由他諸佛悉
皆供養承事無空過者若復有人於後末世能
受持讀誦此經所得功德於我所供養諸佛功
德百分不及一千萬億分乃至筭數譬喻所不
能及須菩提若善男子善女人於後末世有受
持讀誦此經所得功德我若具說者或有人聞
心則狂乱狐疑不信須菩提當知是經義不可
思議果報亦不可思議
尒時須菩提白佛言世尊善男子善女人發阿耨
多羅三藐三菩提心云何應住云何降伏其心佛
告須菩提善男子善女人發阿耨多羅三藐三菩
提心者當生如是心我應滅度一切衆生滅度一切
衆生已而無有一衆生實滅度者何以故若菩
薩有我相人相衆生相壽者相則非菩薩所以
者何須菩提實無有法發阿耨多羅三藐三
菩提者須菩提於意云何如来於然燈佛所有
法得阿耨多羅三藐三菩提不不也世尊如我
解佛所說義佛於然燈佛所無有法得阿耨多
羅三藐三菩提佛言如是如是須菩提實無有
法如来得阿耨多羅三藐三菩提須菩提若有法
如来得阿耨多羅三藐三菩提者然燈佛則不与
我授記汝於来世當得作佛号釋迦牟尼以實無
有法得阿耨多羅三藐三菩提是故然燈佛与我
授記作是言汝於来世當得作佛号釋迦牟尼何
以故如来者即諸法如義若有人言如来得阿耨
多羅三藐三菩提須菩提實無有法佛得阿耨多
羅三藐三菩提須菩提如来所得阿耨多羅三藐
三菩提於是中無實無虛是故如来說一切法皆
是佛法須菩提所言一切法者即非一切法是故
名一切法須菩提譬如人身長大須菩提言世尊
如来說人身長大則為非大身是名大身須菩提
菩薩亦如是若作是言我當滅度無量衆生則不
名菩薩何以故須菩提實無有法名為菩薩是故
佛說一切法無我無人無衆生無壽者須菩提若
菩薩作是言我當莊嚴佛土是不名菩薩何以故
如来說莊嚴佛土者即非莊嚴是名莊嚴須菩提
若菩薩通達無我法者如来說名真是菩薩
須菩提於意云何如来有肉眼不如是世尊如来
有肉眼須菩提於意云何如来有天眼不如是世
尊如来有天眼須菩提於意云何如来有慧眼不
如是世尊如来有慧眼須菩提於意云何如来有
法眼不如是世尊如来有法眼須菩提於意云何

菩提白佛言世尊云何菩薩不受福德須菩提
薩所作福德不應貪著是故說不受福德
須菩提若有人言如来若来若去若坐若卧是人
不解我所說義何以故如来者無所從来亦無所
去故名如来
須菩提若善男子善女人以三千大千世界碎為
微塵於意云何是微塵衆寧為多不甚多世尊
何以故若是微塵衆實有者佛則不說是微塵
衆所以者何佛說微塵衆則非微塵衆是名微塵
衆世尊如来所說三千大千世界則非世界是
名世界何以故若世界實有者則是一合相如
来說一合相則非一合相是名一合相須菩提一
合相者則是不可說但凡夫之人貪著其事
須菩提若人言佛說我見人見衆生見壽者見
須菩提於意云何是人解我所說義不世尊是
人不解如来所說義何以故世尊說我見人見
衆生見壽者見即非我見人見衆生見壽者
見是名我見人見衆生見壽者見須菩提發
阿耨多羅三藐三菩提心者於一切法應如是
知如是見如是信解不生法相須菩提所言法
相者如来說即非法相是名法相
須菩提若有人以滿無量阿僧祇世界七寶持
用布施若有善男子善女人發菩薩心者持於
此經乃至四句偈等受持讀誦為人演說其
福勝彼云何為人演說不取於相如如不動何
以故
一切有為法 如夢幻泡影 如露亦如電 應作如是觀
佛說是經已長老須菩提及諸比丘比丘尼優
婆塞優婆夷一切世間天人阿脩羅聞佛所說
皆大歡喜信受奉行

金剛般若波羅蜜經

真言
那謨薄伽跋帝 鉢羅若 鉢羅蜜多曳
唵 伊哩帝 伊失哩 式嚧馱 毗舍耶 毗舍耶
莎婆訶
咸通九年四月十五日王玠為 二親敬造普施

書 啓不審近日
尊體何似伏惟倍加
重下情待望謹状

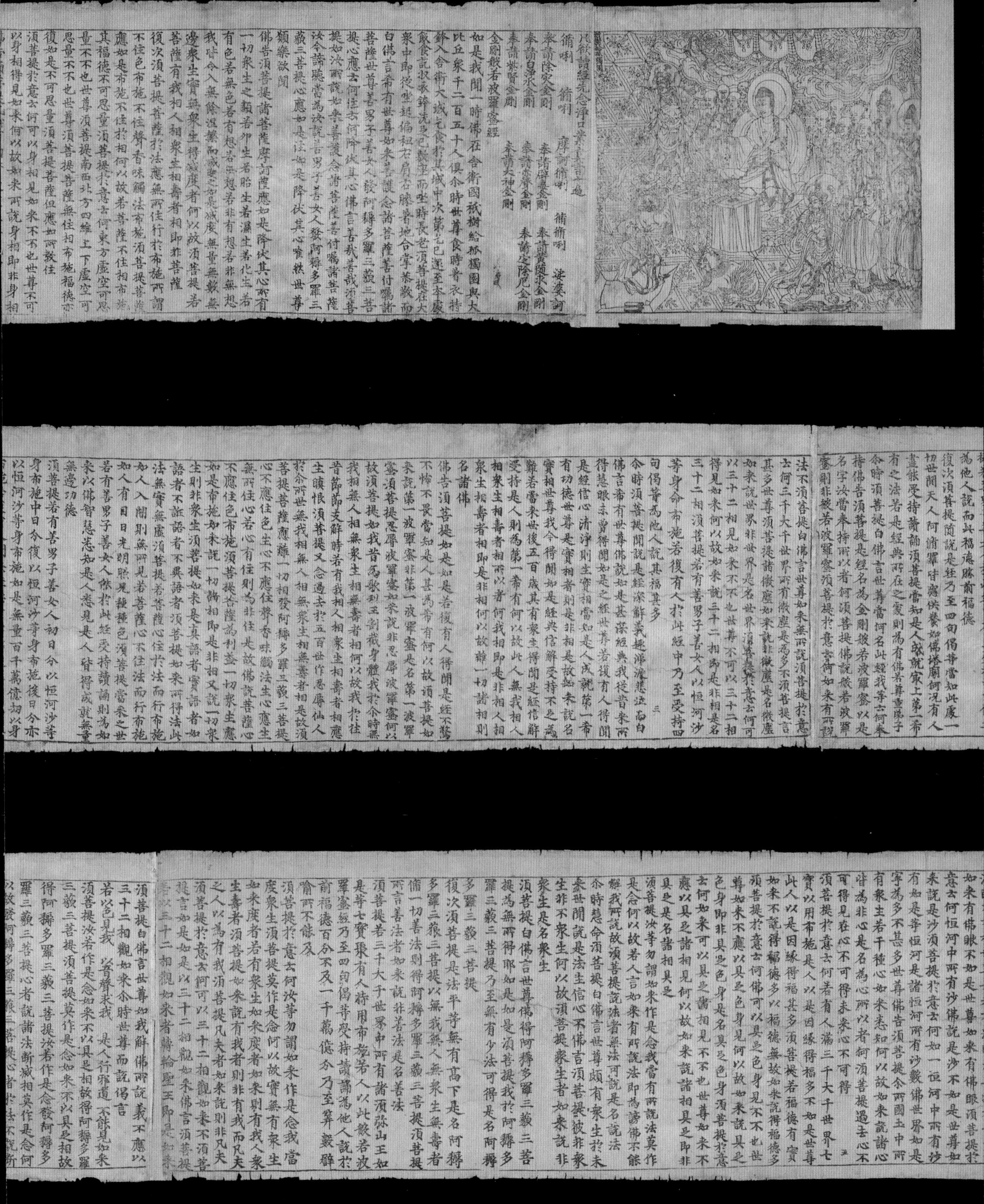

凡欲讀經先念淨口業真言一遍
脩唎 脩唎 摩訶脩唎 脩脩唎 薩婆訶
奉請除災金剛 奉請辟毒金剛 奉請黃隨求金剛
奉請白淨水金剛 奉請赤聲金剛 奉請定除災金剛
奉請紫賢金剛 奉請大神金剛

金剛般若波羅蜜經

如是我聞一時佛在舍衛國祇樹給孤獨園與大
比丘衆千二百五十人俱尒時世尊食時著衣持
鉢入舍衛大城乞食於其城中次第乞已還至本處
飯食訖收衣鉢洗足已敷座而坐時長老須菩提在大
衆中即從座起偏袒右肩右膝著地合掌恭敬而
白佛言希有世尊如來善護念諸菩薩善付囑諸
菩薩世尊善男子善女人發阿耨多羅三藐三菩
提心應云何住云何降伏其心佛言善哉善哉須菩
提如汝所說如來善護念諸菩薩善付囑諸菩薩
汝今諦聽當為汝說善男子善女人發阿耨多羅三
藐三菩提心應如是住如是降伏其心唯然世尊
願樂欲聞
佛告須菩提諸菩薩摩訶薩應如是降伏其心所有
一切衆生之類若卵生若胎生若濕生若化生若
有色若無色若有想若無想若非有想非無想
我皆令入無餘涅槃而滅度之如是滅度無量無數無
邊衆生實無衆生得滅度者何以故須菩提若
菩薩有我相人相衆生相壽者相即非菩薩
復次須菩提菩薩於法應無所住行於布施所謂
不住色布施不住聲香味觸法布施須菩提菩薩
應如是布施不住於相何以故若菩薩不住相布施
其福德不可思量須菩提於意云何東方虛空可思
量不不也世尊須菩提南西北方四維上下虛空可
思量不不也世尊須菩提菩薩無住相布施福德亦
復如是不可思量須菩提菩薩但應如所教住
須菩提於意云何可以身相見如來不不也世尊不可
以身相得見如來何以故如來所說身相即非身相

為他人說而此福德勝前福德
復次須菩提隨說是經乃至四句偈等當知此處一
切世間天人阿脩羅皆應供養如佛塔廟何況有人
盡能受持讀誦須菩提當知是人成就最上第一希
有之法若是經典所在之處則為有佛若尊重弟子
尒時須菩提白佛言世尊當何名此經我等云何奉
持佛告須菩提是經名為金剛般若波羅蜜以是
名字汝當奉持所以者何須菩提佛說般若波羅
蜜則非般若波羅蜜須菩提於意云何如來有所說
法不須菩提白佛言世尊如來無所說須菩提於意
云何三千大千世界所有微塵是為多不須菩提言
甚多世尊須菩提諸微塵如來說非微塵是名微塵
如來說世界非世界是名世界須菩提於意云何可
以三十二相見如來不不也世尊不可以三十二相
得見如來何以故如來說三十二相即是非相是名
三十二相須菩提若有善男子善女人以恒河沙
等身命布施若復有人於此經中乃至受持四
句偈等為他人說其福甚多
尒時須菩提聞說是經深解義趣涕淚悲泣而白
佛言希有世尊佛說如是甚深經典我從昔來所
得慧眼未曾得聞如是之經世尊若復有人得聞
是經信心清淨則生實相當知是人成就第一希
有功德世尊是實相者則是非相是故如來說名
實相世尊我今得聞如是經典信解受持不足為
難若當來世後五百歲其有衆生得聞是經信解
受持是人則為第一希有何以故此人無我相人
相衆生相壽者相所以者何我相即是非相人相
衆生相壽者相即是非相何以故離一切諸相則
名諸佛
佛告須菩提如是如是若復有人得聞是經不驚
不怖不畏當知是人甚為希有何以故須菩提如
來說第一波羅蜜非第一波羅蜜是名第一波羅
蜜須菩提忍辱波羅蜜如來說非忍辱波羅蜜何以
故須菩提如我昔為歌利王割截身體我於尒時無
我相無人相無衆生相無壽者相何以故我於往
昔節節支解時若有我相人相衆生相壽者相應
生瞋恨須菩提又念過去於五百世作忍辱仙人
於尒所世無我相無人相無衆生相無壽者相是故須
菩提菩薩應離一切相發阿耨多羅三藐三菩提
心不應住色生心不應住聲香味觸法生心應生
無所住心若心有住則為非住是故佛說菩薩心
不應住色布施須菩提菩薩為利益一切衆生應
如是布施如來說一切諸相即是非相又說一切衆
生則非衆生須菩提如來是真語者實語者如
語者不誑語者不異語者須菩提如來所得法此
法無實無虛須菩提若菩薩心住於法而行布施
如人入闇則無所見若菩薩心不住法而行布施
如人有目日光明照見種種色須菩提當來之世
若有善男子善女人能於此經受持讀誦則為如
來以佛智慧悉知是人悉見是人皆得成就無量
無邊功德
須菩提若有善男子善女人初日分以恒河沙等
身布施中日分復以恒河沙等身布施後日分亦
以恒河沙等身布施如是無量百千萬億劫以身

如來有佛眼不如是世尊如來有佛眼須菩提於
意云何恒河中所有沙佛說是沙不如是世尊如
來說是沙須菩提於意云何如一恒河中所有沙
有如是等恒河是諸恒河所有沙數佛世界如是
寧為多不甚多世尊佛告須菩提尒所國土中所
有衆生若干種心如來悉知何以故如來說諸心
皆為非心是名為心所以者何須菩提過去心不
可得見在心不可得未來心不可得
須菩提於意云何若有人滿三千大千世界七
寶以用布施是人以是因緣得福多不如是世尊
此人以是因緣得福甚多須菩提若福德有實
如來不說得福德多以福德無故如來說得福德多
須菩提於意云何佛可以具足色身見不不也世
尊如來不應以具足色身見何以故如來說具足
色身即非具足色身是名具足色身須菩提於意
云何如來可以具足諸相見不不也世尊如來不
應以具足諸相見何以故如來說諸相具足即非
具足是名諸相具足
須菩提汝勿謂如來作是念我當有所說法莫作
是念何以故若人言如來有所說法即為謗佛不能
解我所說故須菩提說法者無法可說是名說法
尒時慧命須菩提白佛言世尊頗有衆生於未
來世聞說是法生信心不佛言須菩提彼非衆
生非不衆生何以故須菩提衆生衆生者如來說非
衆生是名衆生
須菩提白佛言世尊佛得阿耨多羅三藐三菩
提為無所得耶如是如是須菩提我於阿耨多
羅三藐三菩提乃至無有少法可得是名阿耨
多羅三藐三菩提
復次須菩提是法平等無有高下是名阿耨
多羅三藐三菩提以無我無人無衆生無壽者
脩一切善法則得阿耨多羅三藐三菩提須菩提
所言善法者如來說非善法是名善法
須菩提若三千大千世界中所有諸須弥山王如
是等七寶聚有人持用布施若人以此般若波
羅蜜經乃至四句偈等受持讀誦為他人說於
前福德百分不及一千萬億分乃至筭數譬
喻所不能及
須菩提於意云何汝等勿謂如來作是念我當
度衆生須菩提莫作是念何以故實無有衆生
如來度者若有衆生如來度者如來則有我人衆
生壽者須菩提如來說有我者則非有我而凡夫
之人以為有我須菩提凡夫者如來說則非凡夫
須菩提於意云何可以三十二相觀如來不須菩
提言如是如是以三十二相觀如來佛言須菩
提若以三十二相觀如來者轉輪聖王即是如來
須菩提白佛言世尊如我解佛所說義不應以
三十二相觀如來尒時世尊而說偈言
若以色見我　以音聲求我　是人行邪道　不能見如來
須菩提汝若作是念如來不以具足相故得阿耨多羅
三藐三菩提須菩提莫作是念如來不以具足相故
得阿耨多羅三藐三菩提須菩提汝若作是念發
阿耨多羅三藐三菩提心者說諸法斷滅莫作是念何
以故發阿耨多羅三藐三菩提心者於法不說斷

03.

Specification	*Scale*
PRINTED COPY OF THE DIAMOND SUTRA China, 868 276 x 4995 mm Or 8210/P.2	

all things have an immutable essence, or soul, in favour of a more fluid and relational view of existence. It was translated several times and between various languages, including Chinese, Tibetan and Khotanese. The version that appears on the copy held at the British Library is the first Chinese translation, which is attributed to the Central Asian monk Kumārajīva around 401 CE. Based on the sermon given by the historical Buddha in Jetavana, near Śrāvasti, in modern-day Uttar Pradesh, India, the text begins with the phrase, 'thus I have heard', as *sutra*s typically do.

As the Diamond Sutra was distributed through China, some ritual textual elements were gradually incorporated before and after the main text. By the mid-ninth century, typical additions included the names of four *bodhisattvas*[2] and eight Vajra deities that vary slightly from manuscript to manuscript, as well as magical incantations, prayers and mantras.[3] In this copy of the Diamond Sutra, a mouth-purifying incantation and a prayer to the eight Vajra deities precede the *sutra*, which is then directly followed by a mantra. These were meant to be recited for protection, indicating that the contents of the sacred book were not only studied, but also said aloud and chanted as part of ritual practice.

Here, the text of the Diamond Sutra and final mantra are followed directly by a colophon that reads as follows: 'On the 15th day of the 4th month of the 9th year of the Xiantong reign period, Wang Jie had this made for universal distribution on behalf of his two parents' (Image 4). This short dedicatory note established the sacred book's claim to fame by authenticating its creation date as 11 May 868. It also informs us that an individual named Wang Jie sponsored the project in order to disseminate the Diamond Sutra widely and for the benefit of his mother and father, whether they were alive or dead at the time. A clue as to why he chose to reproduce the Diamond Sutra lies in the text itself, which encourages its own reproduction as a way to earn merit. The thousands of copies of the Diamond Sutra that were discovered among the documents from the Library Cave speak of the significance and popularity of the *sutra* on the ground.

The British Library's collections contain over 600 copies of the Diamond Sutra that were gathered by Stein and are, for the major part, manuscript.[4] Several possess dedication notes showing that they were commissioned and produced by people from all walks of life: government officials, monks, nuns, and ordinary men and women, hoping that their wishes would be granted in return. One of the most frequently invoked concerns was the well-being of relatives or loved ones. A somewhat surprising colophon reveals how one man asked for his ox to be reborn in the Pure Land. Buddhist devotees equally prayed for benefits in the present life. In 700, a government official, who paid for a copy of the *sutra*, vowed to have one copy made every month if he was promoted, and two if he was further promoted.[5]

A BOOK IN SCROLL FORMAT

This printed scroll of the Diamond Sutra has travelled through time almost completely intact. It measures 276 millimetres high and comprises seven sheets of fine mulberry paper that add up to a total length of 4,995 millimetres. It has retained its beautifully illustrated 'frontispiece' (Image 1), its tapered end piece and its original wooden roller.

For centuries, horizontal scrolls were the most widespread book format in China. They derived from an earlier form of written communication in which text was inscribed on narrow strips of wood or bamboo that were bound together with strings and rolled up for storage or transport.[6] Scrolls were initially made of a long piece of silk, an expensive and valuable material that was used sparingly, and became gradually replaced by paper as a more affordable and convenient alternative. Paper scrolls are constructed of several sheets of paper glued together to create a continuous roll of adjustable length.

Although archaeologists have found scraps of paper dating back to the first and second centuries BCE, according to the official Chinese histories, paper was invented in 105 CE by a court eunuch called Cai Lun. He famously reported to the emperor on paper obtained from a mix of bark, hemp, scraps of cloth and fishing nets. It is clear from the manuscripts and printed documents found in Dunhuang Library Cave that paper was already in common use by the fifth century. By contrast, papermaking was only introduced to Europe in the twelfth century via Arabs who had learned the craft from the Chinese.

Scrolls like this copy of the Diamond Sutra were read from right to left, according to the direction of the Chinese script, by carefully unfurling one segment at a time. The most valuable scrolls occasionally opened with an illustration and had a protective flap designed to be wrapped around them and tied with a fine silk braid. A wooden roller, taller than the height of the paper and sometimes equipped with knobs at the top and bottom for easier handling, was typically fastened to the inner end of the scroll so that the long strip of paper could be rolled around it (Image 3). Several scrolls could then be enclosed and stored together in a wrapper made of bamboo, silk or other cloth.

Every stage in the creation of a book in scroll format required intensive labour and involved the contribution of several skilled individuals. This

03. *Rolled up scroll of the Gem Hip Sutras from Dunhuang with its original wooden roller, protective flap and silk braid,* c. *8th century. (Or 8210/S.351)*

04. *Detail of the colophon of the printed Diamond Sutra.*

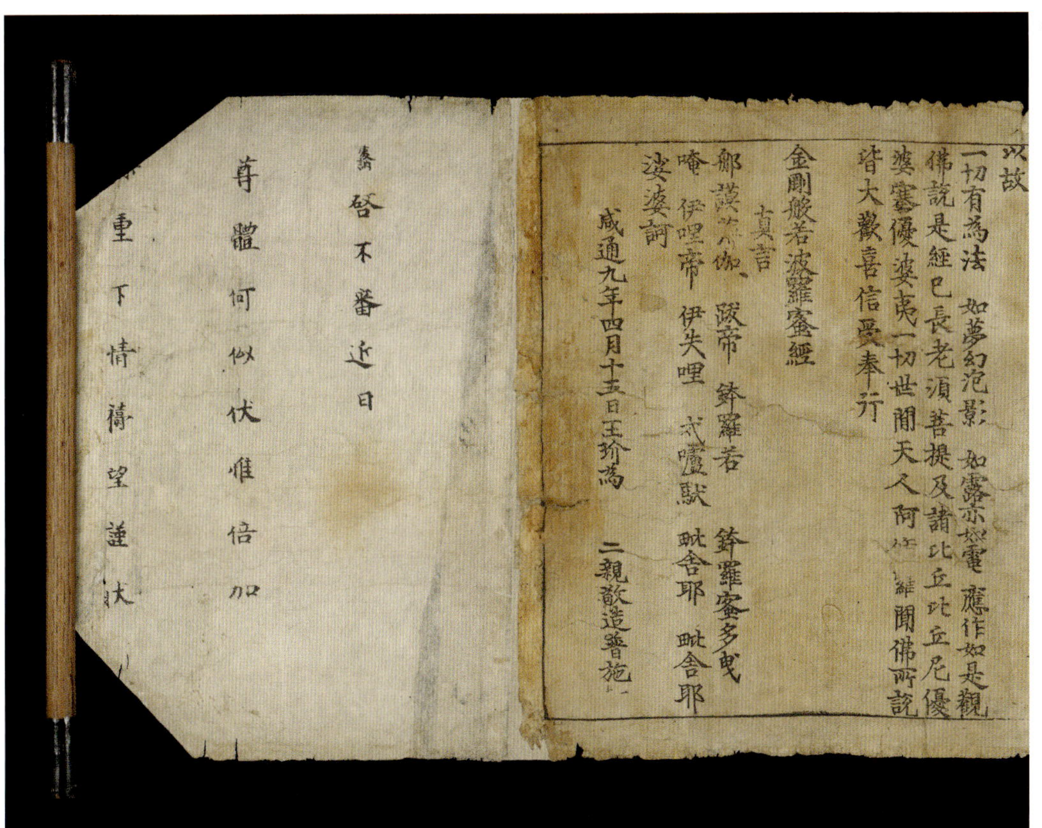

05.

06.

process is particularly well-documented in some of the finest handwritten scroll copies of key Buddhist *sutras* found at Dunhuang. These originally came from the imperial capital, Chang'an, where they were produced according to the highest standard. They contain long tabulated colophons that detail the number of sheets and type of paper used, as well as the names of the paper-dyer and mounter, the scribe, the proofreaders and the superintendents.[7]

Although scrolls were prevalent among the materials from the Library Cave, several other book forms were also represented. This includes booklets that possibly appeared in the ninth century and became increasingly used. Small and portable, they enabled easy access to any part of the text, thus offering the double advantage of being convenient to read and to carry.[8] There was an old man who, between the ages of 82 and 84, copied several booklets of the Diamond Sutra himself. We know this thanks to the dedicatory notes that he appended to each of them. This devout Buddhist did not indicate his name, but he claimed to have written one of the booklets, which can be dated to 906, with a mixture of his own blood and ink.[9]

A LANDMARK IN THE HISTORY OF PRINTING

A particularity of this copy of the Diamond Sutra is that it was produced using woodblock printing. This technique, also referred to as xylography, is believed to originate in China, where it possibly developed during the Tang dynasty (618–907) and spread to the rest of East Asia. It is rooted in reproduction methods that can be traced as far back as the Neolithic period, when potters decorated clay vessels and tiles by stamping patterns on their surface.

To create a woodblock print, the text and/or illustration(s) were first produced in ink on a sheet of paper and then pasted face down on a block often obtained from the wood of fruit trees. Once this was done, an engraver chiselled away the blank parts so that the black lines or characters would appear as a mirror image in relief (Image 8). The block was inked and paper was applied to its surface to take an impression. The sheet of paper was peeled off and put aside and the process could be repeated as many times as necessary. Over 1,000 copies could be taken from the original block.[10] This copy of the Diamond Sutra was printed using seven different woodblocks, one for each of the seven sheets of which it is comprised. Its sophisticated design integrates the remarkable preaching image located at the beginning of the scroll and the Chinese scripture transcribed in beautiful characters.

(07.)

05. & 06. *Depictions of the four* bodhisattvas *and four of the eight Vajra deities, booklet, ink on paper,* c. *9th–10th centuries. (Or 8210/S.5646, ff. 2v–4r)*

07. *The Million Pagoda Charms were printed on thin strips of paper and placed inside miniature wooden pagodas. (Or 78.a.11)*

It bears testimony to a well-established printing industry in which only the most talented artist, calligrapher and woodblock carver could have jointly collaborated to produce this masterpiece. Although the circumstances of its journey to the Mogao Caves are unknown, some scholars believe that the printed Diamond Sutra was probably made in Sichuan, which was an important centre for woodblock printing at the time.[11] Given that it was destined for distribution, it would not be surprising if several copies bearing the 868 colophon had been presented to a number of important Buddhist temples across China, including in the region of Dunhuang, a major Buddhist hub on the Silk Road. However, the copy currently held at the British Library is the only one still in existence.

By turning to printing, Wang Jie would have accumulated good karma on a scale previously unimaginable, while ensuring greater accuracy during the replication process. The 868 printed copy of the Diamond Sutra is the earliest printed book bearing a date, but there exist earlier examples of printing from East Asia. Between 764 and 770, the Japanese empress Shōtoku ordered the production of the Million Pagoda Charms to be distributed among leading Buddhist temples in Japan (Image 7). In 1966, an even earlier printed text, dated to approximately 751, was discovered in the Bulguksa temple in Gyeongju, South Korea. This highlights again the nexus between the development of printing and the practice of Buddhism, anchored in Buddhist doctrine and worship.

Even after the advent of printing, hand-copying remained an important merit-generating activity among devotees, and the documents found in the Library Cave were mostly handwritten. Nevertheless, the Diamond Sutra was not the only printed item found in the cave. For example, the British Library's Stein collection includes a small booklet of the Diamond Sutra printed at Dunhuang in 950 and donated by the local ruler Cao Yuanzhong. Of much coarser quality than the printed scroll of the Diamond Sutra, it identifies the woodblock carver as Lei Yanmei.[12] There are also a few almanacs and several prayer sheets, which contain both text and depictions of Buddhist deities.

AN ILLUSTRATED FRONTISPIECE

The scroll of the Diamond Sutra opens up with a preaching image, which is extremely rich in details and makes it the earliest extant illustrated printed book. Occupying an entire sheet of paper, the picture is placed at the beginning of the book, right before the title and text of the Buddhist scripture, thus serving a decorative function akin to that of a frontispiece.

The scene is set in a grove of trees that a small cartouche on the top right corner identifies as the Jetavana park, where the Buddha delivered his sermon. Foliage is not only visible but also evoked by the flowery patterns of the intricate geometric background. This depiction is directly connected to the content of the Diamond Sutra, whose text begins by describing how, having begged for food in the city, the Buddha ate his meal and settled down to answer the questions of the elderly disciple Subhūti. In the middle of the composition, Shakyamuni is seated cross-legged on his lotus throne and raises his right hand in a teaching gesture (Image 1). Above him are a jewelled canopy and two flying celestial beings followed by long cloud trails. Before him is an altar table with three ceremonial vessels.

The Buddha is surrounded by two *bodhisattvas* identifiable by their princely ornaments and haloes, as well as a group of nine monks of varying ages with shaven heads. The latter are disciples, skillfully rendered with individualised facial features. To the Buddha's left are an emperor and empress, accompanied by servants. He is also flanked by two wrathful guardian deities: one clenches his fists and stands on a rock; the other brandishes a thunderbolt and stands on two lotuses. Two small reclining lions, protectors of the Buddhist faith, are among the Buddha's attendants. Rather than being represented in a frontal view, facing readers, this large assembly is depicted in a more dynamic three-quarter profile, looking towards the elderly figure located in the lower left corner.

This is the disciple Subhūti, to whom the sermon of the Diamond Sutra is directed. His black shoes are neatly placed next to his prayer mat. Having put a knee on the ground and bared his right shoulder, he holds the palms of his hands together in a supplicatory gesture. He looks reverentially at the Buddha, in quest of answers to life's greatest questions. The very layout of the illustration visually establishes the nature of the scripture as a dialogue between the master and his disciple. It also leads the reader's gaze to the content of the conversation that unfolds in the following sections of the scroll.[13]

Among the documents from the Library Cave, there was a small number of Diamond Sutra copies, mostly booklets, that were complemented by hand-drawn illustrations. A couple of these also contain

08. *Woodblock for printing. On the upper right side, an erroneous character was incised and removed. (Or 14251)*

08.

a 'frontispiece', which similarly features Subhūti kneeling in front of the Buddha, with monks and *bodhisattvas* set against a leafy backdrop. Their rendition is simpler than that of the image on the British Library's printed copy of the Diamond Sutra, and the quality of the execution seems to have varied from one manuscript to another, probably dependent on the skills of their creators.

In some instances, additional depictions of *bodhisattvas* and/or Vajra deities were also included. They could precede or follow the image of the Buddha, but could also appear independently of it (Images 5 & 6). In the same way that reciting the name of the four *bodhisattvas* and the eight Vajra deities could generate blessings, these illustrations may have invoked the protective powers of these guardian figures. Perhaps the picture of the Buddha on the frontispiece served a ritual function too – if spreading the word of the Buddha was considered a meritorious act, so was disseminating his image. This practice is exemplified by repeating Buddha images found stamped on paper fragments, or stencilled on the inside of the caves themselves.

The woodblock-printed Diamond Sutra marks an extraordinary achievement in the history of the book and its design. A century after it was created, the printing of the entire canon of Buddhist scriptures was underway in Sichuan, and the first editions appeared during the Northern Song dynasty (960–1127). Nothing comparable existed in Europe, where printing only developed over five centuries later. Even movable type, which proved impractical for Chinese characters, was a technology known in China as early as the eleventh century.[14]

In 2010, the British Library completed a decade-long project to conduct comprehensive restoration and analysis to bring the scroll as close as possible to its original condition.[15] As Joyce Morgan put it, 'It seems ironic that a work which deals with impermanence and life's fleeting illusions is the world's oldest known printed book.'[16] Yet, it can now continue to be shared with a wide audience for generations to come.

THE DEVELOPMENT OF PAPER

LUCY VINTEN

Paper and parchment coexisted for centuries in books in Europe, both manuscript and print. The earliest known book containing paper made in Europe is a Missal now in the monastery of Silos in Spain, made before 1089.[1] Many early printed books in Europe were parchment, including the Mainz Psalter (see pages 74–83) and Gutenberg printed some copies of his Bible on parchment and some on paper. The British Library holds one of each. Ultimately paper became ubiquitous because, being manmade, it was scaleable in a way that parchment, which needed vast numbers of animal skins, could never be. The Lindisfarne Gospels alone used the skins of 130 sheep (see pages 16–25). Although estimates vary, in the first fifty years of printing in Europe between nine million and 12.6 million books were produced, creating a demand for writing surfaces which animal skins could not supply.[2] Paper could be manufactured to meet that demand.

Cai Lun, an official at the Han dynasty court, perfected and recorded papermaking in the first century CE, although some paper had been made earlier. Despite Chinese attempts to keep it secret, the technology spread along trade routes. Paper was made in Central Asia by the eighth century, with centres of excellence at Samarkand and Baghdad.[3] Papermaking spread through Europe from Muslim Al-Andalus in the twelfth and thirteenth centuries, with centres in northern Italy, especially at Fabriano[4] and later in France and Holland.

The papermaking process remained largely unchanged from Cai Lun's time until mechanisation in the nineteenth century. Complex processes transformed plant material into paper, with seventy-two separate stages identified by a Chinese source.[5] Mulberry bark typically provided the fibres for early Chinese paper, seen in the paper used in the Diamond Sutra (see pages 28–37). European papermakers used rags, an already processed source of fibre. These could be old clothes, sails, ropes; the choice would affect the quality of the end paper, and careful sorting was needed. The rags were macerated with copious amounts of water. This process, known as retting, softened the fibres and removed impurities. Next, the fibres were beaten and chopped into small pieces, constantly washed, resulting in a vat of liquid 'stuff', the technical term for the thick soup that was made into paper.

Sheets of paper were formed using a rectangular frame with a mesh surface supported on wooden ribs, surrounded by a mould known as a deckle. This was dipped into the stuff and lifted out horizontally, allowing the water to drain off. The remaining fibres dried to become a sheet of paper. The ribs and wires of the mesh showed as lines in the finished sheet, with the more visible lines of the ribs called chainlines. Papermakers started adding wire symbols to the mesh like bunches of grapes, vases or oxen, which were visible as watermarks, identifying workshops, batches of paper or different sizes and qualities of paper.[6] The British Library Qur'an from Aceh has no dating information other than paper dated by its watermark to 1819, suggesting it was copied in the 1820s (see pages 158–167).

Paper was produced in different sizes, which varied through time; over 300 different English words have been used to describe paper sizes. The quality of paper varied too, chiefly due to the selection of rags. Fine white linens made the best white writing paper, while coloured linen, canvas or a proportion of wool made for lower quality. Coloured paper was produced too, the Aldine Press printed some of its *enchiridia* (see pages 87–93) on blue paper and some artists favoured brown paper for works in chalk or pastel.[7]

01.

02.

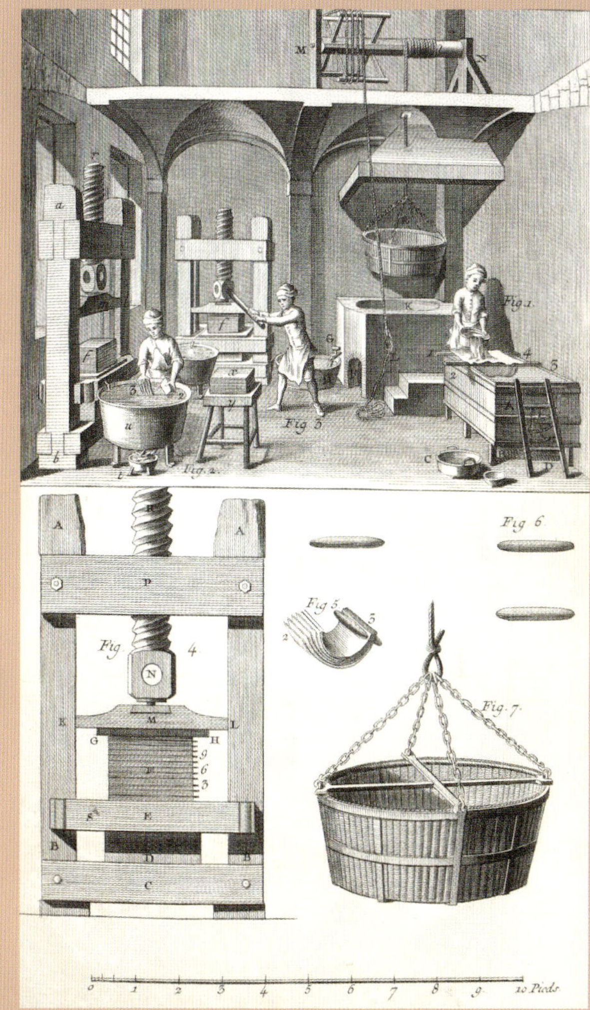

As demand for paper grew, supply difficulties multiplied, especially shortages of suitable rags. Other sources of fibre were trialled including straw, corn husks and seaweed, but none was a commercial success,[8] until Friedrich Gottlob Keller started making paper from wood pulp. This paper was cheap and white, but also brittle and friable, thanks to added chemicals including sulphurous acid, and lignin emitted by the wood pulp.

Mechanisation of the papermaking process started with the adoption of the Hollander Beater in the late seventeenth century, and by the early nineteenth century fully mechanised papermaking was introduced by the Fourdrinier brothers.[9] Essentially the liquid stuff was now poured on to a moving mesh conveyor with the water draining off as it moved, producing a continuous roll of paper.

By 1830 half the paper in England was produced mechanically, and the era of handmade paper came to a close. Henceforward nearly all books were printed on machine-made paper, the few exceptions the result of aesthetic rather than economic decisions. William Morris printed his *The Works of Geoffrey Chaucer* (see pages 204–213) on handmade paper, and it was a popular choice for twentieth-century artists' books.

01. *'Der Papiermaaker' (The Papermaker), engraving from* Het Menselyk Bedrygf (The Book of Trades) *by Jan Luyken, 1694. (12331.dd.1)*

02. *Papermaking, plate from Diderot's* Encyclopédie, *1751–65 (66.g.9)*

III.

THE ARNSTEIN BIBLE

A monastic Giant Bible

KATHLEEN DOYLE

In the late eleventh and twelfth centuries, ambitious projects to create elegant, highly legible and complete Bibles in one or more large volumes were undertaken in scriptoria throughout Western Europe. Together, they are now referred to as Romanesque display or Giant Bibles. Like earlier Anglo-Saxon and Carolingian Bibles, their enormous dimensions indicate that these books must have been read and used communally, rather than individually. Typically, these communal groups were religious, composed either of monks or canons. Most medieval orders, such as Benedictines following the Rule of St Benedict, prescribed daily biblical readings, and it seems likely that these beautiful and very legible books were used in the *opus Dei* (work of God) as part of the daily office in the church or for readings in the chapter house or refectory.

BACKGROUND

The British Library's collections include several splendid examples of these impressive manuscripts, which, with their medieval bindings, can weigh up to 18 kilogrammes. A fine German one is the Arnstein Bible, produced at the Premonstratensian abbey of St Mary and St Nicholas, Arnstein, on the Lahn River about 30 kilometres east of Coblenz. This abbey was founded in 1139 by the last count of Arnstein, Ludwig III (d. 1185), who became a lay brother and donated his castle to the new order, established at Prémontré in northern France in 1120. Ludwig's wife Guda became a hermit who lived in the abbey grounds. The Bible entered the British Library (then part of the British Museum) as one of the foundation collections on the Museum's formation in 1753 as part of the collection of the 1st and 2nd Earls of Oxford, Robert Harley (1661–1724) and his son, Edward Harley (1689–1741).

01. *Evangelist portrait of St John with the first words of his text, his symbol the eagle and, above, Christ blessing and holding a golden book, at the beginning of the Gospel of John. (Harley 2799, f. 185v)*

The Bible can be dated fairly precisely because of historical annals recording important events related to the abbey that were originally included in it.[1] Moreover, we know the name of the man who wrote it, identified in the entry for 1172 as a brother called Lunandus, who asks that whoever reads it should pray that he rest in peace: '*Qui ergo legit, dicat: Anima eius requiescat in pace*.' Lunandus had a formidable task to undertake in planning out the design and layout of this enormous book, which is now in two huge volumes, with Genesis to Malachi in Latin in the first, and Job to Revelation in the second. The text is written out in thirty-nine lines to a page, with generous margins.

PRESENTATION OF THE TEXT

Most of the biblical books and introductory material are presented in two columns of 130 millimetres in width. However, another indication that this Bible is a great monastic book is the inclusion in the book of Psalms of not one version, but rather three translations of this text, in three parallel columns, each 80 millimetres in width. Over a period of nearly twenty-five years, St Jerome (d. 420), one of the four Fathers of the Western Church, worked on translations of biblical texts from Greek and Hebrew into the Latin vernacular, and he completed three versions or revisions of the Psalms. By tradition the first was made from the Greek Septuagint version and is now commonly known as the Roman or *Romanum* Psalter because it was adopted by the Church in Rome. Another is the Gallican or *Gallicanum* version, known as such because it was adopted in Gaul. St Jerome completed this translation between 386 and 391, basing it on Origen's (d. *c.* 254) Greek text of the Psalms from the edition of the Old Testament in Hebrew and Greek. The Gallican text was the version in use at Charlemagne's court, and became the standard version to be included in copies of the Vulgate, the single, authoritative version of Christian Scripture in Latin in Western Europe for over 1,000 years. In the Arnstein Bible, the *Gallicanum* appears in the

02. *Detail of the beginning of the Gospel of John. (Harley 2799, f. 185v)*

03. *The end of Psalms and the beginning of the prologue to Proverbs. (Harley 2799, f. 57)*

first column, accompanied by the *Romanum* and the *Hebraicum* in the second and third columns, the last a translation made directly from the Hebrew that was never used liturgically. This virtuoso display of learning is found in Giant Bibles made in the Mosan and Rhenish regions in particular, although two English examples also survive.

For Lunandus, the transition from two to three columns and back again presented particular challenges. The end of the three comparable versions of the Psalms proper finishes about three-quarters of the way down the page (Image 3). At this point, the reader must switch from comparing variant texts across the page to reading one column and then going to the next, sequentially. However, perhaps because the page was ruled for three columns, the scribe separated the following texts with a series of rubrics (the term rubric is derived from the Latin *rubrica*, the name of the red ochre pigment used to make the colour red). Lunandus then presented the short so-called Psalm 151 in the first column and started the prologue to the next biblical book in the second.

PLACEMENT OF THE RUBRICS

The rubric in the first column summarises the contents of Psalm 151: *Hic p[salmu]s pr[opr]ie scriptus est David [et] extra numerum cum pugnaret cum gloria et in hebraicis codicibus non habetur* (This Psalm was written by David himself and is outside the number [of the Psalms] and is not contained in Hebrew Bibles. It is about the time when David fought with glory.) The short text in seven verses follows. The adjoining rubric is spread out over columns two and three and explains that the Psalms have ended: *explicit liber psalmorum* (here ends the book of Psalms) and that the prologue to Proverbs is about to begin (*incipit*). The start of this prologue begins in the middle column. Here Lunandus left room for an enlarged initial letter on eight lines, the letter 'C' of the first word '*Chromatio*', the name of the original addressee. The rest of the word is written in individual letters vertically to the right of the first letter. The initial itself is embellished with stylised acanthus leaf decoration punctuated with characteristically Germanic bands ornamented by small round dots that are cinched around the foliate form.

This decoration is among the more modest in the book, which, like many Romanesque Giant Bibles is distinguished by the beauty of its drawn and painted initial letters in addition to the elegance of its script. As is typical in these grand Bibles, each biblical book opens with a large initial. This type of embellishment had to be planned carefully, to allow enough space for the enlarged letter. In the Arnstein Bible there is a mixture of initial letters that are designed as foliate forms and more complicated ones that are literally 'historiated', namely with embedded illustrations reflecting or commenting on the story of the text.

FIGURATIVE INITIALS

The historiated initial became a customary feature of luxury biblical codices throughout the Middle Ages. In books without pagination, there is also a functional aspect to this decoration as an aid to finding the different parts or divisions of the work. Different styles are employed in the two volumes, with the Evangelist portraits and the book of Prov-

Incipiunt parabole Salomonis.
Sapientia
Prudentia
Parabole Salomonis
Fortitudo
Iusticia

Specification	*Scale*
BIBLE, IN LATIN Arnstein, Germany, c. 1172 540 x 355 mm Harley 2798–2799, ff. 235 (vol. 1); 243 (vol. 2)	

erbs in the second volume being particularly elaborate, fully painted and illuminated with gold. The image of Solomon illustrating the book of Proverbs on the reverse side or verso of the folio with the end of Psalms is a good example of this (Image 4). It features a crowned Solomon set on a background of gold leaf, writing out the beginning of the text (*Parabole Salomonis*) in the bowl of the first letter '*P*'. The letter dominates the page, filling up most of the second column. The end of the letter indeed spills over into the first column, overlapping the end of some of the chapter lists, and almost obscuring a word of text. This indicates that the painting of the letter took place after the text was written. Little heads emerge and peep out from the end of leaves, and birds and fruit feature among the swirling foliage, while a dragon's body forms part of the letter itself. Four roundels add to the meaning and sophistication of the imagery, featuring personifications of the Virtues identified by scrolls: *Sapientia*, *Prudentia*, *Fortitudo* and *Iusticia* (Wisdom, Prudence, Fortitude and Justice). Each is appropriate to this biblical 'Wisdom' book and exemplifies its contents. Throughout the Middle Ages, ecclesiastical communities reading the Bible understood it on more than one level, interpreting it morally and allegorically, in addition to literally. As in this initial and others in the Arnstein Bible, the most sophisticated biblical illustrations in these books incorporated one or more of these interpretative devices in their designs.

The illustrations at the beginning of each Gospel are even more elaborate: they are not confined to the initial, but become larger combinations of words and images filling most of the page. These impressive initials each include a depiction of the Evangelist who wrote the Gospel, and have been characterised as 'among the most magnificent sets of Evangelist portraits in all of medieval art'.[2] Each Evangelist is in a pose familiar from centuries of Evangelist portraits, seated at a lectern in the act of composing his Gospel, holding a pen and often a knife, too, for corrections. Around the Evangelists intricate foliage, interlace and ornamental clasps adorn the letters of the first word or words of their Gospels. For example, St John's position at the beginning of his Gospel is central, and the arrangement of his initial words multifaceted (Image 1). The large panel takes up most of the page, using forty of the forty-nine lines. Although the first two words are included within this large painting set on gold leaf, they are so embedded and elaborated that they are somewhat difficult to make out.

The '*I*' of the first word '*in*' (in) is barely distinguishable from the curvilinear pattern of stylised vines that are intertwined with it, emerging from the robes of a figure set frontally in the corner of the image. The identity of this man is unclear. One possible interpretation is that the figure is Moses, who was thought to be the author of the first five books of the Old Testament. Genesis begins *In principio* (in the beginning) – the same words as those that begin the Gospel of John. Moreover, later in the first chapter Moses is cited as the recipient of the Law, in comparison with Christ and the new law of grace: 'For the law was given by Moses; grace and truth came by Jesus Christ' (John 1:17). In the illustration, *In principio* is written in red in an open book, together with part of the rest of the verse: '*In pri[n]cipio erat verbum, & verbu[m]*' (In the beginning was the Word, and the Word [was with God, and the Word was God]). Directly above the book Christ with a cruciform halo blesses the Evangelist, holding a golden book over his head, making the point visually that Christ is the Word (Image 2). The scene also makes clear the divine inspiration of the text: St John's symbol of the eagle perhaps literally puts words into his mouth, as it touches St John's lips with its beak.

Lunandus may not have been involved in the design or execution of these large historiated initials. Certainly, sufficient space was left for them at the point when the text was being written. While many of the initials are calligraphic and completed in ink, these more sophisticated painted and gilded ones may well have been made by specialist artists, whether monks within the abbey or others invited in for the purpose. Moreover, the styles of the letters – whether decorated or historiated – are sufficiently distinct that it seems likely that more than one artist was involved. The various stages of production, such as the composition and underdrawing,

04. *Solomon writing* 'Parabole Salomonis', *with busts of Wisdom, Fortitude, Justice and Prudence, at the beginning of Proverbs. (Harley 2799, f. 57v)*

the application of gold leaf and the application of different layers of paint may also have been specialised and involved a team of artists and assistants.

CANON TABLES

Another different but no less complicated design decision involved the layout for a series of tables before the New Testament. These tables, known as canon tables from the Greek word for table, list similar passages in the four Gospels. The system of comparison was devised by the early Church Father Eusebius (d. 340), bishop of Caesarea in Palestine, who developed a list of the passages that narrated the same event in one or more of the four Gospels of Sts Matthew, Mark, Luke and John. As Eusebius explained in a letter to his friend Carpianus, he compiled the tables to help the reader 'know where each of the Evangelists was led by the love of truth to speak about the same things'. There are ten tables in total: the first lists passages common to all four Gospels, the next eight list passages that are common to three or two Gospels, and the final canon lists those that appear in only one Gospel. In order to provide the lists, a numbering system for the verses in each account was required. Eusebius built on a system that he attributed to Ammonius of Alexandria, and these section numbers, which are presented as Roman rather than Arabic numerals, are accordingly known as Ammonian sections.

Canon tables appear in hundreds of copies of the four Gospels, in Greek as well as Latin, and also in many deluxe complete Bibles. As is common in sumptuous copies, in the Arnstein Bible the columns of numbers are themselves framed in an architectural arcade, complete with arches, bases and capitals (Image 5). These architectural columns are actually two columnettes, not unlike those that appear in many monastic cloisters, and are engulfed by swirling tendrils of vines that alternate symmetrically. Within these spaces the Ammonian section numbers are listed in parallel columns for each of the first nine canons. The location and the comparison of the numbers is made somewhat easier (either for the scribe or for the reader) by small brown dots that mark the beginning of each group of five numbers.

Like the rest of the book, the pages of the canon tables are ruled with a series of faint lines. These were created with a straight edge: the pricking holes used to ensure that the lines were straight are still visible in the outer margin of the pages. The preparation for the entering of the rubrics also is still visible in the margins. The rubrics in red would have to be added using a different pen with red ink at a different stage than the text itself, which was written in brown ink. As with the painted historiated initials, it may be that these were added by someone other than Lunandus. Alternatively, he may have written them himself, but at a later stage in the process. There are also notations of what the rubrics should be, written in small letters near the edges of the margins. Presumably these were entered while the scribe had his textual exemplar in front of him. For example, at the top of the page are the rubrics to be entered as headings, reading across: '*canon primus in quo quatuor*' (the first canon in which four [Gospels are compared], with the names of the relevant books below: '*Mathe[us], Marc[us], Lucas and Ioh[an]es*'. These correspond to the red headings that appear just under the arches. The small inscription in the lower margin is somewhat more problematic, because it does not correspond to any rubrics at the end of the page. It reads '*Finit ca-non pri-mus in quo iiii*' (the end of the first canon in which there are four). Given the spacing, which corresponds to the four columns, it seems probable that a rubric was originally intended for the end of the canon, but for whatever reason was never executed. Other decoration, including an unfinished sketch of St Jerome writing at the beginning of the first volume of the Bible, was also left incomplete. Even so, the Arnstein Bible is a stunning achievement in scholarship and design. Every aspect of its production was planned carefully and executed painstakingly by hand. Like other Romanesque great or Giant Bibles, the Arnstein Bible represents a testament to the commitment of its makers to the elegant presentation of the Word of God.

05. *Canon table 1, enclosed in an architectural space. (Harley 2799, f. 152v)*

KING HENRY VIII'S COPY OF THE 'GREAT BIBLE'

KAREN LIMPER-HERZ

The design of a title page could be used as a tool to represent power and authority. In 1538, King Henry VIII's chief minister Thomas Cromwell and Archbishop Thomas Cranmer commissioned the English reformer Miles Coverdale to produce an English translation of the Bible that would improve those of the Coverdale Bible of 1535 and the so-called Matthew's Bible of 1537. In September 1538, Cromwell had issued an injunction ordering every parish to buy a copy of an English Bible and place it in 'sum convenient place' for all to see and read. What became known as the 'Great Bible', due to its impressive size, was the first officially sanctioned translation of the Bible into English and its elaborate woodcut title page reflects this. It was first printed in April 1539 and had been published in six editions and more than 9,000 copies by 1541.[1]

Image 1 shows a special copy of the 'Great Bible', printed on vellum and illuminated throughout. It was presented to Henry VIII by the London haberdasher Anthony Marler, probably in 1542 as a sign of his gratitude to the king for granting him permission to print the Bible but also to protect his own business interests.[2] Marler's presentation inscription faces the title page.[3] This copy was later inherited by Queen Elizabeth I.

The most striking feature of the 'Great Bible' is its woodcut title page which was used to communicate a visual message about Henry's new role as the Supreme Head of the Church, independent of the pope's authority in Rome. In this copy, the woodcut has been painted over and illuminated to make it more luxurious and special, worthy of the intended recipient. At the top God is portrayed in the centre and Henry is kneeling in prayer to his left, receiving the Word directly from God. Below that, Henry is shown wearing his crown and his purple and ermine robes as he hands out the *Verbum Dei*, the Word of God, to Archbishop Cranmer to his right and a bearded man to his left. In the original woodcut for the 1539 edition (Image 2), Thomas Cromwell was placed to Henry's left, but after his execution on 28 July 1540, the woodcut was altered to remove Cromwell's coat of arms, leaving a blank space (Image 3). Tatiana String has convincingly argued that the bearded man shown in Henry VIII's copy is Lord Russell, who succeeded Cromwell as Lord Privy Seal in 1542.[4] Both Cranmer and Russell then pass on the Word of God to clergy and laymen and they, in turn, pass it on to the English people.

The text of this copy is that of the edition printed in April 1540, but the woodcut below the illumination is the one used after Cromwell's execution in July 1540 – the artist has covered the space with green foliage[5] (see Image 1). While the order in which the Word of God is passed down from God to the English people is the same as in the 1539 woodcut (Image 2), the depiction of the main characters, most notably Henry himself, has been refined and is more akin to miniature portraiture than generic woodcut illustration, possibly to be more appealing to its recipient. String suggests that the illumination may have been done by Lucas Horenbout, the Flemish artist and court miniaturist, or his studio.[6]

When illuminating a woodcut in a printed book, an artist's normal practice was to follow the underlying printed illustration. The woodcut on the title page of Henry VIII's copy of the 'Great Bible', however, served only as a guide for the artist who

then painted over it and altered it. This special copy is a good example of how, almost 100 years after the introduction of printing with movable type in the West, in Mainz in the middle of the fifteenth century, the practice of turning individual copies into luxury objects by printing them on vellum and illuminating them continued the centuries-old tradition of illuminating special copies of manuscripts.

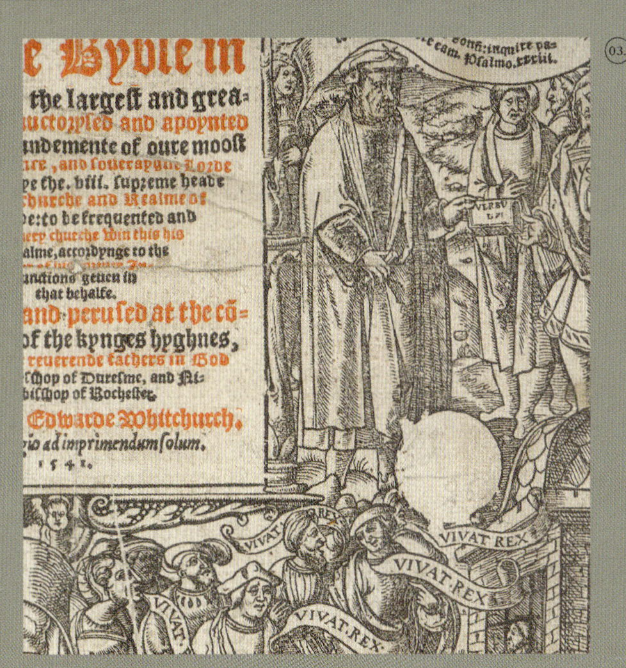

01. *The title page of Volume 1 of Henry VIII's copy of* The Byble in Englyshe *(the 'Great Bible'), Edward Whitchurch, 1540. (C.18.d.10, vol. 1)*

02. *The title page of* The Byble in Englyshe *(the 'Great Bible'), Richard Grafton and Edward Whitchurch, 1539. (C.18.d.1)*

03. *Detail of the title page of* The Byble in Englyshe *(the 'Great Bible'), Edward Whitchurch, 1541 edition. (C.18.d.8)*

01.

THE GOLDEN HAGGADAH

A luxurious Hebrew manuscript from medieval Spain[1]

ILANA TAHAN

HEBREW MANUSCRIPTS AND THEIR DESIGN

After the destruction of the Second Temple in 70 CE, with Judea devastated and Jerusalem, the heart of Jewish religious and spiritual life, in ruins, Hebrew books took on a special significance for the exiled Jewish people. Their books played not only a pivotal role in transmitting Jewish faith and culture, but also ensured the survival of Hebrew – the holy language of Judaism – despite the Diaspora or dispersion of Jews across the world.

Priceless and cherished possessions, books accompanied their Jewish owners wherever they happened to go, be it on voluntary journeys or forced exile to remote lands. Hebrew manuscripts are hence intricately linked to the fate of the Jewish people, offering palpable testimonies of their complex and trying history, their culture and traditions.

The term 'Hebrew manuscripts' denotes hand-copied writings in Hebrew and related languages that use the Hebrew script such as Aramaic, Judeo-Arabic, Judeo-Italian, Judeo-Persian, Judeo-Spanish, Yiddish and various others.

Book production was markedly impacted by the geographical dispersion of the Jewish people. Each geocultural zone produced its own style of Hebrew writing and manuscript design, reflecting the uniqueness of the Jewish community as well as the influence of the host environment.

Medieval Hebrew manuscripts created in Europe and the Near East, for example, were notably affected by contemporary trends prevalent in their respective Christian and Islamic environments. Islam's aniconic approach had a profound and lasting impact on Hebrew books manufactured in Muslim lands. The design and decoration manifest in extant Hebrew Bibles originating from these areas strongly suggest that Jewish scribes and artists would have had access to embellished Islamic manuscripts which influenced their art. Like Qur'ans, early Hebrew Bibles lack human and animal imagery, and their ornamentation is essentially functional. Carpet pages featuring geometric and abstract shapes, patterned and minute lettering, and divisional motifs adapted from Islamic art typify their decoration.

01. *Scenes from Genesis, one of a series of pages with tooled gold-leaf backgrounds in the Golden Haggadah, which give the book its name. (f. 5r, detail)*

Influences from local cultures aside, the design of medieval Hebrew books exhibits certain distinctively Jewish characteristics and motifs:

- The absence of upper-case letters in the Hebrew script led to the ornamentation of initial words.
- There is a lack of painted narratives in medieval biblical codices, particularly those produced in the Islamic Near East and the Iberian peninsula.
- The Hebrew system of writing from right to left meant that the organisation of miniatures usually followed the same direction. The Golden Haggadah is an excellent case in point. The order of its lavish illuminations, which are arranged in groups of four to a page, is: upper right, upper left, lower right, lower left.
- Another design trait often encountered in medieval Hebrew Bibles is micrography.[2] This scribal practice flourished in Egypt and the Land of Israel from the ninth century onwards. It gradually spread to Europe and other parts of the Near East, reaching its peak between the thirteenth and fifteenth centuries. The texts commonly fashioned into micrographic shapes were the Masorah (see description below) and the Psalms.

Peculiar to some Hebrew illuminated manuscripts produced in Germany during the thirteenth and fourteenth centuries (for example, *haggadot* and prayer books) were animal-headed figures or

Specification	Scale
THE GOLDEN HAGGADAH Northern Spain, probably Barcelona, c. 1320 245 x 190/200 mm Add MS 27210	

humans with distorted heads and faces. Theories abound about this intriguing phenomenon. One plausible theory is that this may have been a means of evading the ban (espoused by Jewish pietistic movements) on painting human forms, especially of women.

Given its central role in Judaism, the copying of the Hebrew Bible (Tanakh in Hebrew), both in its entirety and in its constituent parts, continued from ancient times throughout the medieval era. In antiquity the Hebrew Bible and other literary texts were inscribed on scrolls made either of strips of parchment or papyrus. The codex[3] was adopted by Christians for writing and disseminating their holy scriptures in the early centuries of the first millennium. In Judaism, the transition from scroll to codex occurred much later, and no earlier than the eighth century, although bound books may have been in use before then. In the Near East the Hebrew terms used to designate a codex, often mentioned in colophons and owners' inscriptions, were *mitshaf* (מצחף) and *daftar* (דפתר), both loanwords from Arabic.

The tenth and eleventh centuries witnessed a surge in the production of Hebrew Bible codices, some of which have survived to this day. The codex had obvious advantages over the scroll, which was inscribed on one side only, was awkward to consult and handle, and necessitated ample storage space. Due to being written on one side, scrolls were costly to produce, requiring larger quantities of animal hides than codices.

Between the sixth and tenth centuries, scholars in Tiberias, in the Land of Israel, known as Masoretes, developed a system of annotations collectively termed as Masorah (from the Hebrew consonantal root '*msr*' meaning to 'hand down'). The Masorah is fundamentally a corpus of rules on the pronunciation, reading, spelling and cantillation of the scriptural text, which ensured the correct transmission of the Hebrew Bible over the centuries. The Masoretes' foremost contribution was the invention of special signs and vowels that set up in writing the accurate way of reading the consonantal biblical Hebrew script previously fraught with ambiguities. The compact, sturdy and user-friendly codex was seen as the perfect vehicle for disseminating and preserving the authoritative Masoretic text of the Jewish scriptures.

The Torah (Pentateuch or Five Books of Moses) – the most sacred part of the Hebrew Bible used regularly in synagogal ritual – nonetheless continued to be written in scroll format. This millennia-long tradition is still in practice today.

The earliest decorated Hebrew manuscripts were created between the ninth and twelfth centuries in the Islamic Near East, chiefly in Egypt and the Land of Israel. These were largely biblical codices that shared numerous artistic and stylistic characteristics with contemporary Qur'ans. In the Christian West the illumination and decoration of Hebrew books began around the thirteenth century, continuing until the close of the fifteenth century. Throughout this period, schools of Hebrew manuscript painting emerged in Ashkenaz (particularly France and Germany), in Sepharad (Spain and Portugal), and in Italy.

THE PASSOVER FESTIVAL

Passover is a major Jewish spring festival that has been celebrated annually since ancient times. It lasts seven days in the Land of Israel and eight days among the Diaspora Jewish communities, and it commemorates the Israelites' miraculous liberation from Egyptian bondage as described in the biblical book of Exodus. The rituals of Passover enable Jews to re-enact this momentous event.

For Jews, Passover signifies their birth as a free people; consequently, the religious importance of the festival has markedly increased over time. The victorious Exodus from Egypt has become an integral part of Jewish observance. In the Torah where laws or ethical directives are given, there are constant reminders that the Almighty redeemed the Israelites from Pharaoh's oppressive rule. Undoubtedly, one of the most telling examples are the Ten

02.–05. *(top left) An embellished row of initial word-panels (f. 56v); (top right) a decorative panel and foliate scrolls (f. 78v); (bottom left) zoomorphic letters (f. 36v); (bottom right) the* matsah *as a stylised roundel with Islamic style geometric interlacing (f. 44v).*

03.

04.

05.

סדר
הגדה של
פסח
עם שירים מיוחדים, על כל
הנפלאות והנסים, שנעשו
ביציאתם ממצרים
בני חורין
נתנו במתנה הגבירה מרת רוסה
תמ״א בת המפואר כמהר״ר יואב
גאליקו יצ״ו אל המשכיל
חתנה כמ״ר אליה יצ״ו
פ״ה קר״פי

Commandments, which open with the emphatic declaration: 'I am the Lord Thy G-d who brought thee out of the land of Egypt, out of the house of bondage' (Exodus 20:2) (Deuteronomy 5:6).

WHAT IS A *HAGGADAH*?

The pinnacle of the Passover festival is reading the *haggadah*. The *haggadah*, which simply means 'narration' or 'telling' (from the Hebrew consonantal root '*hgd*'), is the Hebrew service book used at home on Passover Eve to guide the order of service at a ceremony known as Seder (order). On the first evening of the festival, as well as on the second in diasporic communities, families and guests of all ages gather around the festive Seder table to recite the story of the Israelites' departure from Pharaoh's Egypt.

Originally an integral part of the Sidur (general prayer book), the *haggadah* became an independent entity sometime in the thirteenth century, soon emerging as the type of Jewish text most suitable for decoration. Its narrative, ritual and educational character, and the fact that it was intended for domestic use, provided ample scope for artistic creativity. This is attested by the broad range of medieval *haggadah* manuscripts still in existence.

THE GOLDEN HAGGADAH

The Golden Haggadah is undoubtedly one of the finest and most remarkable of the *haggadah* manuscripts from fourteenth-century Spain, and the British Library's most famous Hebraic treasure. It has been acknowledged as the most lavishly embellished and best preserved of all extant fourteenth-century illuminated *haggadot* from Spain. Created in Catalonia, probably in or near Barcelona around 1320, this luxurious codex, written and illuminated on vellum, consists of three distinct parts: a preliminary cycle of biblical miniatures; the *haggadah* text; and religious poems for the Passover festival. With some exceptions, this composition is typical of many of the surviving Spanish *haggadot* from that period. It is important to point out that the British Library is the custodian of what is probably the largest and most important collection of *haggadot* originating from medieval Spain, specifically Catalonia.

(07.)

The manuscript opens with a sequence of fourteen full-page miniatures[4] depicting episodes from the books of Genesis (Image 1) and Exodus (Image 9), the midrash (rabbinic interpretations of the Hebrew Scriptures) and ritual scenes showing preparations for Passover (Image 8). The pages with the miniatures are divided into four panels, each containing at least one biblical episode. The panels are framed by blue or brown bands with white pen scrolls or zigzag patterns and have gold squares stamped in their corners. Some panels have foliate pen scrolls extending from the corners. The contemporary captions written at the head and foot of the pages are mostly paraphrases of the biblical verses describing the episodes illustrated in the panels.

Altogether there are seventy-one biblical and midrashic scenes covering the Israelites' history from creation up to liberation from Egyptian slavery. These sumptuous illuminations set against gold tooled backgrounds earned the manuscript its name and were executed by two unnamed artists in the Gothic style predominant in Europe at the time. Their individual methods differ, however, one showing more preference for Italian motifs, the other greater affinity with French conventions.

06. *Probably modelled on frontispiece designs in contemporary printed books, the title page was added in Carpi, Italy, in 1602 by Joav Gallico. (f. 2r)*

07. *The* Seder *ceremony from the Barcelona Haggadah, 14th century. (Add MS 14761, f. 28v, detail)*

Gothic-style decorations also embellish the Hebrew text in the second part of the manuscript (Images 2–5) and include foliage scrollwork, illuminated words, zoomorphic letters and text illustrations of significant Passover symbols: the first cup of wine, the unleavened bread and the bitter herb. Recent studies have shown that the Golden Haggadah was painted in a workshop by a team of craftsmen. Apart from the two principal miniaturists who created the biblical pictorial narratives, other unnamed artists painted the textual illustrations and decorated the poetical pieces.

Various art historians have noted that the biblical miniatures at the beginning of this *haggadah,* as in other fourteenth-century Spanish *haggadot*, while evoking the liberation theme that is central to the Passover festival, bear almost no connection to the *haggadah* text itself, which is a collection of literary works from various time periods. Besides instructions for the Seder rituals which are organised into fifteen orderly steps, the text is a mosaic of biblical passages, blessings, hymns, legends, short dialogues and rabbinic literature.

Theories surrounding the origins and actual role of the biblical illuminated cycles in these manuscripts have thus been wide-ranging. Some scholars have claimed that the biblical narratives were inspired by comparable illustrations in Latin Psalters – volumes containing the book of Psalms and other devotional texts. Developed mainly in England and France during the twelfth and thirteenth centuries, illuminated Psalters included full pages of miniatures depicting scenes from the life of King David, the main author of the book of Psalms, images of saints and episodes from the life of Christ. Interestingly, the illustrations in Christian Psalters are totally detached from the actual text. They are thus akin to the biblical narratives found in *haggadot*, which have no relationship to the text either.

Other scholars have disputed this link to Latin Psalters, contending that the biblical imagery found in Psalters has theological connotations, whereas the pictures in Spanish *haggadot* lack all doctrinal significance.

More recent studies have defined these cycles as didactic tools likely to have been used either before or after the Seder ceremony. Their principal role was to teach biblical history, which is only mentioned generally in the *haggadah* text, and to highlight the unwavering relationship between God and Israel. More significantly, the cycles are seen as message carriers aimed at promoting some of the burning religious issues of the day, particularly criticism against the allegorical exegesis prevalent in the (Christian) host culture, and a revival of traditional midrashic interpretation of the Hebrew Bible. Allegorical interpretation was a method used by Christian medieval theologians to study differences between the Old and New Testaments. Christian commentators believed the Hebrew Bible[5] served as an allegory of New Testament events. For instance, they construed the Old Testament story about Jonah and the whale to be a representation of Jesus's death and resurrection.

The manuscript's last section includes biblical readings for the holiday and a collection of 100 liturgical compositions[6] to be recited in the synagogue during the Passover week. Although intended to enhance the experience of worship, liturgical poems were an optional part of the synagogal service. Many of the authors of the religious poems in the Golden Haggadah are celebrated poets of the Golden Age of Spain (eleventh to twelfth centuries), such as Judah Halevi, Abraham Ibn Ezra and Solomon Ibn Gabirol.

It has been suggested that Spanish *haggadah* manuscripts comprising large numbers of poems were intended for cantors or other officials connected with the synagogue. Accordingly, the Golden Haggadah's original patron could have been a cantor. However, like other *haggadot* created in fourteenth-century Spain, the Golden Haggadah lacks a colophon. Consequently, nothing is known about the original commission, or the identities of the scribe, artists and patron engaged in the production of this timeless masterpiece.

Thorough research work undertaken in the early years of the twenty-first century has nonetheless shed some light on the likely nature of the patron of the Golden Haggadah. He would almost certainly have been an eminent rabbinic scholar-educator and would have overseen the creation of the biblical illuminations, instructing on their contents and messages. The craftsmen responsible for the pictorial narratives skilfully adapted and processed Christian models and motifs for a Jewish audience, weaving legends from the midrash into the biblical imagery. They would have had a close collaboration with and been steered by their erudite patron, indicating that both artists and patron were equally familiar with contemporary trends in Christian art and rabbinic scholarship. It is important to point out that the first half of the thirteenth century[7] constituted a turning point in the position of Spanish Jewry. The Catholic clergy became increasingly hostile towards the Jews, compelling them to wear the yellow badge to distinguish themselves from the Christian population. The papal bull of Pope Innocent IV issued in April 1250 imposed draconian measures on the Spanish Jews, such as forbidding them to build synagogues without permission, to associate with Catholics and live under the same roof, to eat and drink with them, or to employ Christian nurses or servants. At the outset of the fourteenth century, as antisemitism soared, the situation for the Jews throughout Spain became precarious. Recent studies have asserted that the impetus to develop pictorial cycles stemmed from an antagonistic relation with Christianity and its interpretation of the Old Testament and its art. Thus, the message of the pictorial cycles in Spanish *haggadot*, the Golden Haggadah included, were not merely lessons in midrash, but an answer to the rationalist allegorism of the Bible predominant in the Christian host society in which the Jews lived at the time.

An in-depth study of the Golden Haggadah's pictorial narratives undertaken in 2011 addressed the importance of women in the manuscript as well as its possible provenance. Through a systematic analysis of each female character appearing in it and a highly imaginative typology of necessary, corroborative and incidental figures, the study showed that the inclusion of a large number of women in the manuscript had been a deliberate choice by the patron. The analysis yielded several interesting observations:

- the inclusion of episodes from the book of Genesis could have been a deliberate choice so as to include more women
- peripheral or incidental female figures were added to the manuscript because of the creators' desire to involve and thus emphasise women
- there is a visual emphasis on women with children
- females being rescued from death and women grieving at the loss of children are also highlighted.

Relying on the internal iconographic evidence and more specifically on the images portraying women mourning a child's death, the study surmised that the Golden Haggadah may have been originally created for a woman who had suffered the loss of a child. And given the triple appearance of the biblical Rachel in the illuminations, this woman's name could have been Rachel.

The history of this magnificent work of art can partially be reconstructed from later owners' records of sale and censors' inscriptions contained in it, all of which unquestionably prove that the manuscript was in Italy between 1599 and 1863. How and when exactly it reached Italy is uncertain. It has been suggested that the Golden Haggadah was taken there by Jews fleeing Spain shortly after their expulsion in 1492, or maybe before that. Even if that was indeed the case, its fate since its completion up to 1599 is still shrouded in mystery.

The manuscript's earliest known owner was Joav Gallico, rabbi in Mantua in 1602 and formerly a *dayan* (judge) in Governolo. The Golden Haggadah was a wedding gift to Eliah Rava who married Gallico's daughter Rosa in Carpi, on 25 October 1602, as recorded on the title page added on the second page (Image 6) of the codex. Joav Gallico may have acquired his exquisite gift in Governolo or Mantua, or in Carpi itself just before the wedding. It is also possible that the manuscript was already in Carpi as early as February 1599, since Fra Luigi da Bologna, a convert to Christianity and a Dominican, signed it then. Fra Luigi was appointed censor of Hebrew books in the Duchy of the House of Este in the Modena district in 1597. The manuscript remained in the Modena region in the seventeenth century, as indicated by the signatures of Camillo Jaghel and Renato da Modena, two Christian censors who in turn inspected it in 1613 and 1626.

The last private owner was Joseph (Giuseppe) Almanzi (1801–1860), an Italian-Jewish poet, born in Padua, who was an avid collector of rare books and manuscripts. We do not know when the Golden Haggadah entered Almanzi's collection, but in 1864 it was bought by the British Museum and now belongs in the British Library's Hebrew collection.

08 (page 58). *Ritual scenes, with distribution of* matsah *(top left) and Passover preparations (bottom left). (f. 15v)*

09 (page 59). *Scenes from Exodus showing the plagues. Clockwise from top right: frogs, beasts, murrain or livestock, lice. (f. 12v)*

08.

משה
ותעל הצפרדע
אהרן
משה
ותהי הכנם באדם ובבהמה

V.

THE QUEEN MARY PSALTER

A virtuousic display of English painting

KATHLEEN DOYLE

The Queen Mary Psalter is one of the most extensively illustrated manuscripts ever produced, containing around 1,000 images. Prefacing, commenting on and embellishing the Psalms, the illustrations are justly famous for their artistic sophistication in both coloured drawings and paintings. Extraordinarily, all of the illustration seems to have been made by the same person, an artist now known as the 'Queen Mary Master' after this book. The manuscript takes its name not from its original owner but from Queen Mary I (r. 1553–8), to whom it was presented in 1553 by a zealous customs officer, Baldwin Smith, who had prevented its export from England. Although there is no heraldic or documentary evidence that the manuscript's initial patron was also royal, the magnitude and quality of its illustrations makes an owner of such status very likely. Planning, designing and executing the programme of illumination would have been an extensive task.

This manuscript was made in England, probably in London, in the first quarter of the fourteenth century. In size, the Queen Mary Psalter is a large-format book, with each page measuring 275 by 175 millimetres, indicating that it was not intended to be a hand-held devotional book. Indeed, the book would have been much easier to handle (and still is) when placed on a lectern or desk of some sort. Its text is written in large characters and is extremely legible, with very few abbreviations.

CONTENTS

As in any Psalter, the heart of the manuscript is made up of the biblical book of Psalms. This Old Testament book formed the basis of monastic services; monks who followed the Benedictine rule recited all 150 Psalms each week. Laypeople, too, used Psalms in their devotions from an early date. Not surprisingly, therefore, manuscripts containing them in one form or another are the most common type of book to survive from the Middle Ages. In terms of content, a Psalter also includes other devotional and liturgical material such as Canticles, or biblical passages characterised as songs, litanies and prayers. Many hundreds of medieval copies survive, including many very deluxe illustrated ones like the Queen Mary Psalter.

LINE DRAWINGS IN A PREFATORY CYCLE

It is clear that the design and layout of the book – both its text and illustrations – took careful thought and planning. The book begins with an extensive cycle of full-page images, each with a short caption in Anglo-Norman French, one of seven English fourteenth-century manuscripts to feature a long Old Testament picture cycle of more than 100 scenes.[1] In the majority of these manuscripts, including the Queen Mary Psalter, illustrations from the book of Genesis are predominant, perhaps because the text lends itself to narrative. In the Queen Mary Psalter there are sixty-six images, of the total prefatory cycle of 223. Most of the scenes are doubled up two to a page in framed registers or sections, as in the Creation of Adam and Eve, and the Admonition not to eat from the Tree of Knowledge (Image 1). All of these illustrations are executed as line drawings in dark brown ink, and coloured shading and washes in a limited palate of green, purple and brown, with a delicate focus on carefully rendered details. The captions below each drawing summarise the scenes succinctly: below the image of God creating Adam and then Eve the captions read, '*Coment deus crea adam*' (How God created Adam) and '*Coment deu creast Eve de la coste adam*' (How God created Eve from the side of Adam).

01. *The Creation of Adam and Eve, and the Admonition not to eat from the Tree of Knowledge. (f. 3r)*

01.

Coment deus crea adam.
Coment deu creast Eue de la coste adam.
Coment deu baillia a Adam & a Eue paradys terrestre a gardir e lur defendoit le fruyt de cel arbre.

IHESUS
SYMONIS ET IUDE
IOHANNES WA
MARIA VIRGO
IACOBUS MI
IACOBUS MA
IOSEP
MARIA I
ALPHEUS
MARIA II
ZEBEDEUS
MARIA III
Seint anne fu mariee a iij. mariz a joachim a cleophe a salomee. e
de enfaunta les iij. maries. joseph: out la pmere. alpheus la. ij. zebe
deus la. iij. la pmere marie aporta ihu cst. la secunde porta seint. jake
alphei. e seint symō. e seint. jude la. iij. porta seint jake de galice zebedei
e seint. johan euuangeliste.

In terms of production, the red borders around these delicate drawings must have been added after both the drawings and their explanatory captions, because they deviate from a regular rectangular shape in some cases. For example, in the creation of Eve scene the text of the caption regarding Eve extends beyond the frame to the right, and the red is filled in rather awkwardly around the word '*adam*'. Similarly, Adam's left foot in the scene below extends into the border. The figures are drawn directly onto the parchment, without any background colour, so the black border lines and the red colour could not have been in place when the drawings were completed.

POSITIONING THE LAYOUT OF THE GENEALOGICAL DIAGRAMS

Following this long prefatory cycle are four pages with a very different layout, content and style. It is immediately apparent and striking that these are paintings in full colour set on backgrounds of gold, in contrast to the delicate drawings enhanced by light colour washes of the preceding pages. The gold was applied as gold leaf on the pages to form the backgrounds, affixed to a base of gesso, a mix of glue binder and chalk or gypsum. In the Queen Mary Psalter the leaf is decorated with incised diamond shapes or arranged in a checkboard design alternating with painted squares. The washes have been replaced by deeply saturated reds and blues, greens and pinks. The layout is quite different as well: these four pages are painted on only one side of the parchment, in two pairs of facing full-page diagrams. In part, this may result from the different type of content of these pages, which constitute a kind of bridge or transition to the main body of the text. Nevertheless, the figures retain their elegant draftmanship, with carefully drawn features that demonstrate that they were made by the same artist.

02 (pages 62–63). *The Tree of Jesse and the Holy Kinship.* *(ff. 67v–68r)*

The first pair of facing pages feature two genealogical diagrams (Image 2). On the left is a common motif, the so-called Tree of Jesse, showing the ancestry of Christ from Jesse, the father of the shepherd David, who became King of Israel. A branch emerges from the large reclining figure of Jesse at the bottom of the page, twining to form a compartment for David above Jesse, identified by his crown and attribute of a harp. (David is often depicted playing a harp at the beginning of the book of Psalms, which are sacred songs traditionally attributed to him as author.) This imagery is derived from a prophecy articulated in the book of Isaiah (11:1) that 'there shall come forth a rod out of the root of Jesse, and a flower shall rise up out of his root' (*egredietur virga de radice Iesse et flos de radice eius ascendet*). In most medieval depictions of this scene, the rod (*virga*) is interpreted as a reference to the *virgo*, or Virgin, and the flower (*flos*) as Christ, either or both of whom usually appear at the top of the tree.

In the Queen Mary Psalter, however, the lineage of the Virgin Mary is shown in a more extended form on the facing page. This contains an unusual depiction of what has come to be known as the 'Holy Kinship': the relationships between the Virgin and her sisters and nephews. The basis for these relationships is not set out in any biblical account, but instead comes from commentaries and accounts of the lives of saints. One of the most well-known versions of this text occurs in a compilation of the lives of saints made by the Dominican friar Jacobus of Voragine around 1260 entitled *The Golden Legend*.[2] According to Voragine's account, the Virgin Mary's mother, St Anne, had three husbands: Joachim, Cleophas and Salome, and a daughter with each of them, all called Mary.

In the Psalter, Anne appears in the lowest register of the image with each of her husbands. Directly above each pair are the daughters of the marriages together with their own husbands. In the second register, St Joseph and the Virgin Mary are on the left, with Alphaeus and the second daughter Mary (also known as Mary Cleophas, after her father) in the centre, and Zebedee and the third daughter, known as Mary Salome, on the right. The figures in the top two registers are the sons of these unions: here the Virgin is shown again to the left, holding the Christ Child on her lap. Next to them is St James the Less, one of the four sons of Mary Cleophas, and next to him St James the Great, the son of Mary Salome. At the top Christ appears on his own to the left, this time in Majesty, holding a globe of the world, next to the other two sons of Mary Cleophas who became apostles (Sts Simon and Jude), in the centre, and St John the Evangelist, the second son of Mary Salome. Perhaps because this image is much more unusual than the Tree of Jesse, most of the figures are labelled with their names in the band separating the registers. In addition, a short summary is written in Anglo-Norman French below the image that confirms the content. The diagrammatic presentation emphasises the importance of the Virgin and of Christ, by picturing each twice. This prominence may result from a deliberate correspondence with the design and placement of the figures in the branches of the Tree of Jesse on the facing page: the four registers of the Holy Kinship correspond to the levels of the Tree. The Tree begins at the bottom with the recumbent Jesse, the ancestor of David, who is at the same level as Anne, the ancestor of the Virgin. On the right in the Holy Kinship diagram, the Virgin and Christ are featured in the positions they occupy typically in a Jesse Tree.

SETTING OUT THE SAINTS IN THE CALENDAR

The next section of the book is a calendar, and required a completely different layout from either of the first two sections. In the Middle Ages, as today, calendars served to organise time into days and months. Although the names of the months are the same as those we still use, the numbering of the days was based on the ancient Roman system of *kalends* (from which the word calendar derives). The large letters 'KL' at the top of the page are an abbreviation for this (Image 3). In the Psalter, each day of the month is presented on a separate line, with saints' days and holidays noted for the relevant day. The most decorated Psalter calendars often have figurative decoration in addition to the text, consisting of the relevant Zodiac signs and the so-called 'labours or occupations of the months', which show an activity for the month. Thus, in August, three men are busy cutting wheat under the supervision of an overseer, opposite a young woman representing Virgo. Typically, these scenes appear in small roundels in the body of the calendar. However, in the Queen Mary Psalter each month of the calendar is set out on two pages, and the scenes take the form of large images that run across the tops of the page, in a kind of frieze format. The scenes, too, become more elaborated: Virgo is accompanied by three other women who sway as if dancing, together with others who kneel and pluck flowers, mimicking the agricultural activity opposite (Image 4).

ILLUMINATING THE PSALMS

These varied types of images and texts are all prefatory to the heart of the book, which consists of the Psalms themselves. As might be expected from such a lavish introduction, this part of the Psalter is also very extensively illustrated. Both techniques of decoration previously used – watercolour drawings and bright painting in colours on gold backgrounds – are here combined throughout. The gold and painted illumination is utilised at the beginning of each Psalm, which begin with a large initial that is the height of two lines of text, decorated with plant forms, animals or hybrids, faces, or more elaborate scenes, such as figures in prayer. Most verses begin with a one-line illuminated initial executed in gold on a red-and-blue filigree background. Even larger, four-line initials begin the Psalms at the major textual divisions, which assist the reader in identifying them. These divisions separate the Psalter into ten groups. Eight of the groups are derived from the daily recitation of Psalms (two groups

03. & 04 (pages 66–67). *August, with the cutting of corn and Virgo with other women. (ff. 78v–79r)*

03.

KL Prima necat fortem perditque sedua colpertem.

viii	c			Augustus. Aduincula sci petri. .v.	.ix.lc
xvi	d	iiii	N	Sci stephani [illegible] et mris	.iii.lc
v	e	iii	N	Inuentio sci stephi protomris	.ix.lc.
	f	ii	N		
xiii	g	Nonas		Sci osuualdi regis et mris.	.iii.lc
ii	A	viii	Id	Scorum sixti felicissimi et agapiti. mr.	.iii.l
	b	vii	Id	Sci donati epi et mris	.iii.lc
x	c	vi	Id	Ciriaci sociorumque eius. mr.	.iii.lc
	d	v	Id	Sci romani mris. vigilia	.iii.lc
xviii	e	iiii	Id	Sci laurentii leuite et mris.	.ix.lc
vii	f	iii	Id	Sci tyburtii mris.	.iii.lc
	g	ii	Id		
xv	A	Idus.		Sci ypoliti sociorumque eius mr.	.iii.lc.
iiii	b	xix	kl	Septembris Eusebii conf. vigilia	
c		xviii	kl	Assumptio sce marie virg. dup.f.	.ix.lc.

xii d xvii kl'
i e xvi kl' Octaue sancti laurentij . iii. lc
f xv kl' Sc̄i agapiti mr̄is. .iij. lc.
ix g xiiii kl' Sc̄i magni mr̄is .iii. lc
A xiii kl'
xvii b xii kl'
vi c xi kl' Oct' sc̄e marie uirginis ix. lc
d x kl' Sc̄i thymothei & apollinar' Vigil'. ch.
xiiii e ix kl' Sc̄i bartholomei apl'i. Dup' fest' ix. lc.
iii f viii kl'
g vii kl'
xi A vi kl' Sc̄i rufi mr̄is. .iij. lc.
xix b v kl' Sc̄i augustini ep'i & doctoris. d. f. ix. lc.
c iiii kl' Decoll'o sc̄i iohis bapt'e. .ix. lc
viii d iii kl' Sc̄orum felicis & adaucti mr̄. iij. lc. d.
e ii kl' Sc̄e cuthburge uirg' nō mr̄ iij. lc

04.

05.

for Sundays) in monastic practice, and these are placed at the beginnings of Psalms 1, 26, 38, 52, 68, 80, 97 and 109, using the Vulgate numbering. Ultimately these groups echo the Psalmist's reflection that 'Seven times a day I praise you for your righteous laws' and 'At midnight I rise to give you thanks for your righteous laws' (Psalm 119: 164, 62). The other two reflect another, earlier system of division, the so-called 'three fifties', dividing the Psalms into three sections of fifty Psalms (Psalm 1 is part of both systems.)

Another aspect of the planning and design occurs in the subjects of the initials beginning the first words in each of these divisions. All are 'historiated', that is, they are populated with narrative or figurative scenes. Typically, the subjects of these initials are related to the first lines of the text itself, or the Psalm's heading or title. For example, the initial for Psalm 52 beginning '*Dixit insipiens in corde suo non est Deum*' (The fool says in his heart, 'There is no God'), often includes an image of a jester or fool, as is the case in the Queen Mary Psalter (Image 5). In this very literal interpretation, a king points to God emerging from a cloud. A barefoot man wearing a ragged cloak ignores the gesture, instead gnawing on a stone, mistaking it for bread. The fool holds a marotte, the prop stick used by jesters.

Moreover, the Queen Mary Psalter features another type of decoration at these major textual divisions, by including large painted scenes at the top of these pages, and usually of the pages opposite as well. These scenes feature significant episodes from the life of Christ. In addition to emphasising the textual divisions, these images add another layer of commentary on the text itself, by interpreting it Christologically. The series begins at Psalm 1 with the Annunciation, Visitation and Nativity. The scene accompanying Psalm 52 is the Child

05. *The Child Jesus debating with the Scribes and Pharisees in the Temple, above the Fool in the initial for Psalm 52. (f. 150v)*

Specification	*Scale*
PSALTER, IN LATIN London? 1st quarter of 14th century 275 x 175 mm Royal MS 2 B. vii	

Jesus debating with the Scribes and Pharisees in the Temple. Again, the Virgin is prominent in the scene, holding Christ's shoulders, perhaps introducing or propelling him to the scholars.

In this part of the book the two painting techniques are employed side by side, as an extensive cycle of figurative decoration presented in the lower margins, or bas-de-pages, below the Psalter text and the following prayers. These images begin on the second text page of the Psalms and run continuously for 464 pages to the end of the Litany. The subjects, as might be expected from such an enormous corpus, are extremely varied, although many appear in groups, such as miracles of the Virgin or martyred saints, and lengthy cycles of the life of St Thomas Becket and St Mary Magdalene. Other subjects are 'more miscellaneous and disconnected'.[3] The scene directly below the beginning of Psalm 52 features a man on horseback sounding a curved hunting horn, preceded by two dogs in pursuit of a stag. In this instance it is possible to construe this image, too, as a sort of commentary on the text, perhaps viewing hunting as a worldly or foolish pursuit, in contrast to the worship of God. In many other cases, however, particularly with images of various hybrid creatures and animals, it is more difficult to find any relationship. The development of marginal imagery unconnected with the text was an English innovation, and it became particularly pronounced in the fourteenth century.[4] In the Queen Mary Psalter, it adds to the complexity and richness of the book. Collectively, the astonishing breadth and beauty of the drawings and paintings in their complex layout, meaning and design create a moving testament to the importance and fascination of this fundamental biblical book.

THE HARMONIES OF LITTLE GIDDING

FELICITY MYRONE

The Ferrars of Little Gidding and their 'concordances' or harmonies, created between 1630 and 1642, have long attracted attention as highly unusual forms of customised bookmaking.[1] The family fortune originated with Nicholas Ferrar, a Master of the Skinners' Company, a merchant adventurer and member of the East India Company and the Virginia Company.[2] His son, also Nicholas, and the Collets (Ferrars' in-laws) relocated to the country manor of Little Gidding, Huntingdonshire, in 1625 to pursue, in Paul Dyck's words, 'a life expressive of the central concerns of the Christian gospel...: most famously [enacted through] the production of a unique kind of book: a gospel harmony constructed almost entirely of parts from other books'.[3]

(01.)

Harmonies were an established means of demonstrating the concord – the essential unity – across the Gospel accounts. There were numerous printed harmonies,[4] some illustrated,[5] but those created by the Little Gidding community were unique. They were made by acquiring multiple copies of printed books, books of prints and single-sheet prints featuring flora and fauna as well as religious motifs. The women in the family cut these down and reassembled the pieces, sometimes word by word, pasting them on fresh sheets of paper in careful arrangements with red-ink rulings to frame text and image. Some have a fairly simple design broadly mirroring the layout of a printed book, with the illustrated area at the top of the page and text below, others are more elaborate – perhaps particularly one made as a presentation copy for Charles I, in which image and text intermingle.[6]

This Gospel harmony, known as the King's Concordance, is designed to be practical as well as attractive. It employs three methods for recognising and reconciling differences across Gospel texts. These methods were designated 'Collection', 'Comparison' and 'Composition' (Image 2). As Adam Smyth has summarised, in 'The Comparison' the columns of text produced a parallel edition, while in 'The Composition', 'the different accounts...were interlaced to create a single piece of continuous prose... [and] 'The Collection' presents a brief overview in large black letter and then, beneath in a smaller roman font, what was called the supplement: 'details, repetitions and elaborations'.[7] Michael Cop notes that, 'With this method, Little Gidding provides a narrative that conflates the differing Gospel accounts, that limits repetition (i.e., one could read only the blackletter type), but that still allows access to alternate wording (i.e., the roman type)'.[8]

02.

Scholars have identified some of the books that were cut up. Paul Dyck, for example, has identified the provenance of the two different typefaces in the King's Concordance: the black letter type is from a 1631 quarto Bible printed by Robert Barker and John Bill; the roman type is from a 1633 octavo Bible printed by Robert Young. There are other discoveries from Margaret Aston[9] and Malcolm Jones.[10] Five hundred prints with sections missing have now been identified as from the Little Gidding workshop, rather than, as previously thought, collected by Samuel Pepys. Many note the use of the King James Bible, and Michael Cop has recently shown that in the 'King's Concordance Little Gidding cut extracts not only from Bibles, but also from another English harmony, Henry Garthwait's *Monotessaron, The Evangelicall Harmony* (1634), of which they must have owned more than one copy'.[11] They also appear to have sourced some of the engraved flowers and insects they used from John Payne, *Flora: flowers fruicts beastes birds and flies exactly drawne, With their true colours lively described,* using an edition not known to survive complete (Image 3).[12]

The harmonies were not books, or manuscripts, which may explain why the British Library holds examples in both of these collections. They were, however, fit for royalty, and Charles I is said to have received this Concordance by saying, 'Truly my lords, I prize this as a rare and rich jewel, and worth a king's acceptance.'

01. *Binding of the King's Concordance. (C.23.e.4)*

02. *Title page to the King's Concordance. (C.23.e.4, f. 3)*

03 (pages 72–73). *Sections from John Payne,* Flora: flowers fruicts beastes birds and flies exactly drawne. *(C.23.e.4. f. 34r)*

03.

THE SINGLE EIE: & THOUGHT
for things of this LIFE.

CHAP. XLII.

A 6. Take heede that ye doe not your almes before men,
to be seene of them: otherwise ye haue no reward
‖ of your Father which is in heauen.
2 Therefore, * when thou doest thine almes,‖ doe
not sound a trumpet before thee, as the hypocrites doe
in the Synagogues, and in the streetes, that they may
haue glory of men. Uerily I say vnto you, they haue
their reward.
3 But when thou doest almes, let not thy left hand
know, what thy right doeth:
4 That thine almes may be in secret: And thy Father which seeth in secret, himselfe shall reward thee
openly.
5 ¶ And when thou prayest, thou shalt not be as
the hypocrites are: for they loue to pray standing in
the Synagogues, and in the corners of the streetes,
that they may be seene of men. Uerily I say vnto you,
they haue their reward.
6 But thou when thou prayest, enter into thy clo-
set, and when thou hast shut thy doore, pray to thy Father which is in secret, and thy Father which seeth in
secret, shall reward thee openly.
7 But when yee pray, vse not vaine * repetitions,
as the heathen doe. For they thinke that they shall be

heard for their much speaking.
8 Be not ye therefore like vnto them
ther knoweth what things ye haue ne
aske him.
9 After this maner therefore pray
ther which art in heauen, Hallowed be
10 Thy kingdome come. Thy will
as it is in heauen.
11 Giue vs this day our daily bread
12 And forgiue vs our debts, as we
ters.
13 And leade vs not into temptat
vs from euill: for thine is the king
power, and the glory, for euer, Amen.
14 * For, if ye forgiue men their tres
uenly Father will also forgiue you.
15 But, if yee forgiue not men thei
ther will your Father forgiue your tr
16 ¶ Moreouer, when yee fast, b
crites, of a sad countenance: for they d
ces, that they may appeare vnto men
say vnto you, they haue their reward.
17 But thou, when thou fastest,
and wash thy face:

18 That thou appeare not vnto men to fast, but vnto thy father which is in secret: and thy father which
seeth in secret, shall reward thee openly.
19 ¶ Lay not vp for your selues treasures vpon
earth, where moth and rust doeth corrupt, and where
theeues breake thorow and steale.
20 *But lay vp for your selues treasures in heauen, where neither moth nor rust doeth corrupt, and
where theeues doe not breake thorow, nor steale.
21 For where your treasure is, there wil your heart
be also.
22 *The light of the body is the eye: If therefore
thine eye be single, thy whole body shalbe full of light.
23 But if thine eye be euill, thy whole body shall be
full of darkenesse. If therefore the light that is in thee
be darkenesse, how great is that darkenesse?
24 ¶*No man can serue two masters: for either
he will hate the one and loue the other, or else he will
hold to the one, and despise the other. Yee cannot serue
God and Mammon.
25 Therefore I say vnto you, *Take no thought
for your life, what ye shall eate, or what ye shall drinke,
nor yet for your body what ye shall put on: Is not the
life more then meate, and the body then raiment?
26 Behold the foules of the ayre: for they sow not,
neither doe they reape, nor gather into barnes, yet
your heauenly Father feedeth them. Are yee not much
better then they?
27 Which of you by taking thought can adde one
cubite vnto his stature?
28 And why take ye thought for raiment? Consider
the lillies of the field, how they grow, they toile not,
neither doe they spinne.
29 And yet I say vnto you, that euen Solomon in
all his glory, was not arayed like one of these.
30 Wherefore, if God so clothe the grasse of the field,
which to day is, and to morrow is cast into the ouen:
shall he not much more clothe you, O ye of little faith?
31 Therefore take no thought, saying, What shall
we eate? or, what shall wee drinke? or wherewithall
shall we be clothed?
32 (For after all these things doe the Gentiles
seeke:) for your heauenly Father knoweth that yee
haue neede of all these things.
33 But seeke yee first the kingdome of God, and his
righteousnes, & all these things shalbe added vnto you.
34 Take therefore no thought for the morrow, for
the morrow shall take thought for the things of it selfe:
sufficient vnto the day is the euill thereof.

THE MAINZ PSALTER OF 1457

A technological landmark in the development of the European printed book

ADRIAN S. EDWARDS

INTRODUCTION

The Latin Psalter published in 1457 at Mainz, Germany, by Johann Fust and Peter Schöffer is little known outside the world of bibliography. This 'Mainz Psalter', however, represents a significant milestone in the development of the printed book. It was the first to make systematic use of colour as part of the printing process and the first to include music notation, albeit added by hand after the pages had left the press. It is also the first to clearly state the names of its publishers and the first to cite its date of publication.

The book was printed with movable type, a recent technological advancement developed in the workshop of Johann Gutenberg (*c.* 1400–1467/8), whereby mechanical methods were used to produce multiple copies of a text more quickly and more cheaply than could ever be achieved through handwriting alone. But Gutenberg's output had been mainly monochrome and used only one style of typeface. Every copy of his famous Latin Bible had to be finished by a skilled scribe or artist if it was to match the luxuriousness of a richly coloured illuminated manuscript. New techniques were needed, and it was Fust and Schöffer who took Gutenberg's idea and developed it further. Their large Latin Psalter was produced for use in religious houses and churches. At its heart is the book of Psalms from the Old Testament, but this has been supplemented with devotional material, and the whole presented for use in religious rituals according to the liturgical calendar.

PRINTING WITH MOVABLE TYPE

Movable type consists of mass-produced individual letters or characters (*sorts*) that can be assembled into a text for printing, and then disassembled and reused. There are records of clay stamps for reproducing individual characters in China as early as the eleventh century, and metal type appears to have been used in Korea since the thirteenth century. In Europe handwritten texts remained unchallenged until Gutenberg's innovations with metal movable type and a printing press. His method, in fact, required a number of connected innovations, ranging from the mass production of type, to the use of the press, and the development of thick oil-based ink. The process probably took months or years to refine, but the benefits were potentially enormous. Hundreds of identical copies of a text could be produced significantly more quickly and more cheaply than by hand with a pen, and the type itself could be reused. But there were disadvantages too. The production of hundreds of copies at the same time required the supply of thousands of sheets of paper or vellum (animal skin). For editions produced as a purely commercial venture, as opposed to those commissioned by a wealthy patron, this meant that there was a financial imperative to sell the finished books as quickly as possible in order to recoup this investment. Yet there was, at the same time, a genuine risk of saturating the market with unsold volumes if the potential number of purchasers was misjudged.

JOHANN FUST AND PETER SCHÖFFER

Johann Fust (*c.* 1400–1466) had been Gutenberg's business associate and had provided financial backing for the famous Bible. But their business relationship went sour. He filed a lawsuit against Gutenberg, found a new collaborator in the shape of Peter Schöffer (*c.* 1425–*c.* 1503) – a former employee of Gutenberg – and they began work together as Europe's second printing enterprise.

01. *A two-line decorated initial 'A'. (f. 23v, detail)*

01.

02.

Dñicis dieb3 post festū trinitatis · Inuitatoriū.

Regē magnū dñm venite adoremus, ps Venite ·
Dñicis dieb3 post festū ephie Inuitatoriū ·

Adorem9 dñm qui fecit nos, ps venite aīī Seruite ·

Beatus vir qui non abijt in Euouae consilio impiorū et in via pccōrū nō stetit: ⁊ in cathedra pestilēcie nō sedit, Sed i lege dñi volūtas ei9: et in lege eius meditabit die ac nocte, Et erit tanq3 lignū qd plātatū est secus decursus aq̄rū: qd fructū suū dabit in tpe suo Et foliū ei9 nō defluet: ⁊ oīa q̄cūq3 faciet pspērabūt, Nō sic impij nō sic sed tanq3 puluis quē pijcit ventus a facie terre, Ideo non resurgūt impij in iudicio: neq3 pccōres in cōsilio iustorū Qm nouit dñs viā iustorū: ⁊ iter impiorū peribit, Gloria ps

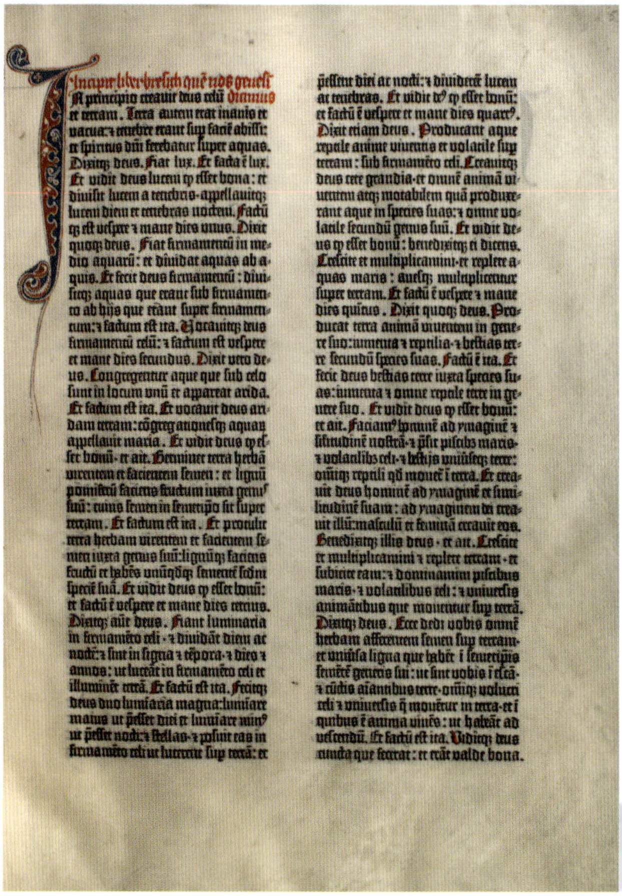

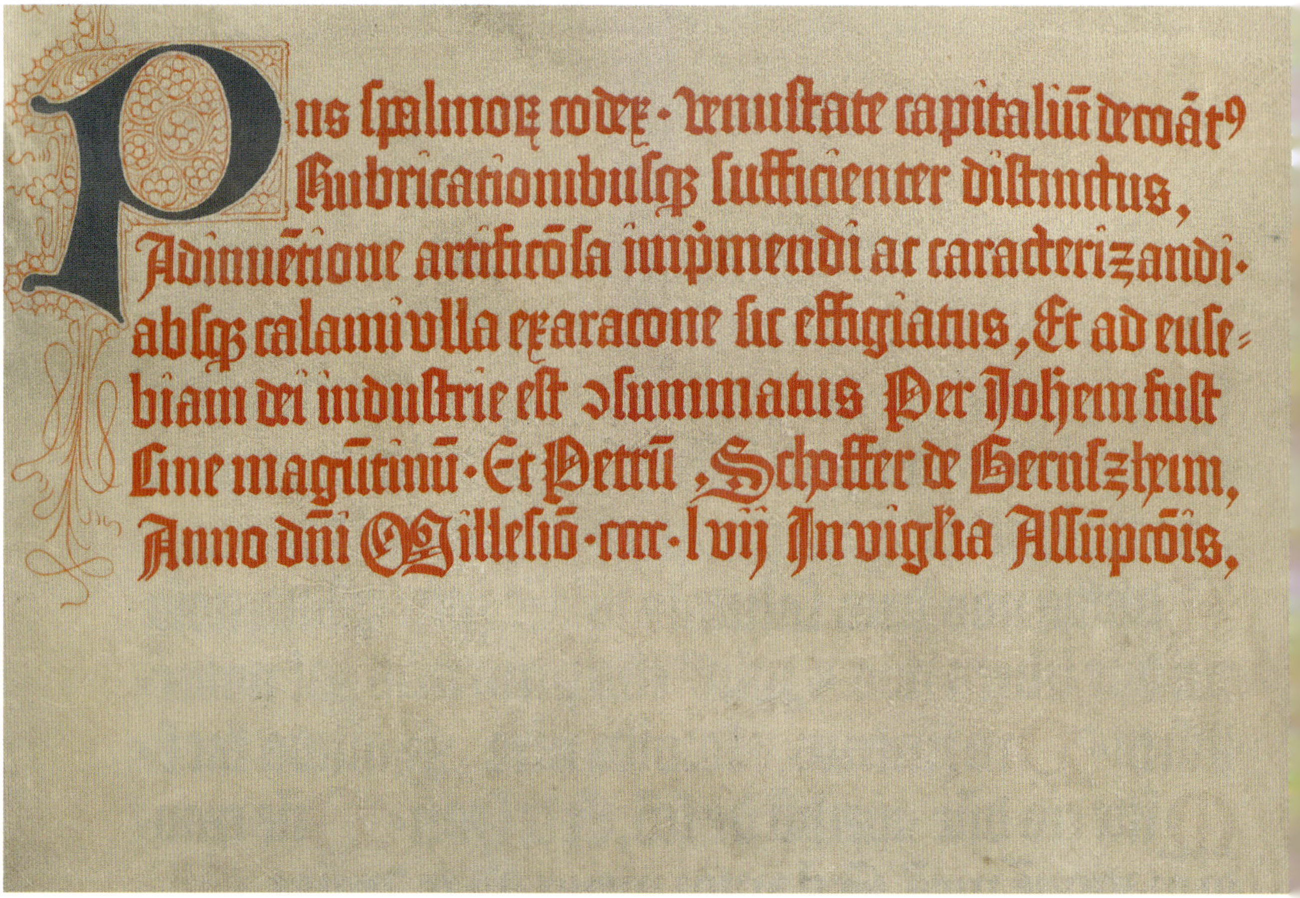

The Psalter of 1457 is their first important collaboration. There may have been attempts to produce an earlier version. France's Bibliothèque nationale holds a single leaf of a Psalter printed with the same type seen in the Gutenberg Bible, but the evidence is too scant to draw any concrete conclusions.

MANUSCRIPT PSALTERS

Fust and Schöffer needed to compete with existing producers of manuscript volumes who had already defined the look and feel of a high-quality Psalter. In design terms, Catholic Psalters across fifteenth-century Europe followed the same broad conventions. They are large volumes read at a lectern. Black gothic letters, in either one or two columns, fill every page. For navigation, the reader relies on larger capital letters (versals) in red or blue ink, although the finest manuscripts sometimes also use gold leaf. Fine flourishes or botanical tendrils frequently surround the largest capitals, and a few may even be historiated, a form of illumination whereby scenes from the text are reproduced in miniature inside the letterform.

The first European printed books were unable to use mechanical processes to recreate the colour and magnificence of these manuscript volumes. The printing in the Gutenberg Bible (1454–5), for example, comprises dense black text, arranged in double columns of forty-two lines of equal length, often achieved by breaking the final word on a line with a hyphen. The colour elements that today fill us with awe, including the richly decorated initials, had to be added by calligraphers and artists after each copy had left the printshop. A few copies do contain a little printed colour in the form of headlines in red, but this seems to have been an experiment that was abandoned part way through production.

FUST AND SCHÖFFER'S MASTERPIECE

Copies of the Mainz Psalter are exceptionally rare. The 'Incunabula Short Title Catalogue' – a database of surviving European books printed before 1501 – records just ten reasonably complete examples, plus around twenty fragments of one, two or three leaves.[1] The Mainz Psalter at the British Library (G.12216) is kept wrapped inside a protective box. The binding is purple velvet fabric over millboard, with doublures (linings) made of plain blue silk. This is much newer than the text block and was probably added in the nineteenth century after the volume had ceased to be used for religious services.

Before arriving at the British Library, the volume had been in the care of the British Museum, which in turn had received it as a bequest from the politician and museum trustee Thomas Grenville (1755–1846). De Ricci, writing in 1911,[2] suggests that it had once been owned by a 'comte de Weißenburg', most probably associated with Weißenburg or Wissembourg in Alsace. In the mid-fifteenth century, the abbot of the town's Benedictine monastery was Philipp Schenk von Erbach (d. 1467), brother of Dietrich Schenk von Erbach (1396–1459), the Archbishop of Mainz. The family connection opens up the possibility that Weißenburg Abbey may have been the first institution to own this copy.

The text block of the British Library Mainz Psalter comprises 143 vellum leaves measuring 333 by 211 millimetres. Longer versions of 175 leaves also exist, augmented with the Vigils of the Dead and other prayers.[3] Vellum had a reputation for longevity, but was expensive to produce and was therefore usually reserved for either the luxury end of the book market or for documents where durability was required. Paper would have been a viable and cheaper alternative, but there is no evidence that this was used for any Mainz Psalter.

There is no title page – this developed as a standard feature of the printed book in the following decades. There is, however, a colophon (statement of publication) printed in red on the final page (Image 4). This tells us that the book was produced using the new invention of printing by Fust and Schöffer, with work completed in 1457 on the eve of the Feast of the Assumption (14 August).[4] In contrast to the Gutenberg Bible, the text in the Mainz Psalter is presented as a single column on each page (Images 2 & 3). The large black gothic letters are interspersed with coloured capitals of

02. *Opening leaf of the Mainz Psalter. (f. 1r)*

03. *Opening leaf of the book of Genesis in the Gutenberg Bible of 1454–5. (G.12226, f. 5r)*

04. *Colophon of the Mainz Psalter. (f. 143v, detail)*

varying size and complexity, and extra words have sometimes been added by pen in red or black. Significantly, gaps have been left on 115 pages for the later insertion of handwritten music. Comparison with contemporary manuscript Psalters suggests that just one element is potentially missing: gold. The application of raised, burnished gilding required the time and skills of an experienced craftsperson, and could not be replicated by Fust and Schöffer's mechanical processes.

THE TYPEFACE

The large black gothic type is designed to imitate the script seen in handwritten church books, and is in a style known as *textura quadrata*. *Texturas* were a family of formal handwriting styles popular across much of fifteenth-century Europe, the name inspired by the apparent similarity between their strong vertical and horizontal pen strokes and the pattern of woven cloth. Two sizes of type are used in the Mainz Psalter: the Psalms, some hymns and the creed[5] are of the larger size with twenty lines per page; the remainder is slightly smaller at twenty-four lines per page. Bibliographers often define type sizes in terms of the average height in millimetres of twenty lines of text: in these terms, the larger type is 286 and the smaller is 234.[6]

THE COLOURED CAPITALS

Small red capitals can be seen on almost every page of the Psalter. They mark the beginning of each phrase, and there are typically eleven to fourteen of them on a full page of text. These capitals are rounder and slightly larger than the surrounding *textura* type, and this – together with their bright colour – helps guide the eye through the text.

Large initials printed in red or deep blue mark a change in content, generally every one, two or three pages. The colours usually alternate, but there are exceptions. Letter shapes are of a broad, rounded style often known today as Lombard capitals. Four categories of these large initials are used in the volume:

- two-line initials of solid colour;
- two-line initials of solid colour surrounded by decoration in a contrasting colour;
- four-line initials with internal patterns surrounded by decoration in a contrasting colour;
- and a single example of a six-line initial with internal patterns surrounded by decoration in a contrasting colour.

Where there is decoration, this resembles fine metal filigree and creates a box surrounding the letter. Decoration may also fill holes (counters) in the letter shapes, extend across to the page edge or creep along the margins. The patterns within the four-line initials comprise small, simple shapes (circles, teardrops, leaves, etc.) created by the absence of ink. The single six-line initial appears on the first leaf, where it comprises the 'B' of *Beatus vir*, the first Psalm (Image 2). The large letter size creates more space for internal decoration, which in the case of the left vertical stem has been filled with a running hound. The style is distinctive, and the artisan who created these larger initials is known to art historians as the Fust Master.

PRODUCTION

The main text in black ink appears to have been produced using the movable-type technology developed in Gutenberg's workshop, and which continued to be the principal method of European book production until the early nineteenth century. The process used for printing the colour elements (Image 6), however, is not immediately obvious.[7] Alan May at Reading University, an expert in reconstructing historical typography, has used practical methods to investigate probable working methods. He has demonstrated how the different colour inks might have been applied before each page was printed with a single pull of the press.[8] This required the metal blocks used for the coloured letters to be inked separately, before being reinserted among the movable type that would already have been inked in black. It would have been a fiddly operation. Mayumi Ikeda also points out that Fust and Schöffer seem to have struggled with

05. *Black, red and blue inks are printed on the opening page, alongside hand-drawn lines. (f. 1r)*

06. *Two-line initial 'L'. (f. 17v)*

05.

06.

07.

cõfessione

illi Laudate nome

in eternū misericordia eius.

ratione et generationem veritas eius

Sederat super thronu

Gloria et honor & benedictio

secula seculorum

De us.

Deus deus meus: ad te de

luce vigilo Sitivit in

anima mea: qm multiplicite

In terra deserta in via

their blue ink, and needed to overpaint the initials in some copies before the pages left the workshop.[9]

Specification	*Scale*
THE MAINZ PSALTER Mainz, Germany, 1457 333 x 211 mm G.12216	

THE MUSIC

The printers left spaces throughout the Psalter for the later insertion of music (staves with musical notation and the words to be sung). This was done by a scribe using a pen, as Fust and Schöffer lacked the technical capacity to print music mechanically.[10] In the British Library copy the staves are in red but not uniform: some appear to have been hand-stamped and others ruled with a pen. Each stave generally comprises four lines, although some are of five, and the notes are indicated with a combination of pen-drawn squares and 'nails' (known as *Hufnagel* notation) (Image 7).

The accompanying words, in black and red, have been written in a small *textura* hand to match the printed text. Several styles of majuscule letter are used, but the most striking are the large black gothic capitals with red highlights. Somewhat later – the handwriting style suggests the early seventeenth century – 'Alleluias' have been added.[11]

OTHER HANDWRITTEN ADDITIONS, LOST LEAVES AND FACSIMILE REPLACEMENTS

Returning to the main text, there are numerous places in the British Library copy where handwritten phrases have been added.[12] The clearest example is on the first leaf (see Images 2 & 5), where four lines of text have been inserted before the decorated initial. The purpose of these additions is most often to accommodate local preferences.

Not all the pages in this copy are original. Leaves 28 and 137–143 have been lost, with three of these being replaced with pen-and-ink facsimiles (28, 142 and 143, although the last is inaccurately executed).[13] The facsimiles are not signed, but they are likely to be the work of John Harris (1791–1873), a craftsman who worked for both Thomas Grenville and the British Museum, and who is recorded as having produced facsimile specimens of Fust and Schöffer, Caxton, and other early printers.[14] The original leaves have been washed, resulting in some damage to the text. This cleaning had already occurred by 1895 when the Hebraist Russell Martineau (1831–1898) wrote that the 'letters damaged by this process [were] painted over in black, so as frequently to change them into other letters'.[15]

CONCLUSION

Gutenberg's method of printing was still new when Fust and Schöffer developed it further for the production of their Psalter. In design terms, their aim was to replicate the page layout, letter shapes and use of colour seen in the luxurious handwritten liturgical books owned by Germany's cathedrals, churches and monasteries. What they achieved was outstanding, especially in terms of colour printing. But there were also limitations. The clearest example is the music, which had to be added later by hand.

In 2014 Eric White of Princeton University considered how the Mainz Psalter might have been used in the performance of the liturgy.[16] He noted the large typeface, the use of coloured capitals to guide the eye, and the absence of words broken with hyphens at the turn of a page. He suggests that these were deliberate design decisions chosen to support 'effortless reading', essential when reading or singing aloud during a religious service. Other scholars have observed that the use of initials of varying sizes and colours also results in openings that are visually distinct from one other. This would have helped with navigation through such a large volume of uniform text. Did Fust and Schöffer have any of these design considerations in mind when they produced their monumental work? Or were they simply following a model provided by existing manuscript Psalters? We'll never know, but it all adds to the layers of interest in this masterpiece of early printed book production.

07. *Printers left spaces throughout for the addition of handwritten music. (f. 16r)*

08 (pages 82–83). *Typical opening, showing the use of three-colour printing and the addition of handwritten music. (ff. 3v–4r)*

me fac ꝓpter misericordi
morte qui memor sit
ɔfitebit' tibi Laboraui
uit ꝑ singlas noctes l
meis stratū meū rigabo
furore oculus meus: inuetera
inimicos meos. Discedite
operamini iniq̄tatē: q̄m exaudiuit
fletꝰ mei Exaudiuit dn̄s depca
dn̄s orationē meā suscepit Eru
conturbent' vehemēter omēs inim
ɔuertant' et erubescant valde velocit

Seruite domino in timore Exultamus

Domine deus meꝰ in te speraui: saluu
me fac ex omnibꝰ ꝑsequentibꝰ me et
libera me Ne quādo rapiat ut leo animā
meā: dū non est qui redimat neq̄ q̄ saluū
faciat Domine deus meꝰ si feci istud: si ē
iniq̄tas i manibꝰ meis Si reddidi retri-
buentibꝰ michi mala: decidā merito ab

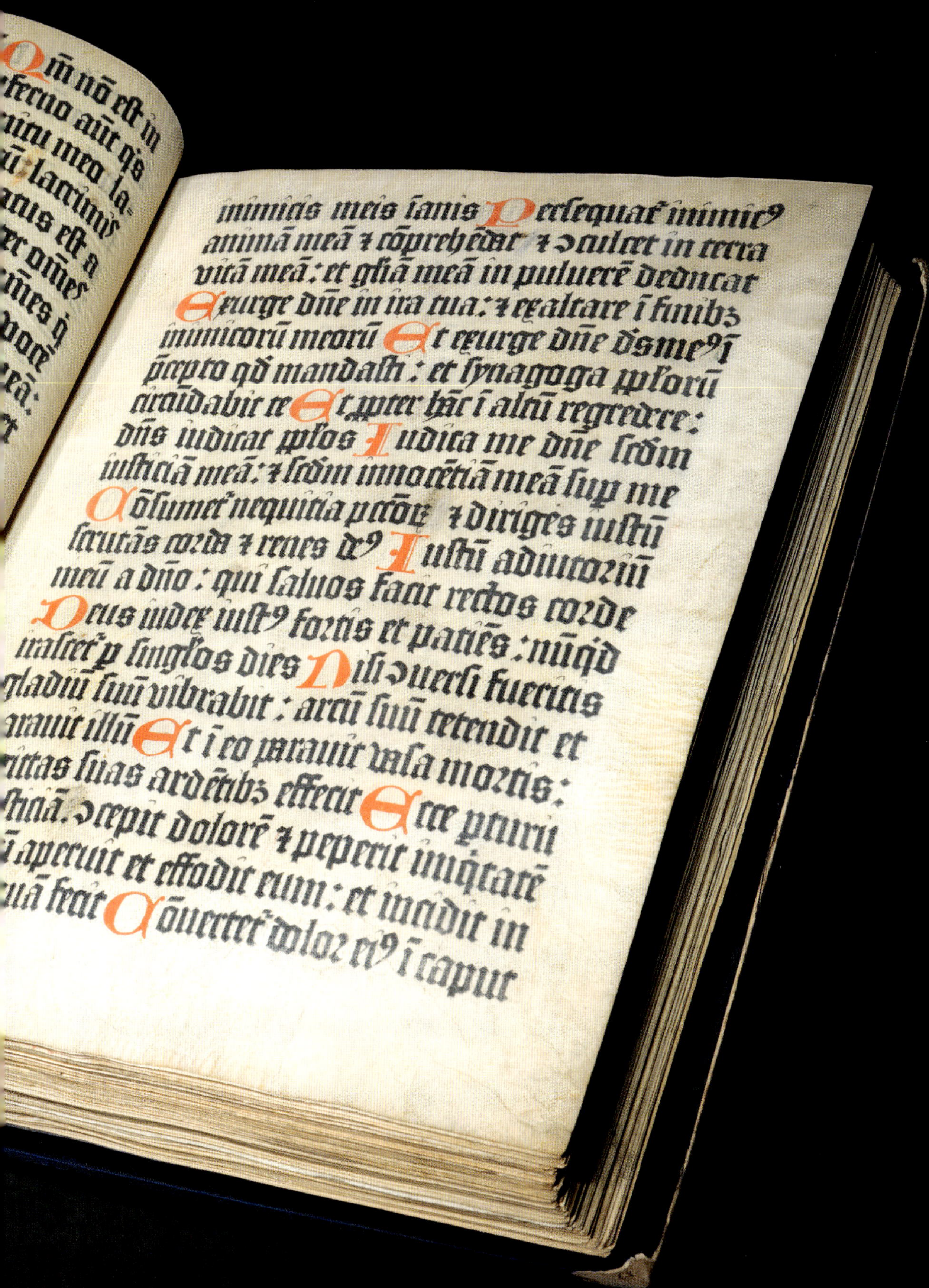

Q̄m̄ nō est in
ferno aūt q̄s
itu meo la
ū lacrimis
atus est a
er oīes
mes q
uoc
eā
et

inimicis meis inanis Persequat inimic⁹
animā meā ⁊ cōprehēdat ⁊ ɔculcet in terra
vitā meā: et gl̄iā meā in puluerē deducat
Exurge dn̄e in ira tua: ⁊ exaltare ī finibꝫ
inimicorū meorū Et exurge dn̄e ds̄ me⁹ ī
p̄cepto qd̄ mandasti: et synagoga p̄ploru
circuidabit te Et ꝓpter hāc ī altū regredere:
dn̄s iudicat p̄plos Iudica me dn̄e sc̄dm
iusticiā meā: ⁊ sc̄dm innocētiā meā sup me
Cōsumet nequitia pctōꝝ ⁊ diriges iustū
scrutās corda ⁊ renes de⁹ Iustū adiutoriū
meū a dn̄o: qui saluos facit rectos corde
Deus iudex iust⁹ fortis et patiēs: nūqd
irascet p singlos dies Nisi ɔuersi fueritis
gladiū suū vibrabit: arcū suū tetendit et
parauit illū Et ī eo parauit vasa mortis:
agittas suas ardētibꝫ effecit Ecce ptuit
stitiā. ɔcepit dolorē ⁊ peperit iniq̄tatē
ū aperuit et effodit eum: et incidit in
uā fecit Cōuertet dolor ei⁹ ī caput

...ERE ET LHORA, E...
...GLI APPARVE IN SOMNO D...
VARSI IN VNA QVIETA ET SILENTE PIA...
CVLTO DISERTA . DINDI POSCIA DISAV...
CON GRANDE TIMORE INTRO IN VNA IN...
OPACA SILVA.

HYPNEROTOMACHIA POLIPHILI.

AVRORAE DESCRIPTIO.

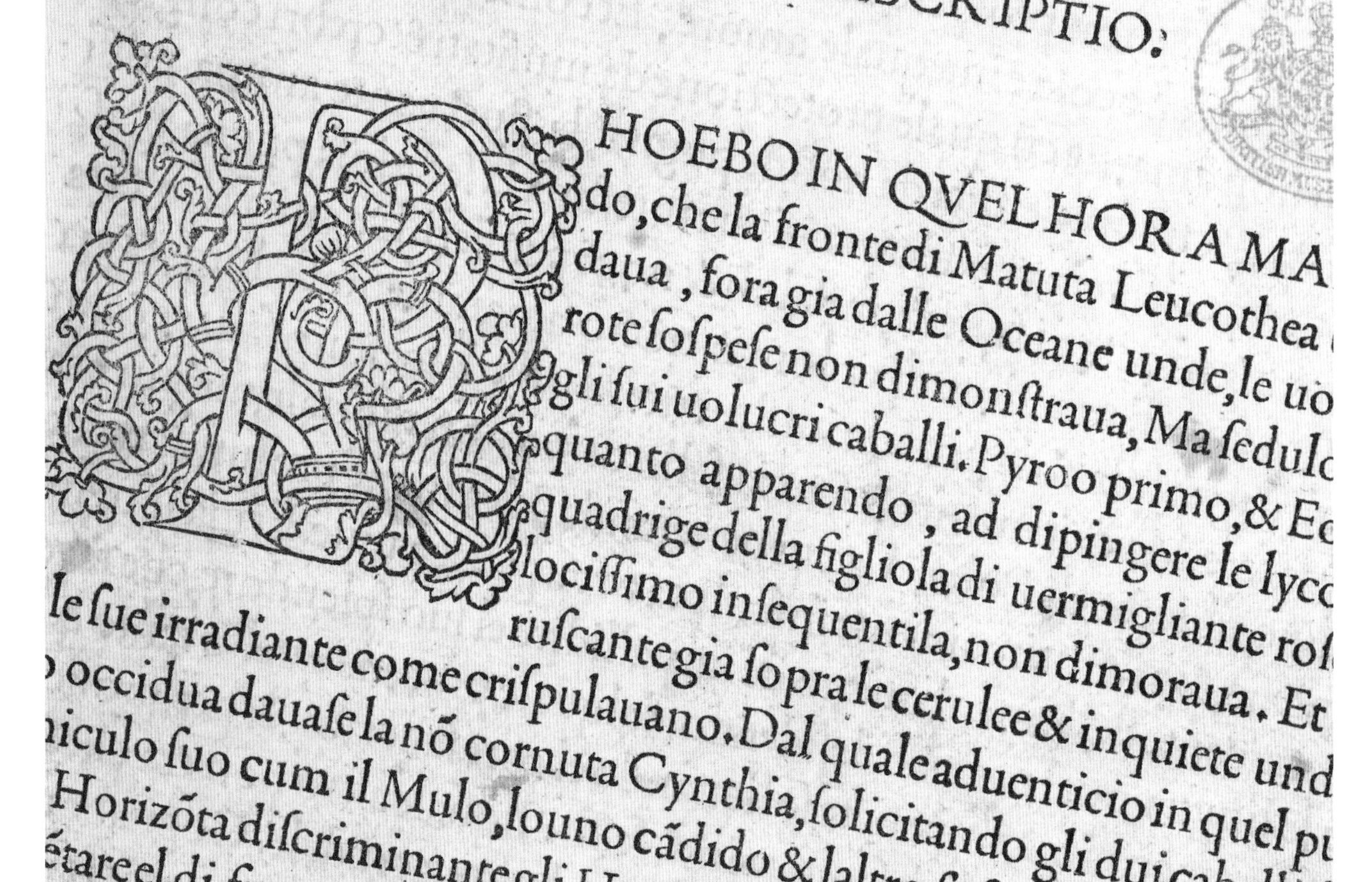

HOEBO IN QVEL HORA MA...
do, che la fronte di Matuta Leucothea ...
daua, fora gia dalle Oceane unde, le uo...
rote ſoſpeſe non dimonſtraua, Ma ſedulo...
gli ſui uolucri caballi. Pyroo primo, & Eo...
quanto apparendo, ad dipingere le lyco...
quadrige della figliola di uermigliante roſ...
lociſſimo inſequentila, non dimoraua. Et
ruſcante gia ſopra le cerulee & inquiete und...
le ſue irradiante come criſpulauano. Dal quale aduenticio in quel pu...
...o occidua dauaſe la nõ cornuta Cynthia, ſolicitando gli dui caballi d...
...niculo ſuo cum il Mulo, lo uno cãdido & laltro fuſco, trahẽti ad lulti...
Horizõta diſcriminante gli Hemiſperii peruenuta, & dalla p̃uia ſtella...
...ẽtare el di, fugata cedeua. In quel tempo quãdo che gli Rhiphæi mõ...
...no placidi, ne cum tãta rigidecia piu lalgente & frigorifico Euro cũ
...rale flando quaſſabondo el mandaua gli teneri ramuli, & ad ĩquieta
...mobili ſcirpi & põtuti iũci & debili Cypiri, & aduexare gli ...
...mini, & agitare gli lenti ſalici, & proclinare ...
...li Tauro laſciuianti. Q...

VII.

HYPNEROTOMACHIA POLIPHILI

Aldus Manutius and his importance in the development of book design

STEPHEN PARKIN

INTRODUCTION

Aldo Manuzio (*c.* 1450–1515), or, in the Latinised form he himself adopted and which is still commonly used to refer to him, Aldus Manutius, is without question one of the most important and innovative figures in the history of the printed book. Historical perspective enables us to distinguish and understand more clearly the sometimes contrasting elements which have fused together to form his enduring reputation and his charisma. He emerges from the early and still exploratory period of the new technology of printing and the nascent publishing industry in the second half of the fifteenth century. By the end of his career in the second decade of the sixteenth century he had established many of the features which have more or less defined – up to the recent arrival of electronic or digital publishing – what printed books as common artefacts look like and how they are read and used. But it is noteworthy that this perception of his significance dates back to his contemporaries who bought and read his publications (and who – at least the wealthier among them – were often portrayed holding an 'Aldine octave' like a fashionable accessory, Image 2). They, and the immediately succeeding generations, were aware of his technical achievements in book production and the way his editions reset the relationship between readers and the volumes they hold in their hands, carry round with them and put on a shelf. For example, in 1530, only fifteen years after Aldus's death, the Spanish scribe Juan de Yciar referred to his typographical achievements as having been awarded 'by general consent, the palm in the art of printing' and a model which he would therefore follow in his own scribal practice. As the typographer Peter Burnhill remarks, the tribute is a striking inversion of what is often assumed to be the usual relationship of scribe and type designer, since in this case the excellence of the Aldine printed letter forms provides the model for the calligrapher. Somewhat later, in the second half of the sixteenth century, the Florentine writer and merchant Lodovico Guicciardini, who spent most of his life in the Netherlands, refers to Manutius in the history he wrote of his adopted country, in relation to Harlem's (unfounded) claim to have been the cradle of printing, that it was Aldus who brought the art of printing to perfection with his 'order and regularity'. This comment on his qualities is echoed five centuries later in Peter Burnhill's detailed analysis of the typography and layout of Aldine editions, when he asserts that '[as] even a cursory glance at [his] pages shows, Aldus had a passion for structural clarity'.[1]

01. Hypnerotomachia Poliphili, *1499. (a2r)*

ALDUS'S EARLY CAREER AND MOVE TO VENICE

Aldus's origins were seemingly far removed from the world of the new technology of printing and the commercial activity of publishing. He was born in Bassiano, a small town near Rome, in the Papal States, the territory directly ruled over by the papacy, in the middle of the fifteenth century. While he was still in his teens the invention of printing reached Italy some ten years after its first appearance in the northern European city of Mainz, at first in the Benedictine monastery of Subiaco 50

02.

kilometres outside Rome and then in the papal city itself, brought there by German printers working under the patronage of leading members of the Roman Curia. After preliminary studies in Rome, Aldus moved north at some point in the second half of the 1470s, to the city of Ferrara, where he followed courses taught by the celebrated humanist scholar Battista Guarino, under whom he mastered Latin and, even more importantly for his subsequent career and ambitions, classical Greek. After his studies, he undertook the traditional path open to a trained humanist scholar by becoming a teacher, a tutor to the two young sons of the deceased prince of Carpi, Alberto and Lionello, whose mother was Caterina Pico, sister of the famous humanist and philosopher Pico della Mirandola. Alberto, who went on to inherit the principality, remained close to Aldus for the rest of his life. He supported him when he decided in the late 1480s – as he was approaching the age of 40, well past what was regarded as the prime of life in this period – to move to Venice to become a printer and undertake the publication of scholarly editions of classical Greek texts. This is a central aspect of the persistent allure of Aldus's achievement in publishing: that it was inspired by what could be called a cultural project or mission, which also represented an underlying continuity with his activity as a teacher in the first part of his career (his interest in teaching Latin and Greek remained strong and manuals and dictionaries for both languages were included in his copious output).

There is abundant evidence over the two decades of his activity in Venice of the commitment and energy with which Aldus carried out this project, not least the testimony provided by the man himself in the numerous and informative prefaces he wrote to each of his editions. He discusses such matters as how he procured the most reliable manuscripts that could be found of the texts he wanted to publish and how he collated and edited them as part of a circle of scholars he managed to build up around him and his printing house – a group of colleagues which was to all intents and purposes an editorial team. What is not so explicit – in fact the evidence is largely implicit only in the physical books themselves – is Aldus's interest in the book as an artefact, a vehicle for communicating to his readers in the most efficient way possible the texts he was interested in publishing. There was nothing inevitable about this interest. Aldus had no technical proficiency in the new technology when he first moved to Venice, where he soon entered into partnership with Andrea Torresani, a printer of his own age. Although an outsider like Aldus himself, Torresani had long been established in the city's printing trade and therefore could have provided – and must have done to a great extent, above all at the outset – his technical and commercial know-how as backing for Aldus's cultural project. Yet the very focus of this project – the printing of the Greek classics, most notably the works of Aristotle, published between 1495 and 1498 – meant that Aldus could not avoid becoming personally involved with the material and technological process of printing, and with its first and fundamental element, the creation of movable type, specifically the manufacture of Greek type. Unlike Latin, classical Greek presents many difficulties, such as its numerous and varying accents and ligatures, for the type designer and type-caster (and by extension, later in the printing house, for the compositor). With his pedagogic concern to make these texts useable and readable, apt for study, Aldus must have become or quickly been made aware of the intrinsic importance of an element of book design – in this case, the type in which a book is printed – for the way a book is read. His search for a Greek type which combined functionality, legibility and beauty must have opened Aldus's eyes and mind to the realities and potentialities of the new medium and to the ways in which printed books might exploit their own identity as printed artefacts rather than printed versions of manuscripts. His experiments with roman type, for which there was already a celebrated model in the production of an earlier Venetian printer Nicolaus Jenson (whose types Torresani had in fact inherited) and the invention of italic at the end of the 1490s, show his continuing engagement with the impact of this primary element of the printed book.

ALDUS'S INNOVATIONS

Thus Aldus's openness to technical exploration and inventiveness was there from the beginning (and arguably must have been part of his personality – what else spurred him in middle age to embark on such a radical career change?). This adventurous thinking in terms of presentation can be seen in his very early productions from the mid-1490s – his first edition, the Greek grammar of Constantinus Lascaris, with its parallel Latin translation and the efforts to devise a didactic efficacy in the layout of the text(s) (Images 3 & 5), or the little edition of the sixth-century Greek poem of the story of Hero and Leander, in both the original version and the Latin translation which could be bound separately or together to form a parallel text. In a recent essay Neil Harris has listed and assessed comprehensively all the innovations in the printed book for which Aldus can be deemed responsible (as said above, largely on the evidence of the books themselves rather than any intentions he explicitly declared).[2] For example, he introduced 'new' punctuation such as commas, semi-colons, quotation marks and diacritics, as well as new paratextual tools such as pagination (as opposed to the foliation commonly employed at the time and for some time after Aldus) and the use of pagination to link index references to the main text. Another such tool was his consistent insertion of lists of errata to correct textual mistakes made in the process of printing. He was the first to publish a work in a sequence of volumes (as units of publication) and to introduce books in series, at least implicitly, with uniformity of visual design and editorial approach. Listing such innovations makes it clear how Aldus must have thought intensively about the book as a 'machine for reading' and how it could be made more efficient in terms of legibility and readers' ability to navigate their way through a volume.

ALDUS'S 'PORTABLE' OCTAVOS

The most influential innovation introduced by Aldus in terms of book design – what books look like and the way readers interact with them – is undoubtedly what he himself first referred to, using a Greek term, as '*enchiridia*' (literally 'which can be held in the hand') and later in Latin as '*libri portatiles*' or 'portable books'. These were volumes published from 1501 onwards in a programme of Latin classics (beginning with Virgil, Juvenal and Martial) and key literary works written in Italian (beginning with Petrarch and, in the following year,

02. *Bronzino (Agnolo di Cosimo di Mariano),* Portrait of a Young Man *(1530s). (The Metropolitan Museum of Art)*

03 (page 88). *Urbano Bolzanio,* Institutiones Graecae grammatices, *1497. (IA.24427, a4r)*

04 (page 89). *Aldus imprint at bottom of erratum list,* Hypnerotomachia Poliphili, *1499. (f. 4r)*

05 (page 89). *Greek original text and Latin translation, Constantine Lascaris,* Erotemata, *1494/5. (IA.24282, a2v–a3r)*

03.

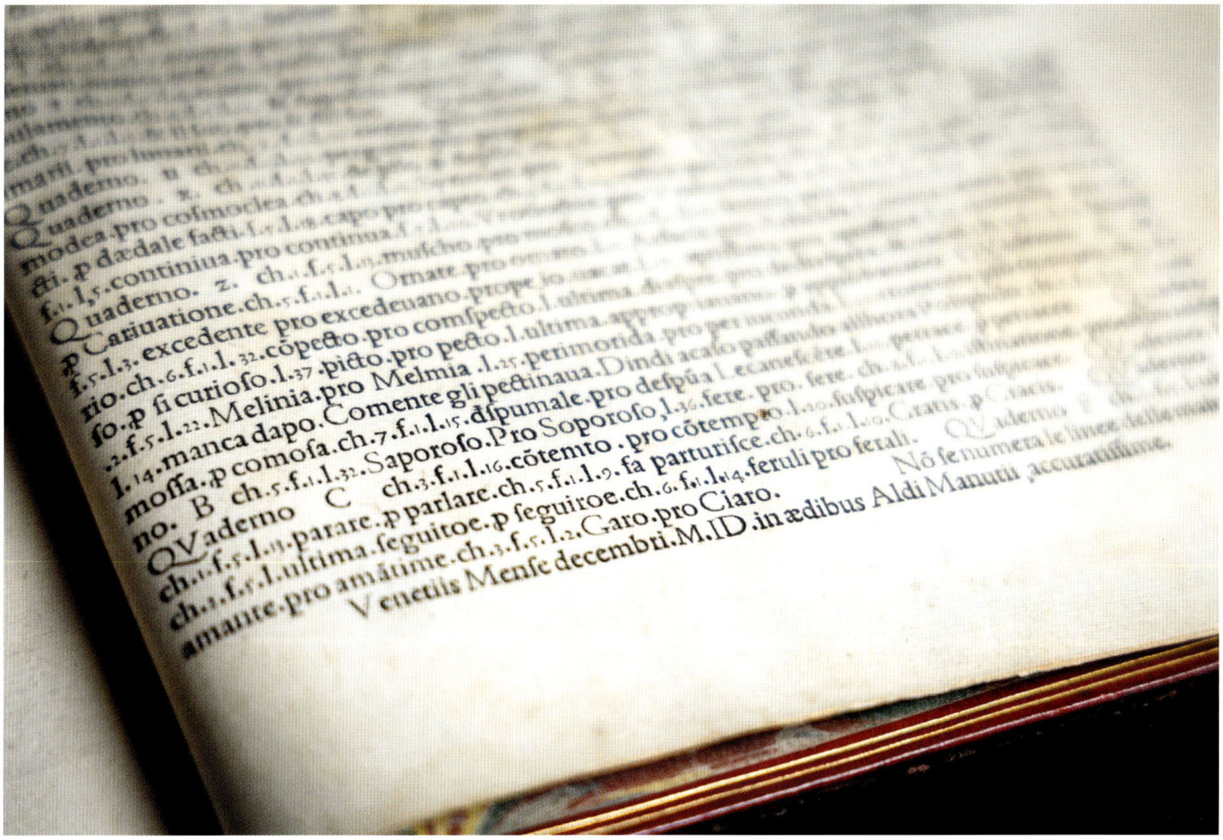
Venetiis Mense decembri. M.ID. in ædibus Aldi Manutii, accuratissime.

04.

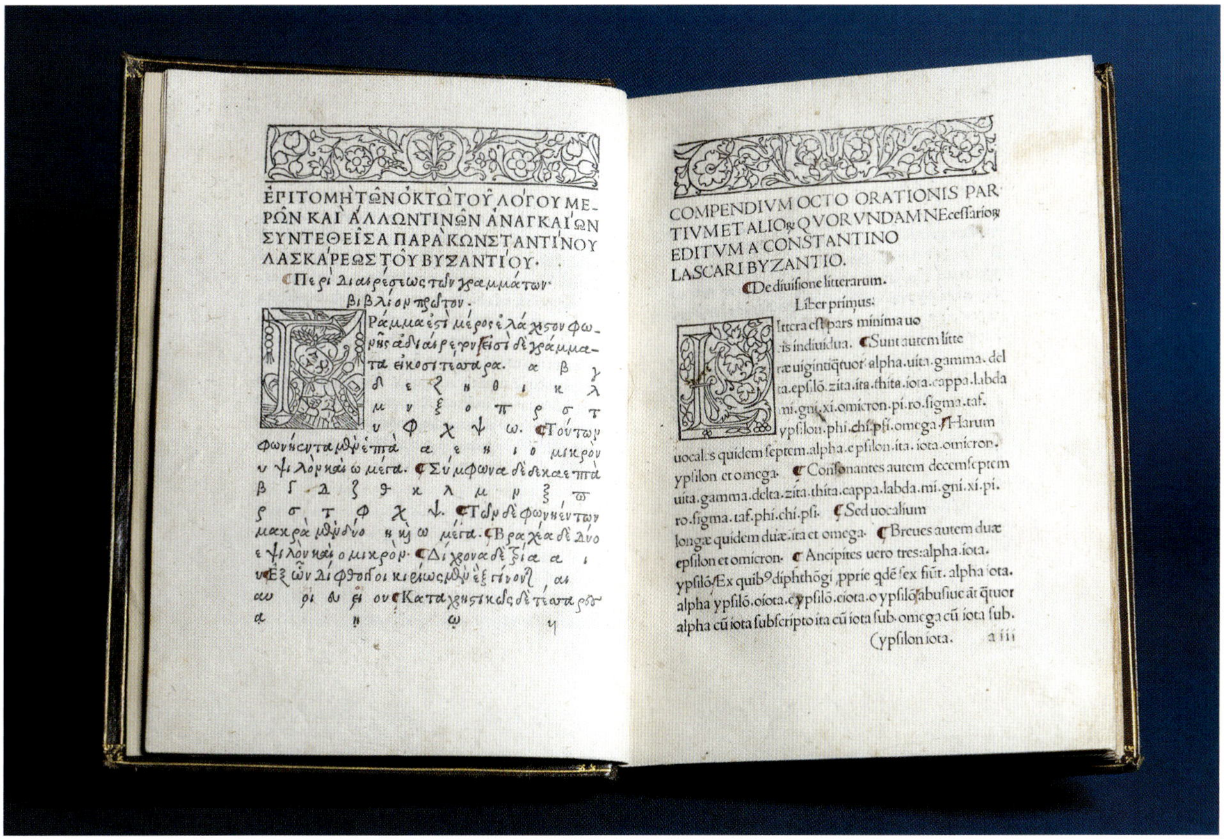
COMPENDIVM OCTO ORATIONIS PARTIVM ET ALIORVM QVORVNDAM NEcessariorum EDITVM A CONSTANTINO LASCARI BYZANTIO.
De diuisione litterarum.
Liber primus.

05.

Dante) in octavo format. In this format the individual sheets of paper used in the printing press were folded three times after printing to form gatherings of eight leaves or sixteen pages. These were then assembled into a complete volume – a complex process of composition and assemblage which required considerable degrees of skill and concentration on the part of all the workers in the printing house, especially the compositors and the 'pressmen' who operated the press. This small format already existed, though it was far from common in early printing while in manuscript production it was largely associated with private devotional texts such as breviaries. As Harris points out, though, the Aldine octavos were different because they used a smaller overall size of sheet which after folding also produced a more slender shape (closer to the harmonious ratio of the so-called 'golden rectangle'), while the quality of the paper itself was also different, being thinner.[3] The result was lighter and genuinely portable books, which led to a change in reading habits and also eventually, as the octavo format became dominant in publishing over the course of the next few decades, to how books were stored, vertically lined up in rows on shelves in what has become the paradigmatic image of a library collection. The presentation of the content of these editions too represented a radical change compared with the earlier publishing history of both the classical and vernacular works included in what was in effect a series: the texts are presented unadorned, without commentary or any other extraneous material (the dedications, prefaces, potted biographies and, in the case of Dante, illustrations) which were a marked feature of previous fifteenth-century editions of such authors. They were still intended to be philologically rigorous and reliable, however. The great Venetian humanist scholar Pietro Bembo, one of Aldus's earliest collaborators, oversaw the texts of Petrarch and then Dante. Bembo was the leading proponent of the adoption of the 'Tuscan' linguistic model, as exemplified in the literary works of these great fourteenth-century authors, for the Italian language in general. Bembo's editions of these culturally iconic texts, together with the immense and widespread popularity of the new octavo format,[4] was an important contribution to the diffusion of the Tuscan dialect, at least among the literate, as the basis for what would come to be seen as standard Italian (Image 6).

06. *Dante Alighieri,* Le terze rime, *1502. Clockwise from top left: title page (a1r); opening of poem (a1v–a2r); end of poem and colophon (H4r); Aldine device (H4v). (C.4.d.4)*

THE *HYPNEROTOMACHIA POLIPHILI* OF 1499

Perhaps the most famous single book ever published by Aldus – and one of the most revered in the history of printing for the outstanding quality of its design – is paradoxically the one which is in several ways atypical of his overall achievements: the strangely named and anonymously authored 'novel' *Hypnerotomachia Poliphili* (Image 1). Poliphilus is the protagonist of the stor,y while the first word is a composite coinage referring to his 'battle of love in a dream', a curious but in fact quite accurate summary of the narrative, in which Poliphilus pursues his beloved, Polia, through various meticulously described dream landscapes and edifices, all related in a hybrid linguistic merging of Latin and Italian. It was printed at the very end of the fifteenth century, in 1499, just when Aldus was embarking on the printing of his *enchiridia* editions. As we have seen, Aldus came to Venice with an intellectual mission to which he thought the still comparatively new technology of printing could be harnessed, and his entire publishing activity from beginning to end was shaped by a more or less coherent and consistent programme in terms of languages, texts, genres and editorial criteria. Although there are numerous elements, both of content, such as its formidable antiquarian erudition and philological/epigraphical focus, and of design, especially the beauty and clarity of its

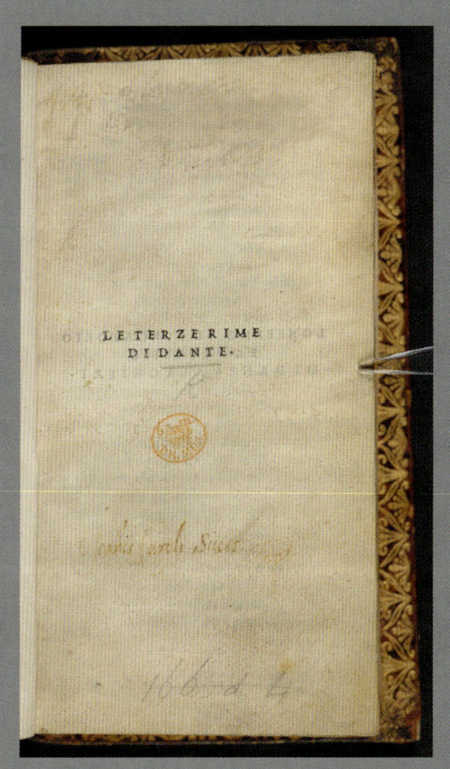

LE TERZE RIME
DI DANTE.

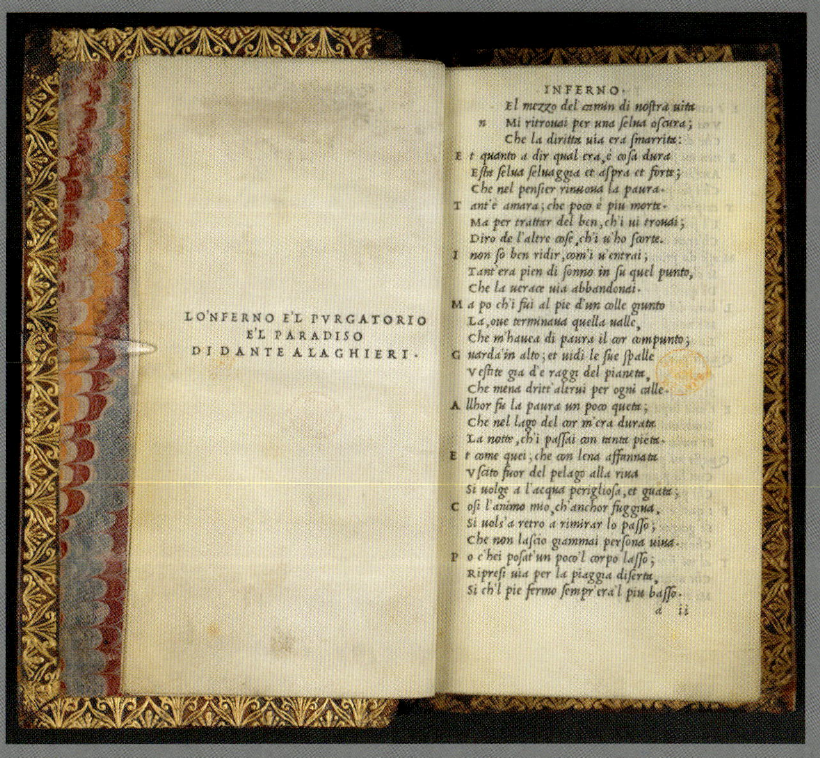

LO'NFERNO E'L PVRGATORIO
E'L PARADISO
DI DANTE ALAGHIERI.

INFERNO.

N El mezzo del camin di nostra uita
Mi ritrouai per una selua oscura;
Che la diritta uia era smarrita:
E t quanto a dir qual era, è cosa dura
Esta selua seluaggia et aspra et forte;
Che nel pensier rinnoua la paura.
T ant'è amara; che poco è piu morte.
Ma per trattar del ben, ch'i ui trouai;
Diro de l'altre cose, ch'i u'ho scorte.
I non so ben ridir, com'i u'entrai;
Tant'era pien di sonno in su quel punto,
Che la uerace uia abbandonai.
M a po ch'i fui al pie d'un colle giunto
La, oue terminaua quella ualle,
Che m'hauea di paura il cor compunto;
G uarda'in alto; et uidi le sue spalle
Vestite gia d'e raggi del pianeta,
Che mena dritt'altrui per ogni calle.
A llhor fu la paura un poco queta;
Che nel lago del cor m'era durata
La notte, ch'i passai con tanta pieta.
E t come quei; che con lena affannata
Vscito fuor del pelago alla riua
Si uolge a l'acqua perigliosa, et guata;
C osi l'animo mio, ch'anchor fuggiua,
Si uols'a retro a rimirar lo passo;
Che non lascio giammai persona uiua.
P o c'hei posat'un poco'l corpo lasso;
Ripresi uia per la piaggia diserta,
Si ch'l pie fermo sempr'era'l piu basso.
a ii

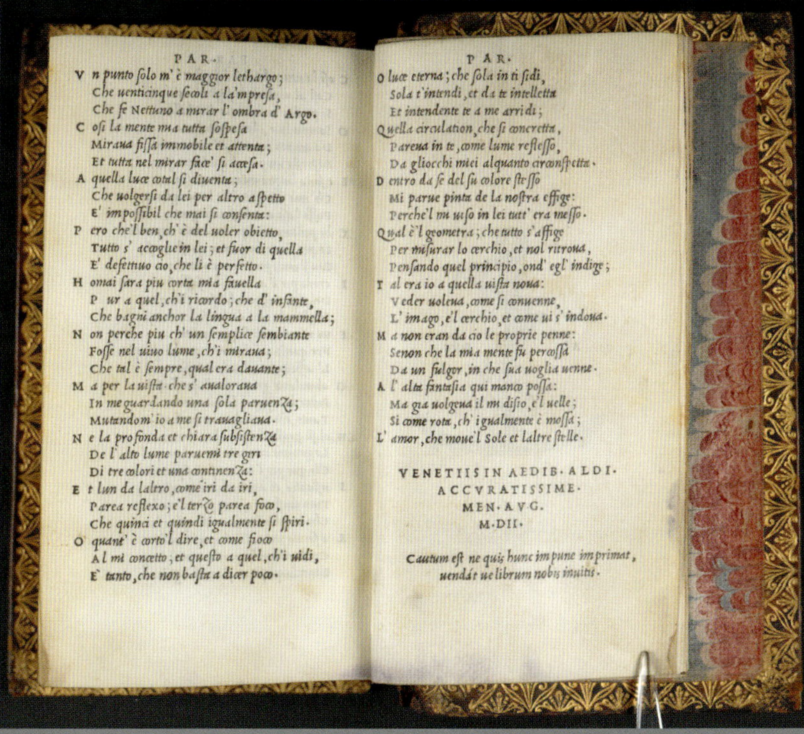

PAR.

V n punto solo m' è maggior lethargo;
Che uenticinque secoli a la'mpresa,
Che fe Nettuno a mirar l'ombra d'Argo.
C osi la mente mia tutta sospesa
Miraua fissa immobile et attenta;
Et tutta nel mirar face' si accesa.
A quella luce cotal si diuenta;
Che uolgersi da lei per altro aspetto
E' impossibil che mai si consenta:
P ero che'l ben, ch'è del uoler obietto,
Tutto s' accoglie in lei; et fuor di quella
E' defettiuo cio, che li è perfetto.
H omai sara piu corta mia fauella
P ur a quel, ch'i ricordo; che d' infante,
Che bagni anchor la lingua a la mammella;
N on perche piu ch' un semplice sembiante
Fosse nel uiuo lume, ch'i miraua;
Che tal è sempre, qual era dauante;
M a per la uista che s' aualoraua
In me guardando una sola paruenza;
Mutandom'io a me si trauagliaua.
N e la profonda et chiara subsistenza
De l'alto lume paruemi tre giri
Di tre colori et una continenza:
E t lun da laltro, come'iri da iri,
Parea reflexo; e'l terzo parea foco,
Che quinci et quindi igualmente si spiri.
O quant' è corto'l dire, et come fioco
Al mi concetto; et questo a quel, ch'i uidi,
E' tanto, che non basta a dicer poco.

PAR.

O luce eterna; che sola in ti sidi,
Sola t'intendi, et da te intelletta
Et intendente te a me arridi;
Quella circulation, che si concretta,
Pareua in te, come lume reflesso,
Da gliocchi miei alquanto circonspetta.
D entro da se del su colore stesso
Mi parue pinta de la nostra effige:
Perche'l mi uiso in lei tutt' era messo.
Qual è'l geometra; che tutto s'affige
Per misurar lo cerchio, et nol ritroua,
Pensando quel principio, ond' egl' indige;
T al era io a quella uista noua:
Veder uoleua, come si conuenne,
L' imago, e'l cerchio, et come ui s' indoua.
M a non eran da cio le proprie penne:
Senon che la mia mente fu percossa
Da un fulgor, in che sua uoglia uenne.
A l' alta fantasia qui manco possa:
Ma gia uolgeua il mi disio, e'l uelle;
Si come rota, ch' igualmente è mossa;
L' amor, che moue'l Sole et laltre stelle.

VENETIIS IN AEDIB. ALDI.
ACCVRATISSIME.
MEN. AVG.
M.DII.

Cautum est ne quis hunc impune imprimat, uendát ue librum nobis inuitis.

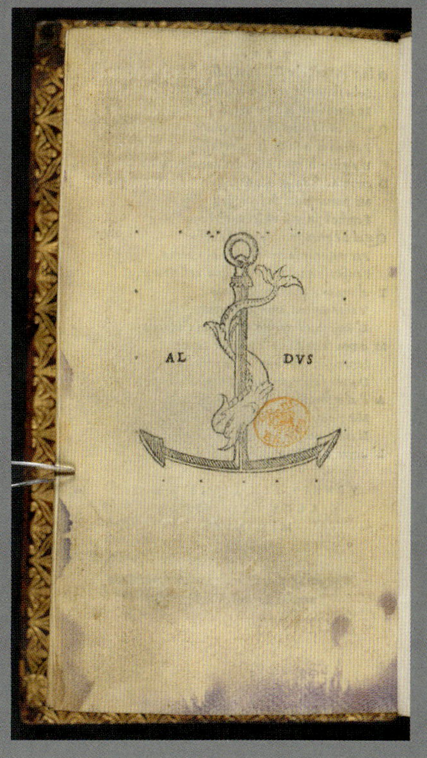

06.

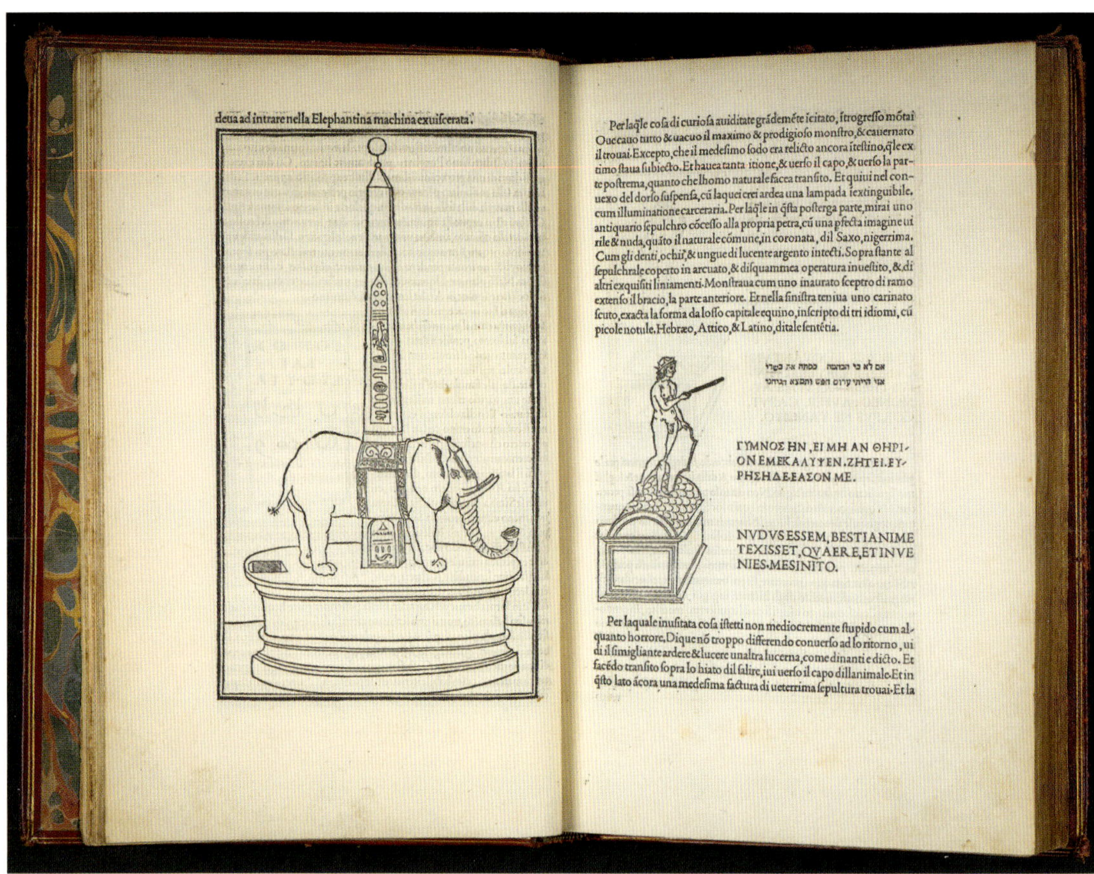
NVDVS ESSEM, BESTIA NI ME
TEXISSET, QVAERE, ET INVE
NIES. ME SINITO.

07.

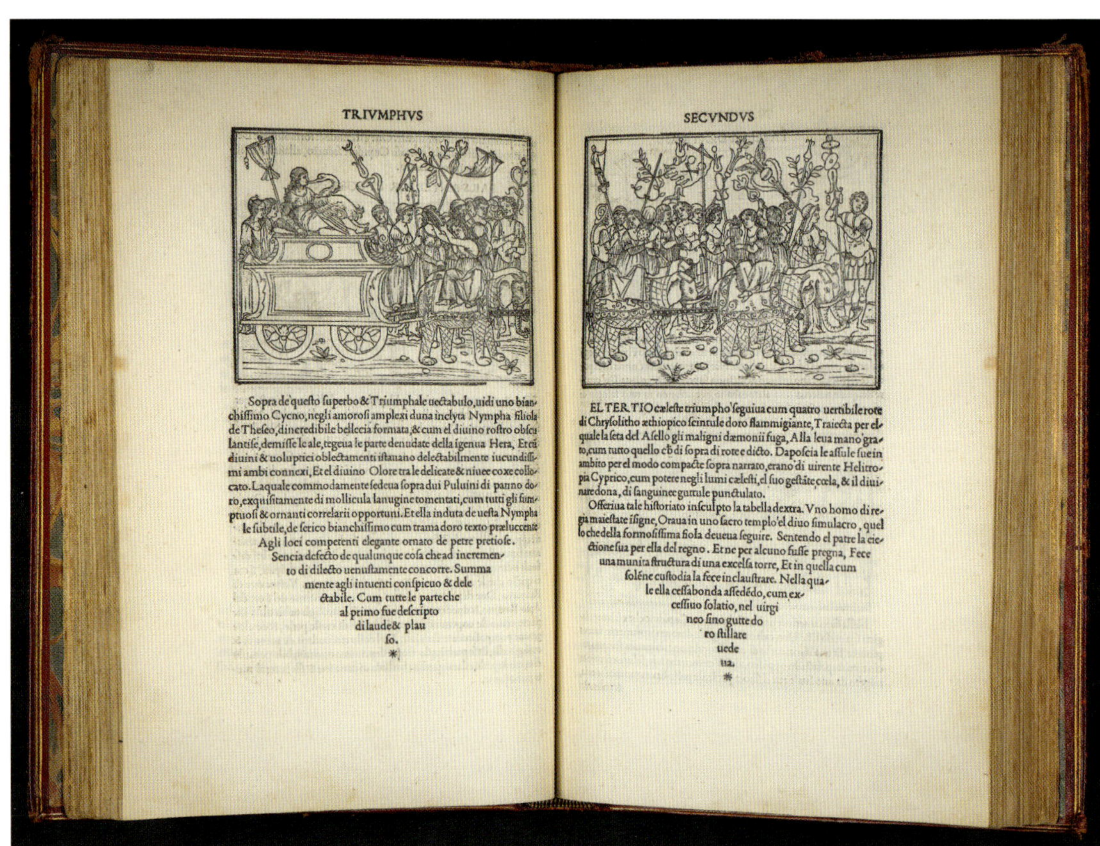
TRIVMPHVS
SECVNDVS

08.

Specification	*Scale*
HYPNEROTOMACHIA POLIPHILI... (Venetiis mense decembri. M.ID [1499]: in aedibus Aldi Manutii). Italy, Venice, 1499 310 x 220 mm 86.k.9	

superb roman type and layout (in no other Aldine edition perhaps is the 'structural clarity' of the page Burnhill praised so evident), which clearly relate to Aldus's interests elsewhere in his production, the *Hypnerotomachia* lies noticeably outside the main direction of this programme. Indeed, in contrast to his other editions, Aldus signs it only discreetly (although this and its other differences also probably reflect the fact that the book was externally commissioned – in other words, it was a job which Aldus took on rather than initiated) (Image 4). To single out the most significant contrast, it is copiously illustrated, whereas Aldus elsewhere showed hardly any interest in adding images to books, perhaps seeing them as superfluous to the textual purity and philological rigour he valued so highly. His previous production had included some books with images such as the Hero and Leander edition of 1494/5 with its two slightly differing woodcuts – one for the original Greek text, one for the Latin translation – depicting Leander's swim across the Hellespont, and the series of illustrations included for one of the component texts in the 1499 *Scriptores astronomici veteres*. Here, in contrast to his attention to producing new and accurate versions of texts, the woodcuts are mostly crude copies from an earlier edition produced by another printer. But he published no other edition in which the illustrations are so important to our understanding and appreciation of the text, which are so often in themselves of superlative artistic quality,[5] and in which such evident care and inventiveness have been deployed in integrating the text and the images in one varying sequence (Image 7). The most spectacular examples are perhaps to be found in the description of the 'Triumphs', with the double-page facing images of the procession each resting on the inverted pyramid of the text in a remarkable combination of monumentality and movement (Image 8), but the care of design can be found everywhere in the book, such as the ingenious and elegant shaping of the letterpress text to fill blank spaces on the page and even in minimal details, like the integration of movable type with engraved inscription in some of the epigraphical illustrations.

07. Hypnerotomachia Poliphili, *1499. (b7v–b8r)*

08. Hypnerotomachia Poliphili, *1499. (k7v–k8r)*

CONCLUSION

Aldus's contributions to the design of printed books as well as the organisation and presentation of their content – pagination, indexing, etc., which are no less a part of overall book design – are the basis of his enduring fame. His inventiveness together with the consistent effort to establish order and clarity are best seen in the evidence of the books themselves; Aldus speaks often of his intellectual projects and ambitions but almost never of the huge and parallel input into design which must have constantly accompanied his concern for the content of his editions. As Peter Burnhill remarks, 'how Aldus co-ordinated the work of his printing staff must remain speculative ... However, [...] little appears to have been left to chance in the detailing of the work ...'[6] Perhaps though the essence of his achievement lies in his ability to combine or synchronise innovations in design – including on occasion those introduced by others – so they become symbiotic. His *enchiridia* editions are the supreme example – an alliance of format, paper, type and text – and have exercised a profound influence down to the present day on our conceptions of what printed books should look like and how we read them.

BODONI'S *MANUALE TIPOGRAFICO* AND HIS FOLLOWERS

VALENTINA MIRABELLA

A neoclassical aesthetic; the science of epigraphy; considering the design of type as an art form: these are the key aspects behind the work of eighteenth-century printer and type designer Giovanni Battista Bodoni, which has inspired generations of designers and typographers.

Giovanni Battista Bodoni (1740–1813), 'Printer to Kings, King of Printers', made the Italian town of Parma the world capital of typography from the second half of the eighteenth century, and an essential stopping-off point for intellectuals and bibliophiles during the Grand Tour.

After completing his studies in typography and oriental languages in Rome, the 26-year-old Bodoni attempted to go to England and work for the famous printer and type designer, John Baskerville. During his journey, he contracted malaria and had to return to his home town, Saluzzo. In 1768, the Duke Ferdinand of Bourbon invited him to establish and manage the Royal Printing Office in Parma, where he would work for the rest of his life.

Bodoni introduced harmony and proportion in book title pages and his bare, epigraphic compositions reflected the neoclassicist taste with geometry and symmetry. The balance between space and lettering offered a pleasant reading experience. The series of crisp and neat 'Bodonian' typefaces that he designed and created are still very popular today, appreciated for the clear contrast between the thickness of strokes and the thinness of rules and serifs. These are still very much in use in magazines and commercial logos.

Bodoni cut his own punches and produced his types from 1771, and he published his first *Manuale Tipografico* (*Inventory of Types*) in 1788, displaying *specimina* ('examples') of his roman, italic and Greek alphabets, in different sizes.

He was certainly influenced by Pierre-Simon Fournier's 1764 *Manuel typographique*, which represented French rococo style and showed the Enlightenment's encyclopaedic spirit in the engravings illustrating punch-cutting, typefounding and printing tools.

For Bodoni, his manual was not just a collection of types, but also an aesthetically pleasing display of typographic skills, including page design and layout.

His types were refined over the course of his life, and the second edition of *Manuale Tipografico* appeared posthumously in 1818 under the direction of his widow, Margherita Dall'Aglio. The 1818 edition, itself a masterpiece of typography, was the fruit of more than forty years of labour: it comprised a variety of roman types, capital letters, Greek and oriental types, borders, ornaments, numbers and musical examples.

More recently typographers including Giovanni Mardersteig and Alberto and Enrico Tallone have followed in Bodoni's footsteps, revisiting his fonts and issuing their own versions of *Manuale Tipografico*. Graphic designers such as Massimo Vignelli and Franco Maria Ricci have adapted Bodoni's work into the digital world.

GIOVANNI MARDERSTEIG

Like many of the early printers working in Italy in the first century of printing before him, Hans or 'Giovanni' Mardersteig came from Germany and established his hand press in Italy. In 1922, the Italian government granted him permission to use Bodoni's original matrices and he set up the Officina Bodoni, which operated out of Verona until Mardersteig's death in 1977. Mardersteig's

01.

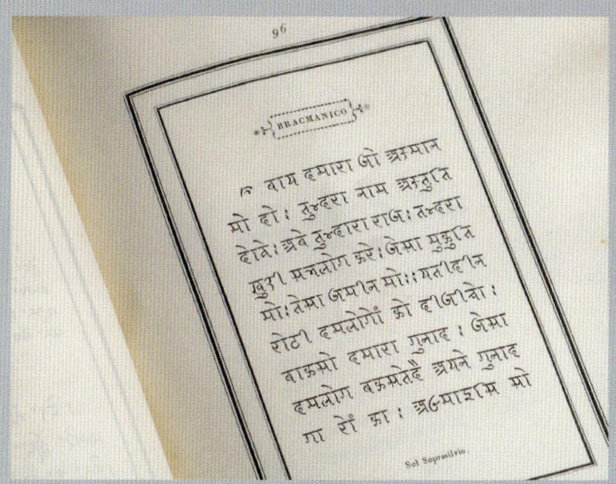

02.

03.

extreme care for detail is shown in his facsimile edition of Bodoni's *Manuale Tipografico, 1788*, recreated with typesetting.

ALBERTO AND ENRICO TALLONE

Alberto Tallone and his son Enrico have worked since the 1930s to honour the book in its material and spiritual aspects. Engravers, typefounders, hand printers and publishers, the Tallone family have honoured Bodoni's idea of a manual, describing, in the four volumes of their own *Manuale Tipografico*, centuries of typography, watermarks, alphabets, title pages and inks used. Each edition produced by Tallone Editore is unique through the choice of book format, typeface, spacing and paper.

01.–03. *Pages from the second edition of Giovanni Battista Bodoni,* Manuale Tipografico, *Parma, 1818. (59.c.19–20)*

01.

نور نظر بزرگواران محراب نماز تاجداران
ای از شرف تو شاهزاده چشم فلک اختشان گشاده
یک تخم بخسروی نشانده از تخمه کیقباد مانده
پر پهر تخت و افسر تاج کاقبال بروی اوست محتاج
مروج دو مملکت بشاهی چون سپ دو رنگ صبحگاهی
شروان ز تو قیروان جلالت خزران ز تو خیزران عدالت

AKBAR'S *KHAMSAH* OF NIZAMI

A Mughal masterpiece

URSULA SIMS-WILLIAMS

The Emperor Akbar's copy of Nizami's *Khamsah* (Or 12208), often referred to as the Dyson Perrins *Khamsah* after its most recent owner, is one of the most perfect productions of the Mughal emperor Akbar's reign (1556–1605). Produced for him in Lahore between 1593 and 1595, this manuscript represents what was without doubt an intensely personal project and combines the work of the best painters, calligraphers and illuminators working at his court.

THE PATRON AND THE POET

Descended from both the fourteenth-century Timur (Tamerlane) and the Mongol conqueror Genghis Khan, the Mughals first established rule in India in 1526. Akbar was the third and the best known of the Mughal emperors and succeeded his father Humayun in 1556 at the age of 12. During his fifty-year reign, he extended his empire to include the independent states of Malwa, Gujarat and Bengal and established capital cities at Agra, Fatehpur Sikri and Lahore, which became centres producing exquisite manuscripts and paintings in addition to other artefacts. Born into a highly educated and literate dynasty, Akbar inherited his ancestors' love of books, although he was illiterate and is thought to have suffered from dyslexia.[1] As his chief minister Abu'l-Fazl recorded,[2] Akbar would never tire of listening to books being read to him over and over again, and at whatever point the reading was interrupted, he would mark the place for a future occasion. In addition to his fondness for literary classics, he also commissioned new works and translations from Arabic, Turkish and Sanskrit texts into Persian, the language of the Mughal court.

01. *Nizami presents his young son Muhammad to the son of his patron Akhsatan, the ruler of Shirvan (r. 1160–97). Artists, Khem Karan and Bulaqi.* c. *1595. (f. 117r)*

Akbar's love of books led to an expansion of the royal library, which at his death in 1605 was recorded as consisting of 24,000 richly bound volumes.[3] Connected to the library were workshops of calligraphers, artists and illuminators, in addition to specialised gilders and binders who created increasingly sumptuous manuscripts. The Dyson Perrins *Khamsah* is one of a small group of luxury Persian manuscripts which also include Jami's *Baharistan*, now held in the Bodleian Library in Oxford[4] and the *Khamsah* of Amir Khusraw, now in the Walters Art Gallery, Baltimore,[5] and were all produced in Lahore between 1593 and 1598. First revealed to the public in 1912, the collector and art historian F. R. Martin wrote of this manuscript: 'Without exception it is the most wonderful Indian manuscript in Europe.'[6]

Among Akbar's favourite books were the five *masnavis* or epic poems, collectively called the *Khamsah* (Quintet) by the poet Nizami (*c.* 1140–1209) of Ganja in present-day Azerbaijan. The individual poems are the *Makhzan al-Asrar* (Treasury of Secrets), a didactic work containing ethical stories, and four romances: *Khusraw u Shirin* (Khusraw and Shirin), the story of the Sasanian king, Khusraw Parviz (r. 590–628 CE) and his love affair with the Armenian princess Shirin; *Layla u Majnun* (Layla and Majnun), about the ill-fated lovers, Qays and his childhood sweetheart Layla; *Haft Paykar* (Seven Portraits), about another Sasanian ruler Bahram Gur (r. 420–438 CE) and the seven princesses; and the *Iskandarnamah* (The Book of Iskandar), a two-part account of Alexander the Great. In his poetry Nizami drew extensively on sources in many different languages, demonstrating his knowledge of mathematics, astronomy, medicine, law and philosophy. He is generally regarded as one of the greatest writers of Persian poetry whose work served as a literary model during the following centuries.

Little is known about Nizami's personal life, details of which are mostly gleaned from the *Khamsah* itself.[7] His favourite wife, Afaq, thought to be the inspiration for Shirin in his second *masnavi*, was the mother of his only child Muhammad. The Dyson Perrins *Khamsah* includes a rare personal portrait (Image 1) in which Nizami presents his son Muhammad to the son of the patron of *Layla u Majnun*, Akhsatan who ruled Shirvan, today in Azerbaijan, from 1160 to 1197.

Nizami's *Khamsah* is one of the most frequently illustrated of Persian manuscripts and Akbar already had several fine copies in his library, including one (Or 6810) produced in Herat at the court of his relative Sultan Husayn Bayqara (d. 1506), which had illustrations by the master-painter Bihzad. Inspired to augment and surpass the collection of his predecessors, Akbar had already commissioned paintings to be added to an earlier small-format *Khamsah*, copied originally in Yazd, Iran, between 1502 and 1506, which is now in the Keir collection, Dallas Museum of Art.[8] Perhaps unsatisfied with the results or thinking of it as a trial run, Akbar decided on another completely new copy and commissioned the Dyson Perrins manuscript, which was completed for him in 1595.

THE DYSON PERRINS *KHAMSAH*

The Dyson Perrins *Khamsah* consists of 325 folios of light brown, polished paper, measuring 302 by 198 millimetres with the text arranged in four columns, each containing twenty-one lines. The manuscript contains a total of thirty-seven out of an original forty-four numbered illustrations, to which an extra painting was added at the end. At some stage the manuscript was repaired and later, probably in Europe in the early twentieth century, sections were extracted. Thirty-nine folios from *Khusraw u Shirin* and the *Iskandarnamah,* including five illustrated pages, were acquired by Henry Walters and are now in the Walters Art Museum Baltimore.[9] The two remaining paintings of the original forty-four are unaccounted for.

02. *The colophon of the* Iskandarnamah, *dated 1595, with an additional portrait of the scribe 'Abd al-Rahim and self-portrait of the artist Dawlat, added in 1609. (f. 325v)*

03. *The story of King Nushirvan the Just and the owls in the* Makhzan al-asrar *by Manohar. (f. 13v)*

04. *The man carried away by the* simurgh, *story told by the Indian princess. Artist, Dharamdas. (f. 195r)*

04.

05.

06.

07.

08.

09.

Specification	*Scale*
NIZAMI, *KHAMSAH* (QUINTET) Lahore, 1593–5 302 × 198 mm Or 12208	

Four of the six colophons[10] are dated between October 1593 and December 1595, of which the earliest at the end of *Khusraw u Shirin* gives the full name of the scribe, 'Abd al-Rahim, son of the scribe 'Abd al-Hayy, son of the scribe 'Ala' al-Din Muhammad of Herat. Descended from a long line of calligraphers 'Abd al-Rahim gained a reputation for his beautiful *nasta'liq* (downward-slanting) and *naskh* (clear and written on a straight line) scripts while working for the Mughal statesman 'Abd al-Rahim Khan-i Khanan before he moved to the imperial studio.[11] Granted the title *'Anbarin Qalam* (Ambergris Pen), 'Abd al-Rahim's reputation was such that the artist Dawlat was instructed by Akbar's successor Jahangir (r. 1605–27) to add his portrait at the end of the volume (Image 2). This was completed, according to the inscription in the wall decoration, in January 1609[12] and portrays, identified by further inscriptions, 'Abd al-Rahim together with a self-portrait of the artist, Dawlat, surrounded by the tools of their trade.

Adjacent to five of the six colophons is the statement that the manuscript was overseen by an official Sharif, 'at the ready (*pa bar ja*), disciple of the four ranks of loyalty' (*ba-ihtimam-i murid dar char martabah-i ikhlas*) who also 'completed' the illustrations (*surat itmam paziruft*). While it is not clear exactly what 'completed' means, these inscriptions suggest a general supervisory role for the project as a whole, a role which Sharif also had in another luxury manuscript, the Jaipur *Razmnamah*.[13] The allusion to the four ranks of loyalty refers to the promise to sacrifice to the emperor property, life, honour and religion which Akbar demanded of courtiers in AH 988 (1581/82 in the Gregorian calendar).[14] The unique phrasing of the inscription allows him to be identified with Muhammad Sharif, son of the Iranian court painter 'Abd al-Samad, who was himself the artist of a hunting scene in *Khusraw u Shirin*.[15] Muhammad Sharif had an official role in Akbar's library and his seal dated AH 1003 (1594/5), with the same inscription, is stamped on several major manuscripts of the period.[16] He was also a painter whose two paintings in the previously mentioned Keir *Khamsah*[17] are inscribed with the same wording.

05. *The much-damaged initial rosette (*shamsah*), inscribed minutely beneath the lowest of the 12 points 'work of the illuminator Husayn'. (f. 1r, detail)*

06. *Heading to* Haft paykar, *inscribed 'work of Khvajah Jan, illuminator, in the year 1004' (1595/6). (f. 169v, detail)*

07. *The heading to the* Iqbalnamah, *the final part of the* Iskandarnamah, *combines the art of the illuminator and gilder with images of the legendary* simurgh *and intricate patterns of flowers and small birds. (f. 285v)*

08. & 09. *Rhinos (f. 282r, detail), and an elephant attacks a tiger. (f. 204r, detail)*

AKBAR AND THE ART OF PAINTING

Many Iranian artists, including the senior painter 'Abd al-Samad, had migrated to India with the emperor Humayun in 1555 after his return from exile in Safavid Iran. During Akbar's reign Iranian writers and artists continued to seek patronage at the Mughal court resulting in a fusion of artistic traditions which was also inspired by European paintings and engravings, brought to India by travellers and merchants. In his *A'in-i Akbari*, Abu'l-Fazl wrote:

'*Most excellent painters are now to be found, and masterpieces, worthy of a* Bihzád, *may be placed at the side of the wonderful works of the European painters who have attained worldwide fame. The minuteness in detail, the general finish, the boldness of execution, &c., now observed in pictures, are incomparable; even inanimate objects look as if they had life. More than a hundred painters have become famous masters of the art.*'[18]

Regarding their origins, he added: 'This is especially true of the Hindus: their pictures surpass our conceptions of things. Few, indeed, in the whole world are found equal to them.'

The Dyson Perrins *Khamsah* is a perfect example of this fusion of techniques. While some of the paintings follow traditional two-dimensional Iranian styles with their use of bright colours, geometric design and attention to detail, the use of colour and perspective is new. This is especially evident in the treatment of landscapes filled with architectural details more often associated with European art. Altogether a team of twenty-two painters were involved in varying major and minor roles: 'Abd al-Samad, Bhem Gujarati, Bhura, Bulaqi, Dawlat, Dhanraj, Dharamdas, Farrukh Chela, Jagannath, Kanak Singh Chela, Khem Karan, La'l, Maddu Chela, Madhu,[19] Manohar, Miskina, Mukund, Nand Gwaliyari, Nanha, Narsingh, Sanwala and Sur Gujarati, to which should be added Shivdas whose painting survives only in the Walters section of the manuscript.

In Image 3, the story of Nushirvan and the owls by Manohar from the *Makhzan al-asrar*, is part of the second discourse 'On justice and maintaining rectitude'. Here the Sasanian king Nushirvan (Khusraw I), famous for his good administration and tax reforms, goes hunting accompanied by his vizier and comes to a ruined village where two owls are discussing a bride-price. One asks for the village in return for the other's daughter in marriage. The second owl replies that if the king continues with his destructive policies, he will soon be able to provide 100,000 such ruined villages. Nushirvan asks his minister what they are saying. On learning their message, he bitterly repented his ways and ruled justly henceforth. Although this particular episode was illustrated in other copies of the *Khamsah*, it would have doubtless had a particular significance in this manuscript comparing Akbar with the legendary Nushirvan the Just.

Image 4 illustrates a story from the *Haft Paykar*, about the Sasanian ruler Bahram Gur and his seven wives. The king visits each princess, housed in a differently coloured pavilion, on successive nights of the week and is entertained by each with a story. In the story of the black pavilion, illustrated here, the Indian princess relates how a king went in search of the City of the Senseless where all wear black. On his way he became imprisoned in a tower, but escaped by holding onto a large bird, here depicted as the legendary *simurgh*, Iranian in origin but derived from Chinese iconography. With the foreground dominated by the immense tower and the bird, the reader's eye, as is characteristic of this style, is led past agricultural scenes and the City of the Senseless into the distance.

10. *Back cover, originally the doublure, featuring a swirling* simurgh *and lion attacking a dragon.*

OTHER DESIGN FEATURES

Although calligraphy, primarily, and painting were prized above all, illumination and other forms of decoration contributed equally to the overall luxury of the Mughal book.[20] Specialist illuminators were employed to design opening pages and headings and to fill the borders with intricate gold patterns. Deluxe Iranian manuscripts frequently began with one or two folios containing a circular or oval rosette (*shamsah*) often inscribed with the title of the text or the name of the patron. Additionally, the opening text page of each work would carry an illuminated headpiece (*'unwan* or *sarlawh*), at the beginning of the text.

Rivalling the most luxurious Safavid manuscripts, the Dyson Perrins *Khamsah* includes eight ornamental rosettes separating the works and six highly illuminated headings introducing the poems.[21] Two illuminators are named. The first, Husayn, signs his name in the opening *shamsah* (Image 5). An inscription, 'work of Husayn' (*'amal-i Husayn*), on the lowest of the twelve points identifies him as the same *Husayn naqqash* (painter) who contributed a *shamsah* and heading in the Walters *Khamsah* of Amir Khusraw.[22] He has also been identified with the marginal illustrator of the Bodleian *Baharistan*[23] and at least eleven manuscript illustrations.[24] Now much damaged, the original central circle has been overpainted in gold with birds added around the edge, and several inscriptions surrounding the decoration, probably dating from Akbar's reign, have been systematically effaced. The central circle of the rosette bears traces of the pear-shaped seal of the Mughal emperor Shahjahan (r. 1628–58) or Aurangzeb (r. 1658–1707) which are visible in a raking light and on the verso.[25]

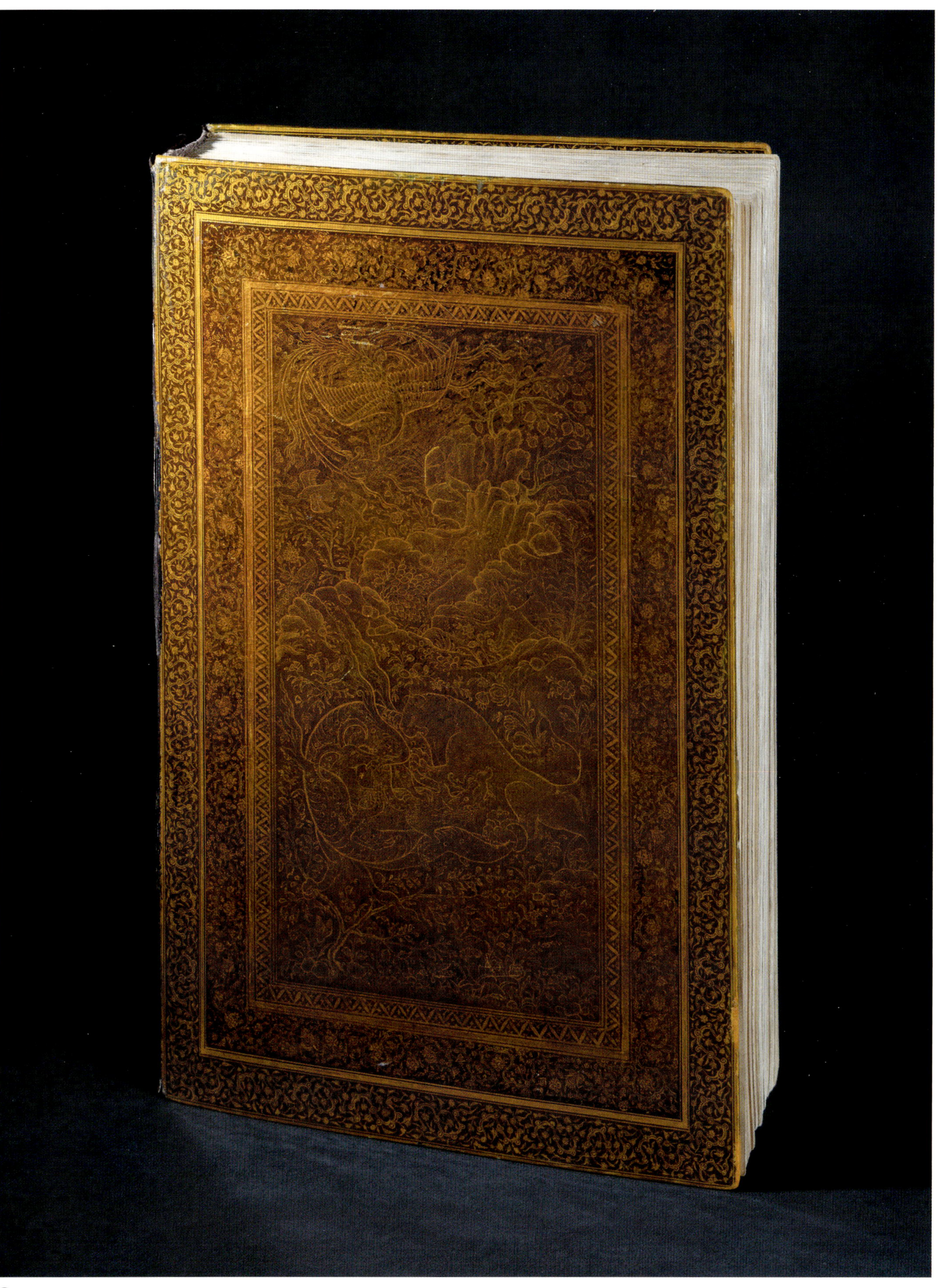

10.

11.

12.

13.

A second illuminator is Khvajah Jan of Shiraz, who signed his name in the headings of *Khusraw u Shirin*[26] and *Haft Paykar*[27] where he added his profession *muzahhib* (gilder) to his name and a date AH 1004 (1595/6) (Image 6). Khvajah Jan also completed a heading in the Walter's *Khamsah*[28] in which he added the epithet *Shirazi* to his name, and a copy of Sa'di's *Gulistan* (Flower Garden)[29] copied between 1582 and 1583 in Fatehpur Sikri.[30] Marginal decorations, illuminated in various shades of gold, took their inspiration from imperial Safavid masterpieces such as Shah Tahmasp's *Khamsah* of Nizami (Or 2265). This art was further developed under the Mughals from the traditional floral arabesques and creatures, real and mythical, which owed their inspiration to China, to include people at work and indigenous animals such as rhinos and elephants.[31] The margins of the Dyson Perrins *Khamsah* include only three human figures,[32] but a full range of flora and fauna in addition to pages containing only arabesque or geometric designs (Images 7, 8 & 9). The names of the artists responsible for the marginal decoration would have been recorded on the outer edge of the page but were unfortunately cut off when the manuscript was trimmed. By good fortune such annotations have mostly been preserved in the Bodleian *Baharistan* whose named artists include Balchand, Husayn, Ikhlas, Khem, Khizr, Madhava, Mukhlis, Nand Chela, Shivdas and Sulayman Kalan.[33] It is likely that these same artists were responsible for the margins of the Dyson Perrins *Khamsah* which was completed in the same year.

THE BINDING

The *Khamsah*'s lacquered binding is of exceptional quality although the doublures and the outer covers were reversed during restoration in the nineteenth or twentieth century. Lacquered bindings first appeared on Persian manuscripts in the early fifteenth century, and became increasingly popular in the sixteenth century, with intricate hunting scenes and princely receptions painted on to pasteboard providing a more stable support than leather. The two current doublures are pictorial scenes which would have originally formed the outside covers. Of particular note is the scene, originally the front cover, of the king in the likeness of Akbar, surveying the results of a hunt (Image 11). Here, enthroned, the king inspects the dead animals, while an official records the details. On the right a horse and other spectators look on. The format and some of the details of this scene resemble the famous 'Akbar orders the slaughter to cease' (Image 12), a detached folio from the first imperial *Akbarnamah* (History of Akbar) of *c.* 1595. The rear binding carries the more orthodox hunting scene of a prince in pursuit of his prey (Image 13), while the two original doublures depict a swirling *simurgh*, lions and dragon (Image 10).

11. *Akbar inspects the catch from a hunting expedition, original outer front binding.*

12. *The emperor Akbar, seated under a tree, informs his courtiers that the slaughter of animals should cease,* c. *1595. (Johnson Album, J.8.4)*

13. *A prince in pursuit of his prey, original outer rear binding.*

RECENT HISTORY OF THE DYSON PERRINS *KHAMSAH*

Little is known about the Dyson Perrins manuscript immediately after the reign of Jahangir. The traces of the pear-shaped seal on folio 1r, suggest that it was still in the royal library during the reigns of Shah Jahan or Aurangzeb – since they are the only two rulers with seals of that shape. Presumably it was sold or removed from the library during the eighteenth century, perhaps as a result of Nadir Shah's invasion of Delhi in 1739. An illegible rectangular seal in Arabic script on folio 325v indicates that it passed into the hands of a Muslim owner before ending up with a dealer in Paris. F. R. Martin in 1912[34] wrote that it reached Paris in the summer of 1909 'where it was vainly offered for sale, until it was purchased by Mr. Bernard Quaritch'. Quaritch, the famous London bookseller, sold it to the collector and philanthropist Charles William Dyson Perrins – grandson of William Perrins, co-originator of the Lea and Perrins secret recipe for Worcester sauce – and Dyson Perrins bequeathed it to the British Museum at his death in 1958. In 1973 it was transferred from the British Museum to the newly formed British Library.[35]

IX.

THE SHAKESPEARE FIRST FOLIO OF 1623

The most famous book of English literature, and the only source for 18 of Shakespeare's plays

ADRIAN S. EDWARDS

INTRODUCTION

Few books in the English-speaking world are as famous as the Shakespeare First Folio. Printed in London in 1623 by Isaac Jaggard and Edward Blount, this hefty tome contains thirty-six plays and a portrait of William Shakespeare (1564–1616) that has been reproduced so many times that it is now instantly recognisable the world over (Image 1).

First Folios are not particularly rare: there are five at the British Library and a worldwide census published in 2012[1] references 232 survivals, although only around forty to fifty are more or less complete. But without the First Folio, performances of eighteen of Shakespeare's plays, including *The Tempest*, *Twelfth Night* and *Macbeth*, would not be possible today, as this is the only version in which they survive. Other plays had appeared in print before, but the Folio text is often different and therefore of interest to both theatre directors and researchers. Original First Folios are also keenly sought after by institutional and private collectors; in 2020 a rare complete copy sold for over US$9.9 million at auction.[2]

Before the First Folio, there was no long-standing tradition of gathering the collected works of an English playwright into a single, published volume. The creators had just one direct model for inspiration – a volume of works by the Bard's near contemporary, Ben Jonson (1572–1637). Jonson's folio had been produced in collaboration with a living writer; Shakespeare's folio, however, was issued seven years after the playwright's death. The publication would therefore need to stand as a lasting memorial to the great man himself.

But, of course, 'First Folio' is not the title of the work itself: this is a descriptive name added in later centuries. The volume's full title is *Mr. William Shakespeares Comedies, Histories, & Tragedies. Published according to the True Originall Copies.*

01. *Title page portrait of Shakespeare. (C.39.k.15)*

FOLIOS AND QUARTOS

The term 'folio' relates to the format or physical structure of the volume, produced by printing two pages on each side of a sheet of paper and then folding it in half to make a bi-folium, much like a greetings card. Several of these folded sheets would then be nested inside one another to create a gathering called a quire. Folios were expensive, primarily because of the large amount of paper they required in comparison to other standard book formats, all of which achieved more pages from each sheet of paper. They were also large and heavy, and became most closely associated with church Bibles, standard reference works, the collected editions of classical authors, and other works that a reader might expect to consult at a table or lectern. Economically, the publication of a folio was a risky undertaking, particularly given the quantity of paper – an imported and expensive commodity – that needed to be sourced before printing could begin.

Popular plays were instead almost always printed as individual editions in a quarto format. Quartos were produced by printing four pages on each

(01.)

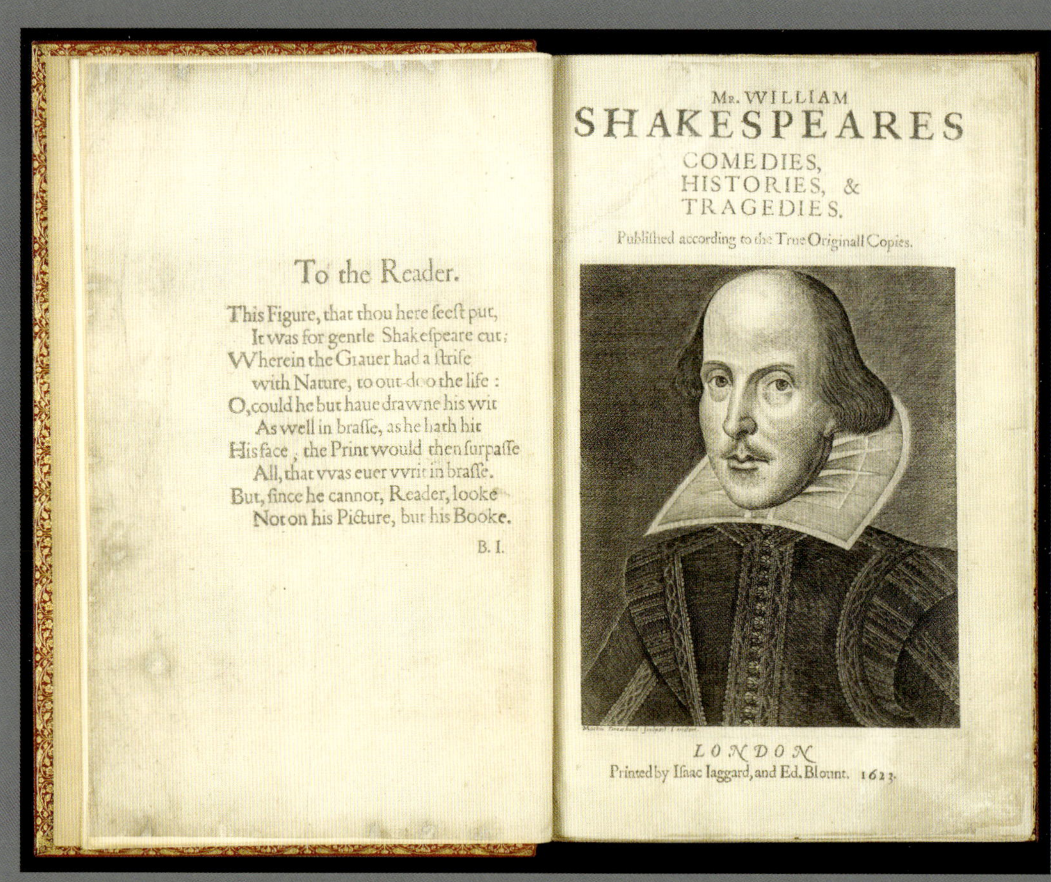

To the Reader.

This Figure, that thou here seest put,
It was for gentle Shakespeare cut;
Wherein the Grauer had a strife
with Nature, to out-doo the life:
O, could he but haue drawne his wit
As well in brasse, as he hath hit
His face, the Print would then surpasse
All, that vvas euer vvrit in brasse.
But, since he cannot, Reader, looke
Not on his Picture, but his Booke.

B. I.

Mr. WILLIAM
SHAKESPEARES
COMEDIES,
HISTORIES, &
TRAGEDIES.
Published according to the True Originall Copies.

LONDON
Printed by Isaac Iaggard, and Ed. Blount. 1623.

02.

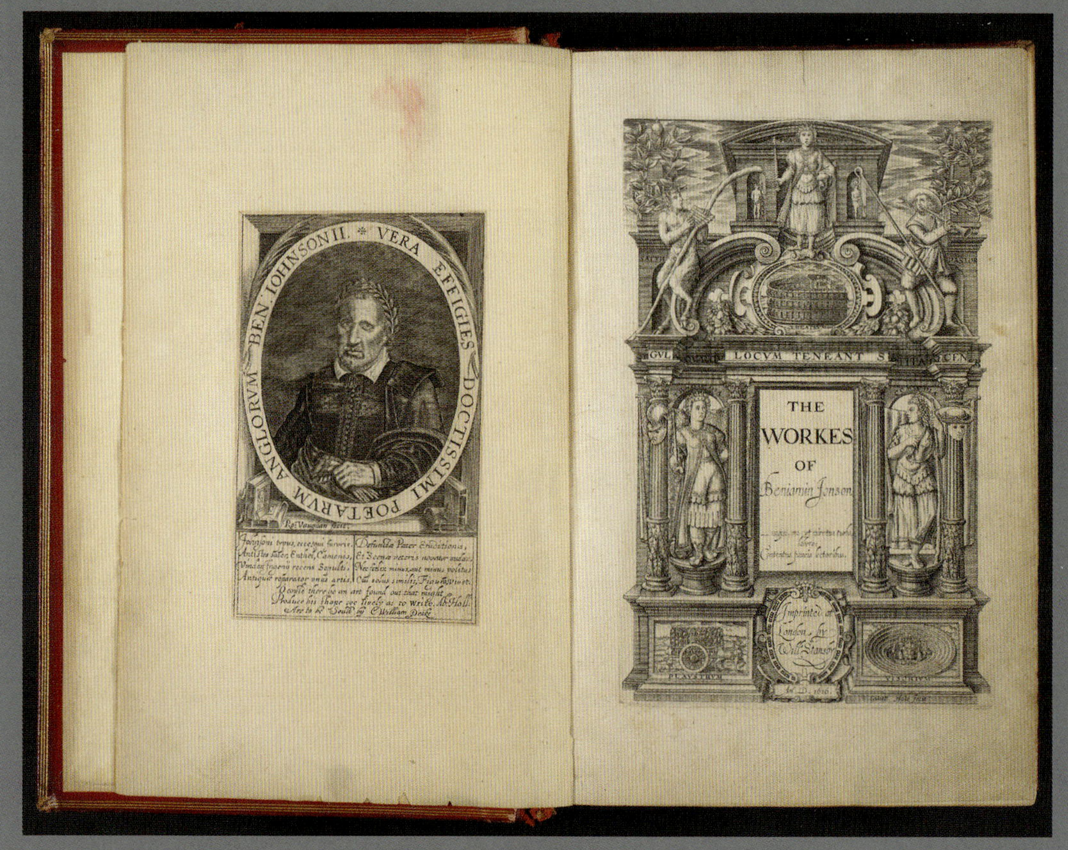

03.

side of a sheet of paper, then folding it twice. The resulting volume was small, fitted comfortably in one hand, and could easily be carried from place to place. Nineteen of Shakespeare's plays in some fifty-eight individual editions and variants had already appeared in print prior to the First Folio. These were all quartos, with the single exception of the 1595 edition of *Henry VI Part 3*, which is in the slightly smaller octavo format.

Some English literature was, nevertheless, beginning to be published in folio volumes by the end of the sixteenth century. These were all single works of prose or poetry: never collections and never plays. Examples include Philip Sidney's *The Countess of Pembroke's Arcadia* (1593) and Thomas Heywood's *Troia Britannica* (1609). The publication in 1616 of a volume of *Workes* by the 44-year-old writer Ben Jonson signalled a change. This volume comprised epigrams, masques and other forms of poetry, alongside nine complete plays, all preceded by a frontispiece portrait of Jonson and an ornate engraved title page (Image 3).

THE PEOPLE RESPONSIBLE FOR THE SHAKESPEARE FIRST FOLIO

The First Folio was the result of a collaboration between three groups of people. First, John Heminges (1566?–1630) and Henry Condell (1576?–1627), who had worked alongside Shakespeare as part of the acting company known as the King's Men. Heminges and Condell may have been particularly close to Shakespeare as they both received money in his will to purchase *memento mori* rings.

Second, a publishing syndicate responsible for finances, obtaining publication rights and sourcing the paper. Four names are given on the last leaf of the volume: William Jaggard (*c.* 1568–1623), Edward Blount (1562–1632), John Smethwick (d. 1641) and William Aspley (d. 1640). Blount, Smethwick and Aspley were literary publishers, whereas Jaggard was primarily a printer.

And it was the printers that formed the third group. The title page states that these were William Jaggard's son Isaac (d. 1627) and the aforementioned Edward Blount. The work was undertaken at the Jaggard family printshop on Aldersgate Street in the City of London. Isaac Jaggard would have overseen production as his father was blind by the 1620s and in fact died in October 1623. It is not clear what role Blount played, but he may have supplied materials or manpower.

PRODUCTION

Production began in 1622 and took at least a year and a half, in part because the printing presses were halted at several points to focus on other publications. The first steps would have been to edit the 'copy-texts' (source documents, whether manuscripts or existing quarto editions) and decide on a running order. Once the format, choice of type and use of ornamentation were settled, the page breaks could then be calculated and marked up on the copy-texts in a process known as 'casting off'. Only at this point could the compositors start work reproducing the text in metal type and supplying completed pages (formes) to colleagues who operated the presses.

Printing seems to have been completed in November 1623. As was usual in seventeenth-century book production, customers were free to choose how their acquisition would be bound. They might request a standard vellum, calf- or goatskin covering via their bookseller, or have loose sheets sent to their preferred bookbinder. There is evidence that an unbound copy retailed in London for 15s. and a bound one for £1 (that is 20s.),[3] but these prices would have varied according to choice of binding and other factors. The figures place the

02. *Title page opening of the Shakespeare First Folio. (C.39.k.15)*

03. *Title page opening of the Ben Jonson Folio of 1616. (G.11630)*

Specification	*Scale*
MR. WILLIAM SHAKESPEARES COMEDIES, HISTORIES, & TRAGEDIES. *Published according to the True Originall Copies* London, 1623 302 x 191 mm C.7.c.14, C.21.e.16, C.39.i.12, C.39.k.15, and G.11631	

First Folio at the luxury end of the book market. Experts vary in their estimates of how many copies were produced, citing anything from 250 to 1,200. The academic Peter Blayney suggests 750 'and perhaps fewer',[4] and this assessment has become broadly accepted, not least because it would help explain why there was enough demand to produce a second edition nine years later.

CONTENTS

The First Folio omits a substantial portion of Shakespeare's creative output. The sonnets are not there, nor are the poems 'Venus and Adonis', 'The Rape of Lucrece' or 'The Phoenix and the Turtle'. Also missing are two plays now accepted as part of the Shakespeare canon: *Pericles* and *The Two Noble Kinsmen*. There may be others too, depending on how you view the evidence for *Love's Labours Won* and *Cardenio*, and his input into *Sir Thomas More*.

The 898 pages of the First Folio are instead dedicated to the thirty-six plays for which members of the publishing syndicate owned the rights. Eighteen had been previously published at least once as quarto editions in the previous twenty-eight years; the texts, however, are rarely identical and sometimes substantially different. The other eighteen appear in print for the first time. And because no contemporary manuscript versions survive, we can be sure that the First Folio is the only reason that we can see these plays performed today.

Nine leaves of preliminary matter precede the plays. They begin with a short verse by Ben Jonson, bound facing the title page, in which he confirms the portrait's likeness of 'gentle Shakespeare'. A series of dedications and commendatory verses follows, signed variously by Heminges and Condell, Ben Jonson again, and the poets Hugh Holland (1569–1633), Leonard Digges (1588–1635), and 'I.M.' – believed to be James Mabbe (1572–1642). A letter from Heminges and Condell confirms they supplied the original play scripts for the publication and, finally, there are two lists: 'The Names of the Principall Actors in all the Playes' (twenty-six names, beginning William Shakespeare) and a contents page or 'Catalogue' (Image 4).

04. *Contents list, although* Troilus and Cressida *is omitted. (C.7.c.14, Preliminaries, 'A Catalogue')*

DESIGN FEATURES

Title page and portrait

Seventeenth-century luxury editions often begin with an engraved portrait. Whereas this is generally placed on a separate leaf, the publishers of the First Folio chose to produce a combined title page with portrait. This decision would not have been taken lightly, because the design required the paper to pass through two printing devices, quite probably in separate workshops. First, a rolling press to print the portrait from its original engraved plate of copper, and then a common screw press to add the title and printing statement using movable type. The illustration is by Martin Droeshout (1601–*c.* 1650), originally from Flanders but based in London, and is the only surviving portrait of Shakespeare known to have been authorised by people who knew him well (Heminges, Condell and, indeed, Jonson). There is no guarantee, however, that Droeshout ever met his subject. Small changes were made to the engraving during the course of the print run, which many researchers take as evidence that the portrait was most likely printed by the artist in his own workshop.

A CATALOGVE

of the ſeuerall Comedies, Hiſtories, and Tragedies contained in this Volume.

COMEDIES.

The Tempeſt. Folio 1.
The two Gentlemen of Verona. 20
The Merry Wiues of Windſor. 38
Meaſure for Meaſure. 61
The Comedy of Errours. 85
Much adoo about Nothing. 101
Loues Labour loſt. 122
Midſommer Nights Dreame. 145
The Merchant of Venice. 163
As you Like it. 185
The Taming of the Shrew. 208
All is well, that Ends well. 230
Twelfe-Night, or what you will. 255
The Winters Tale. 304

HISTORIES.

The Life and Death of King John. Fol. 1.
The Life & death of Richard the ſecond. 23
The Firſt part of King Henry the fourth. 46
The Second part of K. Henry the fourth. 74
The Life of King Henry the Fift. 69
The Firſt part of King Henry the Sixt. 96
The Second part of King Hen. the Sixt. 120
The Third part of King Henry the Sixt. 147
The Life & Death of Richard the Third. 173
The Life of King Henry the Eight. 205

TRAGEDIES.

The Tragedy of Coriolanus. Fol. 1.
Titus Andronicus. 31
Romeo and Juliet. 53
Timon of Athens. 80
The Life and death of Julius Cæſar. 109
The Tragedy of Macbeth. 131
The Tragedy of Hamlet. 152
King Lear. 283
Othello, the Moore of Venice. 310
Anthony and Cleopater. 346
Cymbeline King of Britaine. 369

05.

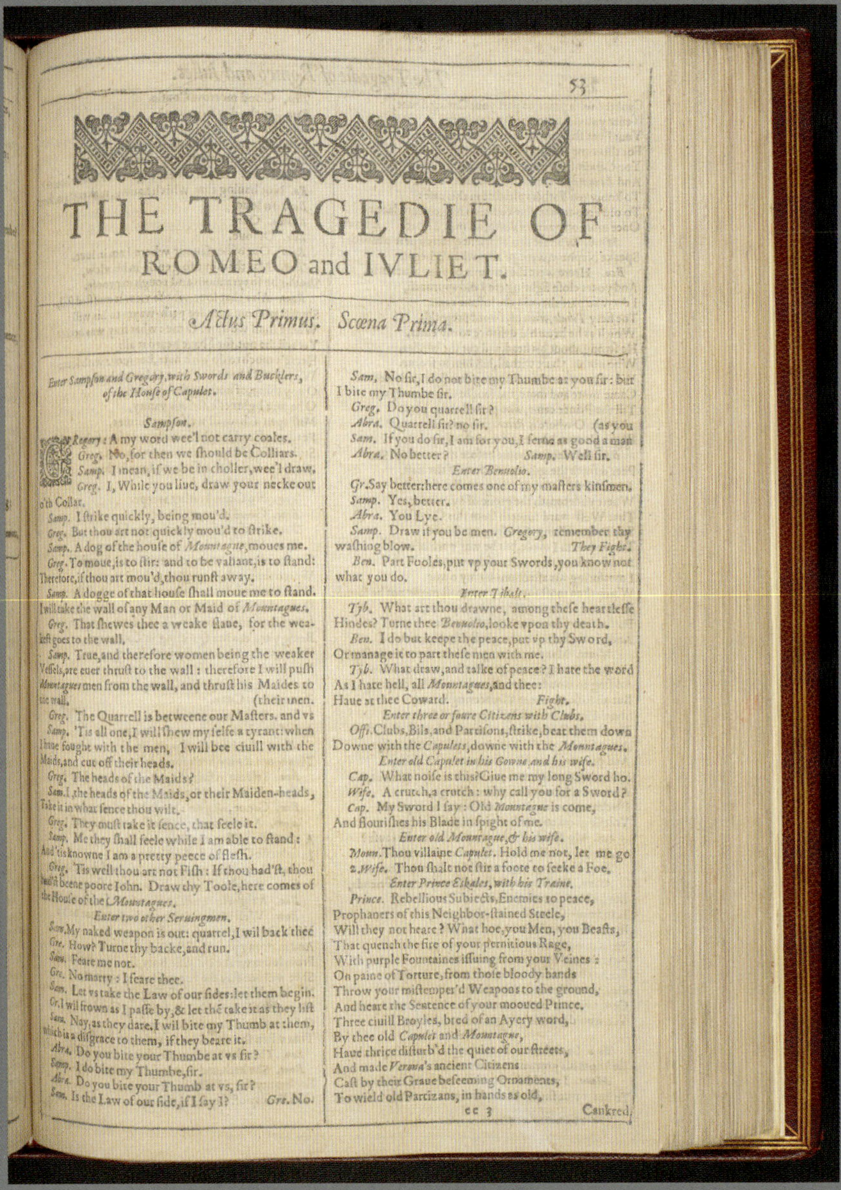

53

THE TRAGEDIE OF ROMEO and IVLIET.

Actus Primus. Scœna Prima.

Enter Sampson and Gregory, with Swords and Bucklers, of the House of Capulet.

Sampson.

Gregory: A my word wee'l not carry coales.

Greg. No, for then we should be Colliars.

Samp. I mean, if we be in choller, wee'l draw.

Greg. I, While you liue, draw your necke out o'th Collar.

Samp. I strike quickly, being mou'd.

Greg. But thou art not quickly mou'd to strike.

Samp. A dog of the house of *Mountague*, moues me.

Greg. To moue, is to stir: and to be valiant, is to stand: Therefore, if thou art mou'd, thou runst away.

Samp. A dogge of that house shall moue me to stand. I will take the wall of any Man or Maid of *Mountagues*.

Greg. That shewes thee a weake slaue, for the weakest goes to the wall.

Samp. True, and therefore women being the weaker Vessels, are euer thrust to the wall: therefore I will push *Mountagues* men from the wall, and thrust his Maides to the wall. (their men.

Greg. The Quarrell is betweene our Masters, and vs

Samp. 'Tis all one, I will shew my selfe a tyrant: when I haue fought with the men, I will bee ciuill with the Maids, and cut off their heads.

Greg. The heads of the Maids?

Sam. I, the heads of the Maids, or their Maiden-heads, Take it in what sence thou wilt.

Greg. They must take it sence, that feele it.

Samp. Me they shall feele while I am able to stand: And 'tis knowne I am a pretty peece of flesh.

Greg. 'Tis well thou art not Fish: If thou had'st, thou had'st beene poore Iohn. Draw thy Toole, here comes of the House of the *Mountagues*.

Enter two other Seruingmen.

Sam. My naked weapon is out: quarrel, I wil back thee

Gre. How? Turne thy backe, and run.

Sam. Feare me not.

Gre. No marry: I feare thee.

Sam. Let vs take the Law of our sides: let them begin.

Gr. I wil frown as I passe by, & let thē take it as they list

Sam. Nay, as they dare. I wil bite my Thumb at them, which is a disgrace to them, if they beare it.

Abra. Do you bite your Thumbe at vs sir?

Samp. I do bite my Thumbe, sir.

Abra. Do you bite your Thumb at vs, sir?

Sam. Is the Law of our side, if I say I? *Gre.* No.

Sam. No sir, I do not bite my Thumbe at you sir: but I bite my Thumbe sir.

Greg. Do you quarrell sir?

Abra. Quarrell sir? no sir. (as you

Sam. If you do sir, I am for you, I serue as good a man

Abra. No better? *Samp.* Well sir.

Enter Benuolio.

Gr. Say better: here comes one of my masters kinsmen.

Samp. Yes, better.

Abra. You Lye.

Samp. Draw if you be men. *Gregory*, remember thy washing blow. *They Fight.*

Ben. Part Fooles, put vp your Swords, you know not what you do.

Enter Tibalt.

Tyb. What art thou drawne, among these heartlesse Hindes? Turne thee *Benuolio*, looke vpon thy death.

Ben. I do but keepe the peace, put vp thy Sword, Or manage it to part these men with me.

Tyb. What draw, and talke of peace? I hate the word As I hate hell, all *Mountagues*, and thee:
Haue at thee Coward. *Fight.*

Enter three or foure Citizens with Clubs.

Offi. Clubs, Bils, and Partisons, strike, beat them down Downe with the *Capulets*, downe with the *Mountagues*.

Enter old Capulet in his Gowne, and his wife.

Cap. What noise is this? Giue me my long Sword ho.

Wife. A crutch, a crutch: why call you for a Sword?

Cap. My Sword I say: Old *Mountague* is come, And flourishes his Blade in spight of me.

Enter old Mountague, & his wife.

Moun. Thou villaine *Capulet*. Hold me not, let me go

2. Wife. Thou shalt not stir a foote to seeke a Foe.

Enter Prince Eskales, with his Traine.

Prince. Rebellious Subiects, Enemies to peace,
Prophaners of this Neighbor-stained Steele,
Will they not heare? What hoe, you Men, you Beasts,
That quench the fire of your pernitious Rage,
With purple Fountaines issuing from your Veines:
On paine of Torture, from those bloody hands
Throw your mistemper'd Weapons to the ground,
And heare the Sentence of your mooued Prince.
Three ciuill Broyles, bred of an Ayery word,
By thee old *Capulet* and *Mountague*,
Haue thrice disturb'd the quiet of our streets,
And made *Verona's* ancient Citizens
Cast by their Graue beseeming Ornaments,
To wield old Partizans, in hands as old,

cc 3 Cankred

06.

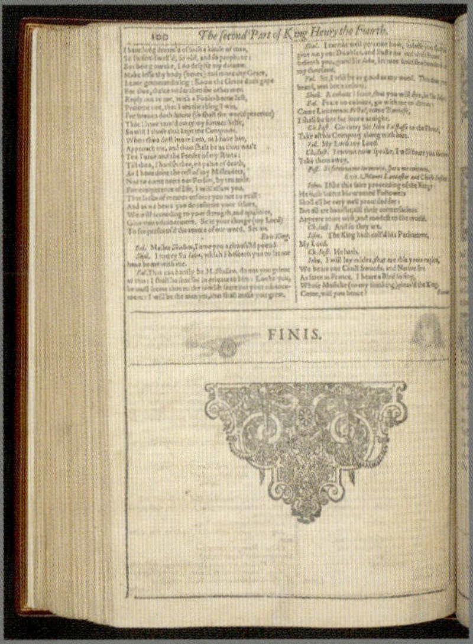

100 *The second Part of King Henry the Fourth.*

FINIS.

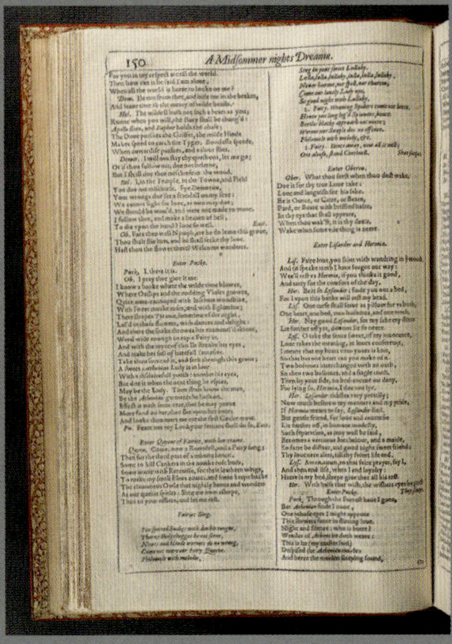

150 *A Midsommer nights Dreame.*

07.

Arrangement of the plays

This was the first time that Shakespeare's plays had been divided into their now familiar categories of comedies, histories and tragedies. Within the body of the volume, however, there are no subtitles to indicate the transition from one category to the next. Instead, the break is evident only from the change in pagination. The plays selected to open and close the volume, *The Tempest* and *Cymbeline*, were both written towards the end of Shakespeare's writing career in around 1610, and neither had been printed before. The decision to place them at these key points in the volume may therefore have been a deliberate one to catch the eye of potential buyers.

Page layout, ornaments and type

The preliminary matter shows little in the way of consistent page design, although there is a tendency to set headings in roman type and the body of the text in italic. The plays themselves, however, follow the same broad template. Each one begins on a fresh page with a horizontal ornament followed by the play's title (Image 5). These ornaments, four designs used randomly, catch the eye and help the reader navigate around the volume. The main texts are presented in double columns, with decorative initials marking the start of the dialogue. The whole is framed with printer's rules (lines) that also enclose running titles and page numbers as well as the headings for any act or scene changes. The overall effect is to break the densely printed page into more manageable segments. Each play ends with the word 'Finis'. Where there is still space to fill, a large triangular ornament has been inserted (Images 6 & 9).

05. *Opening leaf of* Romeo and Juliet. *(C.7.c.14, 'Tragedies', p. 53)*

06. *Closing page of* Henry IV, Part 1, *showing the use of ornamentation. It is not known who added the drawings. (C.7.c.14, 'Histories', p. 100)*

07. *Typeface switches to italic for the fairies' song in* A Midsummer Night's Dream *(C.39.k.15, 'Comedies', p. 150)*

08. *Title page of George III's First Folio, made from three elements fused together (C.7.c.14, detail)*

In terms of typeface, the plays in the First Folio are printed in a combination of roman and italic. The roman typeface is used for the dialogue, whereas italic is used for speech prefixes (i.e. the name of the character who is to speak), any stage directions, and for most proper nouns. Songs, such as those in *Twelfth Night* or *A Midsummer Night's Dream*, are also printed in italic (Images 7 & 10). Recent research has proposed that the font design was of French origin and that the type itself was fairly old: having been cast in London in 1603 or 1608.[5]

Expanded and compressed text

Although page layout was usually the result of deliberate choices, miscalculations in casting off – where the copy-texts were marked up with page breaks – could result in the compositors having to find imaginative ways to fill unexpected gaps or squeeze text into spaces that were tighter than anticipated. Adjustments seen in the First Folio include adding or removing spaces around scene headings and stage directions, breaking pentameter verse lines into half-lines, abbreviating speech prefixes, cutting stage directions and, on rare occasions, rewriting a line or two of Shakespeare's text (these latter two categories can be identified through comparison with earlier quarto editions).[6]

VARIANTS, VARIATIONS AND IMPERFECTIONS

Surviving copies of the Shakespeare First Folio are rarely identical. Higgins[7] notes that 107 of the 898 pages exist in more than one state. For the most part, this is because of stop-press corrections, when printing was halted in order to adjust a piece of type, change spacing or punctuation, or amend a spelling. Sheets that had already gone through the press were retained due to the high cost of paper. But there is also more significant variation around *Troilus and Cressida*. The majority of copies include the play and its prologue, despite its absence from the list of contents. There are, however, copies that either omit the play completely, or include the play but without its prologue. Blayney[8] demonstrated how these variations likely relate to a changing understanding around the ownership of publishing rights.

Many of these variations can be seen in the five copies of the First Folio held at the British Library.[9] Three (C.21.e.16, C.39.k.15 and G.11631) contain an original title page, with the portrait in the second of these in its exceedingly rare first state. One (C.39.i.12) has only two later facsimile title pages, and the other (C.7.c.14), once owned by King George III, contains a composite leaf made from three elements glued together (Image 8): an eighteenth- or nineteenth-century replica title across the top, and a portrait and an imprint statement salvaged from two other Shakespeare Folios.

THE LONG-TERM VIEW

Historians don't know whether the First Folio was an immediate commercial success, but they do know that two members of the publishing syndicate, Blount and Aspley, were 'almost bankrupted by it'.[10] Nevertheless, the appearance nine years later of a second edition with essentially the same content suggests that the venture must eventually have become profitable. Collected editions of the plays of William Shakespeare have continued to be produced right through to the present day, although interest in the First Folio itself waned in the early eighteenth century alongside a growing preference for modern adaptations of the plays. An interest in the earliest editions was rekindled by David Garrick's Shakespeare Jubilee of 1769, but by then many copies had been lost, mutilated or disbound. Book dealers were forced to supply their customers with imperfect volumes that they had repaired or 'sophisticated', and this is the likely explanation for the state of the title page in the copy once owned by George III.

09. *Detail of closing page of* Henry VI, Part 2. *(C.39.k.15, 'Histories', p. 119)*

10. *The song 'Come Away, Come Away Death' from* Twelfth Night *shows use of italics. (C.7.c.14, 'Comedies', p. 262)*

CONCLUSIONS

Sitting with the first folios of both Ben Jonson and William Shakespeare in front of me, it's easy to see both the similarities and the differences. On balance, however, it's the differences that stand out most, particularly around the layout of the text on the page: Jonson's plays are printed in one column, Shakespeare's in two, for example. The role of Jonson's publication is perhaps primarily one of having paved the way for a single-volume collected edition of English plays. In particular, it demonstrated that there could be a market for a large literary folio, a format firmly associated with weighty and durable content such as religion, law and the classics.

The folio format, along with the extra costs associated with printing the illustrated title page, point to a determined effort to place the First Folio at the luxury end of the book market. It is therefore curious that the printers used an old set of type and stopped the presses during production in order to work on other publications. Could this indicate differences in aspiration among those involved? Or maybe the near bankruptcy of two of the publishing syndicate is evidence of a serious cash-flow problem? It does, however, suggest that the Jaggards and their collaborators had scant awareness of the long-term importance of what they were doing. Little did they know that the First Folio would come to be regarded as a pinnacle of literary publishing, nor the role it would play in ensuring Shakespeare's reputation as the finest writer in the English language.

09.

Enter Clifford.
t that my hearts on future mischeefe set,
eake blasphemy ere bid you flye :
u must : Vncureable discomfite
the hearts of all our present parts.
our releefe, and we will liue
day, and them our Fortune giue.
ord, away.
Exeunt
For (as I heare) the King is fled to London,
To call a present Court of Parliament:
What sayes Lord Warwicke
War. After them:
Now by my hand (Lords)
Saint Albons battell wonne by
Shall be eterniz'd in all Age to
Sound Drum me and Trumpets,
And more such dayes as these, to vs
FINIS.

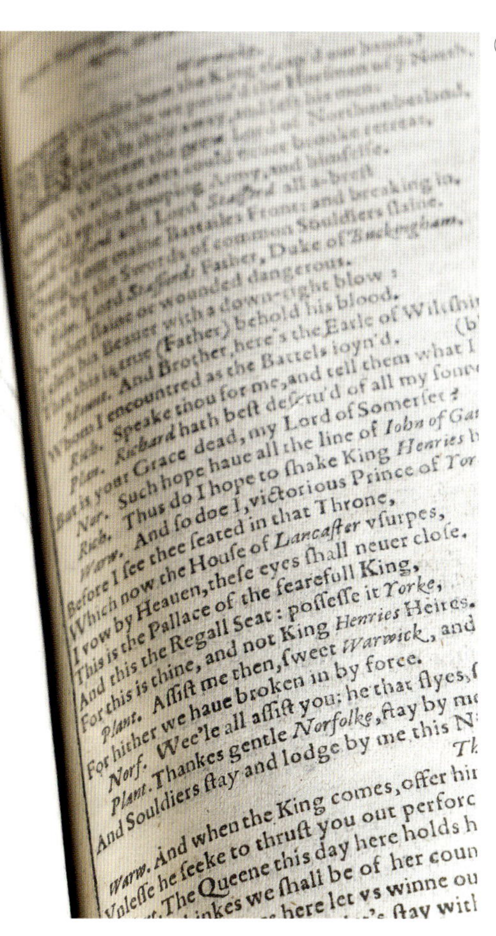

Rich. Speake thou for me, and tell them what I
Plan. Richard hath best deseru'd of all my sonne
But is your Grace dead, my Lord of Somerset?
Nor. Such hope haue all the line of Iohn of Ga
Rich. Thus do I hope to shake King Henries h
Warw. And so doe I, victorious Prince of Yor
Before I see thee seated in that Throne,
Which now the House of Lancaster vsurpes,
I vow by Heauen, these eyes shall neuer close.
This is the Pallace of the fearefull King,
And this the Regall Seat: possesse it Yorke,
For this is thine, and not King Henries Heires.
Plant. Assist me then, sweet Warwick, and
For hither we haue broken in by force.
Norf. Wee'le all assist you: he that flyes,
Plant. Thankes gentle Norfolke, stay by me
And Souldiers stay and lodge by me this N
Warw. And when the King comes, offer hi
Vnlesse he seeke to thrust you out perforc

10.

Clo. Are you ready Sir?
Duke. I prethee sing.
The Song.
Come away, come away death,
And in sad cypresse let me be laide.
Fye away, fie away breath,
I am slaine by a faire cruell maide:
Not a flower, not a flower sweete
Not a friend, not a friend greet
Du. There's for thy paines.
Clo. No paines sir, I take pleasure in singing sir.
Du. Ile pay thy pleasure then.
Clo. Truely sir, and pleasure will be paide one time or another.
Enter Sir Toby, Sir
To. Come thy wayes Si
Fab. Nay Ile come

THE TITLE PAGE AND OTHER PARATEXTS

STEPHEN PARKIN

The term 'paratext' is generally attributed to the French literary critic Gérard Genette and his influential studies *Palimpsestes* (1982) and *Seuils* (1987), which both appeared in English translation in 1997, although the first citation in the *Oxford English Dictionary* entry tracking the word's usage in English dates back to 1974 (where it is spelled with a hyphen). In subsequent decades it has entered academic and more general usage to refer to all those components of books, such as title pages, prefaces, footnotes, indexes, etc., which accompany the main text but do not form part of it. Genette was working within a larger theory of the status and interpretation of specifically literary texts but his term has been found especially useful in the field of book history and has gained wide currency there. In its characteristic application here it has widened its reference in significant ways: Genette focused on paratextual components of books which were themselves textual but as book historians have tended to use the concept it can also refer to non-verbal elements such as illustrations together with decorative features which play a paratextual role in helping to shape and organise readers' perception and understanding of written texts.

All such 'paratextual' elements of course existed centuries before this designation entered the English language in the second half of the twentieth century and were very well known to printers, publishers, librarians and bibliographers (who understood them – like Genette – as 'extra' verbal parts of a book added to the main text). Seán Jennett in *The Making of Books* dedicates a whole chapter to what, using the standard printing house jargon, he calls 'oddments': 'In the printer's mind ... a book properly commences with the introduction or first chapter and ends with the last page of the last chapter; all outside these limits is included, by long custom, under the term "oddments" ... a word of convenience, not of opprobrium'.[1] *Hart's Rules* (now *New Hart's Rules*), the celebrated guide to the practices followed by printers and publishers in the English-speaking world, used initially as an in-house manual by Oxford University Press and then first published in the 1890s, divides a book into three sections: 'preliminary matter (also called prelims or front matter), the main text, and end matter'. It lists seventeen possible items which might be included as preliminary matter: 'half-title page, half-title verso, frontispiece, title page, title page verso, dedication, foreword, preface, acknowledgements, contents, lists of illustrations, figures and maps, lists of tables, tables of cases and legislation (law books), lists of abbreviations, lists of contributors, note to the reader, epigraph'. The list for possible endmatter items is much shorter: 'appendix, glossary, endnotes, bibliography, notes on contributors, index'.[2]

These descriptions and lists belong to the world of printing and publishing: paratexts, including several which now appear as necessary parts of what constitutes a book, proliferated with the development of printing (and of publishing as a business) from the fifteenth century onwards. Some derived from manuscript production while others, now archaic, were once significant paratextual elements, such as the colophons found in scribal practice and early printing or the errata lists typical of hand-press produced books. All have their own complex history over centuries of book production, varying too across different cultures. A rough history and map for at least some of them could be constructed from many of the contributions included in the present volume.

In terms of book design, many paratextual elements involve exactly the same kinds of decisions on the part of printers and publishers – for example, choice of typeface(s), arrangement and page layout, spacing, margins, and so forth – which they would have to make for the main text (and indeed normally in conformity with those if they wish to ensure the consistency and uniformity of the editorial product). The one striking exception to this rule is also the paratext which has undergone the most variety and change in its long history and been subject over time to the direct and combined influence of different factors, functional, material, aesthetic, commercial. It is the title page, which by position and by intention is the most immediately visible paratextual component of a book.

How and why title pages first developed is still unclear. The phenomenon is not only connected with the crucial transition from manuscript to printed book production in western Europe in the second half of the fifteenth century but also reflects a parallel shift in focus in the same period from what *Hart's Rules* calls the 'end matter' to the 'preliminary matter' of published texts. In the lists above much of the sequence in which the items appear is logical – at least according to the logic of printed texts – but it is also in some degree merely conventional. Title pages started to absorb information which in scribal convention was found at the end of a manuscript text – the place and date of production and the identity of the producer (the scribe) – while the concept of a title as the formal identification of a work (and its author) took over from the standard focus on the first line of a text – the so-called 'incipit' – which was the normal place for such identification in manuscript production (and often the space for sumptuous decoration).

Margaret Smith has suggested that the 'invention' of the title page occurred because of the quite specific practical need created by the new technology of printing – the production of multiple copies which needed to be stored before they could all be sold 'to [protect] and [identify] the unbound copies'; the initial blank leaf of the first gathering (i.e. before the actual text began in the customary fashion on the recto of the second leaf) served to protect the first printed page of text from damage in the piles of copies kept in the printer's or bookseller's depository. It then needed something like the title of the work printed on it to identify it and distinguish it from the unbound gatherings of other books produced by the same press.

Once this solution had been devised in response to a challenge created by the new technology, it also opened up a new 'paratextual' space to which information – title, authorship, place and date of publication, etc. – which had previously been found elsewhere in a book could be transferred. But the potential of using the new page as an advertising space was also quickly appreciated: it was used to name the individuals who had printed or published the book, often by displaying their devices (a form of trade mark) prominently, and included images, initially woodcuts and later engravings, which could serve both to represent the contents of the book and attract the attention of potential customers. Again some sense of the waxing and waning of fashions in title-page design can be gleaned from leafing through the contributions in the present volume.

After the initial experiments of the incunabula period, the sixteenth century saw the title page achieve its greatest complexity in terms of visual and verbal information and impact (the bare title pages of the, in all other respects, hugely influential Aldine pocket editions of the classics in the 1500s are the counter-cultural exceptions here – see pages 84–93 – though much later they came to be admired for their classical austerity, for example by Bodoni, and they are certainly much closer in spirit to modern title pages). The hugely complex woodcut title page of the 1539 'Great Bible' is a superlative example, with image and text deployed in this case with ideological rather than merely commercial intent (see pages 48–49).

Throughout the sixteenth and seventeenth centuries title pages feature elaborate architecture (see the Ben Jonson Folio, page 108), portraits (see pages 107 and 108), devices and emblems of various kinds (see page 137). The typical eighteenth-century title page showed more restraint and regularity, even in relatively inexpensive editions such as Thomas Boreman's 1730 children's book – though this, like many publications of this period and later, has an engraved frontispiece which occupies the facing page, thus removing the need for an image on the title page itself (see pages 146–147).

The technical developments of the nineteenth century, and reactions against them, such as those of William Morris, who revived early manuscript and incunable practice by making the first page of the text the main focus (see pages 204–213), produced another period of intense visual elaboration, now not only on title pages but also on mass-produced publishers' bindings. The designed dust jacket and paperback cover can be seen as the end result of this long process, leaving the title page to carry the mere identification details – author, title, imprint, and not much else – which we have come to regard as the norm.

01.

X.

EXCERPTS FROM THE TALE OF GENJI

A seventeenth-century Japanese concertina album of calligraphy and painting

HAMISH TODD

Among the highlights of the British Library's Japanese collection is *Genji monogatari kotoba* 源氏物語詞 or *Excerpts from The Tale of Genji*, a superb album of calligraphy and paintings created at the Japanese Imperial Court in the mid-seventeenth century (Images 1 & 2). It is a lavishly illustrated and decorated example of what is termed in Japanese a *yoriaigaki* 寄合書, a collaborative work produced by a group of calligraphers, poets and artists. This form of artistic expression was much favoured by the cultural elite and literati societies that flourished in Japan during the Edo Period (1603–1868).

The album clearly required considerable organisation and resources to produce, bringing together the talents of calligraphers, artists, papermakers, bookbinders, metalworkers and textile-makers. This chapter will look at the cultural context in which this album was created, its form and design and the process of its compilation.

THE TALE OF GENJI

Genji monogatari or *The Tale of Genji* is widely regarded as the greatest masterpiece of Japanese literature. Written at the very beginning of the eleventh century, it can also claim to be the world's first novel. By any standards, it is a great work, running to over 1,000 pages in its English translations, covering a sweep of seven decades and peopled with scores of well-defined characters. The story follows the life, career and amorous escapades of its protagonist Hikaru Genji, 'The Shining One', a handsome and charismatic son of the emperor by his favourite, Lady Kiritsubo. It vividly conjures up a world of courtly elegance, political intrigue and romantic adventure that continues to fascinate readers today, just as it has for the past ten centuries.

The author of this epic romance was a noblewoman, Murasaki Shikibu (*c.* 978–*c.* 1014–25),[1] usually known in English as Lady Murasaki, who served at the Imperial Court in the city of Heian, modern-day Kyoto. Murasaki Shikibu may be the greatest female writer of the Heian Period (794–1185), but she is certainly not the only one. This was an era when much of the best and most enduring literature was written by women. There is the acerbic Sei Shōnagon, author of the highly entertaining *Makura no* (*Pillow Book*), Izumi Shikibu, poet and diarist, Michitsuna no Haha, the author of *Kagerō Nikki* (*Gossamer Years*) and Takasue no Musume, author of the *Sarashina Diary*, who were all near contemporaries of Murasaki Shikibu.

Why did women have such a leading role in literature at this time? It is an indirect consequence of the influence of Chinese culture on Japan. From its introduction in the sixth century, written Chinese had been the language of the government and Buddhism and the key to unlocking a wide range of knowledge in books imported from China. As such, it was a jealously guarded, exclusively male preserve. Murasaki records in her diary that she used to attend her brother's Chinese lessons – considered rather shocking, 'unladylike' behaviour by her contemporaries. By Murasaki's time there was a strong tradition of native Japanese poetry[2] but fiction was considered frivolous and beneath a man's dignity. In some ways, there is a parallel with the role of Latin in medieval Europe: the business of religion and state was recorded in Chinese.

Meanwhile women, unencumbered by the need to express themselves in what must have been a

01. & 02 (pages 120–121). Genji monogatari kotoba *showing the 'concertina' structure of the album.*

rather restrictive, foreign medium, were able to write fluently in their native tongue, composing lively diaries full of witty and accurate observations. So influential was this male/female, Chinese/Japanese divide that when the famous poet and writer Ki no Tsurayuki wrote *The Tosa Diary*, an account of a journey to a distant province, he pretended it was the work of a woman so that he could write it in Japanese.[3]

We know from Murasaki's diary and those of her contemporaries that *The Tale of Genji* was widely read and copied at court in her own day and its popularity has not waned since. Murasaki's original manuscript has not survived, nor have the copies which were made in her own day and in the following decades. The oldest extant version of the text consists of five chapters copied by the celebrated poet Fujiwara Teika (1162–1241) and based on earlier manuscripts now lost.

The Tale of Genji stood out from the stories and folktales that preceded it by virtue of its scale, complexity and developed characterisation. Through the ensuing centuries, *The Tale of Genji* has taken on huge cultural significance. It has been a popular theme for artists, writers and dramatists, and has been the inspiration for Kabuki plays, musicals, films, television series and *manga* comics. There have been countless scholarly editions, commentaries and studies, and even now, 1,000 years after it was written, these works continue to be published in Japan at the rate of nearly 100 per year.

In its standard form, the story comprises fifty-four chapters. There has been endless debate over the centuries as to whether parts of the text have been added or lost and, as there is a gap of one and a half centuries between the *The Tale of Genji*'s composition and the earliest surviving manuscripts, there has been ample time for additions and deletions.

03. *The front and back covers made of blue brocade embroidered with chrysanthemums in gold.*

04. & 05. *Details showing copper openwork cornerpiece.*

06. *Detail of endpaper decorated with gold and silver leaf.*

The work can be divided into two main parts: the first forty-one chapters follow the exploits of Genji; the last ten concentrate on Kaoru, his supposed son, and Prince Niou, his grandson. In between are three short, transitional chapters, which a number of scholars think are later additions. *The Tale of Genji* spans a period of around seventy years in all.

FORMAT AND DESIGN

The version of *The Tale of Genji* in the Library collection is an example of a binding structure known in Japanese as *orijō* 折帖 (folding album), a variant of the *orihon* 折本 (folding book or accordion-style binding). The *orihon* format originated in China and was introduced to Japan during the late Heian Period. In its simplest form, an *orihon* is composed of either a single long sheet of paper or several smaller sheets glued together with a slight overlap to produce a long, horizontal strip. The pages are then folded to create a form resembling a concertina or accordion. Paper covers can be attached at both ends for stability and often the title is added – either written directly onto the front cover or on a paper title slip pasted to it. Compared to the scroll, the earliest format for written texts in China and Japan, the *orihon* has a number of advantages. It is easier to handle since it does not require rolling and rerolling, and the folding creates pages making it simpler to locate a particular section of the text. The *orihon* became a convenient form for Buddhist texts, calendars, genealogies and travel guides.

The *orijō* was a later development of the *orihon*, similar in structure but using stronger paper. Two sheets of paper were pasted together to form a thicker sheet, a stable base onto which *shikishi* 色紙 (paper squares) inscribed with pictures or poetry could be pasted. During the Edo Period this format was widely used for painting albums, poetry anthologies and collections of calligraphy.

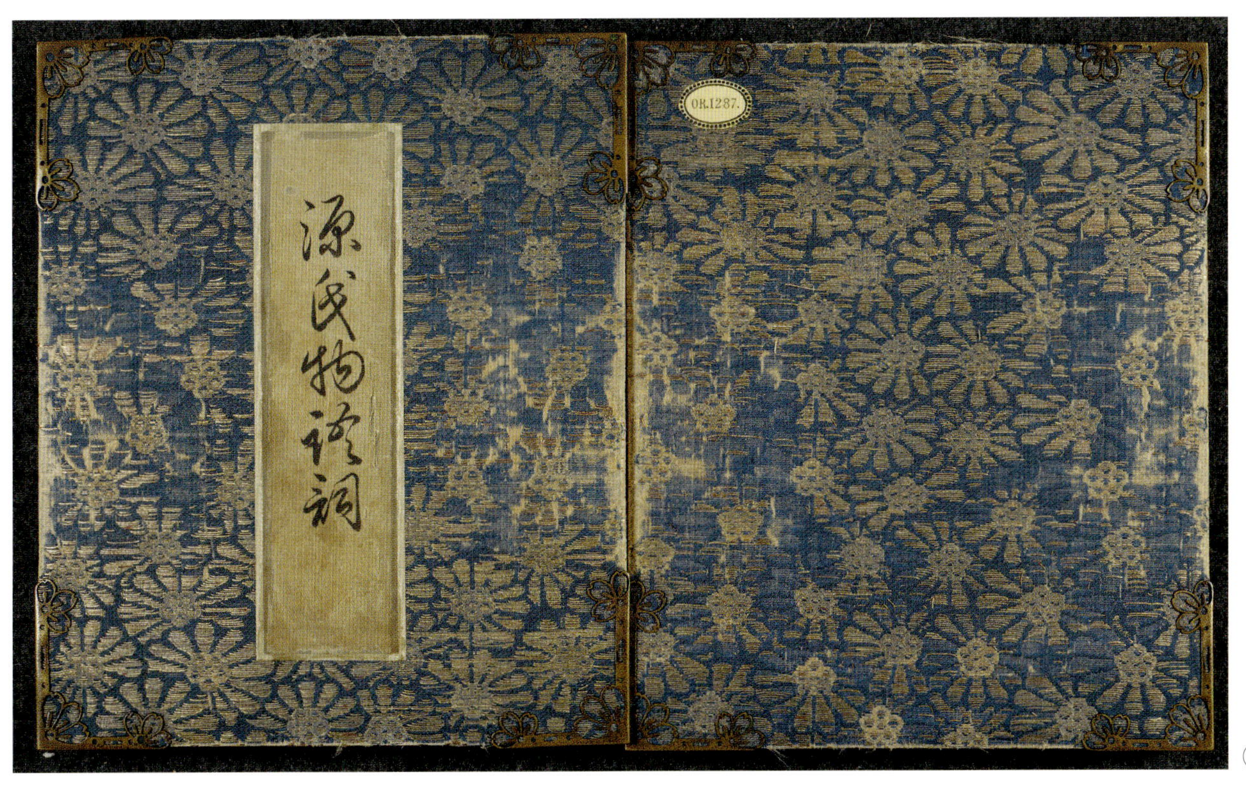

03.

04.

05.

06.

07.

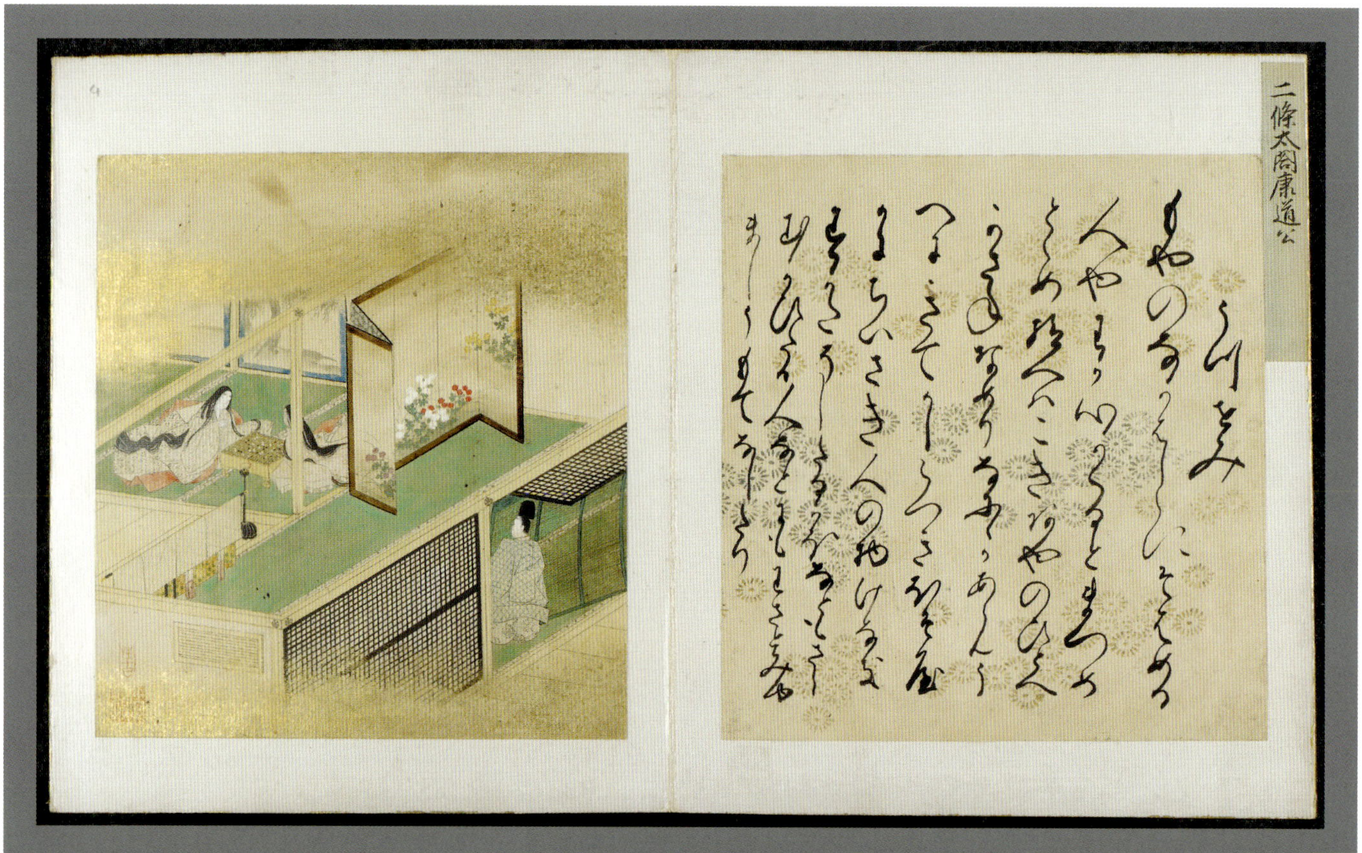

二條太閤康道公

08.

烏丸前大納言資慶卿

Specification	Scale
EXCERPTS FROM THE TALE OF GENJI Kyoto, Japan, 1665/6 230 x 200 mm Or 1287	

The British Library's album measures 230 by 200 millimetres and contains twenty-eight leaves made of *torinokogami* 鳥の子紙 ('hen's egg' paper), high-quality handmade paper with a lustrous sheen and creamy white eggshell hue.

The covers (Image 3) are of dark blue brocade decorated with a pattern of chrysanthemums[4] in gold embroidery, and the corners are strengthened with pieces of copper openwork (Images 4 & 5).

In the centre of the front cover is a vertical paper title slip, or *daisen* 題簽, measuring 175 by 50 millimetres, edged with a white border, which bears the title, *Genji monogatari kotoba* (源氏物語詞). The endpapers (*mikaeshi* 見返し) are covered in gold paper decorated with a pattern of silver clouds and small squares of gold and silver leaf (Image 6).

On the right-hand page of each opening of the album is a famous passage from one of the fifty-four chapters of *The Tale of Genji*, consisting of six to ten lines of text and written in cursive, flowing calligraphy (Image 7). These extracts are written in black ink on *shikishi* (paper squares) decorated with chrysanthemum designs drawn using *kindei* 金泥, a paste made from ground gold foil mixed with a sizing agent and water (Image 11).

In all but one case, to the upper right of the text is a thin vertical slip of paper bearing the name and titles of the calligrapher (Images 9 & 10).

On the left-hand side of each opening is a painting of a scene from the relevant chapter of *The Tale of Genji*. Each painting bears two seals: 'Sumiyoshi' 住吉 in red ink on a white ground and 'Hōkyō' 法橋 in white on a red ground (Image 12), identifying the artist as Sumiyoshi Jokei 住吉如慶 (1599–1670). *Hōkyō* (literally 'Bridge of the Law') was originally a religious title awarded to members of the Buddhist clergy. Later its use was extended to certain eminent sculptors and artists who created Buddhist works.

The illustrations are characteristic of the work of Jokei, and the Tosa School of painting in general, with their use of an elevated perspective, vibrant colours and fine detailing to bring the scenes to life. The subtlety and fineness of the drawing, one of the hallmarks of Jokei's work, is used to great effect, for example, to convey the costumes, facial features and expressions of the characters, and in the depiction of the bamboo hanging blinds (*sudare*) on buildings (Image 8).

THE COURT OF RETIRED EMPEROR GO-MIZUNO-O

As mentioned at the beginning of the chapter, *Genji monogatari kotoba* is a collaboration between calligraphers and artists of a type which was particularly popular in Japan from the seventeenth to nineteenth centuries. The significance of the British Library manuscript lies both in its high quality and in the light it sheds on cultural activity among the highest ranks of Japanese society, in particular the circles at the court of Retired Emperor Go-Mizuno-o.

Emperor Go-Mizuno-o (1596–1680) was the third son of Emperor Go-Yōzei and reigned from 1611 to 1629 when he abdicated in favour of his daughter Empress Meishō (1624–1696). Such abdications were common in Japan until the nineteenth century. It freed the emperor from the burden of performing an extensive schedule of religious duties and elaborate court ceremonies. As the new sovereign was generally a young child, the Retired

07. Genji monogatari kotoba. *Chapter 3 Utsusemi ('The Cicada Shell') with calligraphy by Nijō Yasumichi. The illustration shows Genji watching Lady Utsusemi and her stepdaughter playing 'go'. (ff. 3v–4r)*

08. *Detail from Chapter 34 Wakana. Jō ('Spring Shoots.1'). Jokei's delicate brushwork allows the viewer to see through the bamboo screens. (ff. 35v–36r)*

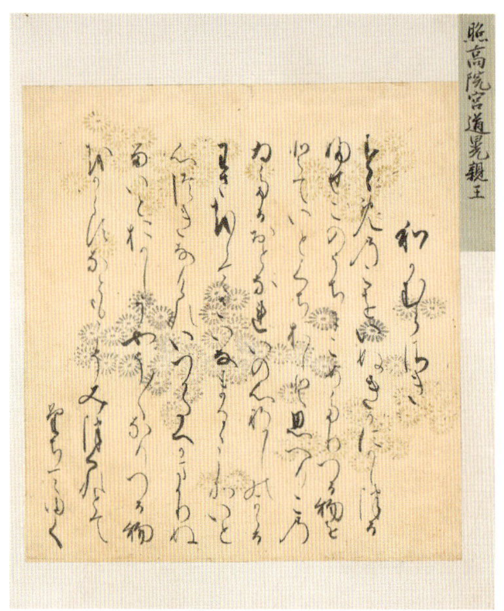

09.

Emperor could then exercise power from behind the scenes, a system known as *Insei* or 'Cloister Government' since the retired sovereign frequently took up residence in a Buddhist temple. By the seventeenth century real power had long since passed from the hands of the emperors in Kyoto to the Tokugawa Shoguns in Edo. In fact, Go-Mizuno-o's empress, Tōfukumon'in, was the daughter of the second Tokugawa Shogun Hidetada. The marriage had brought much-needed wealth to the Imperial Court but interference from the Shogun was another reason behind the emperor's abdication. Go-Mizuno-o continued to conduct *Insei* for over half a century during the reigns of no fewer than four of his children (Empress Meishō and Emperors Go-Kōmyō, Go-Sai and Reigen). His court became a centre for literary and artistic activity. The official record of his life and reign *Go-Mizuno-o Tennō jitsuroku* contains frequent references to gatherings for composition of poetry and lectures on the classics of Japanese literature – including *The Tale of Genji*. In addition to *Genji monogatari kotoba*, a number of similar collaborative albums are known to exist.

THE CALLIGRAPHERS

Calligraphy in Japan, as elsewhere in East Asia, was traditionally the most esteemed form of artistic expression. It was a necessary accomplishment for anyone with a claim to good taste or social standing, as was the ability to compose poetry. The contributors to *Genji monogatari kotoba* are drawn from the highest echelons of society, including five imperial princes and forty-nine court nobles. The princes were three of Emperor Go-Mizuno-o's half-brothers, one of his sons and his cousin. Another contributor, Nijō Yasumichi 二条康道, was the emperor's brother-in-law, husband of his sister Princess Sadako 貞子内親王. Yasumichi was also one of three contributors who held or had held the post of *sesshō* or 'regent', the highest position in the government and court nobility. Indeed the selection of which calligrapher wrote which chapter seems to be based as much on rank as on calligraphic expertise. The first chapter was written by Takatsukasa Fusasuke 鷹司房輔, regent from 1664 to 1668, Chapter 2 by Kujō Kaneharu 九条兼晴, who held the position of 'Minister of the Right',[5] Chapter 3 by Yasumichi and Chapter 4 by his son Nijō Mitsuhira 二条光平, regent from 1653 to 1664. Then come the imperial princes, followed by other nobles and senior clergy roughly in order of seniority.

As noted above, with one exception, the calligraphers are identified by paper slips attached to the extract they wrote. The slip for Chapter 27 *Kagaribi* ('The Flares') is missing, although traces of it remain. Research by Professor Tsuji Eiko,[6] based on a comparison of the calligraphy with other works, suggests that the missing name is that of Asukai Masaaki 飛鳥井雅章 (1611–1679), a noted composer of *waka* poetry and one of the leading cultural figures at the court of Emperor Go-Mizuno-o. Asukai is known to have been involved in other similar collaborative works and is frequently recorded in official sources as the organiser of poetry readings and other literary events at court. Indeed, it is highly plausible that he was the mastermind behind the creation of *Genji monogatari kotoba*.

09. *Identification slip bearing the name of Shōkōin no Miya Dōkō Shinnō, half-brother of Emperor Go-Mizuno-o. (f. 5v)*

10. *Pages showing the vertical slips of paper bearing calligraphers' names.*

11. *Paper with chrysanthemum designs.*

12. *Artist's seals of Sumiyoshi Jokei. Above 'Sumiyoshi', below 'Hōkyō'.*

10.

11.

12.

13.

THE ARTIST

Sumiyoshi Jokei 住吉如慶, the creator of the finely executed illustrations, was born in 1599. Originally known as Tosa Hiromichi 土佐広通, he was the son, or more likely the pupil, of Tosa Mitsuyoshi 土佐光吉 (1539–1613), fourteenth Head of the Tosa School of painting.[7] The Tosa School was one of the leading artistic schools of the Edo Period and drew its primary inspiration from the styles and themes of classical Japanese painting or *Yamato-e*, rather than the Chinese-style *Kara-e* favoured by the rival Kanō School of painting. The Tosa School was patronised by the Imperial Court and aristocracy in Kyoto but Hiromichi moved to Edo (modern Tokyo), seat of the Tokugawa Shoguns, where he pursued a successful career culminating in his appointment as *Goyō eshi* 御用絵師 (Official Painter to the Shogunate). In 1661 he entered holy orders, taking the name Jokei. In 1663, at the request of Emperor Go-Sai, he changed his surname to Sumiyoshi and founded an independent painting school, the *Sumiyoshi-ha*. Jokei died in 1670 and was succeeded as head of the Sumiyoshi School by his son Gukei 具慶 (1631–1705).

Given their predilection for classical Japanese themes, *The Tale of Genji* was a popular theme for artists of both the Tosa and Sumiyoshi Schools. Jokei himself is known to have created at least eleven works which were inspired by it.[8]

DATE OF CREATION

Genji monogatari kotoba has no colophon and no explicit statement of when it was created. However, there are clues, from the career of the artist and the identities of the contributors. As was noted above, each of the paintings bears two seals used by the artist Jokei – 'Sumiyoshi' and 'Hōkyō'. Jokei assumed the family name Sumiyoshi in 1663 and received the title 'Hōkyō' in the same year, so the illustrations must have been produced between 1663 and 1670 when he died. There is no reason to think that the paintings were created at a significantly different time from the calligraphy or their assembly into the album. Research by Professor Tsuji Eiko[9] into the careers of the fifty-four calligraphers has made it possible to narrow the time frame further through analysis of the name and titles recorded on the paper slips pasted next to their work. This reveals that Nijō Yasumichi, calligrapher for Chapter 3 (see Image 3), was the first of the contributors to die, on the twenty-eighth day of the seventh month of Kanbun 6 (1666) so the manuscript must have been completed by then. The complicated ranks of the traditional court hierarchy and regular promotions provide further dating evidence. The paper slip associated with the text for Chapter 50 *Azumaya* ('The Eastern Cottage') gives the name of the calligrapher as Iwakura Tomoaki 岩倉具詮. Official records show that Iwakura changed his name from Tomoie 具家 to Tomoaki on the twenty-first day of the ninth month of Kanbun 5 (1665) on his promotion to Upper Third Court Rank. Thus at least some of the calligraphy was written in late 1665 to early 1666 and it is highly likely that the whole album was completed at that time.

13. *From left to right, top to bottom: the covers, decorated endpaper and selected openings from the album.*

PROVENANCE

Genji monogatari kotoba is part of the Siebold collection of 1,088 Japanese works, in over 3,000 volumes, purchased by the British Museum in 1868. The collection was amassed by the German Philipp Franz von Siebold (1796–1866), who was employed as physician to the Dutch trading factory on the island of Deshima from 1823 to 1829. Siebold was expelled from Japan for having amassed a collection of maps, possession of which was strictly forbidden by the authorities, but returned thirty years later, following the opening of Japan to Western trade, and stayed for three years from 1859 to 1862. After Siebold's death, his son Alexander von Siebold (1846–1911) sold his father's collection of Japanese books, manuscripts and maps made during his second stay in Japan, as well as those remaining from his first, to the British Museum for £1,100.[10]

A MODERN MESOAMERICAN CODEX

MERCEDES AGUIRRE

Only a small number of codices created by the Indigenous peoples of Mesoamerica before the arrival of the Spanish remain today. For centuries, these complex and detailed pictorial manuscripts were instruments for the transmission and preservation of historical, cultural and scientific knowledge, and those that remain are vital sources for the study of pre-Hispanic Mesoamerica. While the production of codices continued in the decades following colonisation, only a small number of pre-Hispanic codices survived destruction at the hands of the colonisers, or neglect and disappearance following their export to Europe. The tragedy of their loss inspired the contemporary painter and printmaker Enrique Chagoya to re-create the format of the codex to 'tell the stories of cultural hybrids, of political collisions of universal consequences'.[1]

The book *Codex Espangliensis: From Columbus to the Border Patrol*, published in 1998, is a collaboration between Chagoya, the performance artist, radical pedagogue and writer Guillermo Gómez-Peña and the US book artist and founder of the Moving Parts Press Felicia Rice, who originated the project. Chagoya and Gómez-Peña were born in Mexico City and moved to the US in the late 1970s. The work explores Mexican-US border culture and politics by drawing links to the wider history of the Americas, from European colonisation to US immigration policy, globalisation and cultural imperialism.

01.

The design of *Codex Espangliensis* takes some features from the original codices. Like some pre-Hispanic codices, it is accordion-folded, and it reaches more than 9 metres when fully extended. The book is designed to be opened from the right side, although the text in each individual section is read from left to right. *Codex Espangliensis* is letterpress-printed in black and red ink from zinc photoengravings on *amate*, a type of paper made from tree bark, which has its origins in pre-Hispanic Mesoamerica and was one of the materials commonly used for codices. Its name is derived from the Nahuatl word *amatl* ('paper').

Rice's montages combine imagery created by Chagoya and text by Gómez-Peña. Chagoya's compositions juxtapose contrasting figures from different ages and cultures, including pre-Hispanic iconography, European and Mexican prints created in different centuries, and US comic book and cartoon characters. The opening panels (Image 2) show an ominous-looking 'Superman' in red with a skull on his chest flying towards three figures taken from the Codex Tonindeye (also known as Zouche-Nuttall),[2] a Mixtec codex which is believed to have been created in the fourteenth century and is now held at the British Museum. To his right is the reproduction of a work by the renowned Mexican artist and satirist José Guadalupe Posada, depicting the jaws of hell. A question from Gómez-Peña's text, referencing the North American Free Trade Agreement (NAFTA), frames the images: 'What is the difference between free-trade art and a free art agreement?'

Chagoya draws inspiration from the Mesoamerican codices to reflect on the contemporary history

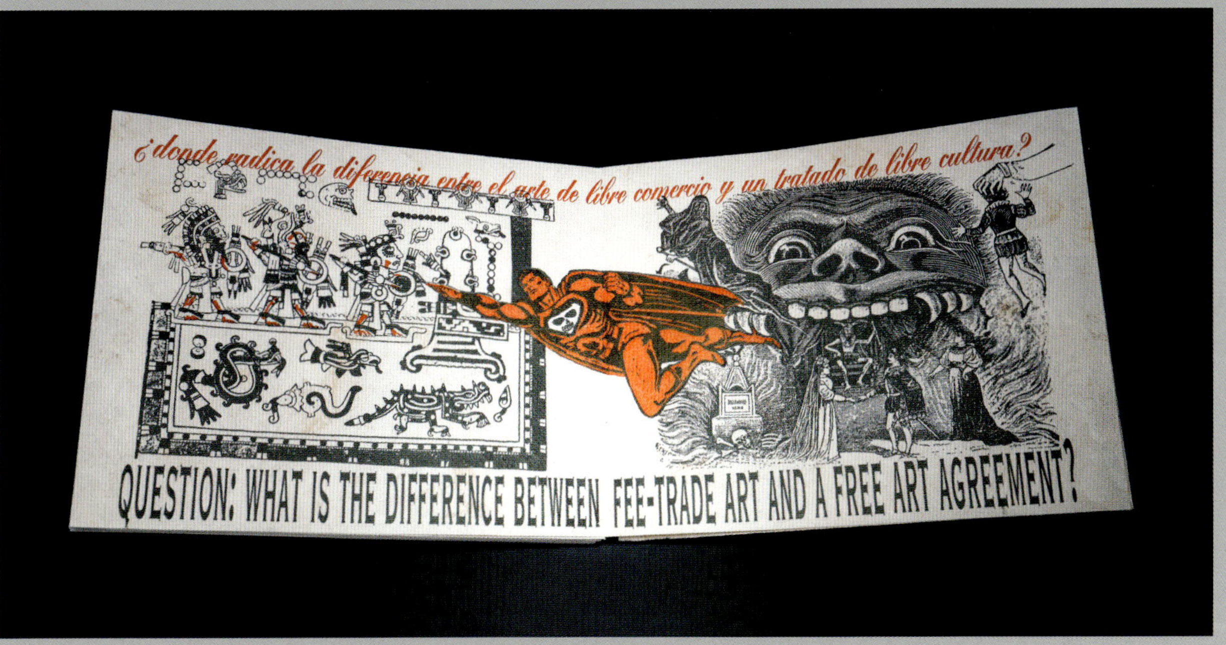

02.

of the Americas. Throughout his career, he has had a long-standing interest in the codex as a format. He created *Tales from the Conquest/Codex* in 1992, to coincide with the 500th anniversary of the arrival of Christopher Columbus in the Americas, and he has continued to use the format in many of his works, including *The Ghost of Liberty* (2004) and *Illegal Alien's Guide to the Concept of Relative Surplus Value* (2009).

In *Codex Espangliensis*, Chagoya's imagery appears alongside poetry and prose writings by Gómez-Peña, in typographic compositions in red and black inks by Rice. The texts, written in English, Spanish and Spanglish, reference border culture, NAFTA and its impact, immigration and transcultural identity. An excerpt from Gómez-Peña's performance poem 'Califas', created in 1987 and reproduced in *Codex Espangliensis*, imagines an American conquest of Europe:

In 1492, an
AZTEC SAILOR
NAMED NOCTLI
EUROPZIN TEZPOCA
DEPARTED FROM THE
PORT OF MINATITLAN
With a small flotilla of
Wooden rafts, 3 months later,
HE DISCOVERED A NEW
CONTINENT AND NAMED IT
EUROPZIN AFTER HIMSELF.

Gómez-Peña's satirical texts echo Chagoya's collages in their adoption of the concept of 'reverse anthropology', imagining a world in which the dominant culture and interpretive lens is Indigenous-American instead of European. Gómez-Peña draws links between the colonisation of the Americas and the relationship between the US and Mexico, exploring economic relations and immigration policy, and questioning damaging stereotypes. Interspersed in different typefaces and sizes throughout *Codex Espangliensis*, the texts stress the multiplicity of voices and influences that make up Mexican and Chicano/a culture.

Despite the thematic cohesion between the visual and textual aspects of the book, Chagoya and Gómez-Peña worked independently, and neither of them knew how Rice was going to combine text and images in the final work.[3] The monumental book took five years to make and became an all-consuming project for Rice. Originally published in an edition of fifty, the *Codex Espangliensis* remains one of the most spectacular and celebrated publications of Rice's Moving Parts Press.

01. *View of* Codex Espangliensis: From Columbus to the Border Patrol. *Its accordion-fold binding reaches more than 9 metres when fully extended. (RF.2008.b.36)*

02. *Detail from the first panels of* Codex Espangliensis, *letterpress-printed in black and red inks from zinc photoengravings. (RF.2008.b.36)*

WILLIAM LEIGHTON'S *THE TEARES OR LAMENTACIONS OF A SORROWFULL SOULE*

The tablebook format: a visually striking approach to the layout of music notation

JAMES RITZEMA AND CHRISTOPHER SCOBIE

European music publishers of the late Renaissance looked for possible solutions to a long-standing question: how best, and most economically, to print music in multiple parts? Two formats which accommodated the music assigned to separate performers in different ways, the choirbook and the partbook, had come to dominate both the manuscript and printed traditions of the sixteenth century. Choirbooks were large tomes with the separate voice parts displayed adjacently on one opening of the book; they were placed on stands or lecterns, most commonly in churches, so singers and instrumentalists could gather round and look up to their parts together (Image 5). Through the sixteenth century the use of choirbooks declined, brought about by changes in musical styles less suited to presentation in this format, but also accelerated in many Reformed countries by the disappearance of liturgical choirs. At the same time, the partbook format – which took the form of an individual small book for each performer, containing just their part – was in its ascendency. The turn of the seventeenth century saw the heyday of its popularity, with Europe's publishing houses churning out thousands of editions of music in partbook format between 1560 and 1630, in part to feed the ever-growing market for domestic music-making.

The tablebook format illustrated in this chapter represents a third design of music book from this period. It was a format whose success was short-lived and legacy small, but one which typifies a period of transition and experimentation in the printing of music. A single tablebook contained all the music assigned to the separate performers, like a choirbook, but displayed so that the individual parts faced outwards from an imaginary central point. If the book were to be read 'normally' then some parts would appear to be printed at 90 degrees, or others upside down. But, laid open flat on a table with the performers gathered around, the parts faced out to each performer.

Tablebooks were principally associated with recreational music-making in people's homes, often containing music for a combination of voices and instruments such as the lute. In these domestic settings they offered an alternative medium to partbooks, elegantly bringing all the musical information together into one volume, thus reducing the risk of individual parts going missing (a frequent problem if today's surviving sets of parts can be taken as any indication). Parts using tablature notation (a form of notation which shows performers of fretted stringed instruments where to place their fingers) were particularly vulnerable as they required more space, and, in partbook format, often appeared in a larger format to the rest of the set, ending up with them being folded or otherwise damaged on the shelf.[1] Surviving examples of tablebooks often demonstrate the great care that went into designing the layout of the parts on the page, with thought given to not only the space on the page but the implications for how players and their instruments would be positioned around the table – particularly important if large instruments were

01. *The presentation copy of Leighton's* Teares. *The volume is bound in white vellum with Charles I's coat of arms (as Prince of Wales) tooled in gold. Ribbon ties would have been laced through the holes on the right-hand side.*

(01.)

02.

03.

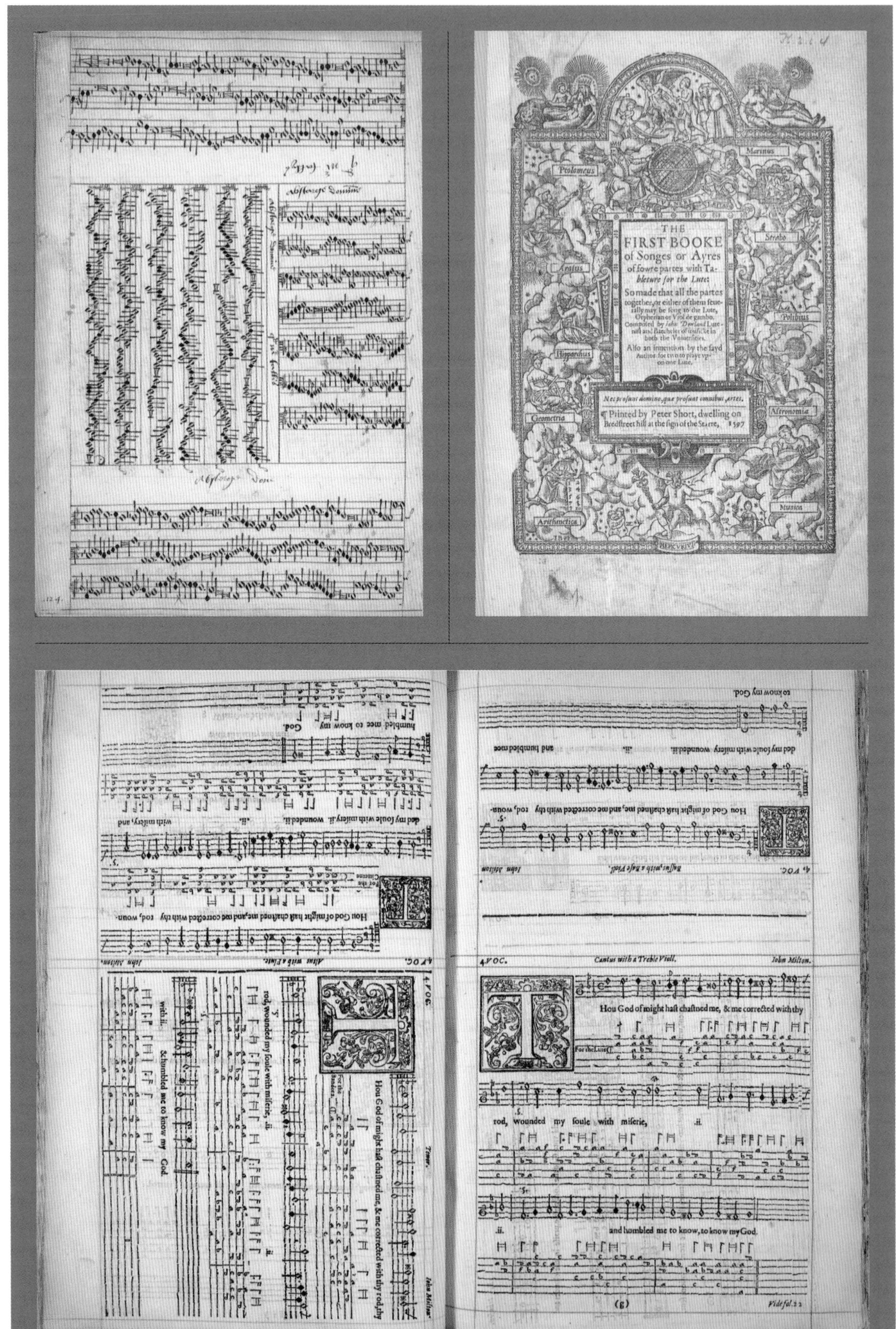
THE FIRST BOOKE of Songes or Ayres of fowre partes with Tableture for the Lute:
So made that all the partes together, or either of them seuerally may be song to the Lute, Orpherian or Viol de gambo.
Composed by John Dowland Lutenist and Batcheler of musicke in both the Vniuersities.
Also an inuention by the sayd Author for two to playe vpon one Lute.
Nec prosunt domino, quæ prosunt omnibus, artes.
Printed by Peter Short, dwelling on Bredstreet hill at the signe of the Starre, 1597
Ptolomeus
Marinus
Strabo
Aratus
Polibius
Hipparchus
Geometria
Astronomia
Arithmetica
Musica
4 VOC.
Cantus with a Treble Viall.
John Milton.
Hou God of might hast chastned me, & me corrected with thy
rod, wounded my soule with miserie, .ii.
.ii. and humbled me to know, to know my God.
For the Lute

04.

to be involved. This was no mean feat as into the mix had to be added the fact that different forms of notation (stave and tablature), text and often illustrations all had to fit onto a single opening.

Jacques Moderne, an Italian printer who worked in Lyons, issued the earliest printed music book in what we might describe as tablebook layout. This edition, *Le paragon des chansons* (1530), displayed four voice parts in such a way that two pairs of singers sit opposite each other to read their parts.[2] This directional arrangement of the music on the page had been foreshadowed in manuscript; an earlier Italian manuscript of four-voice songs laid out in the same way on the page is one surviving source that shows the technique in use.[3] But while this novel layout fostered an interesting social scenario by dictating the position of singers, implying two couples, the layout offered no particular advantage to the publisher, composer or performers. Instead, books of instrumental music from the Low Countries were the first to show some practical benefit from this layout. Pierre Phalèse the Elder's *Hortus musarum* (1552) positioned music for two lute players so that the performers could sit opposite each other, with the advantage of separating the bulky instruments, placing them at either end of a table rather than squeezed in on the same side (as they would need to be if their parts were printed to be read in the 'normal' way).[4]

TABLEBOOKS IN ENGLAND

English music publishers lagged behind their continental counterparts in several respects, often being slow to take advantage of new technology and catering for a smaller base of purchasers. Tablebooks were not printed in England for some

02. *Manuscript tablebook copied c. 1578, entitled 'A booke of In nomines and other solfege songs'. (MS 31390, ff. 104v–105r)*

03. *Title page of John Dowland's* First Booke of Songes or Ayres. *(K.2.i.4)*

04. *Layout of 'Thou God of might' by John Milton, with parts interspersed with tablature and spaced to allow for large instruments in Leighton's* Teares. *(f2v–g̃r)*

05. *Clerics gathered around a lectern to sing, from the St Omer Psalter. (Yates Thompson 14, f. 103)*

(05.)

time, with the first examples appearing towards the end of the 1590s. There are earlier exemplars of this layout in manuscript however, such as that now held by the British Library titled 'A booke of In nomines and other solfege songs'.[5] (Image 2) Bearing the date 1578, this substantial volume was probably copied around that year in Chichester, being heavily associated with an English singer, organist and composer named Clement Woodcock, who was Master of the Choristers at the cathedral there.[6]

But, while slow at first to capitalise on the tablebook's possibilities, English publishers ultimately did so with the greatest vigour, producing more editions of this type than anywhere else in Europe. The first (Image 3), John Dowland's *First Booke of Songes or Ayres* (1597), came some six and a half decades after the first tablebooks printed in France; however, this greatly successful edition was subsequently reissued another four times in the years to 1613, and its financial success probably resulted in the large publishing contract for Dowland's *Second Booke* (1603).[7] The *First Booke*'s success was at least partly due to the effective presentation of the lute tablature, interspersed with the vocal melody. This layout, possibly conceived by Dowland himself, was to become standard for the presentation of this style of mixed instrumental and vocal music, and was replicated many times by London printers over the following twenty years, including the volume that is the subject of this chapter.[8]

Laid me down to rest and slept, and in the morning rose
a-gain, in the morning rose again, God me sustaind & safely kept, & safely kept, &
by his grace, .ii. did mee main- taine his Angels pitcht me round
a-bout, sleeping and waking keeping me, kee-
going out, .ii. and going
security, they guard me with security,
Laid me downe to rest and slept, .ii. and
in the morning rose a- gain, God me sustaind, and safe ly kept, God me sustaind and
safely kept; and by his grace did me maintaine, His Angels pitcht me round about,
sleeping and waking, .ii. kee- ping
out, .ii. they guard me with security,
me with se-cu-ri-ty.

5. VOC.
Cantus secundus.
Laid me downe to rest and slept, and in the morning rose againe, God me sustaind, .ii. and safe-ly kept, & by his grace did me main- tain: His Angels pitcht me round
about, sleeping and waking, .ii. keeping me, both comming in
and going out, they guard me with security, securitie, with
Aa 2

WILLIAM LEIGHTON

The obscure origins and peculiar content of *The Teares or Lamentacions of a Sorrowfull Soule* are closely tied to the unusual personal circumstances of the creator, Sir William Leighton. Born to a family of Shropshire gentry around 1565, Leighton had ingratiated himself into the Elizabethan court by the 1590s. Returned as Member of Parliament for Much Wenlock in 1601, he was knighted upon the accession of James I in 1603, most likely in response to the publication of a book of his poetry entitled *Vertue Triumphant*, which he dedicated to the new king. Thereafter things deteriorated quickly: no stranger to the law courts, Leighton was relentlessly pursued for debt, heavily fined for supporting the farcical legitimacy claim of the young Robert Dudley, expelled from the Gentlemen Pensioners (the monarch's ceremonial bodyguard), and finally outlawed by letters patent in 1608. His father's will disinherited him the same year and a court ordered him to the Marshalsea Prison for debt in 1609.[9]

From prison Leighton turned once more to poetry to restore his fortunes. He published a collection of repentant verse under the title *The Teares or Lamentacions of a Sorrowfull Soule* in 1613, which he dedicated to Prince Charles (later Charles I). This collection of penitential poetry perhaps implied a public act of contrition, although its veiled references to Leighton's 'afflictions' and 'misfortune' attempted to avert blame from the author. Significantly, this edition announced the forthcoming publication of a corresponding book of music, partly his own compositions, but with some musical settings 'by expert and famous learned men in that science and facultie'. By means unknown, Leighton had secured contributions to his music book from almost all of England's foremost composers while still imprisoned in the Marshalsea.

06 (pages 136–137). *Layout of 'I laid me downe to rest' by William Byrd in Leighton's* Teares. *(Aa1v–Aa2r)*

07. *Title page bearing the music puzzle surrounded by the names of musical contributors.*

THE TEARES OR LAMENTACIONS OF A SORROWFULL SOULE (1614)

The reputations of the musical contributors to Leighton's *Teares*, published in 1614, a year after its words-only forerunner, were its greatest strength, and the book capitalised on their respected names and compositional renown. The enticing title page proudly lists the composers who set Leighton's poetry, displaying their names and academic credentials around an eye-catching musical illustration (Image 7). Whereas the music contained within the volume was printed with the conventional small pieces of type, this lavish design was created using a single woodblock. Considerable skill would have been required to carve the musical detail and flowing italic script for the composers' names, all of which would have been inscribed as a mirror image so that they appeared the right way round when the block was pressed upon the page. The individuals listed include the most widely published composers of the day, among them William Byrd and John Dowland; musicians of the Chapel Royal, such as Orlando Gibbons and Thomas Tomkins; and composers of Italian patrimony, Thomas Lupo and Alfonso Ferrabosco, whose continental connections probably made them fashionable contributors. The illustration itself takes the form of a 'puzzle canon', presumably devised by Leighton himself. In this, the voice parts can be followed round (and inside) the circle, entering in canon (one voice after another, in imitation), ingeniously fitting together to produce a short piece of music as well as a striking graphic.

Within the puzzle, the letters C and P (denoting Carolus Princeps) identify Prince Charles as the recipient of Leighton's dedication once more. This woodblock illustration also displays Charles's heraldic arms between a rose and thistle, symbolising his father's kingdoms of England and Scotland, while the carver's virtuosic skill is further employed in the depiction between C and P of

THE TEARES OR LAMENTACIONS OF A SORROWFVLL SOVLE:

Composed with Musicall Ayres and Songs, both for Voyces and diuers Instruments.

Set foorth by Sir WILLIAM LEIGHTON *Knight, one of his Maiesties Honourable Band of Gentlemen Pensioners.*

And all Psalmes that consist of so many feete as the fiftieth Psalme, will goe to the foure partes for Consort.

LONDON

Printed by *William Stansby.* 1614.

07.

a crown with feathers, the crest of the Prince of Wales. The latter is a curiously pre-emptive addition, because Charles was not invested as Prince of Wales until 1616. This woodblock carving was evidently considered a success by the book's creators, who further employed it on the reverse of the title page and on the back page.

Sadly, the intricate cover design and pantheon of compositional talent displayed in Leighton's *Teares* were not matched in the quality of the rest of the book's production. The printing was undertaken by a publisher named William Stansby, notorious for his erroneous presswork and unseemly personal conduct: the Stationers' Company (London's guild of printers) not only reprimanded him for poor workmanship, but also fined him on multiple occasions for using foul language before their company court. Leighton's *Teares* did not escape Stansby's haphazard standards of workmanship, and the heavy music type shows through much of the thin paper on which it was printed. Nevertheless, the publication conveys the musical contents clearly, partly because the tablebook design enabled a layout which was sufficiently economical with space that all the parts of each piece could be fitted onto a double-page spread.

Alongside pieces that were written solely for voices are others written for mixed ensembles of voices and instruments. It was common practice at this time for musicians to substitute parts in vocal music with viols (a family of stringed instrument related to the violin); indeed, most books of vocal music published at this time would have some phrase akin to 'fit for voices or viols' on their title pages as a way of stressing the versatility of the repertoire contained within. However, a considerable number of instruments are specified and called for across the different pieces of Leighton's collection, including the flute, lute, cittern (a metal-strung plucked instrument related to the modern guitar) and bandora (a bass cittern). Ensembles combining such forces, not restricted solely to viols, are known as 'broken consorts', and music printed specifically for groups of these instruments comprise the first third of the volume.

A good example can be seen in 'Thou God of might', a consort song by John Milton, father of the poet (Image 4). The printing of Milton's piece helps to illustrate the considerable care taken in the design and layout of Leighton's *Teares*, particularly regarding the practical issues of the large instruments of a broken consort being gathered around one book. Looking at the bottom half of these two pages, the left is occupied by music for the tenor voice which is interspersed with tablature for the bandora, while the music on the right is for cantus voice (the tune at soprano pitch) accompanied by tablature for the lute. These instruments both have long necks which extend to the left, and thus the music to the left of each part is printed so that each performer is round a page corner from each other, to avoid getting in the other's way. On the top right the bassus (bass) voice is accompanied by a bass viol, while the music at the top left has the altus (alto) singer being accompanied by the flute: the alto singer and the flautist have clearly been placed to the right of the bass parts because the body of the flute extends to the right (towards the top left corner of Image 6), and avoids competition for space. Some inevitable crowding arises on this side because the altus 'corner' of the book also includes some tablature for the cittern, but this is mitigated by the fact that it is the instrument with the smallest neck or fretboard.

THE PRESENTATION COPY

Upon publication, it was typical for a copy of a new edition to be presented to a dedicatee as a gift, which in turn might be met with a financial reward.[10] It has been suggested, on the basis of

Specification	*Scale*
WILLIAM LEIGHTON, *THE TEARES OR LAMENTACIONS OF A SORROWFULL SOULE* London, 1614 570 x 390 mm K.1.i.9	

the binding of this volume, that this was one such gift, the so-called presentation copy (Image 1). This claim can perhaps be supported by evidence from other surviving exemplars: copies of this same edition in the Royal College of Music in London and the Folger Shakespeare Library in Washington share some identical corrections applied by hand, suggesting they might have been emended in the printing house before being sold.[11] These consistent corrections are missing from the Charles I copy in the British Library, giving the strong impression that it was immediately taken from the printing house upon completion to be given to the prince, before any other copies were made publicly available. While lacking the corrections, Charles's copy is however heavily decorated with red lines and borders, drawn in ink on every page (see Image 6). Its binding also provides evidence of this. Bound in white vellum, the volume is decorated with gold tooling which depicts Charles's coat of arms before his accession to the throne. Virtually identical bindings relating to Charles, including one on an Italian book about artillery published this same year, confirm his ownership of this volume.[12]

CONCLUDING REMARKS

The design of Leighton's *Teares* was characterised by practical and aesthetic objectives, both of which were underpinned by commercial benefits. The choice of the inherently functional tablebook design overcame some of the problems associated with presenting instrumental music in other formats, while its compact configuration allowed for an economical use of paper. At the same time, aesthetic concerns were to the fore; through the clever use of decoration, particularly in the eye-catching woodblock illustration on the title page, and the almost virtuosic skill involved in conceiving and executing the layout of the parts on the page (even if, in this case, it was not matched by the quality of the printing).

The functionality of tablebooks, while striking and undeniable, should nevertheless perhaps not be overstated. The difficulty of reading the often small print from a distance, behind an instrument, would have been a significant problem. For practical purposes, it has been suggested that manuscript copies in specially made up partbooks were probably made. Certainly an individual partbook containing a cantus and lute part for the consort songs at the front of this volume lends some credence to this (British Library, Royal Appendix MS 63).[13]

The tablebook's popularity declined sharply after this period, although some books with musical notation facing in different directions continued to be printed as late as the 1670s. Into the tablebook's place came the modern music 'score', where parts were printed together, piled up vertically and 'scored' together with lines on the page, helping one reader to follow multiple parts at once – a practice actually foreshadowed in part in some of the tablebook editions.

While the tablebook design might not be taken as a 'breakthrough' as part of a linear progression towards modern scores, it cemented the trend towards gathering different parts in one printed volume, while also anticipating some elements of the music scores which would ultimately replace them. These design elements are also fascinating in their evocation of the time, and thus editions like Leighton's *Teares* allow the modern reader to conjure images of the social gathering and interactions behind well-known pieces of music.

APPAREIL
L'AUDITION
ANATOMIE ET PHYSIOLOGIE
PAR
G.-J. WITKOWSKI
PARIS
1877
RETINE
Papille
Muscle
DROIT EXTERNE
MALAIRE
Muscle ORBICULAIRE DES PAUPIÈRES
STIQUE

01.

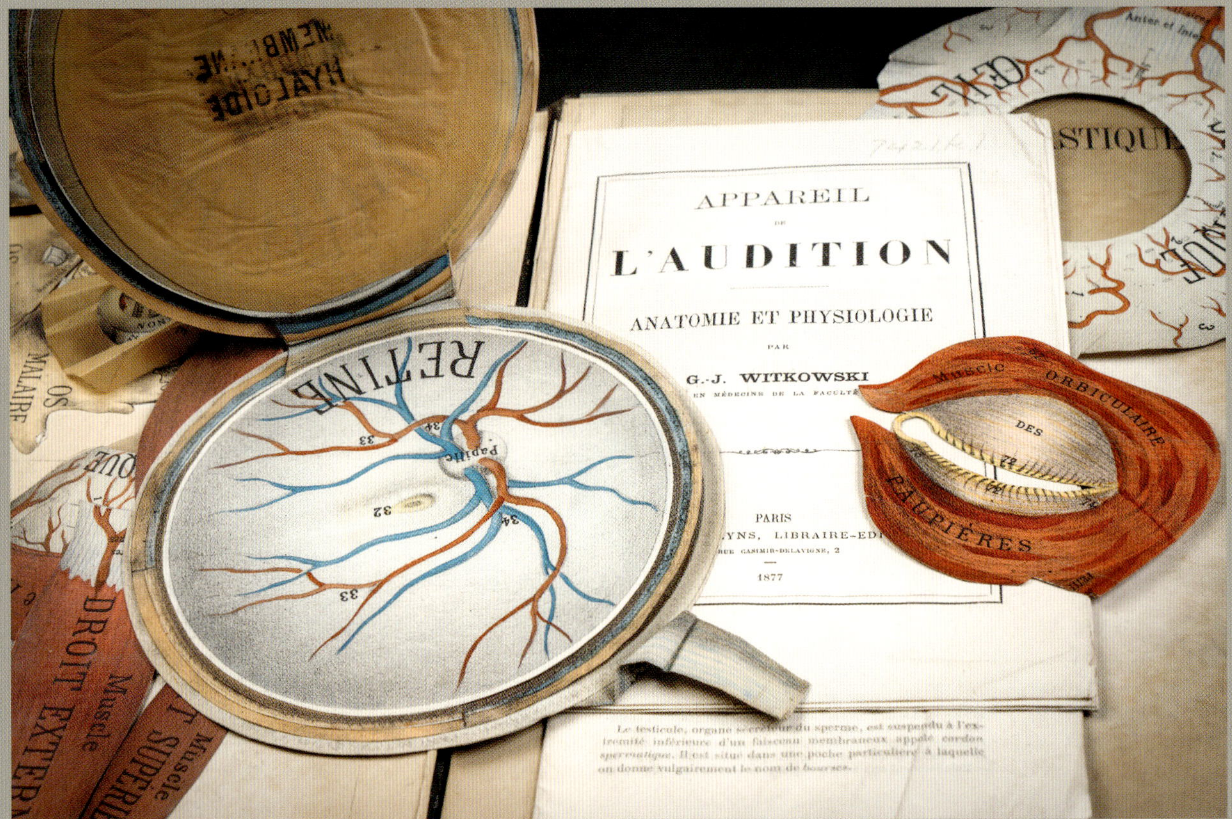

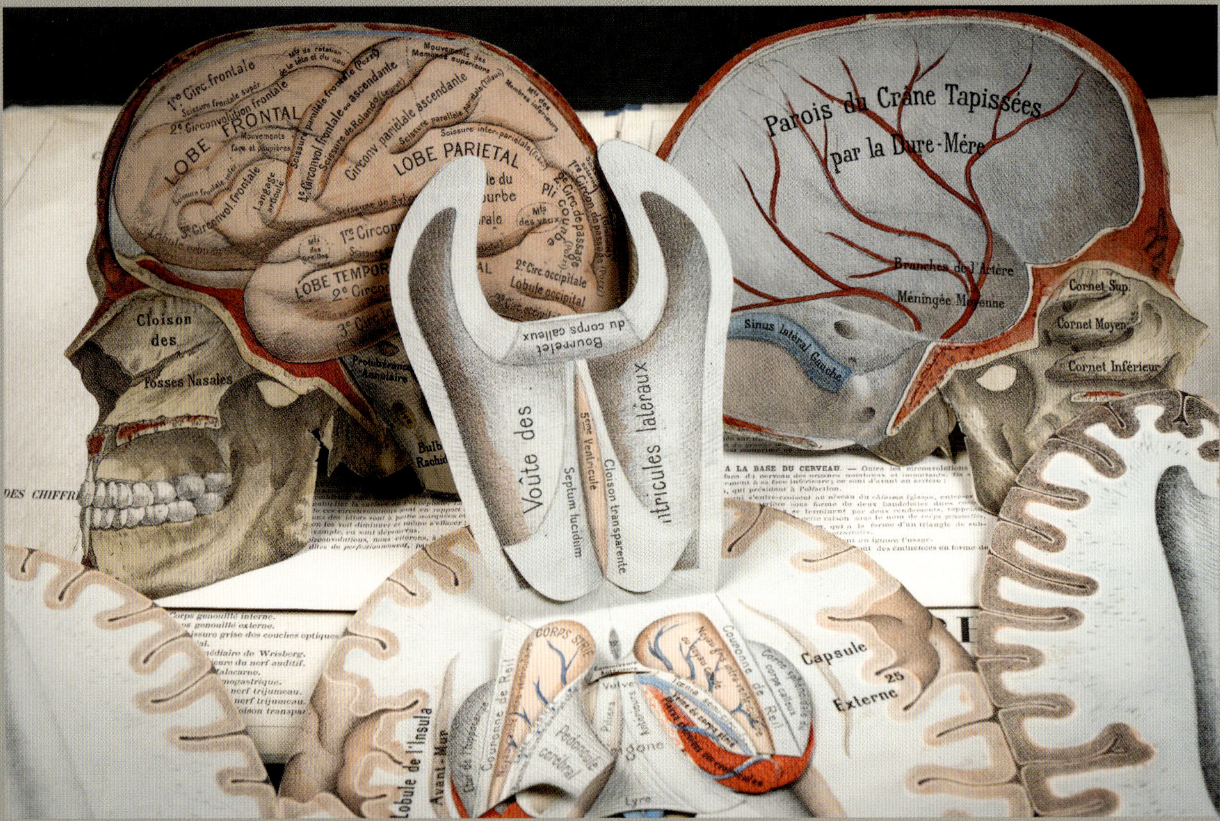
1re Circ. frontale
LOBE FRONTAL
LOBE PARIETAL
Circonv. pariétale ascendante
LOBE TEMPORAL
Lobule occipital
Cloison des Fosses Nasales
Parois du Crâne Tapissées par la Dure-Mère
Branches de l'Artère
Méningée Moyenne
Sinus latéral Gauche
Cornet Sup.
Cornet Moyen
Cornet Inférieur
Bourrelet du corps calleux
Voûte des
Ventricules latéraux
Septum lucidum
Cloison transparente
CORPS STRIÉ
Couronne de Reil
Lobule de l'Insula
Avant-Mur
Capsule Externe
Lyre

02.

THE DESIGN OF HUMAN ATLASES

SOPHIE DEFRANCE

The desire to represent the human body in all its wonderful complexity has long been a source of ingenuity. It led to innovations in book design and advanced the production of flap books, in which the hidden parts of an illustration are revealed by lifting a paper part, and pop-up books or books in three dimensions.

The body has traditionally been seen as a territory: 'anatomists explore the body lying before them as an uncharted ocean', writes author and curator Hugh Aldersey-Williams. Books of illustrated anatomy were called 'atlases', as they continue to be called today. As with actual maps, artists and scientists had to find ways of expressing three-dimensional relationships, in this case between different tissues and organs, while encapsulating them in the format of a book. Clever design outcomes were devised to resolve this challenge. The resulting anatomy fugitive sheets, flap books and pop-up books formed a printed, iconographical and textual genre of their own. As Andrea Carlino wrote in *Paper Bodies* (1999), they constituted a solution to 'the problem posed by the need to represent visual data which are intrinsically topographical: the body is a map, a collection of forms, parts and spatial relations hidden away under the skin'. The main design idea was to show different parts of the human anatomy printed on paper flaps that could be lifted to reveal layers deeper within the body – so skin, nerves and blood vessels, muscles, organs – also constructed as flaps. If these illustrations were surrounded or accompanied by printed text, it was often brief and on the periphery, like the legend on a map.

The fashion for designing books with flaps in Europe goes back to the Renaissance. Early items date from the sixteenth century. One of the most famous anatomy books at the time was Andreas Vesalius's *De Humani Corporis Fabrica Libri Septem* (Basel, 1543), literally meaning 'On the fabric of the human body in seven books', commonly known as the *Fabrica*, a set of which is in the British Library.

A professor at the University of Padua, Vesalius subjected ancient beliefs about anatomy to rigorous experiments through his own practice of dissection. Vesalius's book consisted of 659 pages and 277 plates of illustrations by artists from Titian's workshop.

To accompany the *Fabrica*, Vesalius published the shorter and cheaper *De Humani Corporis Fabrica Librorum Epitome* (or *Epitome* for short), which was a summary of the *Fabrica* books.

The *Epitome* is divided into two parts: the first includes six chapters describing the human body, the second is made of anatomical plates with indices. These plates are not mere illustrations: through them, Vesalius invites his readers to be active and interact with the books, by cutting out and layering the cut-outs over each other, so as to build a human three-dimensional figure that could be studied alongside the text. It created a multi-dimensional construction, allowing 'dissection' without dissection, an examination within the multiple layers of the body without having to approach a dissected corpse.

In the following centuries, many beautiful and even artistic anatomical atlases were produced, but the fashion for paper-engineered books passed; works were sometimes produced for rich patrons and book collectors rather than anatomy students. Some of the most memorable of these beautiful

01. & 02. *The human eye and the motor centres of the brain, from Gustave Joseph Witkowski's* Anatomie iconoclastique, Atlas complémentaire de l'anatomie et de la physiologie humaines *('Iconoclastic Anatomy: Complementary Atlas of Human Anatomy and Physiology'). (14001.g.15)*

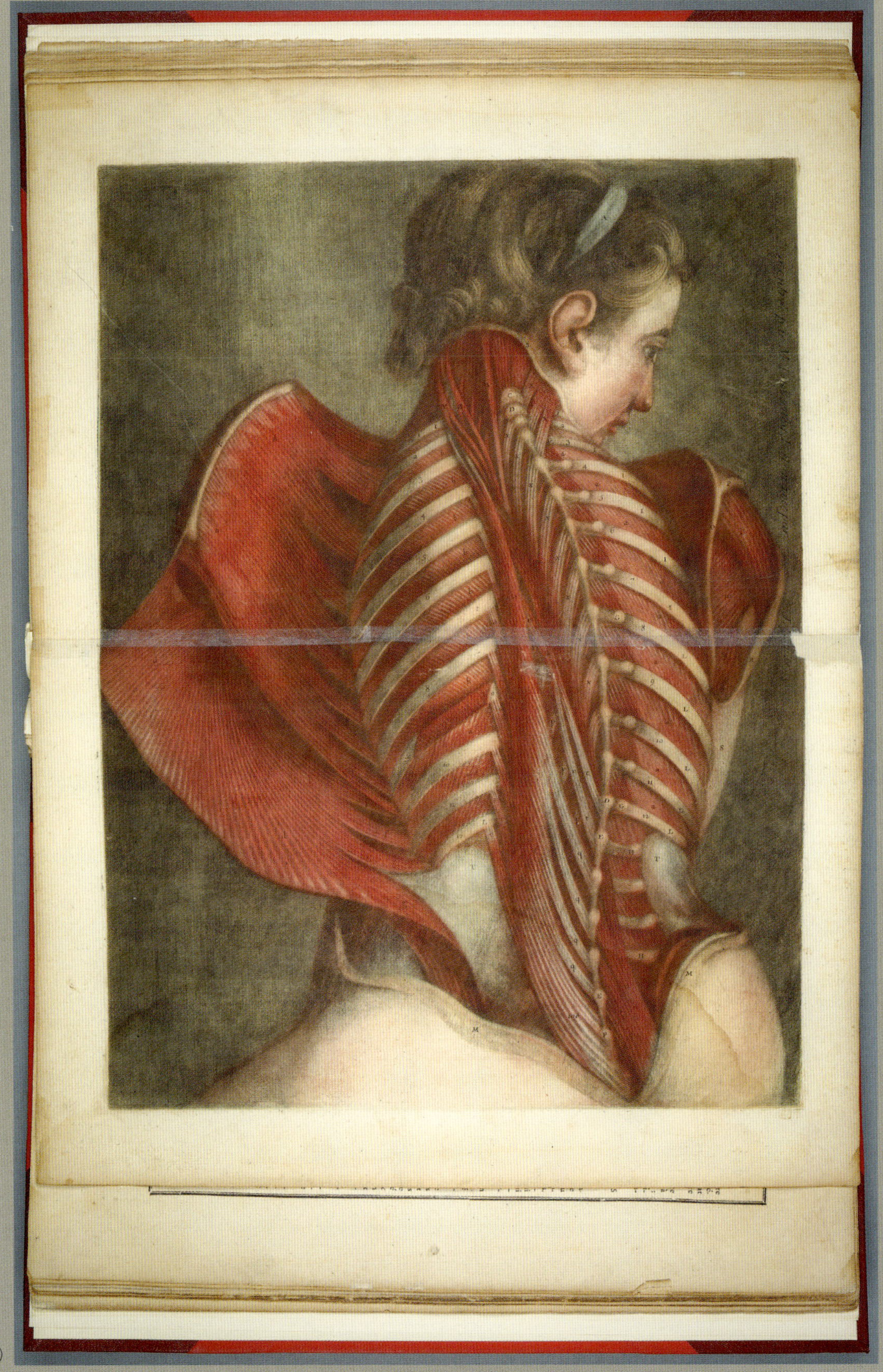

03.

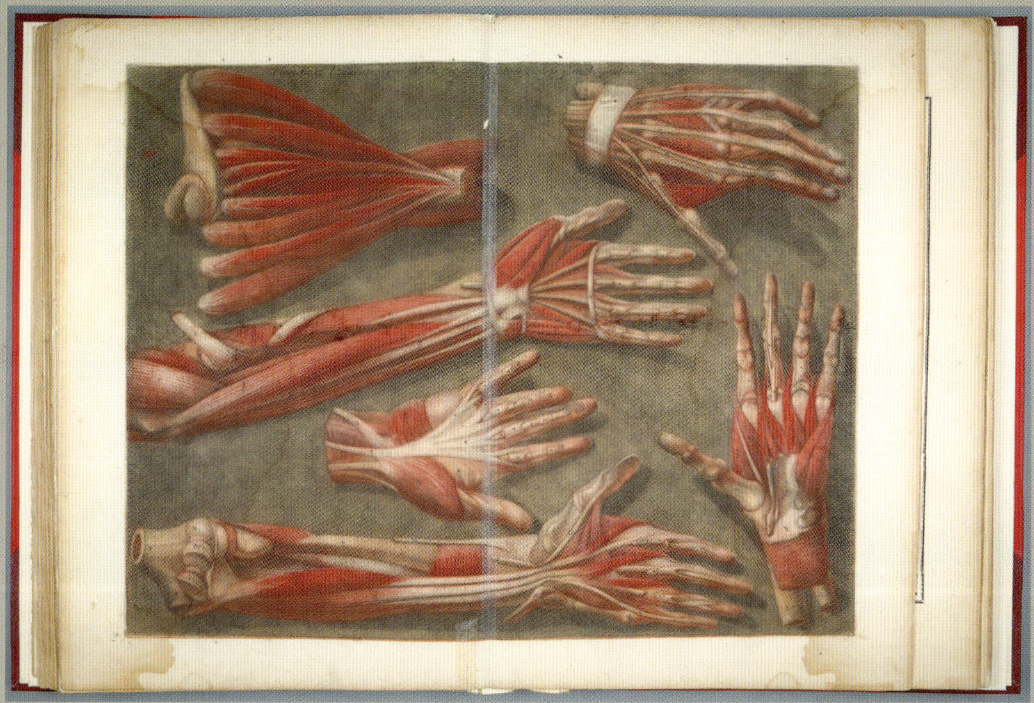

(04.)

'flat' atlases are the work of French artist and anatomist Jacques Fabien Gautier d'Agoty (1710–1785) who invented a new mezzotint process and was one of the first to produce an atlas in full colour (Images 3 & 4). The figures were represented alive as healthy, adorned and coiffed, but with an inside view as if their skin had become transparent.

The idea that slices of the body could be peeled off and put back in layers persisted, however, and the nineteenth century would see a revival, and even a 'golden age' of anatomical flap books.

In England, flap books had been revived with works such as Edward William Tuson's *A supplement to myology* in 1828. Meanwhile, in France, Achille Comte had reinvigorated flap books as an amusement 'for socialites' with *Physiologie pour les collèges et les gens du monde, expliquée sur onze planches à l'aide de figures découpées et superposées*, in 1834. During the same decades, in an even broader attempt to touch a new public, Dr Louis Auzoux started to make large-scale models, with papier-mâché for educational use. The models were called '*anatomies clastiques*' (or 'dismantable', that can be 'taken apart') and soon won international success.

These revivals of human anatomy in its three-dimensional expressions certainly influenced Gustave Joseph Witkowski's *Anatomie iconoclastique, Atlas complémentaire de tous les ouvrages traitant de l'anatomie et de la physiologie humaines. Composé de planches ... coloriées et superposées, etc.* (Paris, 1875–78), the title of which combined the idea of the geographical atlas, Auzoux's 'clastique' dismantability, and the Greek word (*eikon*/icon) for 'image'. Witkowski, a medical doctor for a railway company, had a vocation for popularisation, and wrote widely on a variety of subjects. The volumes of his *Anatomie iconoclastique* consist of coloured chromolithographs, linked together by paper constructions and strings, and they can either pop up or sometimes be taken out altogether to be better examined and manipulated (Images 1 & 2). They use a variety of materials, including coloured string, transparent paper and glassine to imitate the vitreous part of the body. Almost 450 years after Vesalius, design was once more used to replicate and sanitise for students, and the general public alike, that most frightening scientific act, the dissection of a human body.

03. & 04. *Plates 14 and 17 from Jacques Fabien Gautier d'Agoty's* Myologie complette en couleur et grandeur naturelle, composée de l'essai et de la suite de l'essai d'anatomie, en tableaux imprimés, *1746. (1832.e.17)*

01.

DESCRIPTION

OF THREE HUNDRED

ANIMALS;

VIZ.

BEASTS, BIRDS, FISHES, || SERPENTS, AND INSECTS.

WITH

A Particular Account of the *Whale-Fishery*

Extracted out of the Best Authors, and adapt ed to the Use of all Capacities; especiall to allure Children to Read.

Illustrated with COPPER PLATES, where is curiously Engraved every BEAST, BIR FISH, SERPENT, and INSECT, descri in the whole Book.

by Tho. Boreman, a Bookbinde

For every Beast of the Forest is mine, and the Cattle a thousand Hills. I know all the Fowls of the M tains, and the wild Beasts of the Field are mine.

LONDON

Printed by J. T. for *Rich. Ware* at the *Bible* and in *Amen-Corner*, *Tho. Boreman* the Corner of *St* ment's Lane without *Temple-Bar*, and *Tho. Game* *Bible* in *Prince's-street*, against *Stanhope-street*

M.DCC.XXX.

XII.

A DESCRIPTION OF THREE HUNDRED ANIMALS

Colour and innovation in publishing for children

LUCY EVANS

What is a children's book and why do we see such an explosion in popularity of literature written specifically for children in the eighteenth century? Seth Lerer writes that 'ever since there have been children, there has been children's literature',[1] and it is reasonable to assume that children with access to printed material were reading and consuming books for entertainment. Early printed works had a strong focus on education, both moral and pedagogical, although they sometimes contained elements meant to entertain. Books really intended for adults were also read or used by children. Some earlier books for children would have been cheaper than material printed for adults, hence the proliferation of chapbooks for children and the use of crude woodcuts which were more economical. Owning or having access to printed material was a privilege that not every child would have had. Even chapbooks would have been out of the price range of many families and without a formalised education system access to printed material was rare or non-existent for many children.

What changed in the eighteenth century? One idea was the changing perception of childhood itself, popularised by Enlightenment thinkers such as Jean-Jacques Rousseau (1712–1778). Childhood began to be seen as an important and formative period of life, rather than children simply being considered miniature adults or even somehow less than human. Now there was a greater focus on learning through entertainment and a desire to engage children, as John Locke (1632–1704) espoused. As child mortality rates declined there was no longer the need to focus quite so exclusively on the improvement of souls and the very real possibility of an early death. There was a new middle class, with parents who were more likely to be literate than their ancestors, and to have sufficient disposable income to buy books for their children. As the century progressed access to schooling and formalised learning became available to more children.

ENGAGE AND EDUCATE

The biggest revolution in children's literature in the eighteenth century was the increased production of books to amuse, inspire and entertain, as well as to educate. A huge part of this was down to book design. Key to this development was the publisher, Thomas Boreman (active between approximately 1730 and 1743). Boreman had a disproportionately large impact on the appearance and form of children's books. Not only did he spearhead the idea of books which would specifically appeal to children through their design, he recognised that they must also appeal to those with the purchasing power by being educational as well as entertaining.

Pictured here is Boreman's first edition of *A Description of Three Hundred Animals* (1730), of which only two copies are recorded[2] in the UK.[3] The book is considered the first work on natural history written for children.[4] It features attractive and detailed copperplate engravings, with a striking title page in red and black and a frontispiece plate (Image 1). The engravings face their descriptions on the opposite page. Engraved illustrations, in which the lines are cut into a metal plate in order to hold the ink, were more common in works produced for adults, whereas juvenile books more often relied on cruder woodcut illustrations, as they were quicker and cheaper to produce, although they were not so refined in detail. The benefit of the engraved illustration is in the level of detail. Although the illustrator of Boreman's work remains anonymous these illustrations were influential on later book production.

01. *Title page of* A Description of Three Hundred Animals *by Thomas Boreman.*

The text within *A Description of Three Hundred Animals* was based on works which were widely read and considered reputable sources, such as Edward Topsell's *History of Four-Footed Beasts and Serpents* (1658). Alongside those 'beasts, birds, fishes, serpents and insects' that would have been common in any work of natural history we also find the manticora, the unicorn and the tiger (Images 2, 3 & 4). The influence of Topsell can also be seen in the playful nature of Boreman's later *Gigantick Histories*; they certainly share similarities with the medieval bestiary.

The combination of both teaching and entertainment is clear not only from the production and design of the book, but also from Boreman's own words in his introduction to the work: '...with short descriptions of animals, and pictures fairly drawn (which last experience shews them to be much delighted with) to engage their attention.' Boreman certainly seems to have tapped into a niche market; the novelty of this beautifully illustrated work at this time would have been powerful. In the eighteenth century alone there are twenty-three separate editions recorded on the English Short Title Catalogue, not to mention two supplements.

Boreman's work was certainly innovative, and we can draw a line from *A Description of Three Hundred Animals* to the contributions of Thomas Bewick (1753–1828) in both the field of children's books and illustration in general. His works on the same subject had a far greater level of technical accomplishment. Bewick was passionate about natural history and had a deep love of the English countryside from a young age. At fourteen he was apprenticed to the engraver, Ralph Beilby (1744–1817), and began engraving on wood. Whereas woodcuts were traditionally created by cutting along the grain of the wood, Bewick's innovation was to cut across the grain. This meant that the wood could stand closer cutting, and thus more detailed images. In 1777 Bewick and Beilby went into partnership together and over the next thirteen years they produced over eighty books for children.

02., 03. & 04. *Pages from* A Description of Three Hundred Animals *showing illustrations and layout. (pp. 19–20, 5–6, 3–4)*

Two works of natural history confirmed Bewick's reputation as an engraver: *General History of Quadrupeds* (1790) and *History of British Birds* (1797–1804), which were both immediately successful. Like Boreman, Bewick sought to combine attractive and appealing images with facts and the opportunity to learn. In his *Memoir*, he recalled:

'When I first undertook my labours in Natural History, my strongest motive was to lead the minds of youth to the study of that delightful pursuit; ... I illustrated them with all the fidelity and animation I was able to impart to mere woodcuts without colour; and as instruction is of little avail without constant cheerfulness and occasional amusement, I interspersed the more serious studies with tale-pieces of gaiety and humour, yet even in these seldom without an endeavour to illustrate some truth, or point some moral.'[5]

After Bewick's success, it became more common to acknowledge illustrators in published books, for example in *The Happy Family or Winter Evenings Employment* (1801). For the first time, famous illustrators could act as a selling point in a growing market. Through his pioneering work, Bewick not only brought about the revival of woodcut illustration, taking the art of the book to a new level, he also influenced the next generation of children's book creators.

MINIATURE BOOKS

Returning to our innovator Boreman, as well as his impact on illustrated books for children he was also instrumental in the field of miniature books. Produced since the early days of printing, often to make convenient pocket-sized versions of books including devotional works and the Bible, the creation of miniature children's books without a religious slant took children's book publishing in a new direction. Between 1740 and 1743 Boreman produced ten volumes of miniature books, measuring less than 65 millimetres, which were designed for children's small hands. Starting with *The Gigantick History of the Two Famous Giants, and Other Curiosities in Guildhall* the series covered the 'curiosities' of other London monuments such

02.

19 *A Description of* BEASTS.

28. THE HYENA, of which there are several sorts, is in *Cæsarea* about the size of a Fox. It has Bristles, like an Horse's Mane, on his Back. It is said, it can change the Colour of its Eyes at pleasure, a thousand times in a Day. When it is very hungry, it enters the Graves of Men, and eats their dead Bodies; yet is its Flesh, in *Syria*, *Damascus*, &c. eaten by Men. Its Feet and Legs are like a Man's; its Colour like a Bear's: and is thought to be engender'd of a Bear and a Dog. It is a Beast of great Subtilty, that barks, and makes an hideous Noise in the Night. This Creature is said, when it goes to drink at the River *Nile*, to take a Sup and away, for fear of the Crocodile.

29. THE MANTICORA, (or, according to the *Persians*, *Mantiora*) a Devourer, is bred among the *Indians*; having a triple Row of Teeth beneath and above, and in bigness and roughness like a Lion's; as are also his Feet, Face, and Ears like a Man's: his Tail like a Scorpion's, armed with a Sting, and sharp-pointed Quills. His Voice is like a small Trumpet, or Pipe. He is so wild, that 'tis very difficult to tame him; and as swift as an Hart. With his Tail he wounds the Hunters, whether they come before or behind him. When the *Indians* take a Whelp of this Beast, they bruise its Buttocks and Tail, to prevent its bearing those sharp Quills; then it is tamed without danger.

30. THE ANTELOPE is as large as a Goat, of a chesnut Colour, and white under the Belly. His Horns are almost straight from his Head up, tapering gradually, with Rings at a distance from one another, till within an Inch and half of the Top. It has fine large black Eyes; a long and slender Neck, Feet, and Legs; and a Body shap'd like a Deer. There are many in an Herd; when at the same time they have Scouts, who by running give them notice of an approaching Foe. They are taken by Shot, &c. being too swift for a Greyhound.

31. THE

5

A Description of BEASTS. 6

7. THE RHINOCEROT, so called because of the Horn in his Nose, is bred in *India* and *Africa*. His Colour is like the Bark of a Box-Tree. He is said to be in shape somewhat like a Wild Boar, and not much unlike an Elephant; and near as long, but not so high, having shorter Legs. He has two Girdles upon his Body, like the Wings of a Dragon, from his Back down to his Belly; one towards his Neck and Mane, and the other towards his Loins and hinder Parts. His Skin is so hard, that no Dart is able to pierce it; and cover'd over with Scales like the Shell of a Tortoise. His Legs are also scaled over down to the Hoofs, which are parted into four distinct Claws. The Horn upon his Nose is so very hard and sharp, crooking towards the Crown of his Head, that some say it will pierce through Iron or Stone: He is said frequently to whet his Horn against a Flint, &c. that he may be prepar'd, whenever he is attack'd by an Enemy. He is a mortal Enemy to the Elephant, whom he seldom meets without a Battle; and aims chiefly at his Belly, being the softest Place; which if he misses, the Elephant is too hard for him with his Trunk and Teeth. The Naturalists say, that he grunts like an Hog. The manner of taking him, being so variously and uncertainly related, I thought it not worth describing.

8. THE UNICORN, a Beast, which though doubted of by many Writers, yet is by others thus described: He has but one Horn, and that an exceeding rich one, growing out of the middle of his Forehead. His Head resembles an Hart's, his Feet an Elephant's, his Tail a Boar's, and the rest of his Body an Horse's. The Horn is about a Foot and half in length. His Voice is like the Lowing of an Ox. His Mane and Hair are of a yellowish Colour. His Horn is as hard as Iron, and as rough as any File, twisted or curled, like a flaming Sword; very straight, sharp, and every where black, excepting the Point. Great Virtues are attributed to it, in expelling of Poison, and curing of several Diseases. He is not a Beast of prey.

B 2 9. OF

3 *A Description of* BEASTS.

than a Fox; yet is so fierce and bold, that it seizes either Man, or such Beasts as Cows, Hogs, Sheep, &c. It is reported, that when this Creature seizes his Prey, he makes an hideous Noise, which gives notice to the Lion, who immediately comes, if within Hearing; at whose Sight the Jaccall goes a little aside, till the Lion has fully satisfied his Hunger, and marches off; and then returns, to feed on what the Lion has left. His Head is like a Foxe's, and his Body like a Badger's.

4. THE PANTHER is in Shape somewhat like a Lioness, but not quite so large. His Hair is short and mossy, his Skin is of a bright yellow, beautifully mark'd with round black Spots, and is said to send forth a fragrant Smell, and bears a great Price. He is a very fierce and cruel Beast, greedy of Blood, very swift, and catches his Prey by leaping. It is the Nature of this Creature, in some Places, to hide himself amongst the thick Boughs of Trees, and to surprize his Prey, by leaping upon it suddenly. His Tongue in licking grates like a File.

5. THE LEOPARD is both in Shape, Nature and Colour, very much like a Panther, being spotted like that Creature, and is said to be engender'd between a Panther and a Lioness, &c.

6. THE TIGER is in Shape somewhat like a Lioness, but has a short Neck. His Skin is beautifully spotted, not with round Spots, like a Panther, nor with several different Colours. It is very wild and fierce, exceeding ravenous, and of a prodigious Swiftness. He spares neither Man nor Beast, but, if he can satisfy his Hunger with the Flesh of Beasts, he'll not attempt on Mankind. It is seldom taken, but in defense of its Young.

7. THE

4

4

A PANTHER.

5

A LEOPARD.

6

A TIGER.

03.

04.

05.

06.

as the Tower of London (Image 5) – although some of the 'facts' presented should definitely be taken with a pinch of salt! With bright floral paper wrappers[6] (thought to be used for the first time on a juvenile book in England),[7] crude woodcut illustrations and a list of child subscribers, Boreman appealed directly to the juvenile reader in a fresh and exciting way. A closer look at the subscriber's lists across the volumes does suggest some of the child subscribers might be less than credible, for example, 'Miss Cockey Halfhide'! He married the idea of creative vision with marketability at a time when technical advancements in the field of printing were occurring. The list of juvenile subscribers gave readers a sense of ownership over the books and even the publishing process, which was common in adult publishing but novel in children's book publishing. And what of Thomas Boreman, a man known only through his publications? After 1744 there is no further trace of him or his works.

Where Boreman led, many followed, and one of the most notable of those publishers is John Marshall (1756–1824). His miniature books included *The Infant's Library* (Image 6), published in approximately 1800, as a collection of sixteen volumes with glazed paper covers which covered themes such as boys' and girls' names, games, flowers and animals. The box they came in looked like a miniature library bookcase. The pleasure of the book is not only in its size and illustrations but in its housing; you can imagine a child reader rearranging the books and perhaps reading to a doll or younger sibling. The line between book and toy was blurred with these sets of books, and Marshall later branched out into producing games. John Harris (1756–1846) was among several printers who looked to emulate Marshall's success, including in 1802 with *The Cabinet of Lilliput*. This tiny revolution in children's books would stretch across publishing history into the twenty-first century. As miniature books came onto the market we also begin to see further innovation in the field of children's book publishing, with colour printing.

05. Curiosities in the Tower of London, *second edition, printed for Thomas Boreman (London), 1741. (Ch.740/7)*

06. The Infant's Library, *printed and sold by John Marshall (London),* c. *1800. (C.194.a.945)*

COLOUR PRINTING

Colour printing began to take root in the eighteenth century. Colour printing with woodblocks had been common in Asia and Europe for many centuries, as had the pairing of words with illustrations. However, it was more time-consuming than printing with black ink alone and this meant that it was often reserved for more costly books. Colour in children's book illustration only became common from the early nineteenth century, although prior to this there had occasionally been colour in some form in children's books. The exceptionally rare *Tommy Thumb's Pretty Song Book* (c. 1744), one of the earliest surviving collection of nursery rhymes in English, was printed in red and black and featured copperplate engravings, but this was relatively unusual. Hand-colouring in children's literature was more prevalent, as seen in the John Marshall printed edition of *Cinderella* (1817) (Image 7). Colour in children's books represented something perhaps not seen before in juvenile literature – luxury and expense being spent on children in creating something beautiful for them. Not only was it about making the works attractive there was also an argument that colour illustrations had an impact on learning.[8] As colour began to appear more regularly in children's books, the appetite grew and the stage was set for a revolution in colour printing.

George Baxter (1804–1867), himself the son of a printer, perfected the colour printing process and helped brighten the face of children's literature forever.[9] Baxter combined an engraved metal plate, which provided the outline and detail, with engraved wooden blocks, with each block representing a different colour. This new process meant good-quality prints could be produced at a reasonable cost and in greater numbers. For the first time colour printing was commercially viable, though unfortunately not for Baxter who was declared bankrupt two years before his death. It was Baxter who was 'the central figure from whom radiated almost the whole of the early and mid-Victorian mechanically-coloured pictures'.[10] Despite these developments in colour printing it is important to note that hand-colouring did

Specification	*Scale*
A DESCRIPTION OF THREE HUNDRED ANIMALS viz Beast, Birds, Fishes, Serpents and Insects London, 1730 198 x 122 mm 976.c.14	

not disappear overnight, it remained the cheaper alternative, requiring far less investment, for many years. Black-and-white printed illustrations also continued to be used, often to great effect, in children's books.

When the patent on Baxter's method expired other printers began to use the technique and experiment with improving it. Key to the history of colour in children's literature is Edmund Evans (1826–1905), who helped bring an end to 'the strangely prolonged supremacy of monochrome'[11] by developing a six-colour process of printing. Evans, who was a talented engraver, particularly of landscapes and the natural world, was apprenticed to a pupil of Thomas Bewick. As Evans's reputation grew he worked in conjunction with the publisher, Routledge. He began to produce some of the most beautiful colour illustrations the industry had ever seen. Routledge and Evans (among other London printers) produced what became known as toy books, formed of six pages of text and six pages of colour illustration printed on one side of the leaf only. Evans wasn't the first to produce more-affordable colour printed books for children but perhaps his biggest contribution was employing illustrators whose impact we still feel today, among them Randolph Caldecott (1846–1886). Caldecott drawings feel real and immediate, even today. They didn't soften the story for a juvenile audience. When it comes to the design of the children's book it is not just Caldecott's beautiful illustrations which made them a landmark but his understanding of the page and the relationship between text and illustration,[12] he had a way of leaving blank space which drew the reader's attention to the pictures. Caldecott was one of many illustrators influenced by Bewick and his natural history drawings and in turn was highly influential on later illustrators including Maurice Sendak (1928–2012) and Kate Greenaway.

Kate Greenaway (1846–1901) was another of Edmund Evans's protégés. She developed her own 'Queen Anne' style and the subtle colours of Evans's process work perfectly for the stories she told. Her illustrations are both delicate and economical and, like Caldecott, she had an instinctive talent for using the page and blank space. Pictured here is what is considered by many to be her best work, *The Pied Piper of Hamelin* by Robert Browning (1889). The text and pictures have a synergy not always present in some of her earlier works. The colour choice is typically Greenaway, with a muted palette of autumnal colours. Her work is perhaps more intimate than Caldecott's. It is testimony to the enduring power and popularity of Greenaway's work that her illustrations are instantly recognisable in the twenty-first century. Her delicate colour choices and nostalgic images featuring vaguely eighteenth-century children give her work a timelessness. Greenaway's work might not have had the wit of Caldecott but she is still considered a 'minor master'.[13] Even John Ruskin, with whom she had a fraught friendship, declared: '[The Pied Piper of Hamelin] was the grandest thing she had ever done.'[14]

Kate Greenaway's works were part of what came to be known as a golden age of illustration. As the nineteenth and twentieth centuries progressed, children's books became both more beautiful and elaborate, but also more numerous as book production technology advanced. From gift books and movables[15] to cheaply produced stories and primers, books became part of daily life for many children. Looking at the picture books available in the twenty-first century and how colour is a part of daily life in general, it is hard to believe that it was just over 100 years ago that colour printing really became a commercially viable prospect.[16] From the innovation of Boreman, Bewick, Marshall, Baxter and Greenaway, among so many others, our childhood memories are not only deeply associated with stories and pictures but with the physical book we held in our hands.

07. *Pages from Marshall's edition of the popular story of* Cinderella, or The Little Glass Slipper, *printed and sold by John Marshall (London), 1817. (012806.de.21(6.))*

08. The Pied Piper of Hamelin *by Robert Browning and illustrated by Kate Greenaway, George Routledge & Sons, 1889. (11648.f.39)*

07.

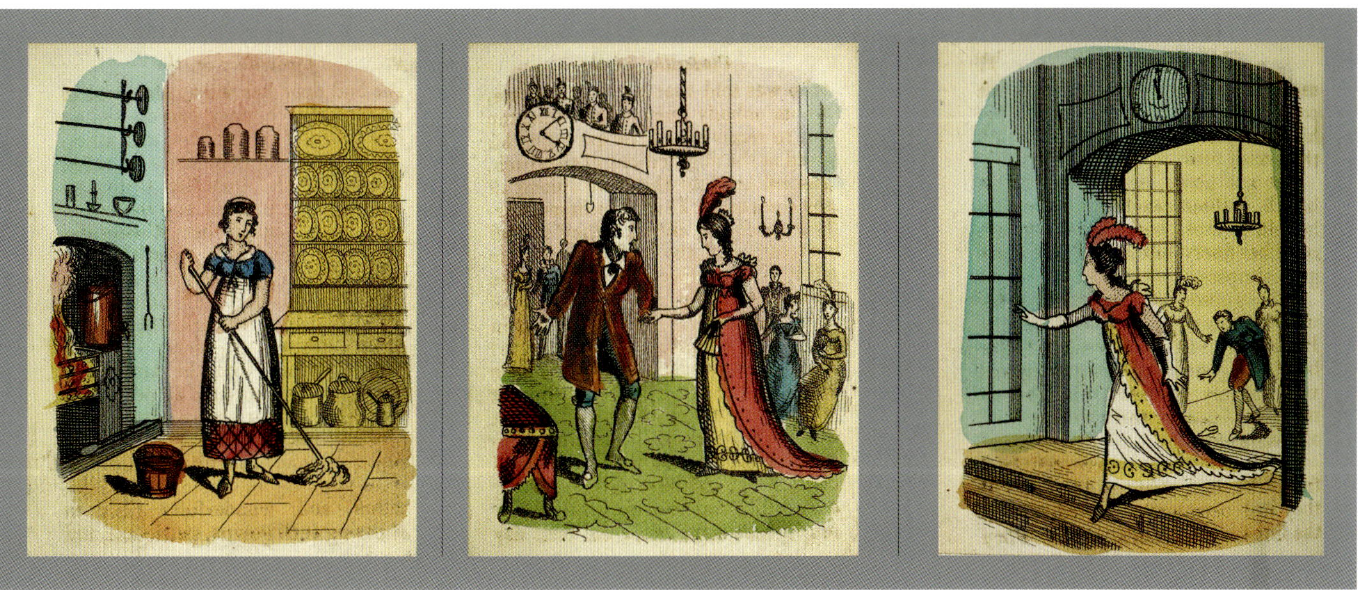

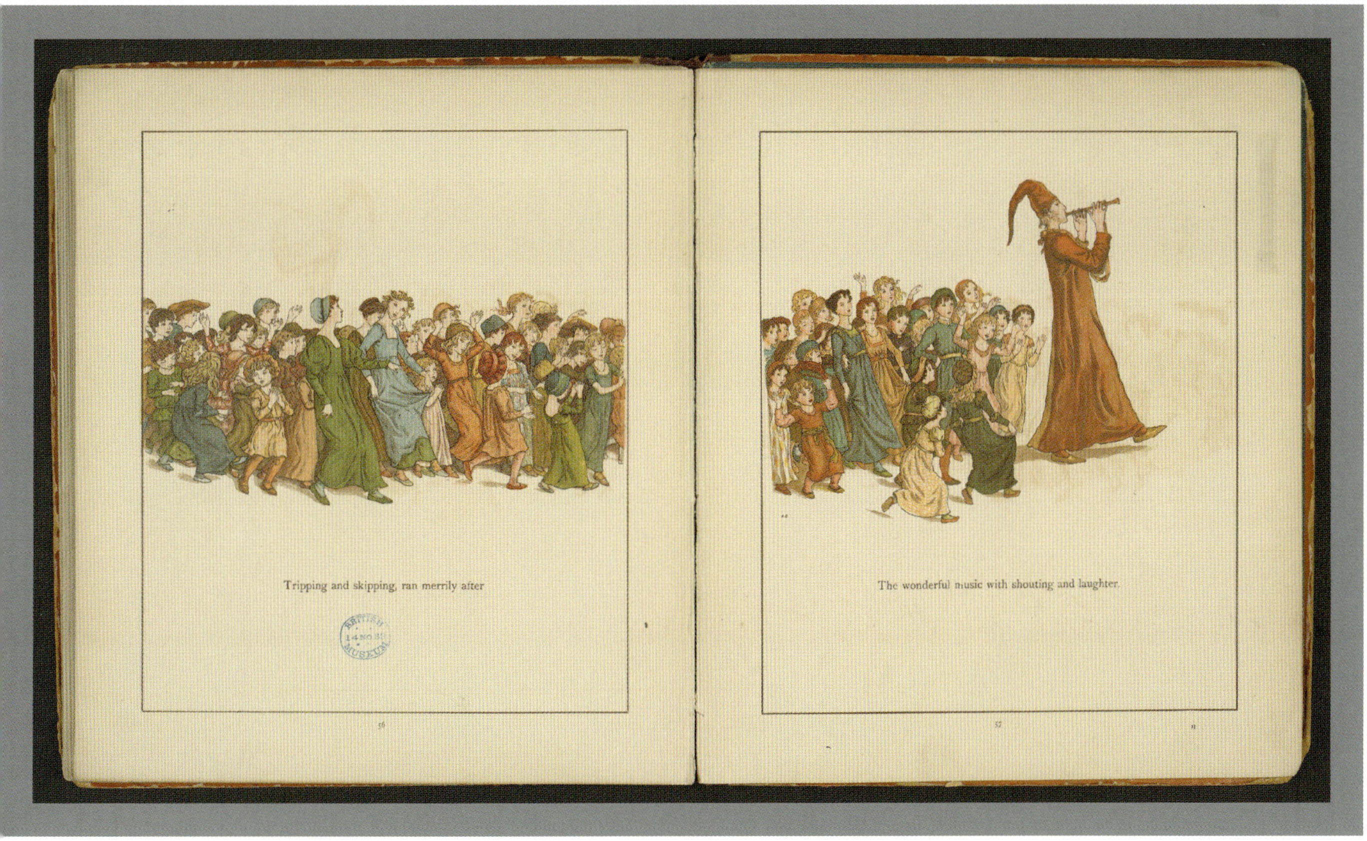

Tripping and skipping, ran merrily after
The wonderful music with shouting and laughter.

08.

01.

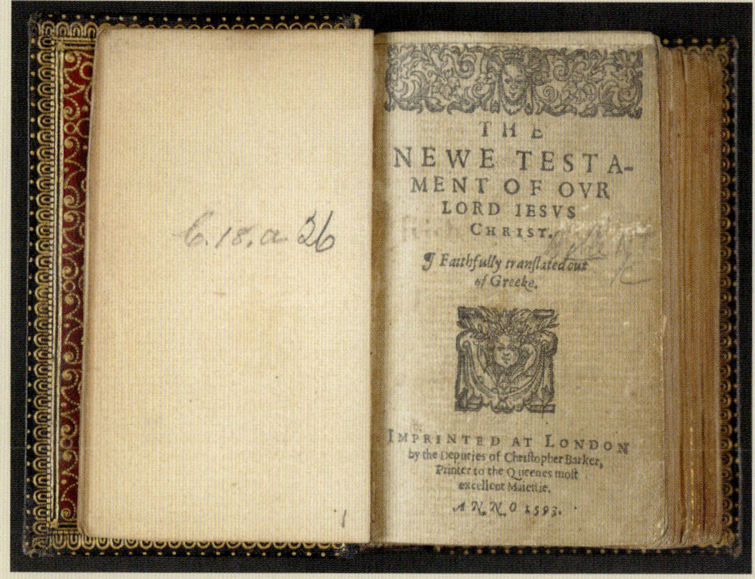
C.18.a.26
THE
NEWE TESTA-
MENT OF OVR
LORD IESVS
CHRIST.
Faithfully translated out
of Greeke.
IMPRINTED AT LONDON
by the Deputies of Christopher Barker,
Printer to the Queenes most
excellent Maiestie.
ANNO 1593.

02.

03.

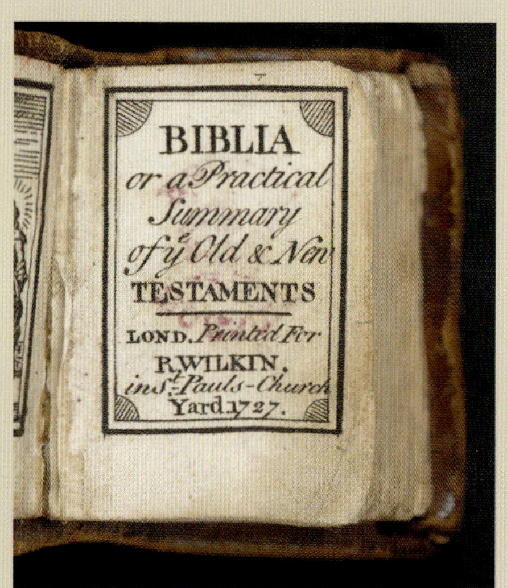
BIBLIA
or a Practical
Summary
of ye Old & New
TESTAMENTS
LOND. Printed For
R.WILKIN.
in St. Pauls-Church
Yard.1727.

MINIATURE BOOKS: THEIR CHARM AND PURPOSE

HELEN PEDEN AND ANNALISA RICCIARDI

Miniature books in both manuscript and printed format may measure no more than 76 millimetres in width, height or depth[1] yet a variety of subjects have been represented in this format. Religious texts for private meditation, works for ready reference and a whole library of favourite texts that would take little space when packed for travel could be ready for use whenever desired. Small books are also easy for small hands to hold, and many books for children and younger readers appeared in miniature size.

The production of these books demanded exceptional craftsmanship and use of the finest materials. Tiny letters and illustrations were printed on the thinnest paper, and presented in bindings that show the most delicate treatment to match the elegance of the pages. The challenge to present a great deal of information in the smallest and most portable format often resulted in miniature works of art,[2] as can be seen in this selection of printed miniature books from the British Library's collections.

This Bible of 1593 (Image 1) is one of the earliest printed miniature books in the British Library and is small enough to have been carried around and used for private contemplation. It is the first of two editions (the second edition was published in 1598) and among the books that are considered to mark the beginning of English miniature book production.

The decorations and type, together with the handsomely decorated binding, inner edges and end papers, reflect the printer's aim to create a beautiful design. The book bears witness to the strong religious feelings and convictions of the age, and also the artistic perfection that dominated the period.

A fashion for miniature or 'Thumb' Bibles developed during the seventeenth century. These contained abbreviated histories of the Bible in prose or verse but it was not until the publication of *Biblia, or a Practical Summary of ye Old & New Testaments*, printed in London for R. Wilkin, 1727, that we see the first children's abbreviated Bible printed in England intended to instruct children in Bible stories (Image 2).

Developments in printing technology throughout the nineteenth century allowed printers to produce even smaller books. David Bryce (1845–1924) of Glasgow was a prolific and successful maker of miniature books of the highest quality, with a particular interest in sacred works. After starting with Christian texts, in the mid-1890s he began publishing miniature Qur'ans for the large Indian market. These were printed on the thinnest India paper, then bound in red morocco with gilt-stamped decorations. They were issued with a magnifying glass set in a metal locket allowing these tiny books to be read and worn as protective amulets. Indeed, during the First World War the British authorities responded to the religious needs of Muslim troops by producing, acquiring and distributing, with the help of individuals, charities and official bodies, copies of Bryce's miniature Qur'ans to soldiers in hospitals and on the front lines.[3] The British Library holds an example (Image 3) of the kind of miniature Qur'an produced by Bryce which was owned by Indian soldiers fighting in the British army.[4]

Notable among English miniature almanacs is *The English bijou almanac*. The first almanac for 1836 is the smallest, and established the inclusion of portraits of famous writers, musicians, painters or stage

01. The Newe Testament, *Christopher Barker (London), 1593. (C.18.a.26, 75 by 51 mm, width by height)*

02. Biblia, or a Practical Summary of ye Old & New Testaments *(London), 1727. (C.180.a.5, 41 by 29 mm, width by height)*

03. *The Qur'an, David Bryce (Glasgow), c. 1900. (Or 70.a.3, 27 mm in height, in metal case 29 by 36 by 13 mm, width by height by depth)*

HEMANS.
THE
ENGLISH
Bijou
ALMANAC
FOR
1836.
Poetically Illustrated
by L.E.L.
LONDON.
Schloss, 2, Gt. Russell St.

BIJOU
ALMANACK.
1836.

THE
MITE

MITE.
Grimsby:
E A Robinson
1891.

THE
SAFEST SERIES
FOR
CHILDREN

London
Characters
PICTURES BY
JOHN HASSALL
VERSES BY
JESSIE POPE
London:
GRANT RICHARDS
1904

04.

05.

06.

07.

performers, accompanied by poems in praise of the personalities shown. The poems themselves are often the first appearance in print of the work of up and coming authors of the period. The early poems of L.E.L. (Letitia Elizabeth Landon, 1802–1838), who published a number of volumes of poetry and novels in 1837, is included here (Image 4).

When issued in 1891, *The Mite* was the smallest English book printed from movable type (Image 5). It contains statistical details and gems of printing information, including the invention of printing by Gutenberg. Attractively printed in red and black inks and bound in decorated leather, a copy of this unusual book forms part of the miniature Library of Queen Mary's Dolls' House.

Miniature curiosities include this little book (Image 6) disguised as a box of matches. It features coloured illustrations of London trades and professions by John Hassell (1868–1948), with verse by Jessie Pope (1868–1941), a successful writer of humorous verse. John Hassell worked from 1895 as an advertising artist for David Allen & Sons and may be better known for his posters using flat colours enclosed by bold black lines that encouraged people to explore England by train and London by the Underground.

Finally, this incredibly tiny book (Image 7) was the smallest printed book in the world in 1985, and remains the smallest printed book in the British Library. It was produced in Paisley, Scotland, in 1985 at the Gleniffer Press, an independent hobby press run by Ian and Helen Macdonald for forty years from 1967. *Old King Cole* was printed using offset lithography in a limited edition of eighty-five copies. The book measures 1 by 0.9 millimetre (width by height) and is mounted on a card that measures 28.5 by 37 millimetres (width by height). Since this is predominantly a presentation piece that demonstrates the skills of the Press, the printers included the text of three copies in a separate uncut sheet.

04. The English Bijou Almanac *[for 1836], Schloss (London), 1835. (C.17.b.10/1, 18 by 13 mm, width by height)*

05. The Mite, *Ernest A. Robinson (Grimsby), 1891. (C.0.a.6, 21 by 13 mm, width by height)*

06. London Characters, *Grant Richards (London), 1904. (C.0.e.5, 58 by 38 mm, width by height)*

07. Old King Cole, *The Gleniffer Press (Paisley), 1985. (RF.2005.b.171, no. 15 of 85 copies printed, 1 by 1 mm, width by height)*

XIII.

A QUR'AN FROM ACEH

An exemplar of the Acehnese style of manuscript illumination

ANNABEL TEH GALLOP

The northern tip of the island of Sumatra in present-day Indonesia was the site of the earliest Islamic kingdoms in Southeast Asia in the thirteenth century. By the sixteenth century Aceh had grown to become the most powerful sultanate in the region, and a renowned centre of Islamic learning, with close links to the holy cities of the Arabian peninsula. Aceh was a hive of literary and scribal activity, with a widespread network of religious schools where large numbers of Qur'ans and other Islamic manuscripts were copied, many of which are still held in Aceh today, in libraries, museums and private collections.

There are probably more illuminated Qur'an manuscripts from Aceh extant today – with more than 130 documented – than from any other region in Southeast Asia. In nearly all these Qur'ans, there is an extraordinary degree of conformity to a highly distinctive Acehnese style of illumination.[1] This style can be defined in terms of preferred decorative formats, palette and motifs common to all the manuscripts, while at the same time allowing for a considerable range of artistic sensibilities and technical competence. A finely illuminated Qur'an manuscript from Aceh in the British Library (Or 16915), dating from the early nineteenth century, can be regarded as an exemplar of the Acehnese style, exhibiting all the characteristic features of this artistic school.

Illumination in Qur'an manuscripts fulfils two main aims, the primary one being to adorn and beautify the Holy Book and hence honour the Word of God to evoke a sense of reverence and awe in the beholder. The second is mainly functional: illumination serves to guide the reader through the text, by signalling key junctures through strategically positioned graphic devices, particularly necessary in a book culture where pages were not traditionally numbered. These decorative elements range from tiny, coloured circles which serve to separate the verses, to grandiose illuminated frames across two facing pages, symmetrical across the gutter of the book. The artistic unity of the double-page spread is not unique to Aceh but is an integral component of the aesthetics of many Islamic manuscript cultures. In many Latin-script books (read from left to right) the text will begin on a right-hand page, with its own design scheme, with the opposite left-hand page either left blank or decorated in its own right (as can be seen in the Lindisfarne Gospels). In Arabic-script books (which are read from right to left) the text will usually begin on a right-hand page and then continue onto the facing left-hand page, with decoration applied equally and symmetrically across both pages.

In this British Library Qur'an from Aceh, the opening illuminated frames function as a symbolic gateway into the Holy Book, surrounding the entire first chapter, *Surat al-Fatihah* (which translates as 'Chapter of the Opener'), on the right-hand page, and the first verses of the second chapter, *Surat al-Baqarah* ('The Cow'), on the left-hand page (Image 2). All the key elements of the Acehnese style of illumination can be seen in these double decorated frames. The small text blocks on each page are surrounded by decorated rectangular panels, the outer vertical borders of which are extended upwards and downwards, with the tips sloping inwards. On the three outer sides of the panels there are arches, in this case composed of triangles adorned with small foliate motifs in alternating red and yellow, topped by a finial, with the arches on the outer vertical sides flanked by a pair of 'wings'. The palette is limited to red, yellow

01. *Brown cloth binding of the Qur'an with a cut-out appliquéd paper pattern inscribed with the* shahada *and its leather wrapper.*

01.

03.

Specification	*Scale*
QUR'AN Aceh, Indonesia, *c.* 1820s 330 x 205 mm Or 16915	

and black, but the most important 'colour', which carries the main motifs, is 'reserved white', which is not a pigment at all, but the background colour of the cream paper which has been left uncoloured to pick out the design. In these frames, the high proportion of white against a ground of red and yellow imbues the traceried patterns with lightness and an ethereal delicacy.

Double frames are also found at the end of the Qur'an, enclosing the two final chapters: *Surat al-Falaq* ('Dawn') on the right, and *Surat al-Nas* ('Mankind') on the left (Image 3). Although each of the building blocks of these frames is different from those at the beginning of the manuscript, exactly the same architectural principles are adhered to: decorated panels around the text blocks extend upwards and downward on the pages, and are adorned on the three outer sides with arches. On these pages the arches are ogival domes rather than triangles, but those on the vertical sides are still flanked by small foliate tendrils. The same colours of red, yellow and black are used and, again, reserved white plays the dominant role in carrying the scrolling floral motifs, albeit in completely different designs from those found at the beginning. Of particular interest is the plaited rope picked out in the arches at the top and bottom of the frames, for this motif is one of the most distinctive features of Acehnese illumination, but is not encountered in any other Southeast Asian Qur'an manuscripts.

A third pair of illuminated frames – similar to those at the end, but with different floral patterns – is found in the centre of the book (Image 5). The placement of the illuminated frames in the middle of a Southeast Asian Qur'an manuscript is an important indicator of its regional origin: in Qur'ans from Terengganu and Patani on the east coast of the Malay peninsula it is the beginning of *Surat al-Isra'* (Q.17, 'The Night Journey') that is highlighted; manuscripts from Java and Sulawesi mark the beginning of *Surat al-Kahf* (Q.18, 'The Cave'); while in Aceh it is always verse 75 of *Surat al-Kahf* which is illuminated, marking the exact midpoint of the Qur'anic text, at the beginning of the sixteenth *juz'* or thirtieth part of the Qur'an.

These three similar-yet-different pairs of illuminated frames in the British Library's Aceh Qur'an illustrate well the basic tenets of Acehnese illumination, namely double frames faithfully constructed according to an acknowledged set of architectural principles, filled with an infinite variety of scrolling floral and foliate motifs, realised in a palette centred on red, yellow and black – in some manuscripts supplemented by other colours such as green or blue – but with the primary role always accorded to reserved white. Unlike in some other parts of Southeast Asia, gold is never used in illuminated Acehnese Qur'an manuscripts, and there may be (as yet unidentified) theological reasons for this reticence in a region otherwise famed for fine gold-working skills, including the weaving of textiles with gold thread.

Throughout Southeast Asia, the impact of the beautiful double, decorated frames is heightened by the fact that illumination in Qur'an manuscripts is applied sparingly, leaving most pages essentially plain (Image 6). The layout of these text pages is very typical of Acehnese Qur'an manuscripts: the text is written in black ink, with fifteen lines per page, neatly justified on each line through the Arabic script's innate ability to extend or compress horizontal ligatures between letters in order to fit into an alloted space. On every page the text block is enclosed by frames comprising four parallel ruled ink lines, in alternating colours (from inside to out) of red-black-red-black. It is notable that even simple features like this can be regionally distinctive: this particular combination of red and black ruled frames is uniquely found in Aceh, and by itself would be almost sufficient to identify the Acehnese origin of a Qur'an manuscript. It is

02. *Opening pages of the Qur'an, with* Surat al-Fatihah *on the right-hand page and the beginning of* Surat al-Baqarah *on the left. (ff. 2v–3r)*

03. *Final decorated frames at the end of the Qur'an, enclosing* Surat al-Falaq *on the right-hand page, and* Surat al-Nas *on the left. (ff. 254v–255r)*

04 (pages 162–163). *Opening decorated frames displayed against leather wrapper.*

evident that the frames were only added after the text was first copied and then carefully checked, for at the top of one page the frames artfully step up and down around a few added words which had originally inadvertently been left out (Image 7).

Even on the relatively plain text pages, graphic devices may be placed to help the reader to navigate through the book, notably to signify textual divisions. The Qur'an is divided into 114 chapters or *surah*s, which are not organised chronologically but by length, with the exception of the first short chapter. Thus, the second chapter, *Surat al-Baqarah*, is the longest, with 286 verses, while the briefest chapters – some containing as few as three verses – are clustered together at the end. In this manuscript all the *surah* headings are set in panels bordered by red-black-red ruled frames, with the *surah* title written in red ink, stating the number of verses it contains, and whether it was revealed in Mecca or Medinah. In the double frames at the beginning and end of the manuscript, the *surah* headings are set in bespoke panels above and below the text block in decorative calligraphy in reserved white on coloured ground. In the first chapters the script of the *surah* headings is relatively staid (see Image 2), but in the final ones it is bold and elaborate, weaving letters around and in between purely decorative flourishes in a dazzling and almost modernist composition (see Image 3).

For readers and memorisers of the Qur'an, more important than the arrangement of the chapters is the division of the full text into thirty parts of equal length, called *juz'* (plural form *ajza'*), which cut across the *surah*s. This mode of division is of particular benefit in planning the recitation of the complete Qur'an within one month, especially in the holy fasting month of Ramadan. Each *juz'* can also further be divided into two, four or eight parts of equal length, so that the daily recitation portion of one *juz'* can be spread equably across the hours.

The division of the Qur'an into *juz'* and parts thereof plays a crucial role in the design and mise-en-page of Qur'anic manuscripts, because these divisions can be marked in manuscripts with a variety of graphical devices, usually in a scale of complexity in direct proportion to the size of the portion of text signified. In the Aceh Qur'an, each new *juz'* is heralded in manifold ways: an elaborate ornament is placed in the centre of the vertical margin of the page; the exact starting point in the text is marked with a composite roundel; and the first line is set within red frames, with the text written in red ink (all shown in Image 5). Subdivision of a *juz'* into halves (*nisf*), quarters (*rubu'*) and eighths (*thumn*) is similarly indicated with a decorative medallion, albeit on a less elaborate scale, placed in the middle of the outer vertical margin, while the exact point of commencement of the respective part is indicated in the text with a smaller decorative roundel (all shown in Image 8).

Each of these marginal ornaments – whether indicating a *juz'* (see Images 6 & 10) or one of its fractions (see Image 8) – is composed on a standard template of between two and five concentric circles, in different colours, each separated with a thin circle of reserved white. In the centre is a pattern made up of intersecting arcs, allowing for great variation through the symmetrical colouring of different portions of the pattern. From the circumference, clusters of small dots and rays may emanate, usually constructed on a four-fold or eight-fold principle. The ornaments which indicate *juz'* are adorned with more elaborate and expansive foliate tendrils and finials than accorded the subdivisions. The astonishing fact is that this somewhat limited range of constituent components and a simple palette of red, yellow, black and reserved white has yielded an almost infinite range of ornaments – to be precise, every single one of twenty-eight *juz'* markers (note that *juz'* 1 and 16 are heralded by double decorated frames) and 210 indicators for parts of *juz'* is unique, reflecting the artist's skill for endless improvisation on a single theme. It is perhaps not entirely surprising that towards the end of the volume the artistic energies of the illuminator begin to flag, for the *juz'* ornaments reduce in scale to match the medallions for the smaller textual divisions, and from the twenty-eighth *juz'* onwards, most of the marginal ornaments are uncoloured and undeveloped concentric circles.

05. *The centre pages of the Qur'an, marking the start of* juz' *16 (Q. 18:75). (ff. 132v–133r)*

06. *Pages of the Qur'an, showing the start of* Surat al-Hijr *and a marginal ornament indicating the beginning of* juz' *14, with the* surah *heading and the first line of the* juz' *each in red ink and set within ruled frames. (ff. 117v–118r)*

05.

06.

07.

08.

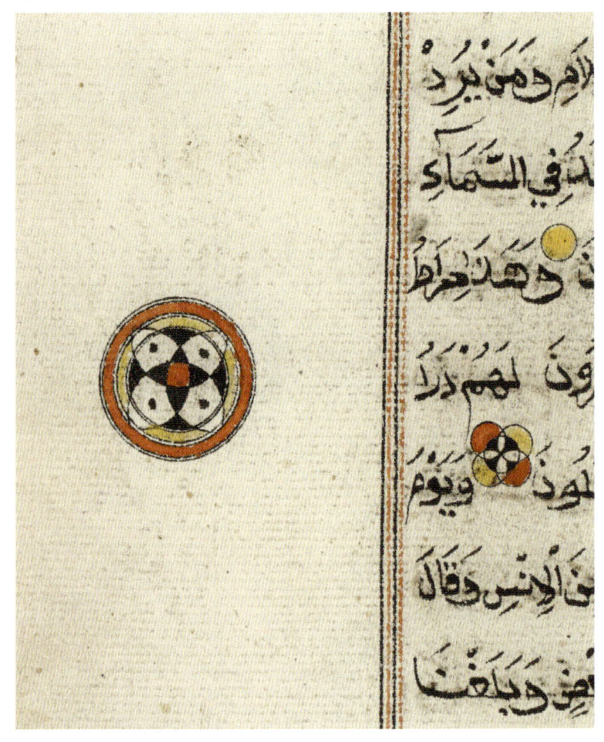

09.

10.

The smallest unit of textual division of the Qur'an indicates verses or *ayah*, and these appear in our manuscript – as in most other Acehnese Qur'ans – as small black ink circles coloured in yellow. These roundels are perfect circles drawn mechanically as if with a compass, but it is not known whether a specific tool was used or a clever scribal technique was employed. And it is these same small circles, combined in multiple intersecting forms and then coloured, which make up the composite roundels placed within the text which indicate the start of fractions of each *juz'* (see Image 8).

Like most Qur'an manuscripts from the Malay world, this manuscript has no colophon with information on the identity of the scribe or artist, or on the place of production or date, but the English paper used is watermarked 'J Whatman 1819', suggesting that it might have been copied some time in the 1820s. Indeed, in studying the art of the Qur'an in Southeast Asia, we are greatly hindered by the complete absence of any referential literature either from within the tradition, or from without. There are no Malay manuals of manuscript illumination which might cast light on the working practices and procedures of scribes and artists, and the otherwise copious and valuable accounts of Western merchant travellers to Southeast Asia from the seventeenth century onwards are noticeably silent on religious book culture. Thus, what we know of how the artists and scribes worked has to be gleaned from a forensic examination of the primary evidence of the manuscripts themselves. As noted above, we do know for certain that the text frames were added after the text was written (see Image 7). We can also surmise from the unfinished marginal ornaments at the end of the manuscript that the base shapes of concentric circles and arced centres were first drawn in black ink throughout the whole manuscript, before being revisited from the beginning, to be coloured in and further elaborated. There are also hints that in some places marginal ornaments which had been completed, were further adorned with foliate flourishes, some of which have been left uncoloured in black ink (Image 9). In view of the relative lack of balance and symmetry of these free-hand additions, they may have been done by someone different and less accomplished than the consummate artist responsible for the double frames.

The covers of this Aceh Qur'an are of considerable interest. It has an original cloth binding of coarse brown cotton, but what is uniquely Acehnese is the appliquéd cut-out paper pattern stuck on to both front and back covers. A number of examples of such paper patterns have been documented, including on another Aceh Qur'an in the British Library, Or 16034, but that found on this manuscript is especially notable for the calligraphic panel across the top in reserved white on a black ground, repeating the first part of the *shahada*, the Muslim profession of faith – *La ilaha illa Allah*, 'There is no god but God' – on the front cover (Image 1), and the word *Allah* on the back cover. The stylish calligraphy, with floriated ends of letters and overlapping strokes, is typically Acehnese and recalls the imaginative *surah* headings in the decorated frames at the end of the Qur'an (see Image 3). Finally, the whole volume is enclosed within a loose, full-leather wrapper in the Islamic style, with an 'envelope flap' and stamped ornamental medallions, cornerpieces and frame bands.

This beautiful Qur'an was purchased by the British Library in 2014, from the London dealer Amir Mohtashemi, who had acquired it at the auction of a deceased estate in Germany. Like many other manuscripts from Aceh now held in Europe – including two others now in the British Library, Or 15406 and Or 16034 – it was probably brought from Aceh in the late nineteenth century following the Dutch invasion in 1873. This attack marked the start of a thirty-year war, during which many manuscripts were destroyed while others were seized by Dutch forces or those in their employ. As a result, Qur'an manuscripts from Aceh can now be found in collections all over Europe, including in Denmark, Belgium and Austria, as well as in the Netherlands and Britain.

07. *The text frames are carefully drawn around a portion of text which has been added above the top line. (f. 207r)*

08. *Marginal ornament for a fraction of a* juz'*, with a composite roundel in the text at the exact point of the division, and a verse marker in yellow. (f. 64r)*

09. *Marginal ornament for a fraction of a* juz'*, with subsequently added foliate decoration in black ink. (f. 49r)*

10. *A marginal ornament marking the start of* juz' *15. (f. 126r)*

XIV.

OWEN JONES'S *THE GRAMMAR OF ORNAMENT*

Experimentation with a new visual language

EDMUND M. B. KING

INTRODUCTION

Owen Jones was an architect, designer and printer. *The Grammar of Ornament*, published in 1856, was a global and historical design sourcebook, based on his design philosophy built up over twenty years' experience. Both before and after 1856, his desire for good design in all forms of artistic endeavour would continue to inform his work to create books for the literate middle classes. The half title page of *The Grammar* (Image 1) shows the obvious visual immediacy and complexity possible using chromolithography. The elaboration of the medieval-style letters, surrounded by dense foliage, strikes the eye immediately. Chromolithography empowered Jones's designs, with much of his work in this medium fitting more generally alongside developments in wood engravings for book illustration in the 1840s and 1850s. The growth of illustrations in books and magazines demanded increased organisation and timely delivery on the part of engravers. The Dalziel Brothers, the workshop of Joseph Swain and the colour printing of Edmund Evans are examples. Increased demand and output led to the systematic use of stereotyping and electrotyping of the original letterpress and engravings.[1] For successful production, the relationships between artist, editor, publisher, author and engraver were complex and occasionally difficult.

Chromolithography – a method for making multi-colour prints – evolved rapidly from its inception in the 1820s. Each colour for an illustration had to be drawn separately on a set of stones (later plates), with the stones applied to the paper one at a time to build up the colours and the image. Each sheet of paper passed through the printing press as many times as there were colours in the final print. To create the print, each stone or plate had to be precisely registered, or lined up using register marks. Exact registration of each colour upon the sheet was critical to its final quality. The more colours used, the greater the need for good registration. A key feature of its adoption in book production was its success, during this period, of astonishingly detailed colour reproductions for expensive books.[2] Mass production was achieved, as very large print runs of sheet music with chromolithographed title pages testify.

From the 1820s onwards, book and magazine publishers sensed new markets. In this period, there were dozens of daily and weekly newspapers published in London (also distributed across the country). Hundreds of advertisements were regularly purchased to publicise the issue of books, magazines and theatre performances, both in London and the provinces. As a beneficiary of this widening of markets, Owen Jones was involved with the production of some fifty-four books for the period 1836–67.[3] The majority of these were advertised, or reviewed, in contemporary newspapers.[4]

IMPACT OF TRAVEL ON JONES'S DESIGN PHILOSOPHY

As Jones developed his architectural studies, he did not find himself in sympathy with the contemporary neo-classical and Gothic Revival fashions of the times. His journeys to Spain, Italy, Greece, Constantinople, India and Egypt motivated him to adopt a cosmopolitan view. Every region had its history of decorative schemes. Perhaps the most inspirational example for Jones was to be found

01. *Illuminated half title page: decorated capital letters and medieval style lettering. (RB.31.c.200)*

01.

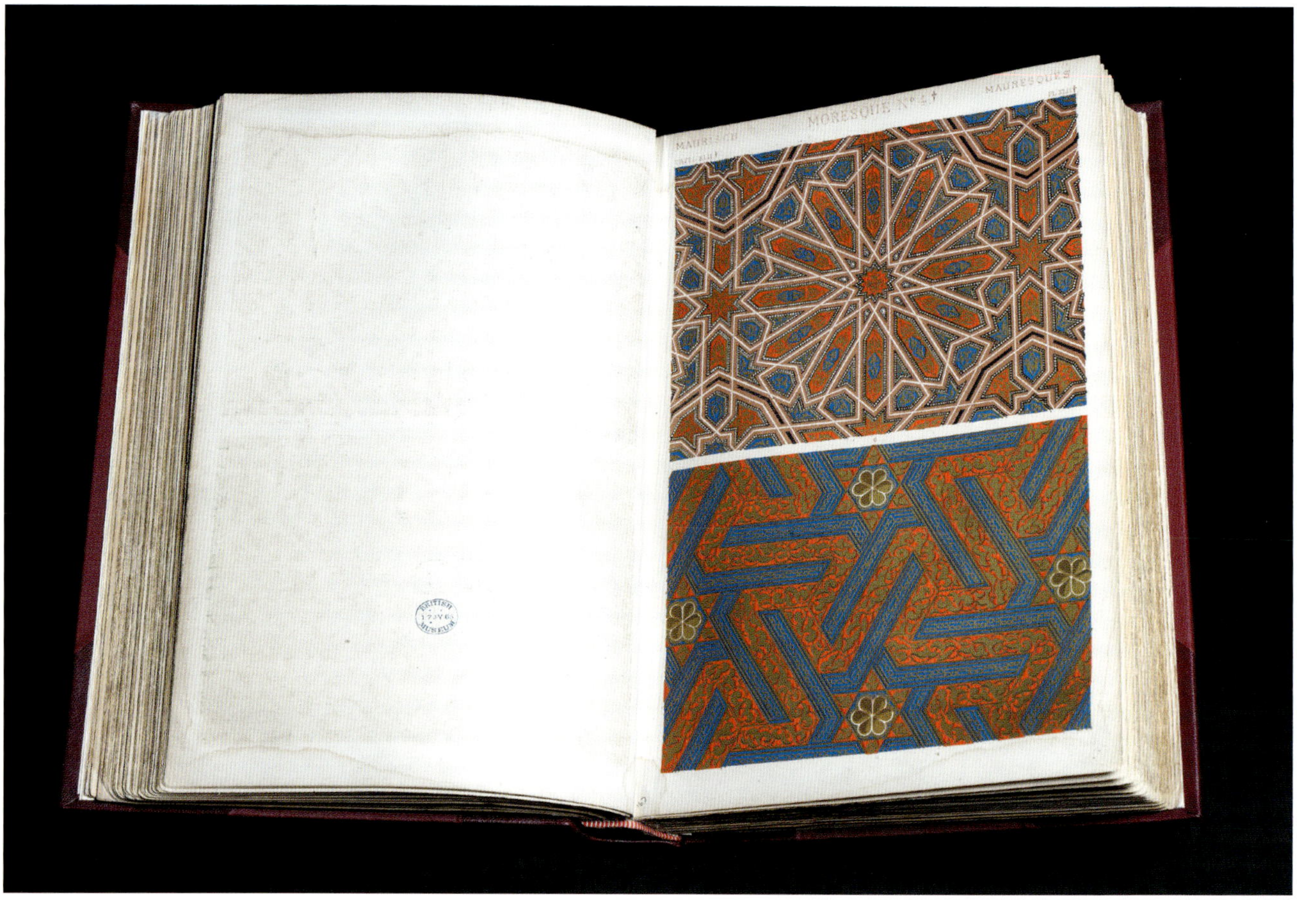

03.

in the Alhambra Palace in Granada, where he explored the vibrant Islamic motifs, polychromy and the underlying geometry. How could these be explained to those at home? A new visual language was needed.

Jones's studies on the Alhambra Palace with the French architect Jules Goury resulted in the publication of *Plans, Elevations, Sections and Details of the Alhambra* (1842–45).[5] Originally issued in parts (from 1836), this book was one of the finest early uses of chromolithography.[6] To ensure a professional standard hitherto unknown in England, Jones undertook the work of producing the chromolithographs himself, setting up a workshop in John Street, London, which he ran for the next ten years. The publication costs were very great, putting a strain on his finances. The prices for the individual parts and the bound volumes could only be afforded by the wealthy.[7]

JONES'S WORK IN THE 1850S

Later, Jones had the role of Superintendent of Works for the Great Exhibition of the Works of Industry of All Nations – the World's Fair held in London's Hyde Park in 1851. The cast iron and plate glass structure to house the exhibition – the Crystal Palace – was designed by Joseph Paxton; Jones worked on the arrangements of the exhibits and the interior decoration of the building, advancing his theories about colour. In 1852, a series of lectures was given to the Society of Arts, summarising the results of the Great Exhibition. Jones lectured on the 'Principles which should regulate the Employment of Colour in the Decorative arts'.[8] Jones ended his lecture with 'a few words on the necessity of an architectural education on the part of the public', advocating bringing art knowledge within the reach of all, stating: 'every town should have its art-museum, every village a drawing-school; every parent should educate himself in art'. In his lecture, one sees the seeds of *The Grammar*.

02. *Plate XLII, 'Moresque no. 4'. Repetition of simple elements to produce complicated effects.*

03. *Plate XLIII, 'Moresque no. 5'. Geometrical combinations.*

04 (page 172). *Cloth upper cover, showing lettering and Greek key border.*

05 (page 173). *Corner detail of Plate XLVI, 'Persian no. 3'.*

Interest in the designs of previous ages had been stimulated by all these developments.[9] Jones went on to design four interior courts for the Sydenham Crystal Palace (built by 1854) – the Egyptian, Greek, Roman and Alhambra. In bringing his *The Grammar* to a wider public, he wished students to 'endeavour to search out the thoughts which have been expressed in so many different languages, so that he may assuredly hope to find an ever gushing fountain [of good design]'. Jones also firmly states 'that the future of ornamental art may be best secured by engrafting on the experience of the past the knowledge we may obtain by a return to Nature for fresh inspiration'.

What sets *The Grammar of Ornament* apart from other contemporary efforts is Jones's introduction and propositions: 'General Principles in the Arrangement of Form and Colour, in Architecture and the Decorative Arts, which are advocated throughout this Work'. With twenty chapters describing styles of ornament of past ages from across the world, arranged chronologically, each has its own commentary. These explanatory texts were accompanied by 100 high-grade chromolithographs, which are numbered as a single sequence across all the chapters. The illustrations clarify meaning through seeing, frequently juxtaposing different sizes of form and colour. It is small wonder that the book became such a success.

The Preface to the Folio Edition states that Jones's pupils engaged in the execution and reduction of the drawings were Albert Warren, Charles Aubert and Mr. Stubbs. For the drawing upon stone, Francis Bedford was assisted by H. Fielding, W. R. Tymms, A. Warren and S. Sedgefield. The

04.

22

ground-breaking nature of the work was Jones's supervision of the whole. *The Grammar* was innovative in its combination of erudition and colour printing. Originally issued in parts, the cost was 4s. 6d. each.[10] The publication of the bound-up parts cost £19 12s. and was most likely offered to subscribers.[11] Even at this price, its sale was advertised in newspapers.[12]

Specification	*Scale*
THE GRAMMAR OF ORNAMENT London: Day & Son, 1865 570 x 390 mm 1756.a.25	

THE IMPACT OF *THE GRAMMAR OF ORNAMENT* ON COVER DESIGNS FOR GUINEA BOOKS

The *Grammar* undoubtedly influenced the production of highly decorated guinea books with oriental ornament. If the distinctiveness of *The Grammar* was its range of historical designs and its folio size, it was part of a continuum, emerging from many other illustrated book designs (including book covers) undertaken before and after 1856. Publishers realised that an audience existed for 'quality' books decorated with wood engravings or chromolithographs, with elaborate cover designs created to make a strong visual impression. Other publishers did avail themselves of the design concepts published in the *Grammar*. A particular market existed for expensive gift books, costing one guinea (equivalent to £136 in 2020), usually published just before Christmas. Frequently the content of these decorated books was poetry, aphorisms, emblems; the texts were recycled from earlier editions, with illustrations specially commissioned from prominent artists. These were high-status books, created by publishers such as Longman, Routledge, Nisbet, A&C Black, David Bogue, Richard Bentley, Cassell & Co. and Smith, Elder & Co. The price enabled the engraving of elaborate brass blocks, often with very dense decoration, for stamping on to covers and spine. Advertisements paid for by publishers or local booksellers, just before or after Christmas, were used to launch sales. Discounts could be offered straight away. Booksellers also discounted published prices in an effort to widen clientele.[13] Considerable costs in the production of guinea books were incurred. The class of reader who purchased these had annual incomes over £300 – professionals, merchants, bankers, industrialists. Images 6–12 show the skill of die-cutters in creating brass blocks for book covers, just as the plates for *The Grammar* show the skills of the artists who drew upon stone.

06., 07. & 08. The Book of Job *(C.109.d.6) was published by Nisbet in 1857. Each cover features a large oval centrepiece, with elaborate tracery, as is also shown for Plate LIII of* The Grammar *(07); we see also the repeating flower head decoration in the corners, similar to those spandril/cornerpiece patterns in Plate XL (08).*

The Book of Job, was published by Nisbet in 1857.[14] Each cover features a large oval centrepiece, with elaborate tracery, as is also shown for Plate LIII of *The Grammar*; we see also the repeating flower head decoration in the corners, similar to those spandril/cornerpiece patterns in Plate XL.

Works of popular authors were issued by different publishers quite quickly one after another. In 1860, both Routledge and Longman published editions of Thomas Moore's popular work, *Lallah Rookh*. The Routledge edition of 1860 has a cover design of interlaced patterns, as illustrated in *The Grammar*, 'Moresque no. 1', Plate XXIX. The book was advertised in time for Christmas sales.[15]

The Longman edition of *Lallah Rookh*, published in 1861 has illustrations after John Tenniel. This cover design has similarities to the patterns displayed in the *Grammar*,'Persian, no. 3', Plate XLVI. Both this book and the Routledge edition have

06.

07.

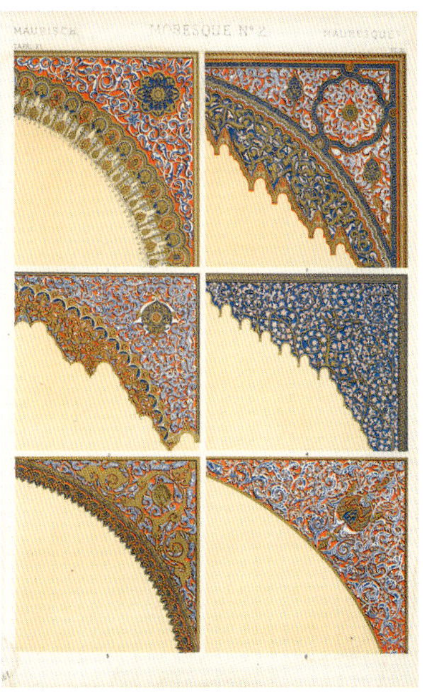

08.

09.

LALLA ROOKH
THOMAS MOORE

MAURISCH
MORESQUE Nº 1.
MAURESQUES

10.

LALLA ROOKH

11.

PERSISCH
PERSIAN Nº 3
PERSES

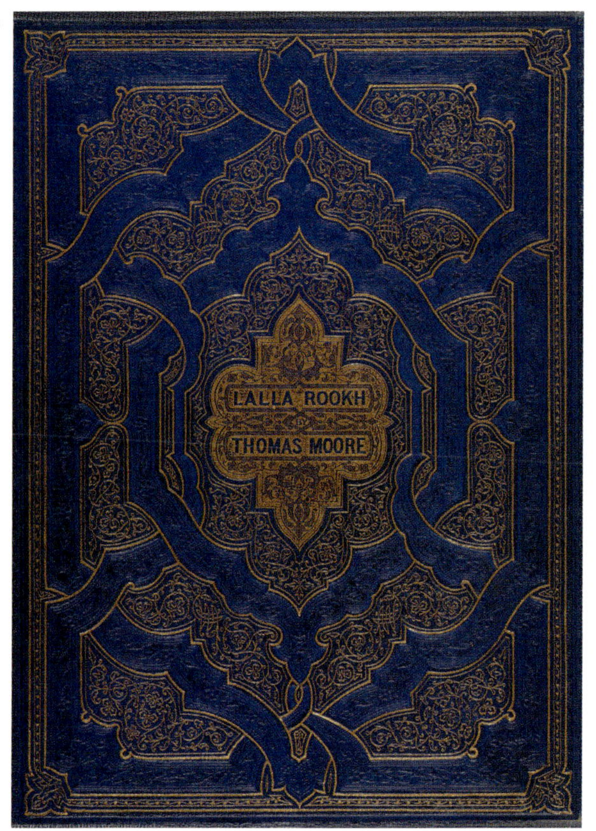

12.

binders' tickets of Leighton, Son & Hodge. The Routledge copy is bound in blue morocco vertical-grain cloth, and the Longman copy is bound in purple coarse pebble-grain cloth.[16]

READERSHIP AND AUDIENCES

Set in the 1880s/90s, Arnold Bennett's *Clayhanger* describes the domestic setting for expensive books. There was a distinctive element of one-upmanship, of conspicuous consumption, between the Orgreave and Clayhanger families, which included the display of books alongside many other household objects. In the Orgreave family, Tom Orgreave collected books with 'rich bindings': 'As Edwin gazed at the bookcase...he saw that a book might be more than reading matter, might be a bibelot, a curious jewel, to satisfy the lust of the eye and of the hand.'[17] Numerous publishers paid for newspaper and magazine advertisements for the sale of the books designed by Owen Jones and his contemporaries, together with the guinea books discussed in this chapter.

CONCLUSION

What seems remarkable to us today is the speed with which this market for luxury books developed from the 1840s (paralleled by the market for cheaper books), and its spread to the whole of the British Isles. Rapid distribution of large quantities of books was enabled by the development of the railways. From the 1830s to the mid-1860s, thousands of expensive books were promoted and sold energetically by publishers and booksellers alike. Owen Jones was, with many other publishers and artists, fully alive to the realities of publishing highly priced books, of selling them, all of which helped to promote his theories of design and art education.

The influence of *The Grammar* has lasted. William Morris is known to have used the work;[18] his emphasis upon the use of natural forms for design echoed chapter XX of *The Grammar*, 'Leaves and Flowers from Nature' (Plates XCI–C). Like Owen Jones, leading Arts and Crafts designers were architects: Christopher Dresser, Edwin Lutyens and, later, Frank Lloyd Wright and Le Corbusier.[19] Owen Jones's studies of the designs of the past, as encapsulated in *The Grammar*, provided a guide for contemporaries and laid the foundations of future progress in the field. In this brief account, it is difficult to convey the multiple impressions on the mind of the 100 plates in *The Grammar*. It is fortunate that copies can still be acquired to provide art education. In addition, scans of the plates are available online.[20]

(13.)

09. & 10. *Works of popular authors were issued by different publishers quite quickly one after another. In 1860 and 1861, both Routledge and Longman published editions of Thomas Moore's popular work,* Lallah Rookh. *The Routledge edition of 1860 (C.109.d.9) has a cover design of interlaced patterns, as illustrated in* The Grammar, *'Moresque no. 1', Plate XXIX. The book was advertised in time for Christmas sales.*

11. & 12. *The Longman edition of* Lallah Rookh *(BM P&D 1992.0406.231), published in 1861, has illustrations after John Tenniel. This cover design has similarities to the patterns displayed in* The Grammar, *'Persian, no. 3', Plate XLVI. Both this book and the Routledge edition have binders' tickets of Leighton, Son & Hodge. The Routledge copy is bound in blue morocco vertical-grain cloth, and the Longman copy is bound in purple coarse pebble-grain cloth.*

13. *Detail from Plate XIV 'Nineveh & Persian no. 3'.*

AMERICAN PUBLISHERS' BINDINGS, NINETEENTH CENTURY

EDMUND M. B. KING

In the nineteenth century, the decoration of American publishers' bindings developed rapidly, mirroring developments in the UK. These were mass-produced books, sold in bindings, most frequently with paper or cloth covers. The blocking of designs onto covers and spines, using gold leaf, became widespread from the 1840s. Binding cases were blocked with decoration and then attached to text blocks. Designs reflected art movements, with Arts and Crafts and Art Nouveau influences becoming prominent from the 1880s, using naturalistic forms. Artists were employed by publishers specifically to create cover designs for a particular book. Blocking in colours as well as gold gave an impressionistic, pictorial immediacy. The sense of adventure and discovery that accompanied American expansion frequently found expression in these bindings, as publishers realised that eye-catching cover designs enhanced sales.[1]

In the early decades, printed paper covers that were cheap to produce were common, for example in *The Art of Angling* ... (1833), which features a full-length fish printed on its front cover (Image 1).

Elaborately blocked gilt designs featured by the 1850s, such as the dense plant and lattice work on the covers of *Town and Country* (1855), (Image 2).

John Feely, an immigrant die-cutter from England, was commissioned over many years to make dozens of designs, such as on Robert Burns's epic poem *Tam O'Shanter* (1868), which featured the title centred, within an 'Arabian'-style oval, with lattice work (Image 3)

Later, the influence of Art Nouveau resulted in 'naturalistic' designs, *In the Tideway* (1897) being a typical example, with a cover design by George Wharton Edwards, known for his Impressionist paintings (Image 4).

A 'frame and foliage' design was provided by Alice Cordelia Morse for Theodore Child's *Summer Holidays: Travelling Notes in Europe* (1889), (Image 5). Her work was inspired by the Arts and Crafts movement. This design provides similarities to Owen Jones's 'rustic frame' cover design for *A Jar of Honey from Mount Hybla* (1848), created a generation earlier. The Henry Altemus Company of Philadelphia published large numbers of books on all subjects; in its Vademecum Series, no. 18, there is a striking multi-coloured design for the work on philosophy, *The Thoughts of Marcus Aurelius* (*c.*1890) (Image 6).

An echo of Toulouse Lautrec's poster art is to be found on the covers of *America and the Americans from a French point of view* (1897), by the travel writer Price Collier, showing a well-dressed man and lady in profile, set against a backdrop of an industrial landscape (Image 7).

Other landscape scenes use contrast on covers between light and dark, as in the explorer Mary Evelyn Hitchcock's account of *Two Women of the Klondike*: *The story of a journey to the gold-fields of Alaska* (1899), their silhouettes shadowed against the snow-covered mountains (Image 8).

The 'American Dream' is exemplified by Edward Sylvester Ellis's story of William McKinley, *From Tent to White House, or How a poor boy became President* (c. 1899). Published by H. M. Caldwell one edition has a cover design of a man driving a motor car, by Harry B. Matthews[2] (Image 9).

Another edition, also issued by H. M. Caldwell, has a cover design of a young man seated against a tree, by Rome K. Richardson.[3]

Cover designs such as these were typical of their time. They convey a contemporary view by publishers as to appropriate enhancement of the book. Decoration on paper covers, on gilded cloth covers, on 'pictorial' multi-coloured covers – all served the purpose of enhancing sales.

Top row: 01. *(C.109.a.57)*, 02. *(C.129. f. 6)*, 03. *(11651.k.14)*.
Middle row: 04. *(C.188.a.401)*, 05. *(10108.de.6)*, 06. *(C.108.n.24)*.
Bottom row: 07. *(10413.e.13)*, 08. *(10470. ff. 22)*, 09. *(C.188.a.396)*.

01.

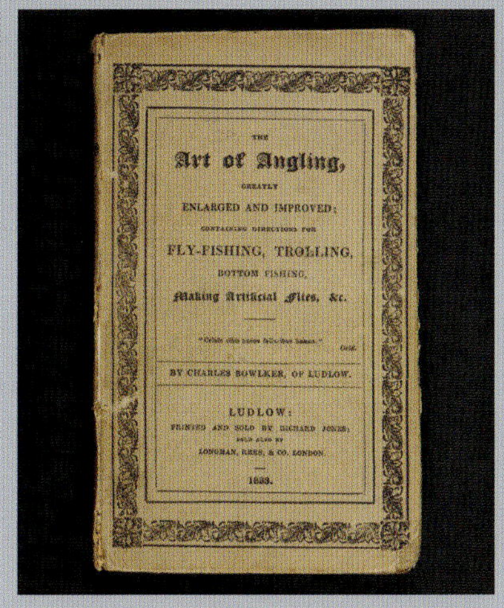

02.

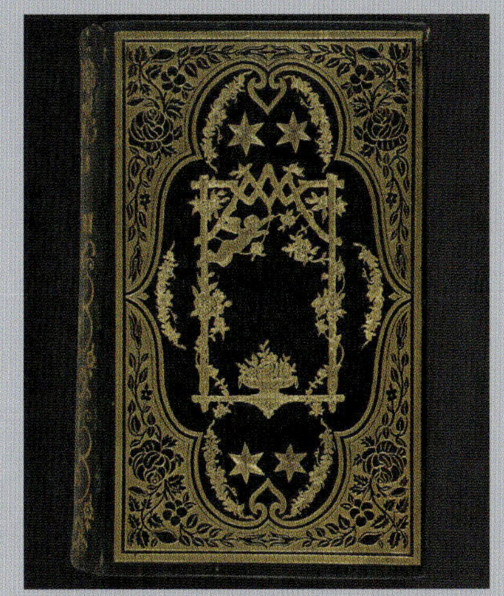

03.

04.

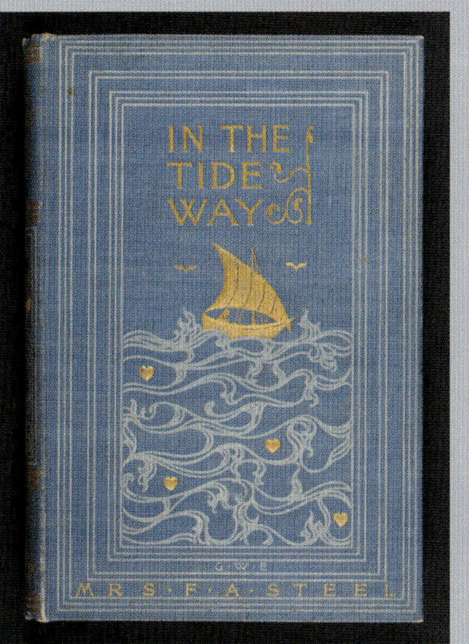

05.

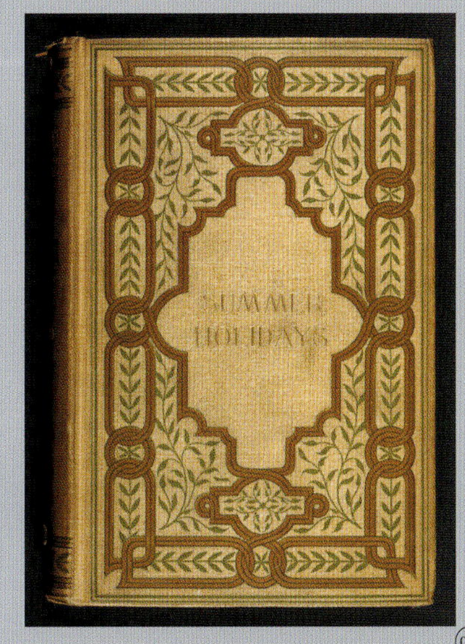

06.

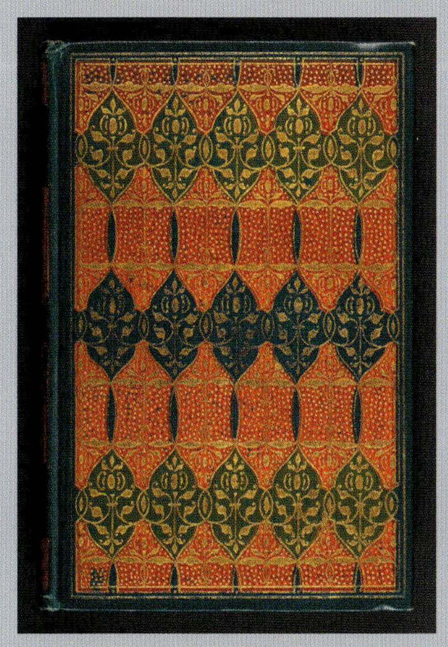

07.

08.

09.

THE BUDDHA'S LAST BIRTH TALE

The art of the palm leaf book

JANA IGUNMA

The earliest manuscripts in South and Southeast Asia were prepared from easily accessible natural materials like tree bark, bamboo slips and the leaves of palm trees. Books made from palm leaves were of particular importance in Hinduism, Jainism and Buddhism, and their use spread from India to Central and Southeast Asia. Although the oldest extant palm leaf books date back to the ninth to eleventh centuries CE, there is archaeological and textual evidence that oblong-shaped palm leaves, designed and bound together in book format, were used as early as the fifth century CE. By the end of the first millennium CE, large libraries holding handwritten palm leaf books had been established across South Asia.

Surviving palm leaf books originate mainly from India, Nepal, Bangladesh, Sri Lanka, Myanmar (Burma), Thailand, Laos, Cambodia, Indonesia and the Philippines. Their production declined rapidly at the beginning of the twentieth century due to the establishment of modern printing presses, which produced large numbers of books more quickly and less expensively.

Texts contained in palm leaf books cover a wide range of subjects including philosophy, religion, history, grammar, literature, music, art, cosmology, laws, mathematics, medicine and biology. Palm leaf books exist as bundles held together with a cord, as loose-leaf manuscripts and in folding book formats, often with wooden covers. The text was applied with an ink pen or incised with a metal stylus, but in the twentieth century text was also printed on palm leaves with modern presses.

01. *Illustrations from the last Birth Tale of the Buddha depicting peaceful scenes with animals, flowers and trees painted on gilded background on palm leaf. Vessantara Jataka, Thailand, 19th century. (Or 16753, f. 1r; Or 1245, f. 25r & f. 26v, details)*

Palm leaf books were illuminated or illustrated depending on the purpose and the text content. Lavish decorations were applied onto the leaves and wooden covers of religious scriptures. In the Buddhist tradition, the creation or commission of artistically outstanding objects was regarded as a meritorious act. Often custom-made cabinets, chests and wrappers were produced to protect the books from damage.

THE BUDDHA'S LAST BIRTH TALE ON PALM LEAVES

The previous lives of Gotama Buddha – the historical Buddha – are the subject of a collection known under the title Jataka ('Birth Tales') in the Sanskrit and Pali languages. There are 547 Jataka stories which show how the Buddha acquired greater virtues and moral stature from one incarnation to the other. Being among the key textual sources of Buddhism, they are attributed to Gotama Buddha himself and are included in the Pali-language Buddhist canon which is well known in the Buddhist cultures of Sri Lanka and Southeast Asia. The Buddha is thought to have narrated them during his forty-year ministry to his followers, using each Jataka to teach the values of compassion, loving-kindness, generosity, honesty, perseverance and morality. In his previous lives Gotama Buddha was incarnated in the form of human beings, various animals, benevolent spirits, or as deities residing in the heavenly realms of the Buddhist cosmos. All of the Buddha's Birth Tales are popular among Theravada Buddhists but the Vessantara Jataka is the best known.

01.

(02.)

Prince Vessantara was the Buddha's last incarnation before he was reborn as Prince Siddhattha who eventually attained enlightenment and became the Buddha. This last Birth Tale, better known as Vessantara Jataka or Great Jataka, is the most popular across Southeast Asia, symbolising the virtues of generosity and compassion. Set in a natural environment, it tells the story of Prince Vessantara, his wife and two children who set up a forest hermitage when they were exiled from their kingdom. After passing a number of tests to prove that his generosity and spirit of compassion were genuine, the family was welcomed back to the royal palace and Vessantara ascended the throne. Unsurprisingly, illustrations relating the story of Prince Vessantara depict natural scenes not only in the design of palm leaf books, but also paper manuscripts and mural paintings.

The popularity and importance of the Vessantara Jataka are not only due to the beauty of the story and its ethical meaning for practising Buddhists, but also reflect a prediction in the Buddhist scriptures: if the Vessantara Jataka was to disappear this would be the very first sign of the departure of Gotama Buddha's teachings, or Buddhism, from the world. Buddhists, therefore, take great care to preserve this Birth Tale for future generations, be it in the form of artworks, written texts, recitations and performances, or audio-visual media.

Kings and other royals, both male and female, commissioned large numbers of Buddhist scriptures, either in the form of palm leaf books or, less often, paper folding books. One outstanding example of such commissioned Buddhist works on palm leaves is held in the Thai, Lao and Cambodian Collections at the British Library (Or 1245). It is a part of an illuminated, multi-volume copy of the Vessantara Jataka made in central Thailand, probably Bangkok, in the nineteenth century. The text in the Pali language was written on palm leaves, in Khmer script, which was used mainly for canonical Buddhist texts or other sacred texts in Thailand (whereas in Cambodia this is still the commonly used script). The beautifully illuminated bundle of this palm leaf book contains two of the standard thirteen chapters of this Birth Tale, chapters eight and eleven. The text describes one of the tests that Prince Vessantara has to pass while living in the forest hermitage: Jujaka, an old Brahmin, asks Prince Vessantara for his children to become servants of Jujaka's young wife. Vessantara realises that true generosity means to renounce much more

02. *Wooden end boards with mother-of-pearl inlay showing a free-flowing floral pattern. (Or 1245)*

03. *Palm leaf bundle containing text from the Vessantara Jataka with the wooden covers, which are decorated with black lacquer and mother-of-pearl inlay. (Or 1245)*

(03.)

than material possessions and grants the wish. However, Jujaka loses his way in the forest and finally arrives at the palace of Vessantara's father, who recognises his grandchildren.

This palm leaf bundle (Image 3) consists of thirty-three leaves which are 580 millimetres long and 60 millimetres wide. The text is written with black ink on twenty-seven leaves, the remainder are blank. The leaves are held together by two lengths of red cord which are tied through holes in the leaves. On each leaf there are two circular markings for the binding holes and five lines of text. Six leaves are illuminated with paired miniature paintings of natural scenes. These images are seen through the eyes of Vessantara and his family, depicting what they would have seen while living in the forest hermitage – trees, flowers, animals, rocks. The embellishment of Buddhist texts with natural scenes and landscapes is not unusual in Thai manuscript and book art as they highlight the close relationship that the Buddha had with his natural environment and all sentient beings. It is believed that in the presence of the Buddha or his previous incarnations as a *bodhisattva* even fierce wild animals and powerful mythical animals become gentle and supportive of him.

In Image 1 the landscape illustrations with blossoming trees and various animals were painted with a fine brush on a gilded background. Brushes for such delicate paintings were usually made from hair from the inside of a cow's ears. The size of the painting is 200 millimetres by 60 millimetres. Red and orange paints were made from vermilion and shellac, which was easy to obtain and therefore used lavishly. The borders in mainly red pigment and gold leaf show the popular flame- or thorn-like pattern and a lotus flower – sacred in Buddhism – in a roundel flanked by foliage on the left side. While painting styles of earlier centuries were not superseded, imported paints such as Prussian blue, synthetic ultramarine, emerald green and chrome yellow helped to develop a more realistic style that benefits from stronger and more contrasting colours.

The skills needed to incise text, illustrate, make paints and all the other decorative practices were passed on from elder monks to novices in monasteries. Similarly, such techniques were taught by secular craftsmen and women to family members and were a valuable source of income.

Specification	*Scale*
VESSANTARA JATAKA Thailand, 19th century 580 x 60 mm Or 1245	

ORIGINS AND METHODS OF MAKING PALM LEAF BOOKS

Palm leaves became a popular writing support in South Asia because of their flexibility, durability and resistance to mould and insects. Often the palm leaf books themselves were objects of worship, and the tradition that they must be treated with due respect survives today.

Both the palmyra and talipot palms were used in the production of manuscripts. The palmyra tree (*Borassus flabellifer*) has an extensive growth range and is cultivated throughout most of tropical and subtropical Asia. It can often be found as a decorative tree around Buddhist temples in Southeast Asia. The leaves are fibrous and of excellent strength and flexibility when fresh; however, over time the natural flexibility decreases. The leaves of the palmyra palm are rather thick compared to those of the talipot tree (*Corypha umbraculifera*). The latter are more commonly used in manuscript production, but it is actually a fairly rare tree with a growth range limited to southwest India, Sri Lanka and parts of Southeast Asia. It needs a wet climate and grows abundantly in moist coastal areas. The leaves are soft, flexible and of a light colour after drying.

Various treatments are needed to prepare the palm leaves for the application of text or illustrations. One method is to boil or soak the leaves in a mixture of water with herbs, for example lemongrass (*Cymbopogon*) or sweet flag (*Acorus calamus*), which are known to be insect repellents. Then they are dried and sometimes smoked or baked in a kiln before being pressed, cut into rectangular shapes and finally written on. If baked in a kiln, the leaves discharge some black oily liquid, which has to be removed with a cloth or hot sand before text is applied. The size of the palm leaves can be between 200 and 600 millimetres long and 40 to 60 millimetres wide. Shorter leaves were traditionally used for secular texts whereas longer ones served for the writing of religious texts. Another method is to glue several long rectangular leaves together at the short ends and roll the resulting sheet to form a scroll. Palm leaves treated in such ways are relatively robust and can last for 500–600 years, even in humid, tropical climates. The edges of the palm leaves can be lacquered or gilded after they are cut to size, which helps to protect them from deterioration and damage by insects. One or two holes are punched through each leaf and then the leaves forming one bundle are strung together with a cotton cord. A complete palm leaf book may consist of one bundle, or more than twenty.

Each leaf contains between three and ten lines of writing, with occasional illustrations or ornaments decorating the text (Image 5). Whereas Buddhist texts and commentaries are usually in the Sanskrit or Pali languages (unless they are translations), secular works and treatises are mostly written in vernacular languages.

The writing is most commonly incised with a hard wood or metal stylus, after which soot or lampblack mixed with oil and resin is applied to the leaves and then wiped off again, leaving the black pigment only in the incisions for better visibility of the text. Other materials used for inking are mixtures of bean plant juice and oil, or pulverised burnt candlenut and coconut oil. In rare cases, specially made black or gold ink is used to write the text onto the palm leaves with a bamboo pen or a brush (Image 4). For the writing of particularly important texts the palm leaves can be gilded or silvered before the text is written on. The scribe or copyist has to be very skilled and must take great care if the text is incised since overwriting or correction are practically impossible.

04. Incipit *of the Vessantara Jataka in the Pali language in Khmer script, written in gold ink on red lacquer. (Or 1245b, f. 1v)*

05. *Fragments from a palm leaf bundle containing five protective texts with illustrations of Buddhist deities, Pancharaksha, Nepal, 12th century. (Or 14000)*

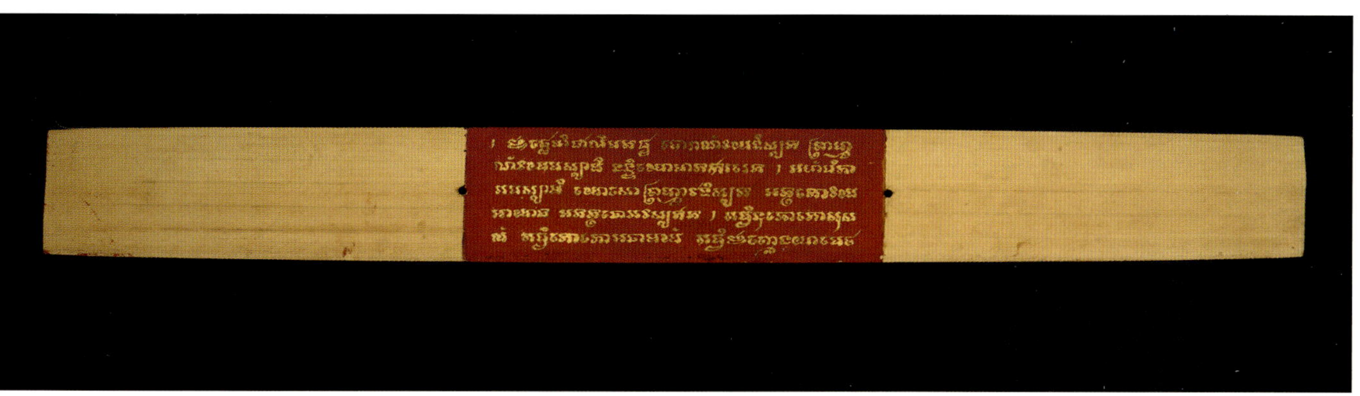

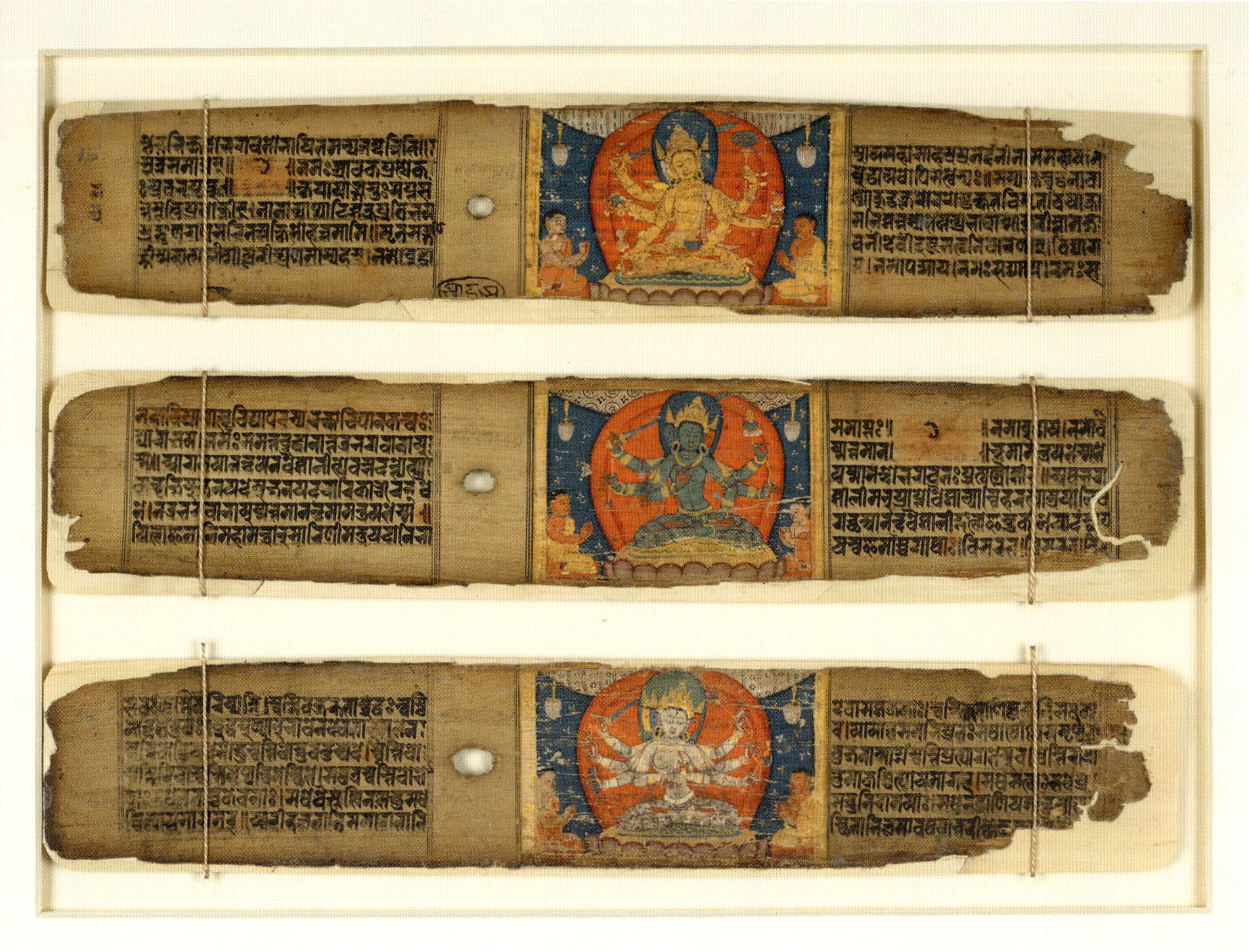

05.

Palm leaf books are often equipped with a title indicator made from a small piece of palm leaf, wood, bamboo, ivory or cloth showing the title or contents of a book, and the names and wishes of its patrons. In the Burmese tradition long handwoven tapes known as *sazigyo* are used for this purpose. Historically, title indicators and *sazigyo* were important means of identifying texts when these were stored together in large wooden cabinets in Buddhist temple libraries, for example.

Valuable manuscripts containing important texts were protected from physical damage with two end boards, made from a variety of materials. Ivory, wooden and bamboo boards were sometimes carved with floral designs. For aesthetic reasons, or to add meritorious value, they could also be lacquered in red, black, yellow or orange colours before being painted (Image 7) or embellished with gold leaf. Lacquer was a popular material as it guarded against damage by water and humidity. It was made from the sap of the Burmese lacquer tree (*Melanorrhoea usitata*) and could be mixed with various natural substances to achieve different colours, for example cinnabar or lampblack. The glossy appearance of black lacquer was an ideal background for gold leaf. Motifs included flowers, plants and foliage, flame-like and hourglass-like designs, but also figures of deities and animals.

ILLUSTRATION OF PALM LEAF BOOKS: SOOT, LACQUER AND GOLD

The long rectangular shape of palm leaves is not ideal for illustration, so various techniques had to be adopted to decorate the text. The most frequent type of illumination are miniature drawings, floral patterns and diagrams which are incised into the leaves with a stylus, and afterwards either blackened with soot (like the text) or wiped with a mixture of oil and natural substances including powdered shellac or cinnabar if different colours were required. Designs could vary, for example the South and Central Asian tradition favoured miniature paintings of the Buddha, *bodhisattvas*, Hindu gods and goddesses, protective deities, and in rare cases images of the sponsors of a palm leaf book. In Buddhist parts of Southeast Asia,

06. *Illustrated Burmese Buddhist cosmology on palm leaves sewn together in folding book format, Burma, 18th–19th century. (Or 15283)*

07. *Palm leaf book with an incised Buddhist text in Sinhalese script, title indicator made from palm leaf and illuminated wooden end boards, Sri Lanka, 18th–19th century. (Or 6600/69, ff. 1v–2r)*

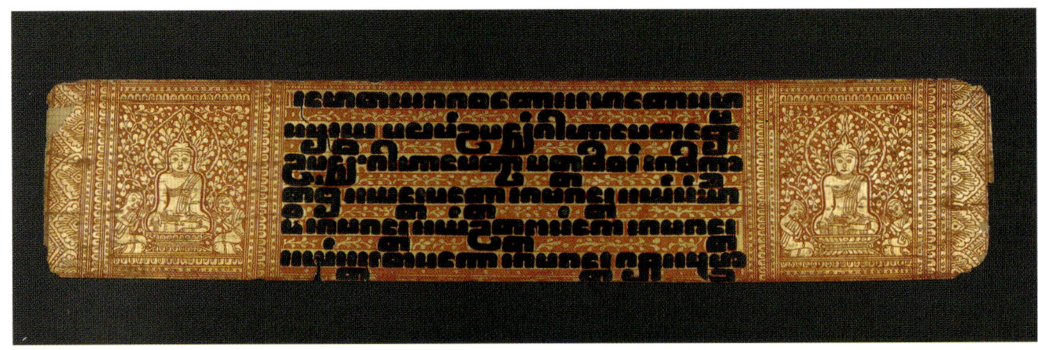

the front leaves of manuscripts commissioned by royalty were sometimes embellished with red or black lacquer and gilt ornaments of royal symbols, flowers and lattice patterns. Gold paint was used to execute the text in fine calligraphy on contrasting black- or red-lacquered palm leaves.

Occasionally the texts of palm leaf books required larger illustrations for clarification of the subject, for example Buddhist cosmologies which explained and depicted the thirty-one planes of existence in Buddhist belief. For that purpose, several palm leaves were sewn together to form a larger surface upon which illustrations and diagrams were incised and blackened with soot (Image 6). These palm leaf books were then folded like concertina books, and it is thought that this is the ancestor of the paper folding book which became the preferred format for illustrated texts in mainland Southeast Asia during the eighteenth and nineteenth centuries.

08. *Sheet from a Burmese Kammavaca manuscript made from palm leaves, with gold and lacquer illuminations of two Buddhas with two disciples each, Burma, 19th century. (Or 12010/b, f. 1r)*

09. *Palm leaf book consisting of multiple bundles strung together with a red cord, and two wooden boards decorated with mother-of-pearl inlay and with a silk brocade wrapper. Buddhist commentaries, Thailand (manuscript) and India (wrapper), 1824–51. (Or 5107)*

10. *A wooden case with gilt and lacquer decorations showing a floral design, custom-made for one Buddhist palm leaf book containing a Kammavaca text in Dhamma script, northern Thailand or Laos, 19th century. (Or 16893, f. 1r)*

In the Burmese, Lao and northern Thai tradition larger surfaces of single folios were created by placing two or three palm leaves next to each other and covering them with several layers of lacquer. This method allows for more space to add lavish gold illuminations and illustrations next to Buddhist ordination texts (Kammavaca) or other sacred scriptures written in highly decorative calligraphy script (Image 8).

PALM LEAF BOOK WRAPPERS AND BOXES

To provide additional protection against dust and mould, palm leaf books were often wrapped in a piece of cloth, which could either be custom-made or simply an unused skirt, a handwoven shawl or an imported piece of cloth (for example, printed Indian cotton). Bespoke palm leaf wrappers were also made from local or imported silk (Image 9). These wrappers had sometimes woven-in bamboo strips to provide extra stability for palm leaf books that lacked end boards. Another method of protection took the form of a long cotton or silk bag that was sewn to fit the size of the palm leaves.

Precious palm leaf books were traditionally equipped with a custom-made wooden enclosure to keep them safe from rodents, insects and water damage. There are three types of such storage caskets: the single manuscript or book case (Image 10), the larger chest with a lid and the cabinet with hinged doors. All three are usually made from wood, often beautifully carved or decorated with lacquer and gilt, or sometimes with intricate mother-of-pearl inlay or mirror glass inlay.

09.

10.

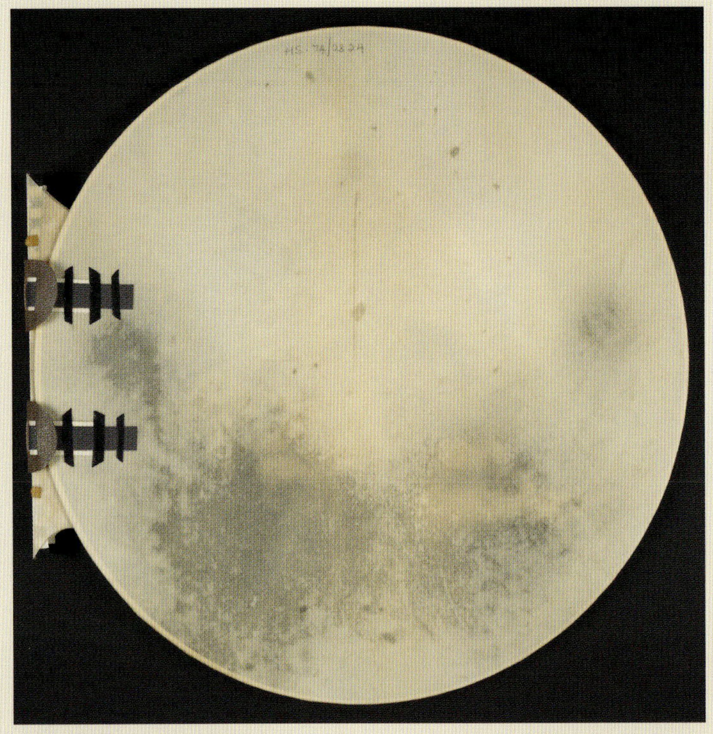

01.

02.

03.

A MATERIAL IDENTITY IN OCEANIA BOOK DESIGN

LUCY ROWLAND

The depths of the British Library basements hold an array of fascinating items. Among them are a handful of books designed from materials found on the opposite side of the world: kangaroo skin and harakeke (New Zealand flax). The oldest examples, both published in London, are Joseph Banks's 1789 copy of *The Voyage of Governor Philip to Botany Bay,*[1] bound in kangaroo skin by his request, and the Scottish scientist John Murray's 1836 treatise, *An account of the Phormium Tenax or New Zealand Flax,*[2] printed on harakeke paper. These early experiments with exported native materials were short lived,[3] yet they share the same space in the basements with a small collection of books also designed from kangaroo skin and harakeke, but published around two centuries later in Australia and Aotearoa New Zealand.

From European colonisation to the mid-twentieth century, book design in Australia and Aotearoa New Zealand was shaped by the domination of British exports; from books and paper, to binding materials and techniques. A distinct Australian or Aotearoa New Zealand identity struggled to flourish during this period, with design dependent on the materials and fashions of Britain or Europe. However, the mid-twentieth century onwards has seen some book artists eschewing traditional binding materials to experiment with those indigenous to the region, including kangaroo skin and harakeke, to create design independent of British and European traditions.

In Sydney, Australia, Sue Anderson and Gwen Harrison of Impediment Press make use of parchment and leather made from kangaroo skin in the bindings of their limited-edition artists' books. Kangaroos, marsupials native to Australia, are harvested from the wild under strict government quotas for their meat and skin, which is widely used in the manufacture of leather products. The skin is light and flexible but still resilient. It can also record the harsh environment in which the animals live, with kangaroo skin showing evidence of blemishes, scratches and scars. It was exactly these qualities which attracted Anderson and Harrison when creating their books *Quaranta Australis* (2008) (Image 1), *Howl for a Black Cockatoo* (2015) (Image 2, back right) and *Phantomwise Flew the Black Cockatoo* (2017) (Image 2, back left), which focus on stories of colonial historical sites: specifically places of female incarceration and institutionalisation. The books were designed to act as monuments to those women who left their marks on the walls over two centuries. When handling these remarkable books with their kangaroo skin covers, the books' users feel connected to the content as though they have already started to 'read' them.

At The Pear Tree Press, a private press in Auckland, Aotearoa New Zealand, typographer Tara McLeod has experimented with harakeke in the bindings of his fine press material. Harakeke (a type of lily rather than a flax) is a tough, fibrous plant with fan-shaped leaves which has great cultural significance for Māori and symbolises *whānau* ('family'). Early Māori used it for a variety of purposes, from weaving clothes, ceremonial cloaks, baskets and fishing nets, to medicinal use and trade with Europeans in the nineteenth century, who valued its use for making ropes and rigging.[4] Today, McLeod sources locally handmade harakeke paper, and has used it to produce bindings for his fine press publications, *The Moa Seen on the Buller* (2013) (Image 3 and Image 2, front right) and *The Kuaka or Godwit* (2017) (Image 2, front left). The harakeke paper covers shown here are less refined than other examples, with strands clearly visible and raised to the touch when handling. The rougher texture is more appealing for use in covers but makes printing difficult, so the covers are left blank. The binding material provides the sole clue to the content: the two books are exquisitely printed extracts about the kuaka or bar-tailed godwit and the extinct moa bird; like the binding, these birds are/were indigenous to Aotearoa New Zealand.

By using materials from flora and fauna native to Australia and Aotearoa New Zealand, these items are distinctive examples of book design that shout their national identity, even in their 'flaws'.

01., 02. & 03. *Kangaroo skin and harakeke bindings. Clockwise from top left: HS.74.2324, HS.74/2412, HS.74/2310, RF.2019.a.9, C.188.a.411, C.188.a.411.*

AUDUBON'S *THE BIRDS OF AMERICA*

A set of four volumes that blur the line between book production, American art history and scientific enquiry

FELICITY MYRONE

The monumental *The Birds of America from Original Drawings by John James Audubon*, 1827–38, has been acclaimed as a landmark in book production, printmaking and American art history. Its sheer size and extent – 435 prints in four volumes, each a metre along the spine – and Audubon's skill in rendering his bird subjects at full size, have been celebrated in multiple historical accounts and surveys, in exhibitions and with the reprinting of the plates themselves. Scarce and much sought after, copies have reached record auction prices. The hand-coloured aquatints are individually striking and collectively constitute one of the most complex and sustained graphic publishing enterprises of the time. Audubon has been heralded as a new kind of native genius. Even the lack of refinement in the draughtsmanship and compositional naivety – particularly in the balance between the birds and their foliage settings – has been interpreted, positively, as reflecting his rugged grass-roots American identity and straightforward manner. The project as a whole has been taken as a coherent testament to his heroic single-mindedness and endurance.

THE PRINTS

Audubon's images were produced on three sizes of plate, corresponding to the size of the specimen, although printed on a uniform size of paper, approximately 1,000 by 750 millimetres, known as double elephant. Most subscribers had their prints bound as the four title pages suggested, in a uniform order of volumes I prints 1–100, II prints 101–200, III prints 201–300 and IV prints 301–435, but in bindings of their own choice. The book appears in that format as a treasured object in many public libraries in the US and elsewhere, including the British Library. Exceptionally large and heavy, the volumes require special handling, with two people needed to turn the pages safely.

While recognising the many exceptional features of the project, and without doubting the continuing visual appeal of the prints and the impressiveness of the volumes as physical objects, the characterisation of *The Birds of America* as a wholly singular project, and the manifestation of a singularly heroic creative imagination, does not capture its more complicated genesis.[1] What we now may be familiar with in reprints, reproductions and in library or museum exhibits as the four volumes were the result of a far more untidy and compromised process. As well as a landmark in book design, *The Birds of America* can be resituated between book and art history, and between science and art. Audubon had developed his plan to publish *The Birds of America* in the US in 1820 but struggled to find support there. In 1826 he removed to England, bringing his drawings, and embarked in 1827 on the publication itself. The production of the plates was a collaborative process. Scottish artist and engraver William Lizars etched plates 1–10, with artist, engraver, publisher and proprietor of the Zoological Gallery Robert Havell Jnr then taking over.[2] They traced Audubon's drawings onto plates, printed them as etching or etching with aquatint, and hand-colourists (Havell employed fifty) completed them with watercolour. The wording and positioning of the text varies over time, usually including plate and part number, title

01. *Barn Owl, Vol. 2, Plate CLXXI.*

01.

and Audubon's membership of relevant societies. Changes were also made to titles, particularly as names of the birds were corrected. The text declares Audubon as the originating artist on all but one of the plates, but others actually provided flowers, foliage, insects and backgrounds, including Robert Havell, Joseph Mason, George Lehman, Maria Martin, and his two sons John Woodhouse Audubon and Victor Audubon.[3]

This division of labour was not uncommon, but demonstrates the capital Audubon had available to him. Moreover, other ornithologists had taken on more labour personally – George Edwards was taught etching by Mark Catesby to reduce the cost of the plates in his *Natural History of Uncommon Birds* (1743–51).[4] Audubon's income was the cause of gossip, Charles Waterton writing, 'I particularly want to know about his keeping shop, because... people really imagine that Audubon was quite independent, and had nothing to do for twenty years but to draw birds and to write their history.'[5]

02. *George Edwards, The hen of the bearded titmouse. (Add MS 5624 f. 139)*

03. *Black-throated Weaver from Thomas Hardwicke's collection, Miscellaneous Drawings. (Add MS 10985, f. 11)*

DID *THE BIRDS OF AMERICA* HAVE A FIXED AND DEFINITE FORM?

The British Library initially acquired its copy of *The Birds of America* in 1835 as part of a collection, not of books or prints as such, but the natural history collection of Major-General Thomas Hardwicke, bequeathed to the British Museum in his will proved April 1835 and listed in the *Additions Made to the Collections in the British Museum in the Year MDCCCXXXV*, 1839. It was not made clear there, perhaps seen as irrelevant, that while Audubon's *The Birds of America* is listed as 'bequeathed by Major General Hardwicke', it had been received incomplete. Hardwicke was a soldier and naturalist who served in India. His collection comprised drawings, manuscripts, books, and specimens including stuffed birds and animals, even an elephant. His will specified that the British Museum would receive everything from his collection not a duplicate of something already held:

'All my books upon Natural History not being duplicates of Books on similar subjects in the Collections of the British Museum and also all my Drawings upon Natural History Collections of Quadrupeds, Birds, Zoological Specimens in Spirits, Cabinets of Minerals, Shells and other Curiosities and Articles in Cabinets into the care of the Trustees of the British Museum to be kept by them in one Collection or different separate and entire Collections according to the different natures of the Particulars contained in this bequest and such Collection or Collections to be named by them and entered in their Catalogues by the name of "The Hardwicke Bequest".'[6]

The curator of printed books at the time of the bequest, Henry Baber, noted that the collection included 300 valuable books, highlighting 'several of the Works so acquired being of considerable expense, particularly Audubon's American Birds' and noting that it had cost Hardwicke 96 guineas (a very substantial sum for a single publication, equating to the annual household income of a skilled tradesman or shopkeeper of the time) and was still in the course of publication.[7] On 11 April 1835, 'The Trustees directed that Mr Baber should add the remaining portion of this Work to the Library, as the numbers may severally appear.'[8] While Audubon's prints became a book, and was listed as such by author, title and date in the Printed Books section of the *Additions*, most of Hardwicke's drawings were listed, grouped and bound by the British Museum in albums arranged by subject matter, size and extent for the Manuscript collection (listed as Add MS 10974 to 11032 and 11808). The collection has been further divided with large transfers to the Natural History Museum,[9] so that works like 'Drawings of Birds', 5 vols, Large folio, (10986–10990) are no longer at the British Library, and the transferred works were again rearranged.

The British Museum did acquire the rest of *The Birds of America*, although librarian Antonio Panizzi noted in 1836 that he had been in touch with Audubon:

'...*and he said that we should not have the continuation, because the former numbers were badly bound by General Hardwicke, and broken; and that he (Mr. Audubon) would never allow such a copy of his book to be in the British Museum as a specimen of what his work is.*'[10]

The British Library copy includes plates 1–10 still as etchings by Lizars, although four of these plates were later reworked as aquatints by Havell. This makes it rare, as Audubon was unhappy with Lizars's work and retrieved some of these from other subscribers.[11] Hardwicke had cut down the prints, and these are now presented inlaid into larger sheets and were rebound by Charles Tuckett, the British Museum binder[12] in goatskin tooled in blind and gold, with the royal coat of arms (customarily used by the British Museum bindery). These bindings would have been expensive, but are not

(03.)

what Hardwicke, the original owner, had in place. Audubon's annoyance suggests that the integrity of the large format was important to him[13] but also that Hardwicke, as a user of his publication, had other ideas.

The context of Hardwicke's collection immediately begs the question of what sort of book *The Birds of America* was meant to be, who it was intended for, what the aspirations for it might have been, and what, in design terms, were the consequences of all this. Importantly the British Museum knew it was not getting a completed work: it was, the librarian noted, 'still in the process of publication'. Audubon's plan had been to issue eighty numbers or parts comprising five prints each (one large bird, one medium bird and three small birds), the series running over sixteen years. 'Ultimately the printing ended after twelve years, completing 87 parts with 435 prints...each instalment costing approximately two guineas.'[14] So when the British Museum received the Hardwicke copy in 1835 there were still three years yet to run. In fact, the museum had both refused to subscribe to the work and to buy the complete first volume when offered several years earlier by the artist, directly, for the price of

£42. Audubon heard this was due to the opinion of one of the Trustees, artist Sir Thomas Lawrence: 'he considered the drawing so-so, and the engraving and colouring bad'.[15]

Subscription publishing was a long-established means of artists financing the publishing of their own works. It had been crucial as a way for artists to secure money directly from subscribers in advance of the work being finished, rather than depending upon publishers. What it meant though, among other things, was that what was originally projected by the artists and publisher – often in deliberately enticing terms aimed at securing all those initial subscriptions and the finance they would bring – was not what necessarily transpired. The world of early nineteenth-century publishing is littered with unfinished publishing projects of this sort, including enterprises involving such eminent figures in the history of art as Turner, Constable and William Blake, as well as a multitude of now less-familiar or forgotten names. While a prospectus or plan might set out a definite timetable and sequence of publication, this rarely proved to be what happened in practice. But this tends to be forgotten when these works enter public collections, particularly when they are bound as books.

The way that Audubon's images were originally encountered was quite different. The prints were sent out in sets of five to the original subscribers in tin boxes. There was a design to the whole, in terms of a stimulating mixture of size of birds, portrait- and landscape-format images, and subjects – the first 200 prints are land birds, 201–350 water birds, 351–435 a mixture. But they were not then, nor would they be until a whole series of parts was issued and the owner chose to bind them together, a book. Subscribers could cancel their subscription,[16] some like Hardwicke would not live to see the work completed, and in the case of Hardwicke's

04. & 05. *Trade cards for Robert Havell's Zoological Gallery. (British Museum, Heal,100.34)*

06. *Four-volume set.*

07. *Common American Swan, Vol. 4, Plate CCCCXI.*

Common American Swan.
CYGNUS AMERICANUS, Sharpless

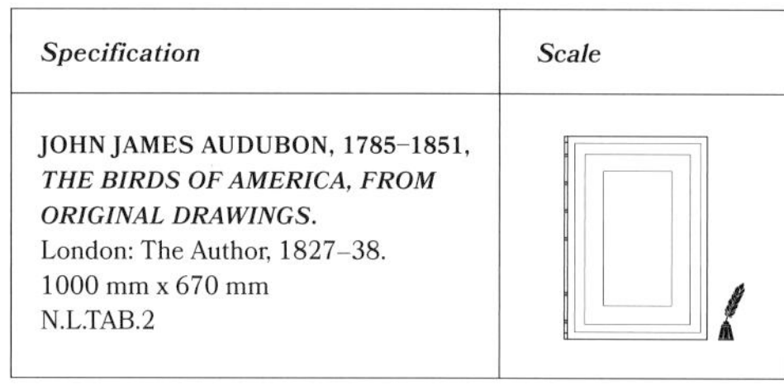

Specification	*Scale*
JOHN JAMES AUDUBON, 1785–1851, *THE BIRDS OF AMERICA, FROM ORIGINAL DRAWINGS.* London: The Author, 1827–38. 1000 mm x 670 mm N.L.TAB.2	

copy we have the evidence that the owner had not taken any particular care to maintain the prints as a set of volumes.[17] At least one critic saw the size of plates as:

'*...needless...the birds are almost overwhelmed, in many cases, by the mass of herbage which surrounds them. If some of the plates were hung up as pictures, they would be taken for botanical instead of ornithological paintings; the figures of flowers are certainly better done than those of the birds.*'[18]

'Badly bound' may just suggest carelessness; 'broken' may also imply that the prints were separated or that Hardwicke had reworked the sheets, cutting them down to the size of the plates as they appear now. It would certainly be a more economical way of storing the images. The popular publisher Henry G. Bohn's advice to Audubon had been that the size of the sheets would be an obstacle:

'*...at present productions of taste are purchased with delight, by persons who receive much company particularly, and to have your book laid on the table as a pastime, or an evening's entertainment, will be the principal use made of it, and that if it needs so much room as to crowd out other things or encumber the table, it will not be purchased by the set of people who now are the very life of the trade. If large public institutions only and a few noblemen purchase, instead of a thousand copies that may be sold if small, not more than a hundred will find their way out of the shops; the size must be suitable for the English market.*'[19]

But this may also point to their status as images not for the purpose of aesthetic enjoyment, but in the context of scientific enquiry. Robert Havell's shop was a Zoological Gallery, where you could acquire specimens as well as images. Hardwicke's natural history collection, as noted, contained specimens and drawings and works in a variety of media and was well known. It was not a rare book collection, nor an art collection, but not yet either a strictly scientific collection in the sense that we might recognise it. At this time the boundaries between intellectual disciplines were still far more porous, and this was manifest too in the range of collections brought together at the British Museum. In the 1830s bird skins donated by Audubon would have been displayed alongside Hardwicke's[20] and printed books and manuscripts were viewed in the same reading room. The collections that were subsequently divided between the British Library, British Museum and Natural History Museum, and the transfers to the National Gallery, had not taken place. The distinctions between art and science, between text and image, between human history and the natural world, were far less decisive.

That lack of distinction is rather obscured by the way that *The Birds of America* has been catalogued in the context of the British Library. Treated as a book, rather than as volumes of prints, the individual images have not been described. So while a reader can easily locate the book itself, someone wanting to identify an image of a flamingo or a specific species of American owl won't be led to the volume. The mid-1830s was a time of reflection about cataloguing standards across the British Museum. Listings of new acquisitions like the one covering Hardwicke's bequest were noted as an inadequate means for a member of the public to locate their holdings, but the cataloguing for his drawings and prints was not revised. Audubon's work is not an isolated case: the contemporary *Illustrations of British Ornithology* by Prideaux John Selby, 'the English equivalent of Audubon's great work'[21] published in parts between 1821 and 1833 and ultimately depicting 218 mainly life-size British birds in two Atlas-sized volumes (approximately 655 by 520 millimetres), is catalogued only as 'Atlas'!

A SINGULARLY HEROIC ACHIEVEMENT?

Audubon's project was a major achievement in the history of book design, but that does not mean it was simply a success. The costs to Audubon were substantial, the disputes with his production team and ornithologists showed the limits of what could reasonably be achieved, the initial lack of interest of as auspicious an organisation as the British Museum must point to some sort of mismatch between his self-perception and ambitions and the institutions of the day. That the copy which came to the museum was imperfect may suggest some kind of failure as well. But if the plates were left unbound, or broken up when they were bound, is that a sign of neglect? Or is it rather a reflection of a project which did not necessarily see the fixed book form which we are now familiar with as the only, inevitable outcome. It may even be, that for visitors to the Zoological Gallery, or for Hardwicke in his natural history collection, that the 'book' was more useful if it was handled as plates.

While the pile of typical wares in Images 4 and 5 includes a bound copy of *The Birds of America*, the interior of Havell's Zoological Gallery also shows what can surely be identified as the prints framed on the wall, as well as one placed prominently under Havell's name in the middle of the image, laid flat on a table. In this setting they were not necessarily encountered as a book.[22]

This was in effect a volume of prints, not a book as such. The only text was the four title pages, one for each volume. The distinction was significant because British copyright law required that books, defined as including text, be deposited with eleven libraries, an expense which would be borne by the publisher. There were good financial reasons to hold off including textual explanations or commentary, and Audubon therefore produced a separate accompanying work, the *Ornithological Biography* co-written with Scottish naturalist and ornithologist William MacGillivray, published in 1831–9. Panizzi later highlighted the case, 'of Audubon's work on American birds: By the Copyright Act we get the letter-press of that work, but we do not get the plates; that is one specimen of the evils inflicted upon us by the Copyright Act, and of its multifarious imperfections. We had the text and not the plates; and the text without the plates is not good for much.'[23]

Audubon also later worked with Philadelphia printer J. T. Bowen to publish a smaller, less expensive and highly popular octavo edition of *The Birds of America*, with lithographic plates. 'While the Havell edition brought celebrity, the Bowen edition provided solid financial support.'[24]

The insistence on Audubon's heroic status, his resilience in pursuing this complex and overstretched publishing project, has overshadowed the original contexts in which such prints might have circulated and been understood in their own time. It has overshadowed too the material realities which had to be in place for Audubon to pursue this project. Audubon was born on a sugar plantation; his family owned and traded slaves. He may have had African heritage, but exploited the labour of his black workers and held racist views. He may have struggled to publish *The Birds of America* in some ways, but nonetheless he had the means to cross the Atlantic, to finance and manage a complex project over many years, and to survive through all that in a way that many others of the time – least of all the enslaved – were simply unable to do. *The Birds of America* may be a seminal achievement in technical and publishing terms, but it may not be a book in the simplified sense we often have in mind, nor may it be simply heroic in the way it is often projected to be.

08 (page 200). *Nuttall's Lesser-marsh Wren, Vol. 2, Plate CLXXV.*

09 (page 200). *Flamingo, Vol. 4, Plate CCCCXXXI.*

10 (page 201). *Blue Jay, Vol. 1, Plate CII.*

11 (page 201). *American White Pelican, Vol. 3, Plate CCCXI.*

08.

09.

10.

11.

'AN ERROR OF TASTE'[1]: SMITHERS, BEARDSLEY AND *THE SAVOY*

ALEX KITHER

Bad luck struck illustrator Aubrey Beardsley in 1895. On 5 April, Oscar Wilde was arrested at the Cadogan Hotel on charges of gross indecency. It was a scandal. Provincial papers seized the story, and all recited one fateful detail: '[Wilde] never for a moment relaxed the grasp of his arm upon *The Yellow Book*'.[2]

The Yellow Book[3] was an illustrated quarterly to which Beardsley was art editor. It became infamous among late Victorian society for its modern prose, audacious illustrations and distinctive yellow cover. What Wilde was truly reading that day has been disputed,[4] but moral hysteria inevitably gathered around *The Yellow Book* and its contributors. The publisher, John Lane, was quick to sever ties with Beardsley and, despite having only the vaguest associations with Wilde, he was promptly sacked.

However, this hardly ruined Beardsley's career. Conversely, his work flourished, and was encouraged by his newly found publisher and friend, Leonard Smithers. Smithers was a man of intense infatuations whom Wilde described as, 'the most learned erotomaniac in Europe'.[5] Professionally, he was a bookseller, and treated his collections with similarly obsessive affection.[6,7] This combination of fancies attracted those marginalised artists who has been exiled following Lane's purge and resulted in a creative partnership between Smithers and Beardsley, which was crystallised in a new illustrated periodical – *The Savoy*.[8]

01.

02.

In substance, *The Savoy* shared a great deal with its yellow-bound rival – not least, poaching some of its contributors. However, it differed in its artistic philosophy. This new serial sought to distance itself from the lurid controversies that had consumed *The Yellow Book*, and instead focus its editorial intentions on the purest aesthetic creed; 'all art is good which good art is'.[9] This ethos was manifested both in its content and design.

The Savoy is recognisable for its lavishly illustrated covers. Sublime line-art depictions of grotesque figures populate the front, blending Japanese-inspired orientalist style with decadent, rococo imagery. The lower covers carry Beardsley's calling card – Pierrot riding Pegasus (Image 2). The design style of these covers was made only more impressive when, following the premature cessation of the journal, Smithers had all eight issues bound and reissued in three hardback volumes, gilding Beardsley's delicate illustrations upon blue cloth bindings (Image 3).

Beardsley's influence further extends to the interior of each issue, and such exquisite illustrations were not to be wasted on shoddy materials here either. The two men debated the merits of a variety of suitable papers,[10] though ultimately Smithers held a fetish for 'old-style', deckle edge paper. He used this for the main 'run' of most of his publications, invariably accompanied by an additional limited run on Imperial Japanese vellum. He held meticulously high standards in production, and entrusted printing and binding to the Chiswick Press, which held a reputation as the premier firm.[11] This perfectionism stands in contrast to John Lane's nasty habit of picking up small lots of remainder paper at bargain prices.[12]

Beardsley's style permeated many of Smithers's later publications: covers, vignettes, borders, initials, frontispieces and cul-de-lampes – all were by Beardsley. Despite his waning health, his artistic

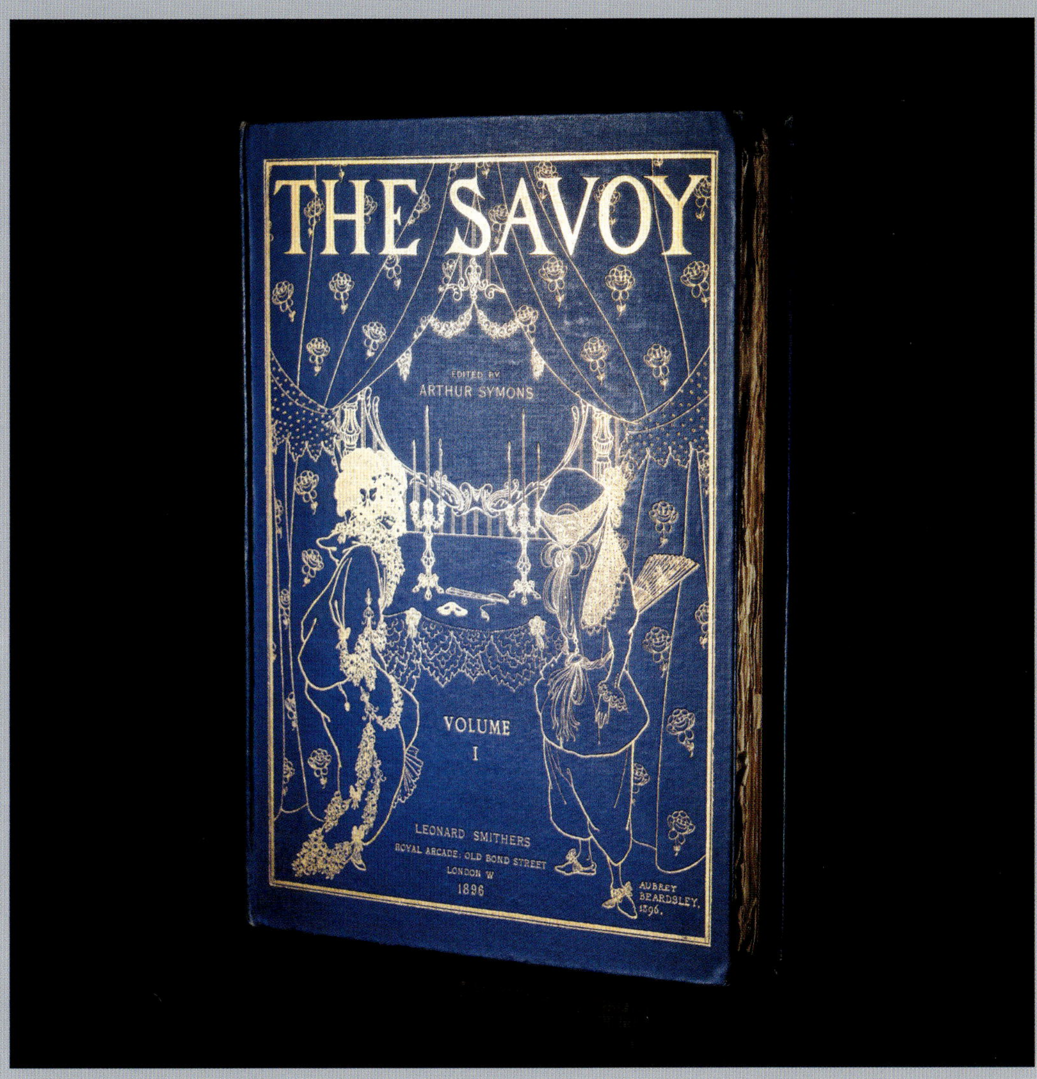

03.

output from 1896 to 1898 was astonishingly vast[13] and of audacious quality. Yet, strangely, he is not formally credited as art editor in *The Savoy*; his name only appears as such in its prospectus[14] and Smithers later claimed the art editorship for himself.[15] However, neither man held authority alone over design. Through their constant correspondence, they married their adoration of books and illustration to guide the design of *The Savoy*, and many other publications.

Beardsley died in 1898. On his deathbed, he converted to Roman Catholicism and begged Smithers to destroy all copies of his 'obscene drawings'.[16] Smithers continued to publish Beardsley's work until his own death nine years later. The books of Leonard Smithers epitomise the best of *fin-de-siècle* publishing. He took risks, publishing the works of *personae non gratae* at great expense and often to a hostile reception. He died, wretched and penniless, but his monastic dedication to beautiful books cemented the art of Aubrey Beardsley in our cultural imagination, and set the standard for modernist book designers of the early twentieth century.

01. *An initial P, illustrated by Beardsley, in E. Dowson,* The Pierrot of the Minute*, 1897. (K.T.C.102.a.6)*

02. *The iconic Pierrot riding Pegasus motif, which appears across most of Smithers and Beardsley's collaborations. The image has been interpreted as a form of mockery towards 'phillistines' and critics of* The Savoy *and other works of the 'decadent' movement.*

03. *Volume 1 of a three-volume set of* The Savoy. *(Eccles 1040)*

01.

XVII.

THE WORKS OF GEOFFREY CHAUCER

William Morris's ideal book

HELEN PEDEN

William Morris (1834–1896) was a master of design. He was also a rebel whose ideas challenged the industrial age and established a new concept of art. His work inspired the Arts and Crafts movement and continues to influence contemporary design.

Morris was fascinated by beautifully produced books, and was drawn to the artistry of these earliest printed texts. His own experiments in fine book production at his own press culminated in *The Works of Geoffrey Chaucer*. This was quickly recognised as his masterpiece, 'by far the most important achievement of the Kelmscott Press'[1] and 'the greatest triumph of English typography' from a press that 'gave to the world the greatest of our decorative artists as an illustrator in pure line'. Morris himself was identified as the artist who 'set the world thinking about questions of paper and margin, and the relation of type to ornament'.[2]

Morris's achievement stood out from the work of contemporary publishers and his desire to produce an ideal book represented a new and unusual approach to book production. While other publishers certainly emphasised the textual accuracy of their reprints of Chaucer – 'to give the text of the *Canterbury Tales* as correct as the MSS. within the reach of the Editor would enable him to make it'[3] – their approach to book production was pragmatic rather than aesthetic. Since mass production and rapidly turned-out wares led to commercial profit, most publications were printed in standard type, using machine-made paper on fast steam-driven presses, and were issued in standard bindings.

However, for Morris Chaucer's tales represented a golden age of art and craftsmanship. His *Chaucer* was therefore 'intended to be essentially a work of art',[4] with a beautiful type and page arrangement that captured the style of the medieval books he found most beautiful. This volume therefore contained the most careful designs and, like all Morris's publications at his Kelmscott Press, it was handcrafted using the purest materials.[5] *Chaucer* essentially became Morris's ideal book.

01. *Pages showing some of the decorative borders from* The Works of Geoffrey Chaucer now newly imprinted. *Hammersmith, 1896. (C.43.h.19)*

Chaucer was to be Morris's final statement against industrial mass manufacture and in favour of traditional craftsmanship that gave a sense of pleasure and joy to both maker and user. With control of the whole design and production process Morris created his *Chaucer* to his own exacting standards. The resulting volume represents Morris's idea of the finest printed book – one that was visually appealing, and had been created from the purest materials, printed on Kelmscott hand-operated presses, and bound and finished by hand. This achievement revealed a new direction for book production and left a legacy adopted by the private presses of the early twentieth century. It remains alive in artists' books today.

THE KELMSCOTT PRESS

Morris had gained early practical editing and publishing experience in 1856 through his work with Charles Whittingham of the Chiswick Press as editor of the first number of the *Oxford and Cambridge Magazine*. Whittingham had subsequently printed Morris's own writings, including *The Defence of Guenevere* in 1858. However, as a designer Morris must have felt that he needed the creative freedom that total control of the whole book production process allowed. In January 1891 he duly founded the Kelmscott Press in Hammersmith, London.

The press was named after the sixteenth-century manor house in the village of the same name in

Oxfordshire that Morris had rented from 1871. Kelmscott Manor had come to exemplify his vision of the harmonious world he perceived in the England of the Middle Ages, in which art or 'work pleasure' was demanded, practised and enjoyed by all. The manor is illustrated on the frontispiece of *News from Nowhere*[6] and is described in Morris's novel as the ultimate, quintessential destination for the people of the story. His Kelmscott Press represented the same ideal.

The press was in close proximity to Morris's London residence (from 1878), originally called The Retreat and renamed Kelmscott House, and the residences of his friends and colleagues Emery Walker (1851–1933), Sydney Cockerell (1867–1962) and Edward Burne-Jones (1833–1898). From 1893 it was also beside the Doves Bindery, founded by the book designer and binder Thomas James Cobden-Sanderson (1840–1922). This was effectively an artists' village where Morris could cooperate with his compositors, press-workers, illustrators and engravers to ensure his book arts thrived.

Morris began work on his typefaces. He had been inspired by the clear, well-defined roman and gothic type designs of the fifteenth-century printers Nicolas Jenson and Jacobus Rubeus and used these as the models for his new designs so that they would be equally pleasing to the eye and clear to read. The three new typefaces he created were named after the titles of the Kelmscott books in which they were intended to first appear. However, although 'Golden' was produced for *The Golden Legend*, due to a difficulty over the paper size it first appeared in *The Story of the Glittering Plain,* which was the first book completed at the Press in 1891. 'Troy' appeared in *Recuyell of the Historyes of Troye* in 1892, and 'Chaucer' (a smaller version of 'Troy') in *The Works of Geoffrey Chaucer* in 1896.

Morris also noted the style and overall design of books and manuscripts of the medieval masters. He considered that if he applied the same principles of page arrangement and included 'really beautiful ornament and pictures, printed books might once again illustrate ... that a work of utility might be also a work of art ...'.[7] However, as Morris also remarked, 'the ornament must form as much a part of the page as the type itself, or it will miss its mark ...'[8] and the transformation would not be achieved.

Like John Ruskin before him, Morris favoured page ornaments that featured stylised representations of natural forms. The challenge he faced was to achieve the same sense of proportion, balance and harmony between his decorations, text and illustrations as he had detected and admired in the earliest printed books.

02. A Dream of John Ball and a King's Lesson. *Issued by the Kelmscott Press, 24 September 1892. This was also the first Kelmscott Press book to contain a full-page illustration – a woodcut frontispiece designed by Burne-Jones. (C.43.e.6)*

03. Sidonia the Sorceress. *Issued by the Kelmscott Press, 1 November 1893, with the chapter title printed in red and a variation of the delicate border around the first page of text. (C.43.f.5)*

THE KELMSCOTT CHAUCER

For Morris the works of Chaucer epitomised the 'romance' of medieval England and a pre-industrial world where craftsmanship thrived. It is not surprising that he wished to produce a magnificent Kelmscott edition. Using the Rev. Walter W. Skeat's scholarly textual analysis of Chaucer's poetry[9] Morris could concentrate wholly on the design and production of the book. Morris had considered this project from his earliest days at the Kelmscott Press. Sydney Cockerell noted in his diary that Morris had first thought of printing *Chaucer* in June 1891 when he spoke of a black-letter font that he hoped to make.[10] The resulting type was displayed in an advertisement on the cover of the second issue of the December 1892 Kelmscott publication list.

By early February 1893 Morris had begun work on his decorations and quickly completed his design for a vine border around the opening pages. An intertwined grapevine was one of the many natural forms that Morris had often used to decorate his initial letters, frames and borders in Kelmscott publications. His first marginal ornament had been a stylised and delicately drawn grapevine around the top corner of the opening page of his poem 'Rapunzel' in the Kelmscott edition of *The Defence of Guenevere, and Other Poems* (1892); the first Kelmscott publication to include a grapevine design

A DREAM OF JOHN BALL.

CHAPTER I. THE MEN OF KENT.

SOMETIMES I am rewarded for fretting myself so much about present matters by a quite unasked-for pleasant dream. I mean when I am asleep. This dream is as it were a present of an architectural peep-show. I see some beautiful and noble building new made, as it were for the occasion, as clearly as if I were awake; not vaguely or absurdly, as often happens in dreams, but with all the detail clear and reasonable. Some Elizabethan house with its scrap of earlier fourteenth-century building, and its late degradations of Queen Anne and William IV. and Victoria, marring but not destroying it, in an old village, once a clearing amid the sandy woodlands of Sussex. Or an old and

02.

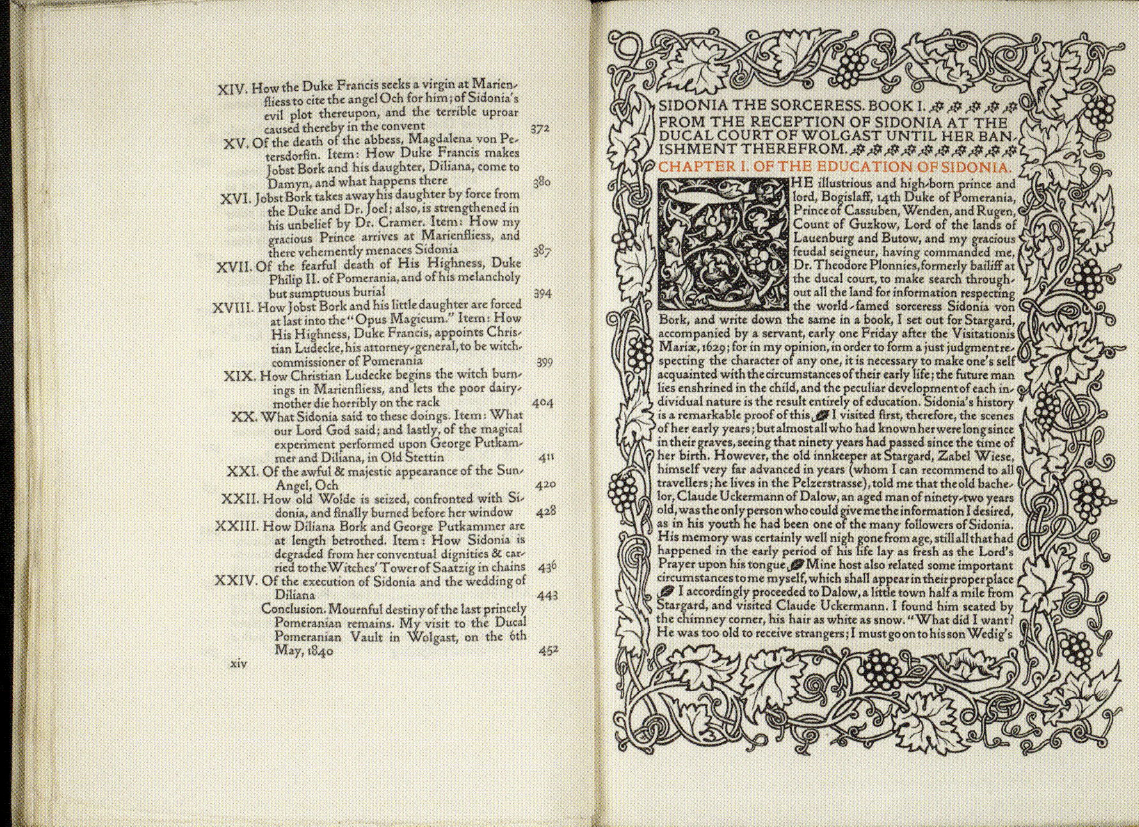

XIV. How the Duke Francis seeks a virgin at Marienfliess to cite the angel Och for him; of Sidonia's evil plot thereupon, and the terrible uproar caused thereby in the convent 372
XV. Of the death of the abbess, Magdalena von Petersdorfin. Item: How Duke Francis makes Jobst Bork and his daughter, Diliana, come to Damyn, and what happens there 380
XVI. Jobst Bork takes away his daughter by force from the Duke and Dr. Joel; also, is strengthened in his unbelief by Dr. Cramer. Item: How my gracious Prince arrives at Marienfliess, and there vehemently menaces Sidonia 387
XVII. Of the fearful death of His Highness, Duke Philip II. of Pomerania, and of his melancholy but sumptuous burial 394
XVIII. How Jobst Bork and his little daughter are forced at last into the "Opus Magicum." Item: How His Highness, Duke Francis, appoints Christian Ludecke, his attorney-general, to be witch-commissioner of Pomerania 399
XIX. How Christian Ludecke begins the witch burnings in Marienfliess, and lets the poor dairy-mother die horribly on the rack 404
XX. What Sidonia said to these doings. Item: What our Lord God said; and lastly, of the magical experiment performed upon George Putkammer and Diliana, in Old Stettin 411
XXI. Of the awful & majestic appearance of the Sun-Angel, Och 420
XXII. How old Wolde is seized, confronted with Sidonia, and finally burned before her window 428
XXIII. How Diliana Bork and George Putkammer are at length betrothed. Item: How Sidonia is degraded from her conventual dignities & carried to the Witches' Tower of Saatzig in chains 436
XXIV. Of the execution of Sidonia and the wedding of Diliana 443
Conclusion. Mournful destiny of the last princely Pomeranian remains. My visit to the Ducal Pomeranian Vault in Wolgast, on the 6th May, 1840 452

xiv

SIDONIA THE SORCERESS. BOOK I.

FROM THE RECEPTION OF SIDONIA AT THE DUCAL COURT OF WOLGAST UNTIL HER BANISHMENT THEREFROM.

CHAPTER I. OF THE EDUCATION OF SIDONIA.

THE illustrious and high-born prince and lord, Bogislaff, 14th Duke of Pomerania, Prince of Cassuben, Wenden, and Rugen, Count of Guzkow, Lord of the lands of Lauenburg and Butow, and my gracious feudal seigneur, having commanded me, Dr. Theodore Plonnies, formerly bailiff at the ducal court, to make search throughout all the land for information respecting the world-famed sorceress Sidonia von Bork, and write down the same in a book, I set out for Stargard, accompanied by a servant, early one Friday after the Visitationis Mariæ, 1629; for in my opinion, in order to form a just judgment respecting the character of any one, it is necessary to make one's self acquainted with the circumstances of their early life; the future man lies enshrined in the child, and the peculiar development of each individual nature is the result entirely of education. Sidonia's history is a remarkable proof of this. I visited first, therefore, the scenes of her early years; but almost all who had known her were long since in their graves, seeing that ninety years had passed since the time of her birth. However, the old innkeeper at Stargard, Zabel Wiese, himself very far advanced in years (whom I can recommend to all travellers; he lives in the Pelzerstrasse), told me that the old bachelor, Claude Uckermann of Dalow, an aged man of ninety-two years old, was the only person who could give me the information I desired, as in his youth he had been one of the many followers of Sidonia. His memory was certainly well nigh gone from age, still all that had happened in the early period of his life lay as fresh as the Lord's Prayer upon his tongue. Mine host also related some important circumstances to me myself, which shall appear in their proper place. I accordingly proceeded to Dalow, a little town half a mile from Stargard, and visited Claude Uckermann. I found him seated by the chimney corner, his hair as white as snow. "What did I want? He was too old to receive strangers; I must go on to his son Wedig's

03.

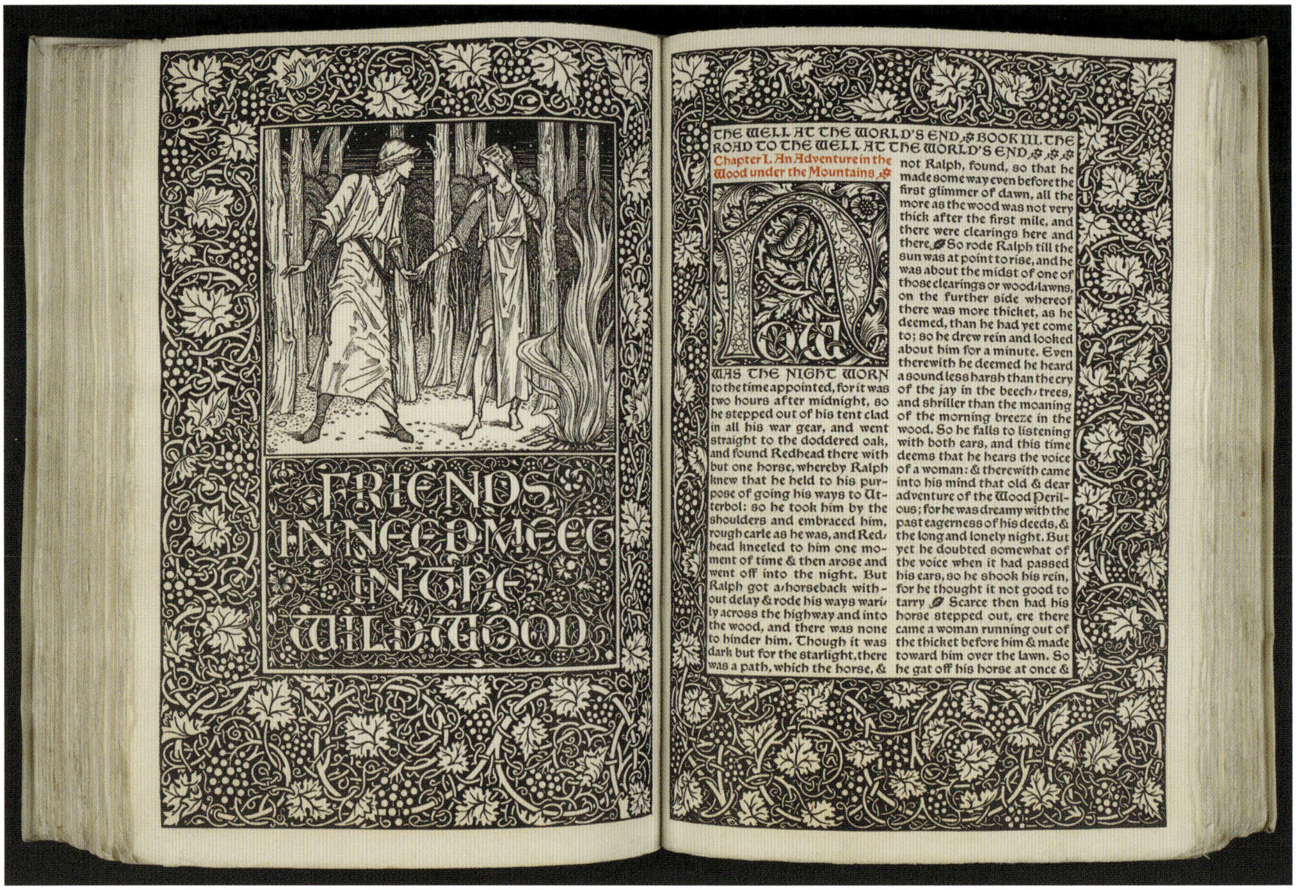

FRIENDS IN NEED MEET IN THE WILDWOOD

THE WELL AT THE WORLD'S END ❧ BOOK III. THE ROAD TO THE WELL AT THE WORLD'S END ❧ ❧ ❧

Chapter I. An Adventure in the Wood under the Mountains ❧

NOW WAS THE NIGHT WORN to the time appointed, for it was two hours after midnight, so he stepped out of his tent clad in all his war gear, and went straight to the doddered oak, and found Redhead there with but one horse, whereby Ralph knew that he held to his purpose of going his ways to Utterbol: so he took him by the shoulders and embraced him, rough carle as he was, and Redhead kneeled to him one moment of time & then arose and went off into the night. But Ralph got a-horseback without delay & rode his ways warily across the highway and into the wood, and there was none to hinder him. Though it was dark but for the starlight, there was a path, which the horse, & not Ralph, found, so that he made some way even before the first glimmer of dawn, all the more as the wood was not very thick after the first mile, and there were clearings here and there. ❧ So rode Ralph till the sun was at point to rise, and he was about the midst of one of those clearings or wood-lawns, on the further side whereof there was more thicket, as he deemed, than he had yet come to; so he drew rein and looked about him for a minute. Even therewith he deemed he heard a sound less harsh than the cry of the jay in the beech-trees, and shriller than the moaning of the morning breeze in the wood. So he falls to listening with both ears, and this time deems that he hears the voice of a woman: & therewith came into his mind that old & dear adventure of the Wood Perilous; for he was dreamy with the past eagerness of his deeds, & the long and lonely night. But yet he doubted somewhat of the voice when it had passed his ears, so he shook his rein, for he thought it not good to tarry ❧ Scarce then had his horse stepped out, ere there came a woman running out of the thicket before him & made toward him over the lawn. So he gat off his horse at once &

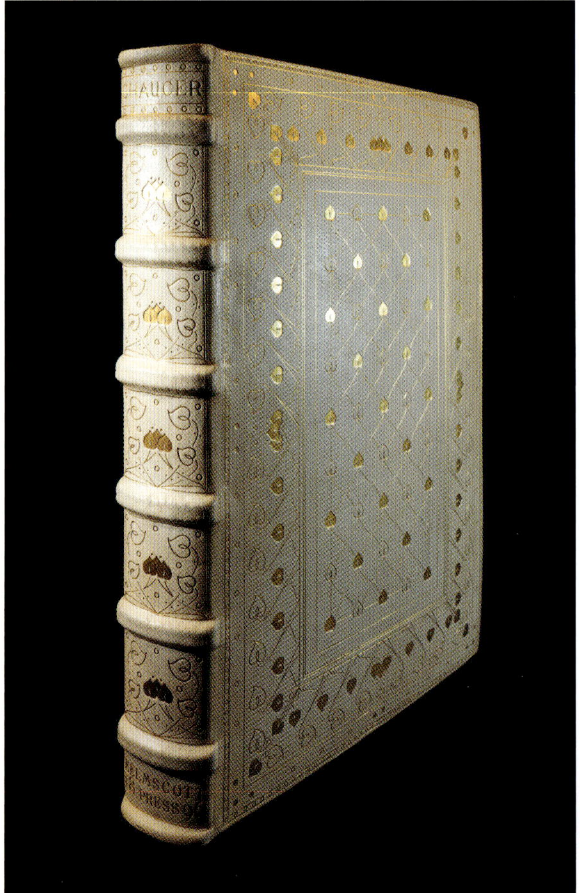

05.

as a full-page border was *A Dream of John Ball and a King's Lesson* (Image 2).

This border shows Morris's preference for a small upper edge that allowed space for a larger design along the lower edge, and for narrow borders at the left and right sides of the page with the narrowest border along the inner edge. A nice counterbalance is created by the juxtaposition of the stylised black line edges of the vines around the opening text, and the thinner, straight-edged and more even border with white leaves on black ink, around the illustration and caption on the facing page. The chapter heading is printed in red ink. Morris used red ink sparingly to highlight shoulder and side titles, and sometimes for a few lines of text and the colophon. This again references the appearance of the earliest printed books.

Both text and decorations were printed in a pure and strong black printing ink made in Hanover by Gebrüder Jänecke. One of Morris's prerequisites for ideal printing,[11] this ink neither clogged the type nor spoiled the impression and could produce exceptional clarity and richness of text and decoration. The printed results could be stunning when executed on the handmade linen paper produced by Joseph Batchelor that Morris favoured.[12] This was made without the use of bleaching chemicals and offered an exceptionally fine surface that could bring a crisp and luminous quality to the pages.

Morris must have been pleased with the overall effect created by this page arrangement and vine border in *Dream of John Ball* as he used it again around the first page of text in *News from Nowhere* (issued 24 March 1893), *The Order of Chivalry* (issued 12 April 1893) and *Utopia* (issued 8 September 1893). The vine border also appeared as a double-page design in *Ballads and narrative poems by Dante Gabriel Rossetti* (issued November 1893), *The Book of Wisdom and Lies* (issued 29 October 1894) and in *Poems chosen out of the works of Robert Herrick* (issued 6 February 1896).

Specification	*Scale*
THE WORKS OF GEOFFREY CHAUCER NOW NEWLY IMPRINTED Hammersmith, London: printed by ... William Morris at the Kelmscott Press, 1896 435 mm x 305 mm C.43.h.19	

However, while this elegant border produces a light and dainty effect here, Morris must have considered it less suitable as a border for text printed in double columns.

Morris resolved the difficulty in another grapevine design. This appears around the title page and facing first page of double-columned text in *The Well at the World's End* (Image 4). The white vine is silhouetted against a black background, within straight border edges. The border, title letters, decorated initial letter and text block are now well defined and the contrast between black letters on white paper and the white decoration on black ink creates an effective counterbalance.

The Well at the World's End was issued in quarto (the British Library copy measures 288 by 220 millimetres) on 4 June 1896 just twenty-two days before *Chaucer* appeared in a much larger folio size (the Library copy measures 435 by 305 millimetres). Although they are of such different sizes, both volumes share a similar arrangement of text, ornament and layout – the text in double columns, with similar vine borders and decorated initials. Morris had observed with reference to large paper copies that margins that were right for a smaller book must be wrong for a larger copy, and that if they were right for the large paper, they would be wrong for the small.[13] Therefore to improve the page arrangement and balance between text and decoration in the larger *Chaucer* volume he adjusted the border dimensions and narrowed the width of the upper edge, to allow for a wider lower edge.

A specimen of the opening page of *Chaucer*, with Morris's vine border, heading, frame around the illustration by Burne-Jones, initial and text, was shown at the Arts and Crafts Exhibition in October

04. The Well at the World's End. *Issued by the Kelmscott Press, 4 June 1896. Decorated title page and facing first page of text of Book III, with an illustration designed by Burne-Jones and the chapter title in red. (C.43.f.11)*

05. *William Morris in his library at Kelmscott House, Hammersmith, in the 1890s. (011903.b.92)*

06. The Works of Geoffrey Chaucer *bound in 1897 in white pigskin with gold tooling by T. J. Cobden-Sanderson at The Doves Bindery. (Ashley 5170)*

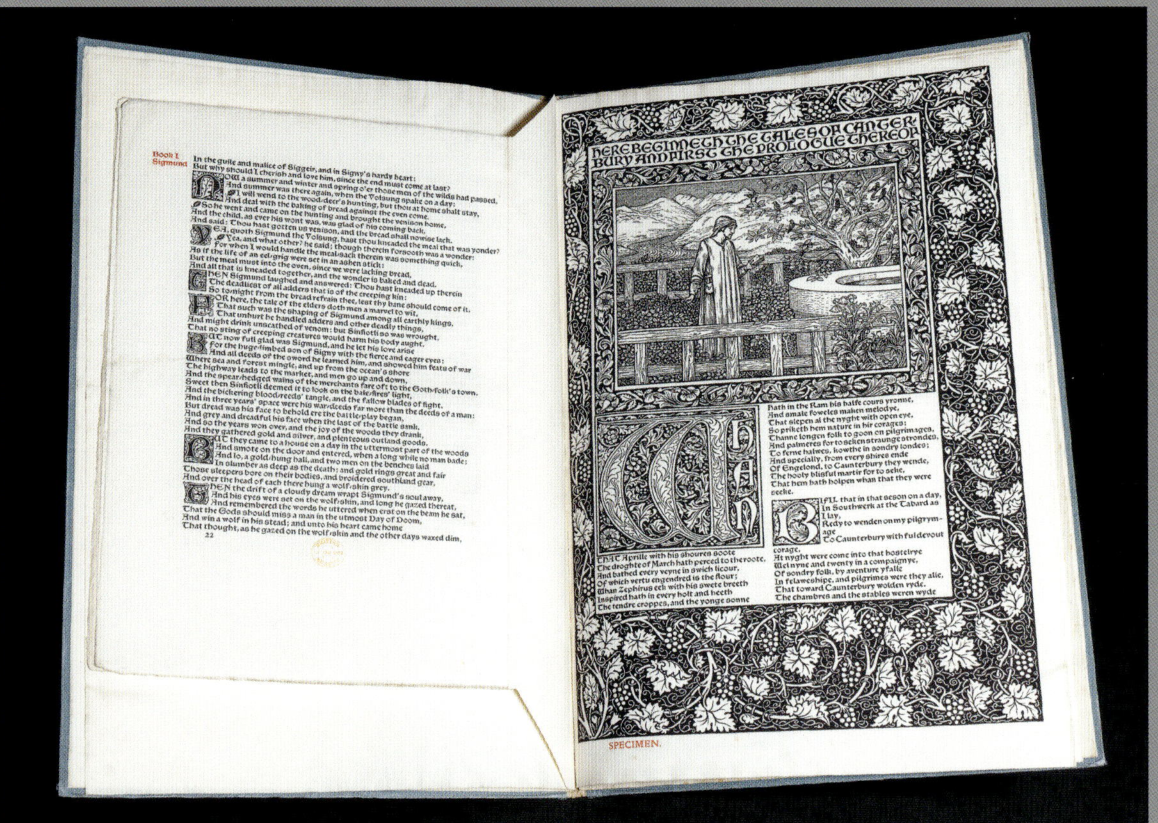
Book I
Sigmund
HERE BEGINNETH THE TALES OF CANTERBURY AND FIRST THE PROLOGUE THEREOF
SPECIMEN.

07.

the works of Geoffrey Chaucer now newly imprinted
HERE BEGINNETH THE TALES OF CANTERBURY AND FIRST THE PROLOGUE THEREOF

08.

09.

and November 1893 (Image 7). Morris's desire for minimal letter spacing that would avoid too much white space on the page, resulted in the specimen being printed with seven lines of verse under the initial word 'Whan', and an extra line at the end of the second column. However, he must have felt this page now showed too little space between decoration and text because in the published version the lines have been moved to the top of the second column and to the next page (Image 8). This decision not only improved the page arrangement but allowed the text to be more legible.

It is interesting to see that in another specimen of the decorations on the opening pages Morris included a heavy black line around the outer edges of the border (Image 9). This does not appear on the published design so it must also have been considered to be a distracting, less harmonious, detail that was out of keeping with the scheme of the book.

07. *The first page of text as exhibited at the Arts and Crafts Exhibition, from Robert Proctor's collection of specimen sheets of the Kelmscott Press. (C.43.h.22, vol. 1, f. 4)*

08. The Works of Geoffrey Chaucer. *Title page and first page of text as published by the Kelmscott Press, 1896.*

09. *Specimen of Morris's decorations on the opening pages showing the thick black edge around the vine border. (C.43.h.22, vol. 2, f. 15, 16)*

Chaucer was a fine volume, and one that Morris had intended to be even finer when finished in one of four bindings handcrafted to his own design.[14] It was a luxury item that could only be produced in relatively low numbers, and offered for sale at a high price – £20 (without a special binding). Today this would represent a purchasing value of approximately £3,404.[15] However, copies of this exclusive book were so highly sought that a Kelmscott Press notice on 14 November 1894 announced 'the demand for the book has been much in excess of the number (325) originally contemplated, and much disappointment has been caused to book-lovers in consequence'. Just over two weeks later, by 1 December 1894, all of the 100 additional paper copies had also been subscribed.

Thirteen particularly exclusive copies were printed on vellum, which, as Morris's daughter May noted, presented particular challenges as a printing surface.[16] These copies were considerably more expensive, being offered at a price of 120 guineas each (£126, the equivalent in purchasing power to £21,446 today).[17] Remarkably by 1 July 1895, all of these had also been sold prior to publication.

The first edition was issued on 26 June 1896. Burne-Jones had predicted that *Chaucer* would be 'like a pocket cathedral – so full of design'.[18] The lavishly decorated volume featured Morris's designs for twenty-six large, engraved initial words and fourteen different large borders (four different grapevine designs, two rose, and eight with flowers and leaves) that were used around a single page or double-page opening. In addition, Morris designed smaller frames and initials throughout the text in such abundance that it is extremely difficult to determine the total number of different designs he created. The published volume also had eighty-seven rather than the sixty wood-cut engravings by Burne-Jones as had been advertised in the December Kelmscott publication list. The visual effect of these printed pages was so stunning that when the book was displayed at the Arts and Crafts Exhibition of 1896, one reviewer felt completely 'overwhelmed with patterns'.[19]

Praise for Morris's work grew. Three months after publication 'This great edition of *Chaucer'* was recognised as 'the crowning achievement of the Kelmscott Press'[20] and copies were highly sought by book collectors. By April 1898 those printed on paper were 'now quickly bought at £30'.[21] This would have been over twenty-two times the weekly wage of a bricklayer or mason in London,[22] or the equivalent in purchasing power of nearly £5,000 today.[23]

Morris certainly regretted the high cost of his books, but recognised that this could not be avoided in his quest for the ideal book. 'I wish, I wish indeed that the cost of the books was less, only that is impossible if the printing and the decoration and the paper and binding are to be what they should be.'[24]

THE LEGACY OF THE IDEAL BOOK

The Kelmscott Press gave Morris a final adventure in design, and the opportunity to indulge his fascination with typography and the book arts. Out of the forty-three works reprinted at the Press, Morris completed forty-two titles before his death, each of which represents an experiment to attain the standard of his ideal book. Morris's pursuit of this harmony that he detected between type and page ornament in fifteenth-century printed books, reached its climax with *Chaucer,* his most decorated volume. In this sense *Chaucer* is the culmination of Morris's experiments, and the venture in which his vision of the ideal book is most perfectly realised. It has also been celebrated as the ultimate Arts and Crafts book and one of the finest examples of English typography.[25]

Morris's respect for the Middle Ages, and his emphasis on traditional handcrafted skills and processes, influenced a growing admiration in late Victorian Britain both for the earlier period and for the aesthetics of book production. The Kelmscott Press closed in 1898 but inspired other printers to form their own private presses. The Essex House Press, founded in 1898 by Charles Robert Ashbee (1863–1942), endeavoured 'to keep living the traditions of good printing that William Morris had revived'. It operated until 1910 using printing presses acquired from the Kelmscott Press and the talents of many former employees. In 1900, Emery Walker established the Doves Press with T. J. Cobden Sanderson and until 1916 continued in the spirit of Morris 'to work with my hands and my head at something ... beautiful, and, as far as human things may be, permanent'.[26]

More widely, Morris's principles influenced artists and designers in Europe and printers in America, including Daniel Berkeley Updike (1860–1941), founder of The Merrymount Press in Boston in 1893. Updike incorporated his own 'Merrymount' type with commissioned illustrations and Kelmscott-inspired initials and borders and produced his books using both traditional hand and machine work. Like Morris, Bruce Rogers (1870–1957) also chose the finest papers, designed his books with attention to type and ornament, and the spacing of these on the pages. His best work, from 1896 to 1912 at the Riverside Press, Boston, shows a 'variety, color and interest hardly to be found in the work of any other producer of books of this time'.[27]

The Works of Geoffrey Chaucer showed how a printed text could be combined with graphic art and the skills of traditional craftsmanship to create the whole book as a single work of art. Morris's particular genius in experimentation, innovation, creativity and craftsmanship set a new standard for book production that continues to be explored by artists like Carolyn Trant, Christine Tacq, Ken Campbell, Natalie d'Arbeloff, Ron King and D. R. Wakefield. As the typeface designer Will Ransom wrote, William Morris 'not only inaugurated a new era – he created it'.[28]

10. The Works of Geoffrey Chaucer, 1896. *Detail of Morris's decorated initial 'A' at the beginning of* The Squieres Tale. *(p. 553)*

10.

Ther may ful many a sighte ysatle
Beth war, I prey yow; for, by
ful many a man weneth to see
And it is al another than it sem
He that mysconceyveth, he mys
And with that word she leep
tree.
This Januarie, who is glad but he
He kisseth hire, and clippeth hire
And on hire wombe he stroketh hir
softe;
And to his palays hoom he hath hire
Now, goode men, I pray yow to be gla
Thus endeth heere my tale of Januari
God blesse us, and his mooder Seinte
Heere is ended the Marchantes Tale of Januarie.

HEERE BIGYNNETH THE S

Incipit prima pars

SARRAY, IN THE LAND OF Tartarye,
Ther dwelte a kyng, that werreyed Ru

TWENTIETH-CENTURY TYPEFACES

PHILIP PARKER

Although calligraphy was of great significance in the age of hand-copied manuscripts, it was only with the invention of printing with movable type in the mid-fifteenth century that the question of typefaces arose. The extended palette of letter forms that gave the book's text both its individuality, in the choice of face, and its uniformity, now that it could be reproduced without variation, became of vital importance.

Advances in the manufacturing processes of printing heralded a golden age of typography, with the invention of hot type machines, beginning with the Linotype in 1886, that allowed the easier compilation of text. The early part of the century was also a time of great flux and inventiveness in the aesthetics of design, an ethos reflected in typography by a growing tension between tradition and innovation. The florid lines of Art Nouveau were transferred into typefaces with variations on Renaissance typography, such as German designer Otto Eckmann's popular Eckmann font, while in Britain the Arts and Crafts movement spearheaded by William Morris yielded a plethora of private presses using typefaces inspired by the spirit of medieval and Renaissance models. In the US the prolific typographer Frederic William Goudy produced more than 100 typefaces, including Trajan, based on the lettering on Trajan's column in Rome, and the more contemporary Goudy Modern.

In the 1920s, the thirst for renewal after the carnage of the First World War helped radical new movements sweep the European artistic scene; the rise of Futurism and Expressionism, typified by the Bauhaus in Germany, led to a preoccupation with geometry in crafting letterforms. The old, curved serif typefaces were increasingly supplanted by san serif faces, among the most prominent of which was Futura, released by the German typographer Paul Renner in 1927. Its enduring appeal led to it being chosen for the lettering on the commemorative plaque left on the Moon by the Apollo 11 mission in 1969. In Britain the best-known exponent of the style was Eric Gill, whose Gill Sans was created after Stanley Morison, the typographic consultant to the Monotype Corporation, spotted his hand-lettering on a shop-front sign in Bristol. Gill produced more traditional serif fonts, such as Times New Roman, first used in 1932 for the layouts of *The Times* newspaper, while faces such as A. M. Cassandre's Peignot, launched for the Paris World's Fair in 1937, and subsequently to become the ubiquitous typeface of the Paris Metro, showed a continued appetite for more classic fonts.

The invention of phototypesetting in the 1950s, and the growth in demand from the advertising industry for posters, generated a demand for a wider variety of typefaces and a means to create them. Swiss designers were at the forefront of innovation, with the san serif Helvetica, designed by Max Mieding and Edouard Hoffman, achieving huge popularity. The following decade, just as designers in music and fashion experimented, typographers began to use the full possibilities of phototypesetting to create faces, such as the futuristic Countdown, that would have been almost impossible using hot metal processes, while Jan Tschichold, the Swiss designer who rebranded Penguin Books, bridged the old and the new with Sabon, which was commissioned as a typeface that would look similar whether manufactured on a new phototypesetter or with hot metal.

The 1970s saw the almost complete victory of photocomposition over older processes, and type

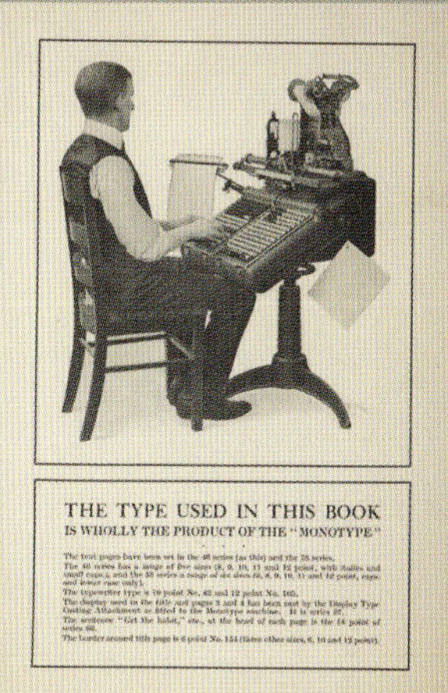

(01.)

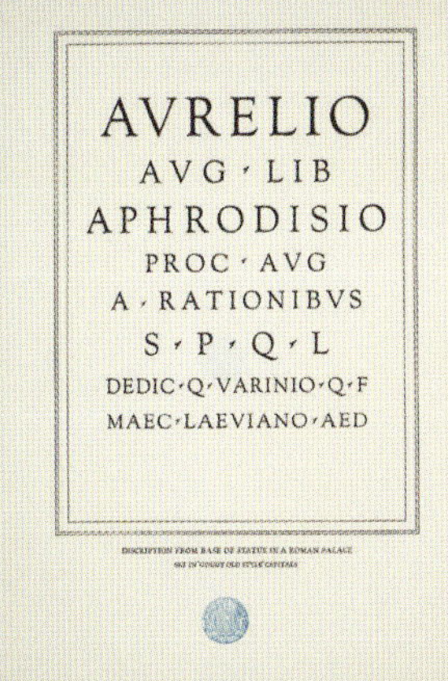

(02.)

(04.)

(05.)

foundries such as the International Typeface Corporation produced ever-greater numbers of innovative fonts. Adrian Frutiger's eponymous Frutiger and his Univers, the first of a scaleable family of san serifs designed to take full advantage of phototypesetting, continued the tradition of Swiss designers being at the vanguard of typography. The 1980s saw even greater changes, with the beginning of the Desktop Publishing revolution, spearheaded by Adobe and Apple (whose first Apple Macintosh computer was launched in 1984). Adobe's creation of PostScript, a page description language that allowed computers to create scaleable vector graphics, opened the way to the world of digital typography. Fonts such as Arial, initially bundled with all Microsoft Windows and Apple OS systems, became by default among the most widespread fonts in printing history, at the same time as the ease and ever-growing sophistication with which typefaces could be produced led to an explosion in the number of type foundries. By the twenty-first century, the variety of typefaces available to book designers was once again almost as varied as the handwriting of their long-ago medieval predecessors.

01. *Frontispiece to* Operating the Monotype Keyboard, *Lanston Monotype Corporation, 1914. (ya.1993.b.3742)*

02.–05. *From* The Alphabet and Elements of Lettering *by Frederic W. Goudy, 1942. (L.R.274.d.17)*

06. *Front cover to* Fourteen type designs selected from the Linotype repertory of book faces, *Linotype and Machinery Limited, 1960s. (Shaw 225)*

XVIII.

SADOK SUDEI AND OTHER FUTURIST BOOKS FROM RUSSIA

Unusual materials and typographical techniques in design

EKATERINA ROGATCHEVSKAIA

Futurism was an avant-garde artistic movement prominent in Russia in the 1910s. As groups of Futurists formed in St Petersburg and Moscow, the most important and innovative art works were created as collaborative projects. Futurists embraced modern technologies and innovations, which they saw as symbolising the industrial, political and artistic revolutions of the period. At the same time, they were interested in such traditional art forms as icons, woodcuts, wooden sculptures and folk tales. They rejected conventional approaches to artistic expressions not only as a representation of the past, but also as a representation of the establishment. Futurists wanted to 'free' all art forms from the rules, combine them to create new meanings and celebrate innovative concepts, in such fields as colour and sound theories, linguistics and the psychology of the consumption of art. It is not surprising therefore that some of their most significant achievements were in book design, which served as an experimental playground for their collaborative pioneering ideas.

BOOKS MADE OF WALLPAPER

'I have a mamma on blue cornflower wallpaper', wrote the 20-year-old poet Vladimir Mayakovski in 1913.[1] This statement was supposed to shock his readers. Not many of them, though, knew at the time when Mayakovski was imagining his 'mamma' on blue cornflower wallpaper that his poems were actually being printed on rolls of wallpaper with different floral patterns. Three years earlier Mayakovski's fellow Futurists (*budetliane* – a neologism made up from the future tense form of the Russian verb meaning 'to be') experimented with their artistic, literary and linguistic theories in a small book called *Sadok Sudei*. This was their first book printed on wallpaper (Image 1).

01. Sadok Sudei *or* Trap for Judges *(St Petersburg) 1910, printed in 300 copies.*

What was it about wallpaper that made it so suitable to promote revolutionary declarations in art? Wallpaper was a sign and product of modernity just like trains, machinery and industrial sounds in fast-growing cities. William Morris aestheticised it by creating designs based on his artistic theories and close observation of nature. Just a couple of decades later, Russian Futurists used it as a symbol of their fight against Modernist aesthetics. The mass production of wallpaper made it economical decoration in the homes of newly emerged petty bourgeois citizens with simple and standardised tastes. Russian Futurists symbolically stripped the walls of such decoration. They used the most uninspiring material for the most unusual artistic expressions. They were endeavouring to renew visual language and find a universal artistic technique. One of the founding fathers of the Futurist movement, the poet David Burliuk (1882–1967), decoded the symbolism of wallpaper in his memoirs: '... we will tear up your entire lives with the fire and sword of literature: under the wallpaper you have bugs and cockroaches; now – let our youthful and cheerful poems live on this wallpaper'.[2] Another participant in the 'project', the artist Vladimir Matiushin (1861–1934), who produced the book in his publishing house Zhuravel', recalled how merrily they all laughed and joked as they thought of the readers who would be made uncomfortable just by looking at the book or touching it.[3]

01.

02.

Въ защиту
Свободнаго
Искусства
ПОЩЕЧИНА
ОБЩЕСТВЕННОМУ
ВКУСУ.
Стихи
Проза
Статьи

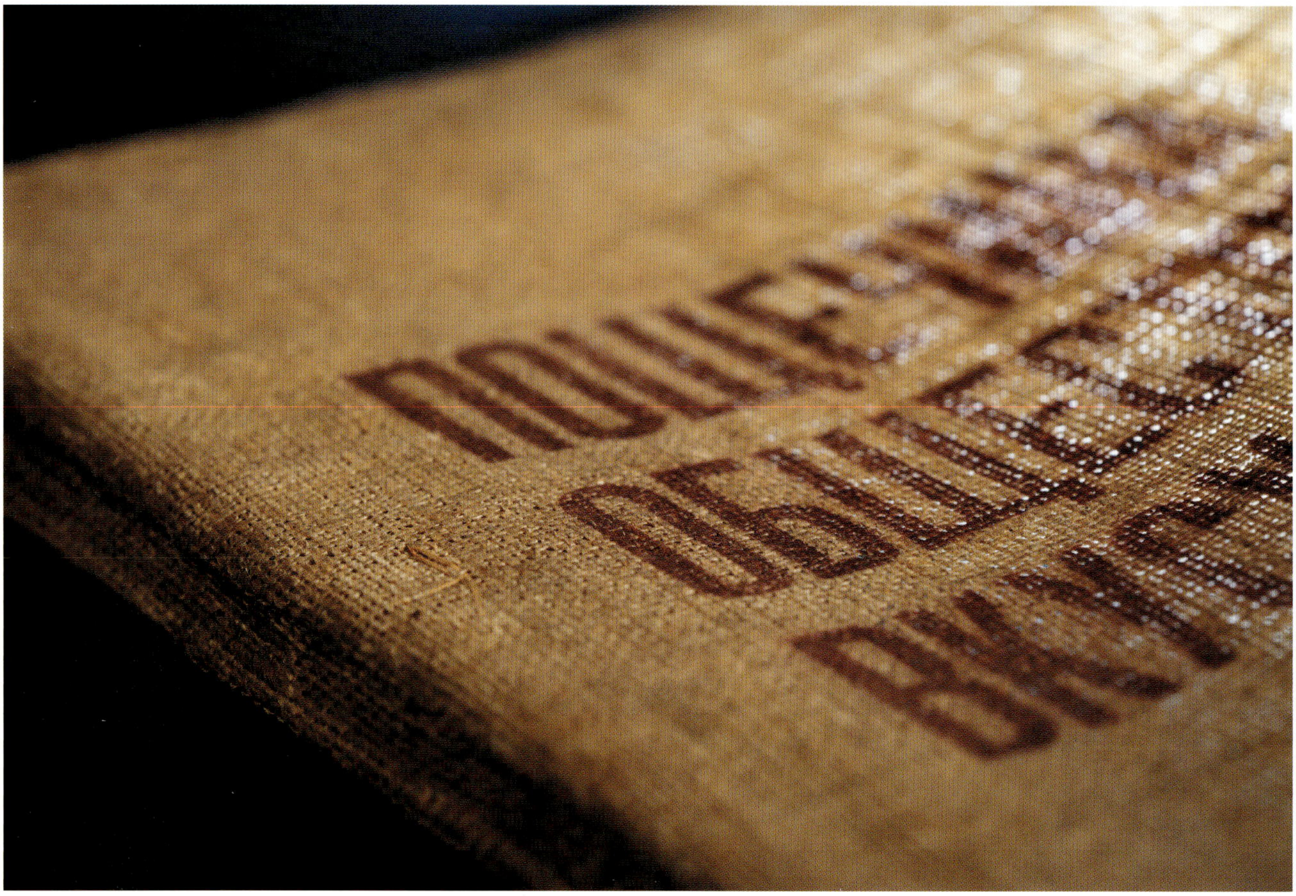

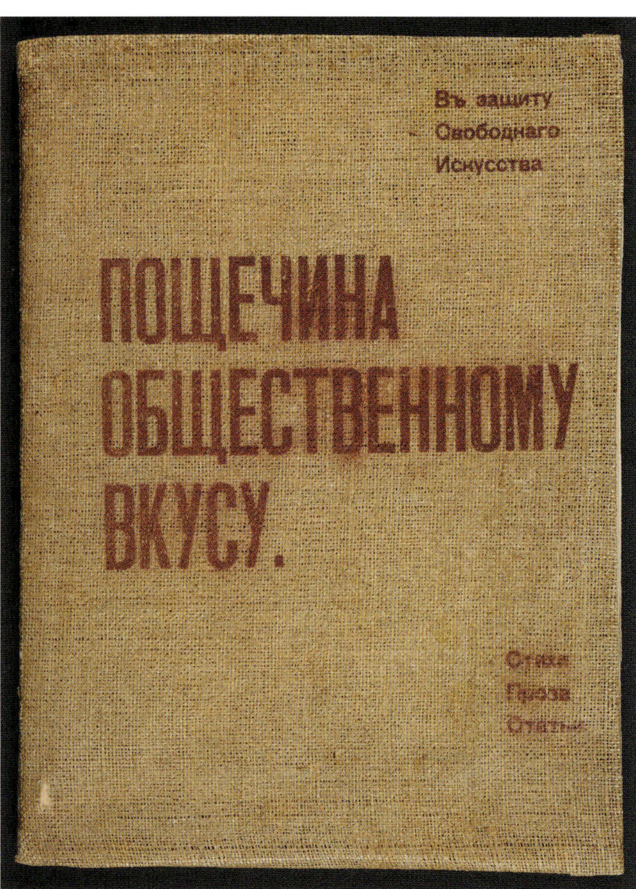

03.

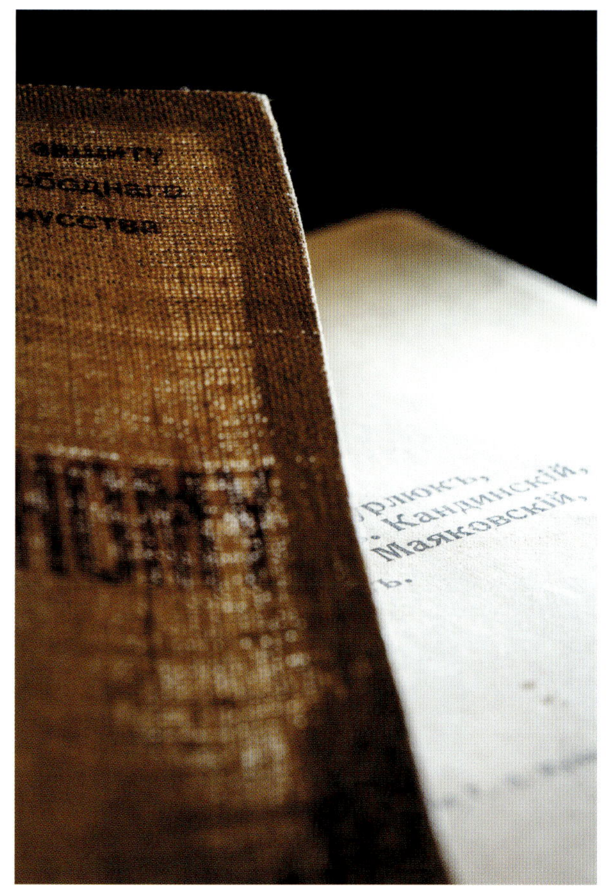

04.

Specification	*Scale*
SADOK SUDEI St Petersburg, Russia, 1910 124 x 100 mm C.104.e.24	

Although *Sadok Sudei* was not the first volume in which Russian Futurists published their poetic experiments, it became a milestone in the development of the Russian Futurist book.

The title *Sadok Sudei*, sometimes translated into English as *Trap for Judges*, was proposed by one of the contributors, the poet Velimir Khlebnikov (1885–1922). It is not intended to make any sense. The first word might mean 'pond', 'cage' or 'fish trap' and the second is a form of the word 'judges', 'experts' or 'connoisseurs', but the relations between the words are ambiguous. The book contains poems and short stories by Vasilii Kamenskii, Ekaterina Nizen (Guro), Nikolai Burliuk, Elena Guro, Sergei Miasoedov, David Burliuk and Velimir Khlebnikov, as well as nine illustrations by Vladimir Burliuk. Texts were printed on the reverse of several rolls of wallpaper, of slightly different shades. Each copy was unique, as the pages had different combinations of texts and patterns. The authors recalled later how difficult it was for the publisher Matiushin to find a printer. No one wanted to take the job on until a small German printing house agreed. We can only guess what the typesetters were muttering while having to clean the cheap and crumbling wallpaper off the type after each run through the printing press! They were never paid in full either, so out of 300 copies printed, only a couple of dozen made it to the readers. The remainder rotted in a warehouse. The authors also wanted to create a new means of distribution for their book, the purpose of which was to 'blow up the old world' and 'start a new epoch', by poking copies *gratis* into the pockets of overcoats left in hallways by owners who were enjoying a party or a poetry reading. These early, cheap-looking books made by Russian Futurists now cost a fortune when they come up for sale at auctions.

As Aage A. Hansen-Löve has observed, the Futurist book wants on one hand to 'retreat into a pre-Gutenberg world of unique objects and handmade [techniques]', but 'on the other, [...] belongs to the sphere of trivial, mass printing products, brochures, posters, slogans and billboards'.[4] The texts in the book, although printed, are reminiscent of pages from manuscripts. For example, the authors' names and the titles of the works were removed from the main text block, creating a visual reference to the marginal glosses often used in manuscripts. Each cover was also made of wallpaper, but with a different pattern to those used for the contents of the book, and had a label with the title pasted on the front.

02., 03. & 04. Poshchechina obshchestvennomu vkusu *or* A Slap in the Face of Public Taste *(Moscow), 1912, printed in 600 copies. (C.105.a.4)*

OTHER FUTURIST BOOK EXPERIMENTS

The authors who had been involved in *Sadok Sudei* in cooperation with other artists gathered again in 1912 to work on a new project. Velimir Khlebnikov, Benedikt Livshits, Nikolai and David Burliuk, Vasilii Kamenskii, Aleksei Kruchenykh and Vladimir Mayakovski were very clear about their intentions. They called the new collection *A Slap in the Face of Public Taste* (Images 2, 3 & 4). They deliberately used grey wrapping paper to print on to evoke cheap grocery wrappers. The books were covered in pieces of sackcloth with a roughly lettered title. Despite unfavourable criticism, this book sold well. It was already difficult to find by 1913, not because everybody rushed to recycle the sackcloth, but because most copies were acquired by students, artists and left-wing intellectuals.

The manifesto at the beginning of the book signed by David Burliuk, Kruchenykh, Mayakovski and Khlebnikov stated that only the authors of this book were the authentic 'face of our Time'. Earlier writers – such as Pushkin, Dostoevsky, Tolstoy – had to be thrown overboard from the 'Steamship of Modernity'. Other contemporary writers did not deserve even that fate.

(05.)

For Russian Futurists, the links between text and medium, the look of the words and the texture of the surface on which they were printed, the sound of poems and the visual presentation of them, were the cornerstones of their artistic method and message. *A Slap in the Face of Public Taste* is a perfect example of such an approach. Under the coarse sacking cover, the Futurists were experimenting with the new language. They aimed to deconstruct old meanings by taking apart the material forms of words and the concepts that these forms denoted. By inventing strange neologisms, new word forms, combining letters in a way that, when read out loud, would affect emotions rather than thoughts, they were creating a system 'where the word itself is an object'. Deconstruction as a method of creating new meanings and forms also applied to the Futurists' approach to the book, which in its traditional form also underwent deconstruction in their early experiments. If in earlier times 'bespoke' bindings indicated the status and

05. Sadok Sudei II *(St Petersburg), 1913, printed in 800 copies. (C.104.e.24)*

taste of the book owner, their replacement in the nineteenth century with affordable mass-produced covers (which were uniform in style) made owners of book copies all equal. To challenge this, modernists saw the book cover as a new medium for their aesthetic ideas. Russian Futurists took this idea to the logical extreme: the book cover should either blend with the content of the book (printed on wallpaper, like the book itself) or provoke disgust in the reader (by its coarse sackcloth texture).

At the same time as making *A Slap in the Face of Public Taste*, Burliuk, Khlebnikov and others were preparing the second volume of *Sadok Sudei*, which appeared just several months later, in 1913.

It was printed on rough paper of two different shades (one bluish and the other greenish, though how many were printed in each colour is unknown). As for the cover, most of the copies I have seen are made from the same wallpaper as the copy held at the British Library (Image 5). However, I have recently located a copy with a differently patterned cover, which reminded me of Mayakovski's blue cornflowers. Was he thinking of this book when creating an image of his 'mamma' – who knows? What we can say for sure is that the authors focused on interweaving drawings and texts into an organic form. Initially, the authors did not pay much attention to the cover of the second volume, so thick blue wrapping paper (the same as inside the book) was considered sufficient. However, Burliuk insisted on creating a visual link between the two books with the same title and the decision was made to use wallpaper again, although this time only for the cover.

The early Russian Futurist book, where text and image organically fuse, reveals the genesis of new systems and a universal language of expression through its experiments not only with typography and page design but also with the actual texture of books. In his *Manifeste technique de la littérature futuriste* of 1912, the Italian poet Filippo Tommaso Marinetti insisted on freeing the new language of modern mass communications that operated in the age of aeroplanes, telephones and radio from the 'old syntax' of traditional grammar. In 1913, Marinetti 'announced that the liberation of the word implied a typographical revolution – that the word should be set free not only from grammar but also from the traditional "bookish" conception of page design and type setting.'[5] The latter could be achieved by 'a use of different colours of ink and of different typefaces for semiotic purposes'.[6] In March 1914, 'a five-sided book of ferro-concrete poems flew out [into the world]'[7] in Moscow (Image 6). The author who set this 'bird' in motion was the Russian poet and aviator Vasilii Kamenskii.

He saw a direct link between aeroplanes and Futurist poetry, and insisted on the influence of technical innovations on modern poetry, suggesting that 'car journeys and flights of aeroplanes, which shrink space, give us a new perception of the world and proclaim "new concepts of beauty"'. Kamenskii intentionally gave his book an enigmatic title *Tango with Cows: Ferro-concrete Poems*. Tango as a dance was coming into vogue internationally at that time and was seen by many as a wanton form of dance. Dancing a tango with cows would make the action look even more audacious. Trying to make sense of the concept of 'ferro-concrete poems', some researchers have suggested that the poems that Kamenskii laid out in various pentagonal shapes on the book's pages represent cement poured into a framework of steel rods.

Tango with Cows was also printed on wallpaper. The use of wallpaper this time was intended not to shock by its ordinariness, but on the contrary – to emphasise the uniqueness of the copy in hand. The trivial and repetitive pattern of the wallpaper used in *Sadok Sudei* – small flowers and poorly traced lines – serve to reinforce the feeling of disharmony between the book's radical ideas and mass-produced 'wrappings'. By contrast, the luxurious pattern of large red flowers on a yellowish background of *Tango with Cows* produced an illusion of a carefully thought through design, as if the author were testing which cut-out or part of the pattern would better suit his experiments with words, lettering and types. The book lacks a separate cover. However, the first sheet bears a pasted-down label

06 (pages 222–223). Tango s korovami: zhelezobetonnye poemy *or* Tango with Cows: Ferro-concrete Poems *by V. Kamenskii (Moscow), 1914, printed in 300 copies with drawings by Vladimir and David Burliuk. (C.114.n.32)*

06.

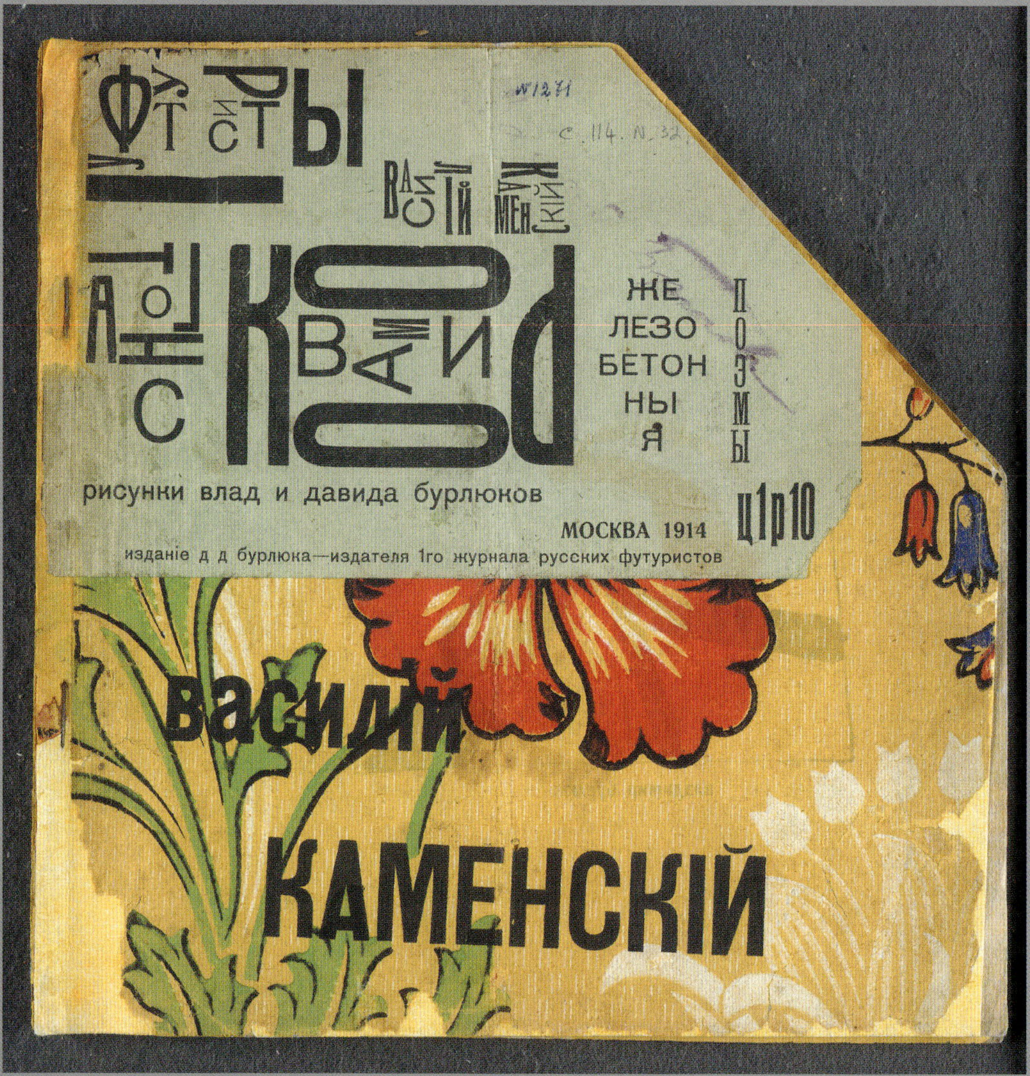
ФУТУРИСТЫ
ВАСИЛІЙ КАМЕНСКІЙ
ТАНГО С КОРОВАМИ
ЖЕЛЕЗОБЕТОННЫЯ
ПОЭМЫ
рисунки влад и давида бурлюков
МОСКВА 1914
ц1р10
изданiе д д бурлюка—издателя 1го журнала русских футуристов
василий
КАМЕНСКІЙ

ЯР
БАР
КАБАРЭ
ЗОН
МАКСИМ
ТАВЕРНА
ШАМПАНСКОЕ
ТАНГО
ШАНСОНЕТКИ
кафэ

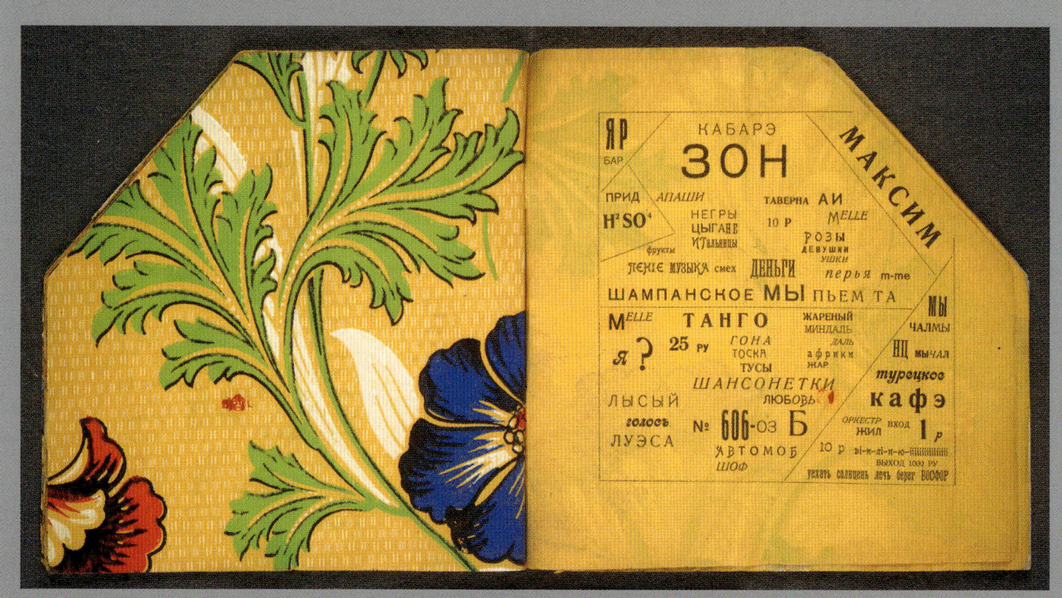

МУЗЫКА
автомобили
босиком по крапиве
ДеТСВО
1884 на КАМЕ
на КАМНЕ
вася КАМЕНСКIЙ
апрель 5 перед ПАСХОЙ
с золотых прiисков
на буксирную пристань
любимова
свистки пароходов
по ночам
и на мачтах огни
мы одни
отдают якоря
от чудес
трое жались
под одним одеялом
вася алёша и петя
(ЧИТАТЬ СНИЗУ ВВЕРХ)

with the title, the author's name and the publisher's details, thus performing the function of a cover. Individual letters are printed using different fonts and are placed in an arbitrary order forming individual shapes for each word. Instead of grammar and syntax, words in Kamenskii's poems are also arranged spatially. Independently from Marinetti's experiments and the ideas developed by Dadaism (a literary and artistic movement which flourished in Switzerland in the 1920s), Kamenskii played with typography using the Russian language and the Cyrillic alphabet. Some of his poems in this book resemble puzzles, other poems can be read like maps. It is now commonly agreed that Kamenskii's poems are early examples of concrete poetry – a term coined only in the 1950s.

Explaining the significance of typographic poems, a modern researcher compares them with what he describes as Gutenberg's '[canonisation of] a certain aesthetic of text design',[8] in which, although there is a wide variety of visual components, these are all confined to the conventional text block. Trying to challenge this, the Futurists became interested in the graphic texture within the book, where 'the words seem to speak for themselves',[9] which made them look into the opportunities offered by lithography.

In the Futurist book, 'the artist is not merely an illustrator', but 'the author of the whole book from its first to last page, from sketching a drawing to writing the text [by hand]'.[10] Drawn handwriting was for the Futurists both a text and an image at the same time. One of the finest examples of this technique is a small fifteen-page book with the cryptic title *Te li le* (Image 7).

TWO WOMEN ARTISTS AND THE BOOKS THEY CREATED

As a rule, copies of this book differ greatly from one another, in both the composition of the pages and the quality of the prints, because multiple copies were produced by means of a hectographic process involving transfer of a master image or text, covered with special dyes, to a pan of gelatine, from which copies are made by pressing paper against it. This book is a remarkable achievement of the extremely talented Olga Rozanova, formed in her collaborative work with Khlebnikov and Kruchenykh, the inventors of the linguistic experiment known as *zaum*. Rozanova collaborated in the design of no fewer than eighteen books, twelve of which were entirely made by her. She saw the book page as a single image, where each element – illustration, letters, punctuation marks and even margins – should relate to each other organically. She experimented with various techniques, including hand-colouring and collages, and paid special attention to choosing the right paper texture for pages and covers.

Another woman artist prominent in Russian Futurism was Natalia Goncharova. Although she took part in several book projects, it is *Mirskontsa* (Image 8) that remains exceptionally famous among art historians and book collectors. Here Goncharova made collage the centre of book design for the first time.

A flower-shaped coloured paper sticker, which comes in multiple variations (so far twelve versions have been recorded), takes up all the space on the cover. The flower comes in black, green or gold, with embossed and marbled patterns; it bends to the right or to the left, or stands straight. It is sometimes concealed behind the text containing the title and author's name and sometimes overlaps with it, or is occasionally placed below it like a support, or pushes down on it from above. The cover evokes the atmosphere of a children's game and invites the book's readers to open the volume with a feeling of naïve excitement. The pages are printed as lithographs, designed as one integral image.

Radical and calm, shocking and magnificent, cheap and expensive, trashed and treasured, Russian Futurist books were a breakthrough in our understanding of art and the world around us.

07. *Pages from* Te li le *(St Petersburg), 1914, printed in 50 copies. (C.114.mm.37)*

08. *Pages from* Mirskontsa *(Moscow), 1912, printed in 220 copies. (C.114.mm.42)*

07.

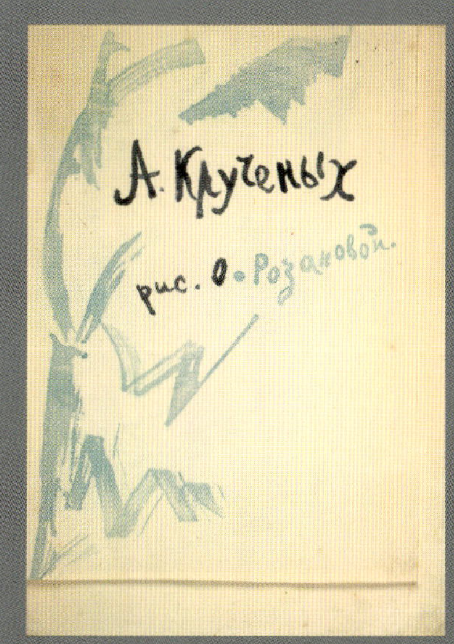

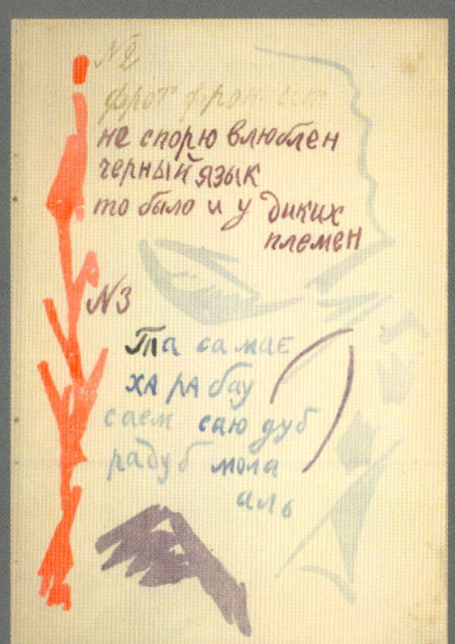

08.

Как трудно мертвых воскрешать...
Труднѣй воскреснуть самому!
Вокруг могилы бродишь тать
Призывы шепчешь одному...

Но безполезны всѣ слова,
И нѣт творящей вѣры в чудо,
Узором шепчут лѣс трава
И ты молчишь... забуду...

М. Ларионов

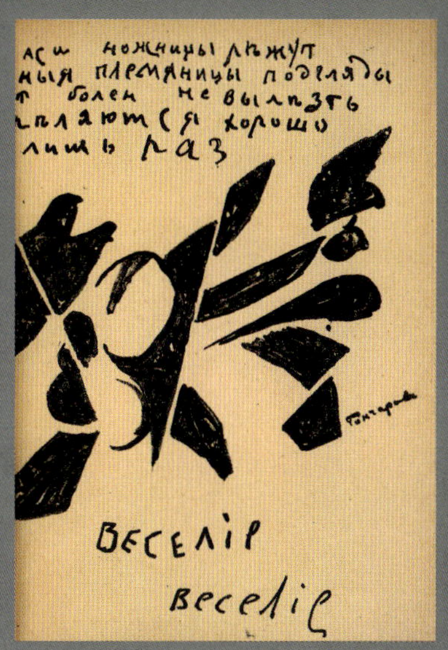

ER
RÀN
CÍA

01.

02.

7 PARA
ARAMI
MIGUEL ÁNGEL MEZA

03.

LA MUJER de
LOS SUEÑOS
del DOMADOR de JACARÉS

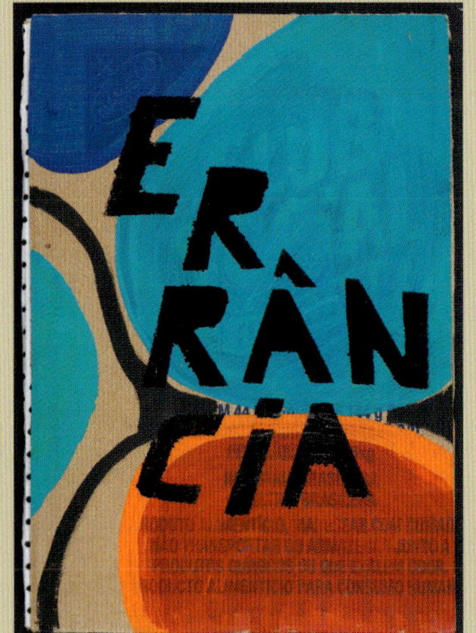

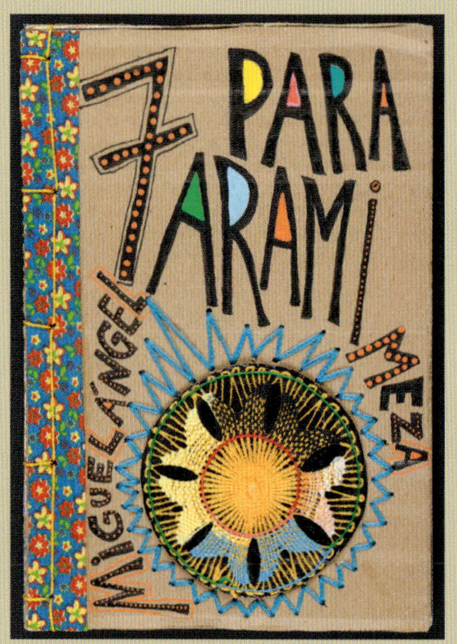

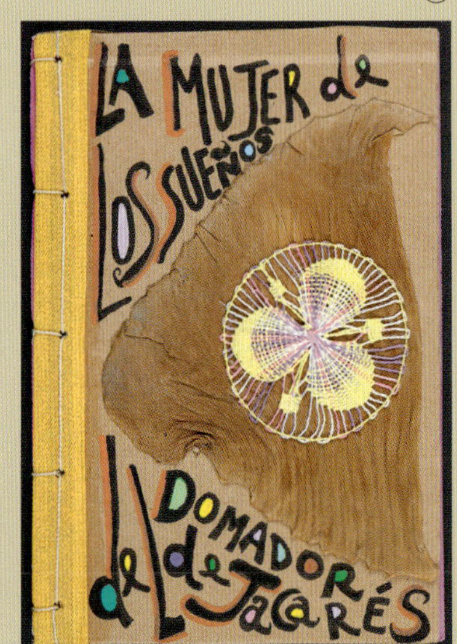

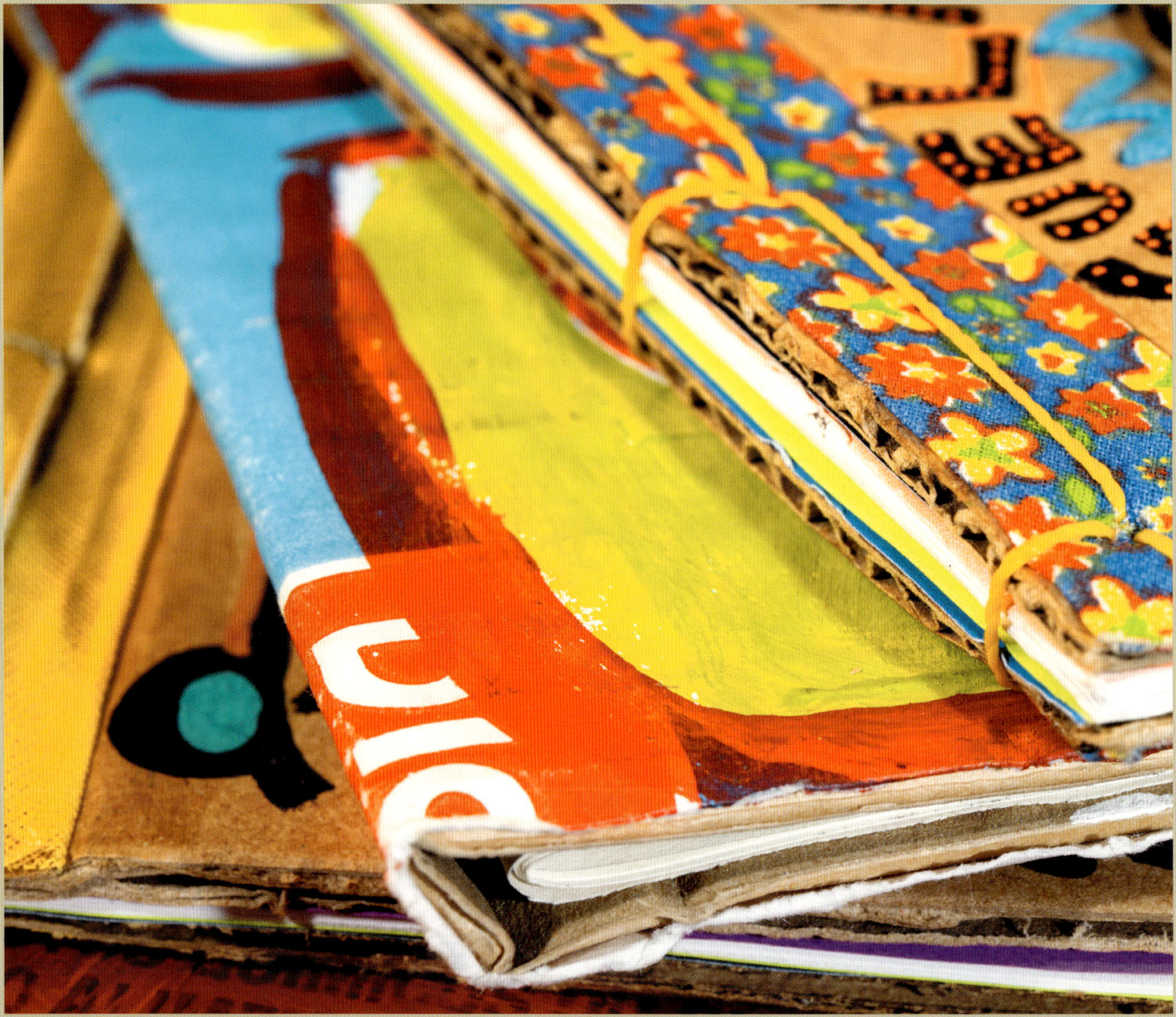

04.

CARTONERA BOOKS AND PUBLISHERS

IRIS BACHMANN AND ANNALISA RICCIARDI

Cartoneras are books of poetry and literature, also pamphlets and translations, made from salvaged cardboard with hand-painted or collage covers. The creators of the illustrated cardboard covers are often anonymous, even when they are famous artists, or the covers are signed by all members of the publishing collective in a clear attempt to promote the community effort over the individual artist. Nonetheless, artistic practice plays a crucial role and many cartoneras are beautiful artefacts. All books are handmade and the cardboard covers become a foil for creative expression through different techniques, from painting and drawing over stitching to collage, stencil and silkscreen printing. Editions have limited print runs and some editions extend and play creatively with traditional book formats, resembling artists' books in so doing.

Originating in South America in the wake of the financial crisis in Argentina in 2003 with Eloísa Cartonera in Buenos Aires, cartonera collectives have worked with underrepresented groups. The phenomenon quickly spread across the region and from the Americas to Europe. Dulcinéia Catadora, for example, are based in a recycling cooperative below a flyover in São Paulo, after emerging from a project at the 27th São Paulo Biennial, a celebrated international arts show.[1] There are cartonera projects in prison, one in Jalisco (Mexico) even creating their own in-house publishing project Bote Cartonero (Cartonera in the Clink).[2] Since its beginnings, Eloísa Cartonera's blueprint for affordable community publishing has allowed other groups plagued by economic and social inequality to appropriate reading and bookmaking practices creatively and in a community-based way.[3] Cartonera collectives often publish original works by non-mainstream authors, but well-known writers have also collaborated with them. Eloísa Cartonera has published works by the renowned authors Ricardo Piglia and César Aira.

The notion of cartonera (*cartón* means 'cardboard' in Spanish) refers to the books and the collectives creating them, and, importantly, it points towards the *cartoneros*, the cardboard-pickers, who inspired the movement and became important collaborators in some of the workshops engaged in creating sustainable literature with very low environmental impact.[4] This is how cartoneras acquired their name according to cartonera lore.[5] The collective at Eloísa Cartonera started paying local cardboard-pickers five times the usual price and reused the collected cardboard to make beautiful books for people who could not otherwise afford them. Thus, Eloísa Cartonera was born and today there are over 250 cartonera collectives in many different parts of the world working at the intersection between literary production, artistic practice and community action.[6]

In the past twenty years, cartoneras have come a long way and are now collected by libraries around the world. The British Library holds around 350 cartonera books from over ten countries and around thirty cartonera collectives. Between 2017 and 2019, together with Cambridge University Library and Senate House Library, the British Library participated in a research project about cartonera publishing led by Lucy Bell at the University of Surrey and Alex Flynn at the University of Durham. In true cartonera spirit, this project led to a number of workshops in Brazil, Mexico and the UK. It also initiated London's first Cartonera Books Festival in 2019 hosted by The British Library and Senate House Library, which brought cartoneras to a wider audience in the UK.

01. *Stencil, drawing and acrylic painting on recycled cardboard, hand-sewn spine (Brazil). (RF.2020.a.76)*

02. *Acrylic drawing, lettering and embroidery on recycled cardboard. Hand-sewn spine on embroidered fabric using Ñandutí, a traditional Paraguayan lace (Paraguay). (RF.2019.a.355)*

03. *Acrylic drawing, lettering and embroidery on native dried plant leaf and recycled cardboard, fabric hand-sewn spine (Paraguay). (RF.2019.a.356)*

04. *Selection of covers showing binding and spines.*

XIX.

CENTURY

Branding and commercial publishing

PHILIP PARKER

The twentieth century saw enormous changes politically and economically, from a world in which European empires were still in their heyday, to one in which decolonisation had long since dismantled them, and nations faced the consequences of the unravelling of the international security system which had preserved them in uneasy stasis during the Cold War. A world in which the motor car was a novelty and international air travel but a far-off dream had become one in which the Internet allowed information to pass from one part of the globe to another in milliseconds.

Book publishing, like most industries, was not immune to those trends and, arguably, as one of the traditional conduits for the dissemination of information, it both reflected and enabled the huge changes in society which took place. By the early twenty-first century, although threatened by the parvenus of the digital information providers, book publishers provided a wider range of titles, to a broader public, at higher quality and in more diverse formats, than ever before.

ADVANCES IN TECHNOLOGY AND TYPEFACES

The key changes which revolutionised the publishing arena arose from the marriage of developments in book design to those in the technology of book production, generating a wholly new field of high-quality illustrated non-fiction in which words and images were fully integrated, rather than uneasily paired by the insertion of sparse (and expensive) colour plate sections.

01. *Ironically for an illustrated title,* Century's *cover employed stark, elegant typography, rather than visual imagery, to enhance its impact.*

Although the introduction of linotype and monotype machines in the 1880s had vastly simplified the process of typesetting, it was another invention of roughly the same time, phototypesetting, in which machines set the type photographically for transfer onto the printed pages, that came into its own in the post-war period. The Intertype Fotosetter, introduced in the US in 1945,[1] enabled the cheaper and faster production of books which enabled the revolution in book design and production that was to follow. In particular, it allowed a sea change in the treatment of illustrations, from a publishing landscape in which they were largely produced from wood engravings, printed on coated paper and bound into books in separate tipped-in sections, to one in which text and images could be fully integrated on cheaper, less glossy paper.

The ability to generate and experiment with new typography was accompanied by more-general developments in the fine arts, in which advertising posters and book covers became legitimate vehicles for aspirant artists to show their talents, especially those at the cutting edge of artistic movements such as the Italian Futurists of the 1920s. The avant-garde typography of designers such as Filippo Tommaso Marinetti and Fortunato Depero was a harbinger of the emergence of professional book designers who concentrated on the look, and eventually the branding, of covers and interior typography, typified by the work of the German designer Jan Tschichold at Penguin in the 1950s.

01.

02.

HAMLYN
London · New York
Sydney · Toronto

Hamlyn
All Colour
Cook Book

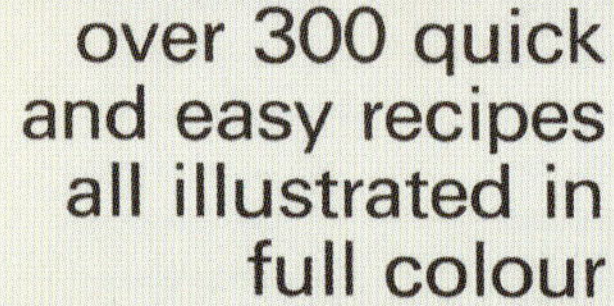

over 300 quick
and easy recipes
all illustrated in
full colour

03.

The aftermath of the War in Europe

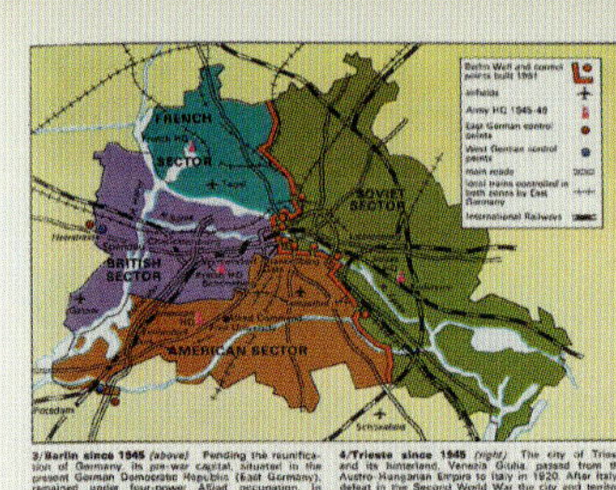

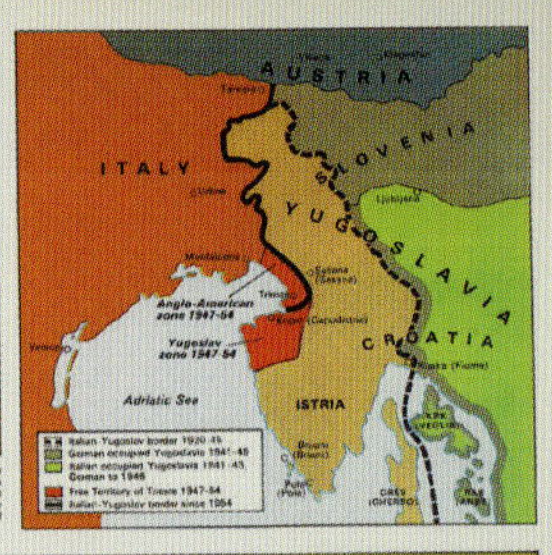

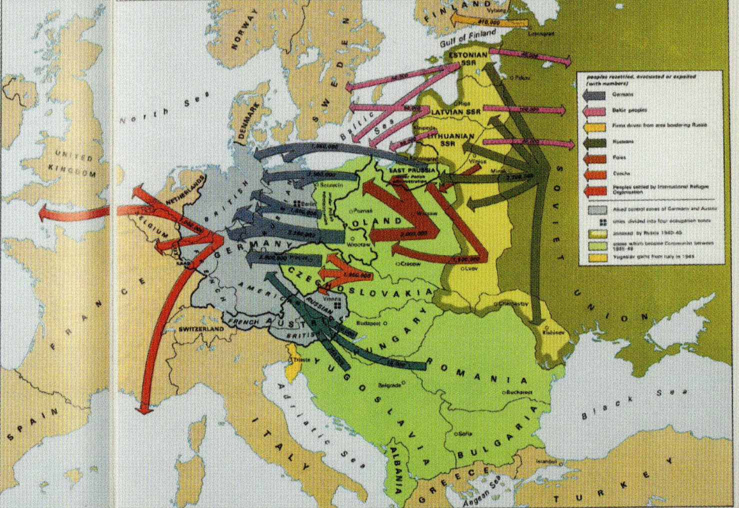

THE COLOUR PRINTING REVOLUTION

As the 1950s opened, publishing in the US and the UK was concentrated in a small number of companies, often founded in the 1920s, many still run by their founders (such as Knopf's eponymous Alfred Knopf and Bennett Cerf of Random House), with hardback lists heavily focused on trade fiction and non-fiction. The pace of change was sedate, but the decade saw the beginnings of larger-scale colour printing in non-fiction titles. The introduction of photocomposition in the 1950s and 1960s (by which photographic images of page layouts were used to create printing plates) and then terminals in which digital typefaces could be stored supplanted the traditional role of compositor, while the advent of affordable desktop publishing from the early 1980s meant that designers could lay out pages directly.

This combined with falls in the cost of colour printing and an increase in the quality produced by the wider adoption of offset litho printing (in which the reversed photographic images were transferred to an intermediate surface such as a rubber sheet before being reversed onto the final printing plate) meant that for the first time high-quality colour books could be created in which images and the relevant text which referred to them could appear on the same or facing pages. A first step in this direction had been taken by the *About Britain* series produced by the typographer Ruari McLean and the former book salesman George Rainbird which, with their focus on improvement and national pride, were an apt reflection of the aspiration of the nation in the 'New Elizabethan Age'.

02. *Advances in printing technology in the 1970s made truly integrated titles, such as the* Hamlyn All Colour Cook Book, *possible for the first time. (X.622/794, pp. 2–3)*

03. *Whereas most previous historical atlases had been in black and white,* The Times Atlas of World History *made use of colour, arrows and shading, together with longer texts and annotations integrated onto the maps, enabling the book to tell a far more complex and nuanced story. (LD.31.b.3745, pp. 204–205)*

The process was accelerated by German-born Paul Hamlyn, who launched his Books for Pleasure in 1949, using cheap colour printing in Czechoslovakia to produce a range of cookery, lifestyle, art and travel titles which appealed to a wider audience, selling them through outlets such as department stores, and pioneering point-of-sale merchandising such as spinners. At once, the stuffy world of traditional bookshops, off-putting to many potential new customers, was challenged to open its door wider. The *Hamlyn All Colour Cook Book*, first published in 1970, with text by cookery writer Mary Berry, became an icon of the new wave of illustrated titles boasting 'over 300 quick and easy recipes all illustrated in full colour' and going through several editions and generating spin-off titles covering a range of culinary tastes, including curries, salads and slow cooker dishes. With each recipe having exactly one picture and half a page of text (including 1970s favourites such as aspic chicken and chocolate butterflies), its bright colours were perhaps a reflection of the fashion tastes of the era.

THE ADVENT OF INTEGRATED PUBLISHING

The revival in illustrated publishing gathered pace in the 1970s as publishers realised that the new technology allowed them to go further than a formulaic placement of text against images. For art publishers in particular, such as Phaidon, Thames & Hudson or Taschen, the opportunities were huge, both in publishing monographs and, as Thames & Hudson did after the appointment of Ian Mackenzie-Kerr as art director in 1957, in creating strong series styles and visual branding epitomised by the striking black backgrounds framing single colour images of artworks of the flagship *World of Art* series (launched in 1958). The sector, too, came to be populated by publishers such as Hamlyn and Marshall Cavendish, producing low-cost titles which sat sometimes uneasily between the spheres of education and entertainment. Many of them were produced by book packagers, the lineal descendants of medieval monastic scriptoria or printers' ateliers, which created books on commission, which were then actually published under the imprint of a major publisher (which thereby was able to buy in specialist design skills and concentrate on the editorial and sales functions in-house). Dorling Kindersley, originally founded as one such book packager in 1974, was by the early 1980s publishing on its own account. Its founders Peter Kindersley and Christopher Dorling developed a distinctive look, sometimes derided as 'lots of white space', but which integrated blocks of text and images in an unparalleled fashion to make the visuals and type work seamlessly to impart information to the reader. Early successes such as Miriam Stoppard's *Complete Child and Babycare,* first published in 1990, enabled the company's rapid expansion, assisted by the large in-house design resource which kept the design and branding tight and a hugely successful series of alliances with US, European and other international publishers for the publication of foreign language co-editions. The company's heady expansion into almost all areas of illustrated reference publishing, including historical atlases, travel guides and cookery books, was only temporarily staunched by a disastrous venture into *Star Wars* merchandising which saw it left with millions of pounds worth of unsaleable stock and led to its takeover by Penguin in 2000.

HISTORICAL ATLASES – A NEW WAY OF TELLING HISTORY

In 1999 DK published its *Atlas of World History,* adding a new entry into an area in which illustrated publishing had pushed the bounds of a traditional reference publishing mainstay – the historical atlas – into entirely new territory. For example, the *Shepherd's Historical Atlas* (first published in 1911 by Henry Holt) had adapted the techniques of traditional cartography to display historical trends and had foreshadowed the integration of text and image on the maps themselves (with bold arrows and areas of coloured shading showing the waxing of empires and invasions by barbarians). They had not, however, been able to include large blocks of text on the map spread themselves, discussing historical developments in an integrated way. *The Times Atlas of World History,* published in 1978 by Times Books (soon afterwards incorporated into Rupert Murdoch's growing publishing interests as part of HarperCollins), made that leap. Although the pre-digital production processes in cartography were still laborious – with the labels for towns, their names and even the arrows showing which way the Huns or Goths had travelled, having to be stuck on layouts by hand – the inclusion of text by leading historians (under the guidance of the medieval specialist Geoffrey Barraclough) meant that readers were presented not just with a series of maps in isolation, but with a book in which the maps and text genuinely worked together to create a historical landscape. The four colour plates (Cyan, Magenta, Yellow and Black) which the photocomposition process normally created was also supplemented by a text black plate on which all the type for town names, and the main text itself, was embodied, allowing the easy translation of the title, and the production of numerous foreign language co-editions which helped fund the hugely expensive project. The bespoke creation of hand-drawn hill-shading (to create impressions of geographical features from the Himalayas or the Andes, to the Gobi or Sahara deserts) further enhanced the effect of something more dynamic than the flat monochrome maps of traditional historical atlases.

By the time of the fourth edition, published in 1993 on the cusp of the age of digitisation, the *Atlas of World History,* now under the editorship of the early modern historian Geoffrey Parker, had expanded to 360 pages with 126 map spreads, each containing as many as nine maps – though some with a single map showing a dramatic global sweep, in deference to the original planners' intention to use the large format (with a page size of some 370 by 260 millimetres) to create a truly world history, rather than a merely parochial European one. The subjects treated ranged from early human migrations to the Aztec empire, the Silk Route, the Napoleonic Wars and the Cold War (only then finally coming to an end) and the incorporation of pictures on each spread as well as maps and text produced a visually integrated approach that gave readers several ways into each subject. On the maps themselves the widespread use of areas of variegated colour shading, annotations with leader lines, bar charts and colour-coded keys allowed the cartographic elements of the book to offer a dynamic historical narrative, which, alongside the text composed by more than 100 leading historians, represented a comprehensive design-led approach to history that could not have been possible in previous decades. The digitisation of the atlas in the late 1990s simply cemented this process, allowing the easier updating of maps, as trends in global politics (and accompanying them, in publishing markets) led to a greater concentration on areas such as Chinese, Korean and African history, as well as the momentous events which had taken place in the thirty-seven years between the first edition and the ninth in 2015, including the Iranian Revolution, the fall of the Berlin Wall, the dissolution of the Soviet Union, the 9/11 attacks on the US, the Gulf Wars, the Afghan conflict and Global Financial Crisis of 2007–08.

Specification	*Scale*
CENTURY London, 1999 270 x 272 mm 99/38592	

CENTURY: 100 YEARS OF IMAGES

One book, published to mark the end of the twentieth century and the beginning of a new millennium, sought to capture many of these developments and at the same time acted a marker both of tradition and innovation in British commercial book publishing. Phaidon's *Century: One Hundred Years of Human Progress, Regression, Suffering and Hope*, published in 1999, made few compromises: at over 1,200 pages long and including more than 1,000 photographic images, it provided a lush visual chronicle of the twentieth century. It became one of the most talked-about (and sold) titles of the turn of the century, both for its sparse, yet rich design and its uncompromising bulk. In many ways it is a nod towards traditionalism, with a single photograph (or occasionally two) per page, accompanied only by brief captions and text-only pages interspersed through the book to give more detailed explanations of the background to the images, and with little of the complex integration of text and illustration which became a hallmark of later twentieth century large-format non-fiction. Its cover, too, is bold in its starkness, with the single word 'Century' in white against a solid black background. Yet the book's ambition (and its success in fulfilling it) lies in the way in which its panorama of photographs encapsulate the essence of the century, including such iconic images as French soldiers being rushed to the front by taxi to head off the German thrust towards Paris in 1914, children waving at an incoming plane during the Berlin Airlift in 1948 and, as if to show for all our technological and economic progress that the despair of war's victims remains universal, victims of ethnic cleansing by Serb militias in Kosovo in 1999.

Phaidon, the company which produced this monumental bookend to a transformative century, had lived through much of it. Originally established in Vienna in 1923, it transferred to England when its founder Bela Horovitz fled the Nazis in 1937.[2] It established its reputation for high-quality art books with Ernst Gombrich's monumental *The Story of Art* (commissioned after Horovitz met the art historian by chance on the upper deck of a London bus), which was published in 1950 and went on to sell over eight million copies. After losing its independence in 1967 to a subsidiary of Encyclopaedia Britannica, and then Elsevier, the company revived in the 1990s with a return to strongly branded titles, playing on the company's reputation for design excellence, which *Century*'s success confirmed.

CONSOLIDATION AND CHALLENGES

By then the cost of keeping up with the very technological developments which had opened up such vast possibilities were taking their toll on the publishing industry. Penguin's takeover of DK was a sign that publishing consolidation was gathering pace, as long-standing independent publishers, such as Hamish Hamilton and Michael Joseph, were swallowed up, as well as Frederick Warne, with whom came the Beatrix Potter titles and even greater opportunities to produce merchandised goods to generate further revenue from loyal readers. The final acquisition of Collins, by Rupert Murdoch's News International, came in 1989 after some years of pursuit. Murdoch merged it with the US publisher Harper & Row to form HarperCollins, which became one of the UK's 'Big Five' publishers in the 1990s, its access to film and TV franchises through the larger News Corporation empire and the large advances which its new owner's deep pockets could finance – setting off an acceleration in payments to star authors, which offered a goldrush to a lucky few but ultimately led to an unhealthy cleavage between a small number of high-earners and others who struggled to establish themselves, as publishers understandably concentrated on marketing those authors whose high advances they needed to recoup. In the US, a similar process of consolidation culminated in the announced merger of Simon & Schuster by Bertelsmann in late 2020.

Yet, although the diversity of the publishing landscape may now be coming seriously into question, with only a few major publishing leviathans, and the consequent lowering of advances paid to most authors making it harder for non-established authors to break into the market, the advances in design and layout software, removing most of the previous, laborious stages between design conception and final camera-ready pages, mean that illustrated titles in all areas of the non-fiction marketplace continue to proliferate. A range of medium-sized publishers, such as Phaidon, Thames & Hudson and units of larger publishers such as DK, ensure that the market is still innovative. The renaissance of illustrated publishing looks set to continue, and book design and the visual impact of books are now as important in the twenty-first century as they were to a sixteenth-century Venetian printer or a tenth-century monastic manuscript illuminator.

04. *Although the pages with* Century's *imagery contained only the briefest of captions, separate text pages fleshed out the background to each of the photographs.*

05. *Striking Polish mill-workers in New York and immigrant garment workers – bearing a Babel of placards – on strike in the same city are two of* Century's *images telling the story for 1913.*

04.

1899–1914

Historical Background

All pictures are referenced by page number.

1899

14. *Organ Grinder* by Eugene Atget. Europeans could be forgiven for feeling light-hearted at the dawn of the century. Europe was at its presumptuous, confident peak: its cities were the envy of the world and its empires spanned the globe. War between these major powers seemed a distant possibility.

15. The drawing room of the Edward Lauterbach residence, New York City. Waves of immigration from Italy and Eastern Europe during the latter part of the nineteenth century helped power a booming economy in which thousands of New Yorkers amassed large personal fortunes. By 1900 approximately 80 per cent of New York's population were immigrants or the children of immigrants. It was at this time that America's largest city became a metropolis, moving from national to world stature in finance, business and the arts.

16. This blacksmith was one of some 2 million Germans who were still working in traditional artisanal enterprises at the turn of the century. The pre-industrial sector was more entrenched in Germany than in Britain or France at the time, but the same cannot be said for the rest of the economy. In his lifetime this blacksmith had witnessed the euphoria of military triumph in the Franco-Prussian War (1870–71) and the emergence of Germany as a unified, modern European nation-state. By 1900 Germany had risen to become an industrial colossus and the most powerful state on the continent.

17 top. British beauty and actress Lillie Langtry striking a pose as Mrs Trevelyan, a character from Sydney Grundy's comic satire *The Degenerates* (1899). Daughter of the Dean of the Isle of Jersey in the Channel Islands, Langtry was one of the most famous women of her time. Known as 'The Jersey Lily', she caused a sensation among the upper classes by becoming the first society woman to have a career on the stage. Eventually she acquired many distinguished admirers, including the Prince of Wales, subsequently King Edward VII.

17 bottom. In the 1890s Russia's industrial growth approached 10 per

intolerable conditions in the countryside often made their way to the industrial cities and found work in huge factories such as this textile plant in the region of Ivanovo. But urban life proved just as difficult for most. This, combined with the unfamiliar pace of factory work and an awareness of continuing rural hardship, caused waves of strikes and demonstrations to break out. By 1905 workers in Ivanovo had set up the first soviet – a council of workers that demanded the right to assemble freely to discuss their grievances and elect representatives.

18. The sinking of the USS *Maine* which had been sent to Cuba to protect US citizens and property after rioting against Spanish colonial rule swept across the island. The mysterious explosion of the American battleship on 15 February 1898 precipitated US intervention in the Cuban struggle for independence. When war broke out between Spain and the US in 1898, newspapers had not yet turned to photography for reporting topical events. Stereographs (of which this and the image on the opposite page are examples) were the closest thing to the news for most Americans. These are three-dimensional images which were produced by looking through a stereoscope.

19. American soldiers during the Philippine campaign of the Spanish-American war. A US naval squadron went into Manila Bay in the Philippines and destroyed the anchored Spanish fleet in a quick, one-sided battle on 13 December 1898. The Filipinos suffered greatly during the US occupation of their country which followed. In response, an unsuccessful guerrilla campaign was waged against the US (1899–1902), foreshadowing similar struggles in other South-East Asian states against foreign domination in future decades.

20. Alfred Dreyfus, seen standing in the central area of the military court in Rennes, France, declaring his innocence on 7 August 1899. Five years earlier the young French army officer had been tried in secret and convicted of treason for passing secrets to Germany. Suspicion had fallen on him because he was Jewish. Prominent writers and French intellectuals began a campaign, which included

famous letter '*J'accuse*', to have Dreyfus exonerated. The controversy flared into a national crisis, dividing French society into Dreyfusards and anti-Dreyfusards. It was not until 1906 that a civilian court finally reversed the verdict.

21. A group of upper-middle-class American women at the Woodbine Settlement School, New Jersey. To these women wearing men's clothing was one of the few ways that they could openly express their sexuality and desire for more autonomy during this period. By the late nineteenth century, distinct limits on female participation in the workplace, coupled with a general tendency across society to view women only in their traditional roles as wives, mothers and homemakers, fuelled a minor backlash among small groups of women in Europe and America. Gatherings of the 'Old Maids' Convention' – as these women ironically referred to themselves – reflected the less aggressive forms of opposition to male domination which preceded the vigorous and sometimes militant women's movements in the West over the next two decades.

1900

22. A Japanese battleship built by the British, leaving Newcastle-upon-Tyne. Shipbuilding was one of the few heavy industries in which Britain still maintained an international supremacy at the turn of the century. British naval technology helped Japan, then a British ally, to develop the fastest and most powerful fleet in the Far East. The British and continental Europeans still regarded Japan as a small, albeit clever nation with no great imperial ambitions in the Far East.

23. A Japanese officer wipes blood from his sword after beheading several Boxer rebels in Tangshan, China. Foreign interference in China's affairs and attempts by European powers to monopolize trade in the country sparked a peasant uprising known as the Boxer Rebellion. The protest was led by members of a secret society (named Boxers by Westerners) which had strong links with the Imperial Court. Foreign legations and religious missions in Peking were attacked. Popular unrest followed, most notably in Tianjin. A six-nation expeditionary force

05.

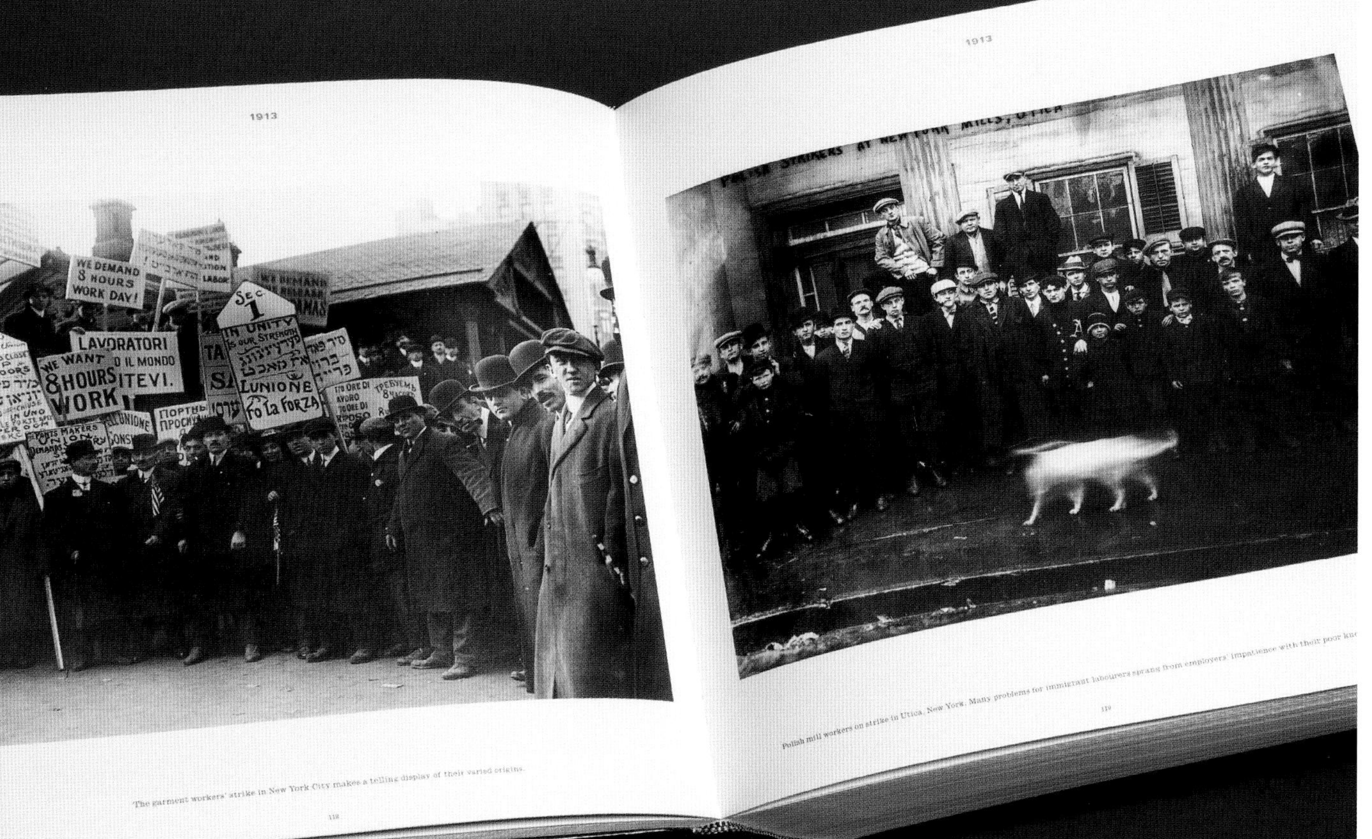

The garment workers' strike in New York City makes a telling display of their varied origins.

Polish mill workers on strike in Utica, New York. Many problems for immigrant labourers sprang from employers' impatience with their poor kn

PENGUIN BOOKS AND THE PAPERBACK REVOLUTION

PHILIP PARKER

In 1935 the publisher Allen Lane came up with an idea that would revolutionise the British publishing market. During a long, dreary train journey back to London he found the reading material on sale at Exeter station particularly dispiriting – all cheap thrillers and romantic novels. His solution – to combine the paperback format of these books with a wider range of titles, ranging from modern literature and ancient classics to art and economics, all linked by strong visual identity – was a stroke of genius. It saved his family company, Allen Lane, from financial ruin and generated an offspring, Penguin, that became a publishing leviathan.

None of this was entirely new. Portable editions arguably dated back to Aldus Manutius's edition of Virgil's *Opera* in 1501 (with its diminutive page size of 77 by 150 millimetres). Series such as Joseph Malaby Dent's Everyman Library and the Albatross range, which were strongly branded according to subject (such as red for crime), had brought higher-brow literature into the paperback arena during the Victorian era. Yet Lane understood that British publishers simply weren't reaching a market that found traditional bookshops rather stuffy but still craved something more inspiring than they could find elsewhere.

Lane succeeded in persuading publishers to sell him paperback reprint rights, and he assembled a list of ten launch titles, including a detective novel by Agatha Christie and *A Farewell to Arms* by Ernest Hemingway (Image 2). The overall series title, Penguin, arose almost by chance from a brainstorming meeting and the Production Assistant, Edward Young, was sent to London Zoo to sketch one of the animals as a logo. Aware of the need for a clear series identity, Lane had Young design a cover style that became iconic, with three horizontal bands, an emphasis on typography and a two-tone colour-coding system, including orange and white for general fiction and green and white for crime.

Initial orders were unpromising until Lane secured one from the department chain Woolworths for 63,000 copies. Before long frantic reprints were in train, and the despatchers were overrun in their ad hoc headquarters in the crypt of Holy Trinity Church, Marylebone, where one of the tombs did double service as a repository for invoice ledgers. By the end of 1935 Penguin had sold over a million books, and as the range grew to fifty titles by July 1936 the total reached three million, a tally helped by the low price point, at 6d., at which Lane had pitched the series.

This unprecedented success encouraged Lane to launch a new brand, Pelican, in 1937, specialising in non-fiction. For the first book in the series, he innovated further by commissioning the company's first original title, achieving the coup of getting George Bernard Shaw to contribute to *The Intelligent Woman's Guide to Socialism, Capitalism, Sovietism & Fascism* (Image 10). With their distinctive light blue covers the Pelicans cemented Penguin's dominance of the paperback market. They were soon joined by further sub-brands including Penguin Specials (on political subjects) and children's books, which began publication under the Puffin brand in 1940, initially as educational titles, but encompassing 'Story Books' the following year.

Penguin weathered paper rationing during the Second World War, and in 1946 launched the Penguin Classics range with a translation of Homer's *Odyssey* by E. V. Rieu. By now, though, despite its enormous commercial success, the company's branding was beginning to look tired (unkind commentators referred to the Penguin icon as looking as though it had appendicitis). In 1947, Allen Lane hired the Leipzig-born typographer Jan Tschichold to rejuvenate the brand. With a background as a radical Modernist influenced by New Typography, Tschichold drafted a set of prescriptive Penguin Composition Rules, both tightening up the design ethos of the imprint and weaning it away from an over-reliance on Times New Roman. He redesigned the Penguin logo to produce a more believably bird-like icon (Image 12), changed the banding on the main Penguins from horizontal to vertical, introduced a rectangular window with embedded

images in it, and placed roundels on the Penguin Classics adorned with delicate line engravings.

In his twenty-nine months at the company, Tschichold designed over 500 titles, establishing a design ethos that endured for decades and reinforcing a Penguin brand which, against increasing competition from rivals such as Pan (launched in 1944), survived to become one of Britain's best-known twenty-first-century publishing brands. In 2011, Allen Lane's little intuition at Exeter station earned his successors worldwide sales of over a billion pounds.

Top row: **01.** *(12208.a.1/1)*, **02.** *(12208.a.1/2)*, **03.** *(12208.a.1/31)*, **04.** *(12208.a.1/5)*.

Middle row: **05.** *(12208.a.1/60)*, **06.** *(12208.a.1/7)*, **07.** *(12208.a.1/16)*, **08.** *(12208.a.1/17)*.

Bottom row: **09.** *(12208.a.1/628)*, **10.** *(12209.d.4/1)*, **11.** *(12208.a.2/1b)*, **12.** *(12208.a.1/746)*.

01.

XX.

SEA AIR

An artist's book by Susan Allix

JEREMY JENKINS

Susan Allix's *Sea Air* is one of the finest recent examples of an artists' book, defined in Joanna Drucker's words as 'any work of original art created in the book format' or where, in Stephen Bury's reverse formulation, 'the book [as an object] is intended as a work of art in itself'.[1] It can be argued that this approach to the physical copy of a book as a precious object in itself – in a sense, the concept of book design taken to its ultimate degree – has been a recurrent feature in manuscript and printed book production over the centuries though the term 'artists' books', in Drucker's and Bury's sense, is generally used to refer more narrowly to works in book format created by independent artists in the period from the 1960s onwards. They are usually issued in highly limited editions.

Sea Air is described in its prospectus as 'Prints of the Sea with poetic interludes and interventions. Extracts from the poetry of Rossetti, Byron, Shelley, Wordsworth, Coleridge, Kipling, Arnold & Swinburne designed and printed with aquatint, etchings & woodcuts by Susan Allix'.[2] It explores seascapes or more precisely the coastline where sea and land and sky meet by bringing together words and images, juxtaposed and connected in a great variety of ways, and employing a wide range of different techniques and contrasting styles. Allix was first a painter, then a printmaker. In looking for alternative ways of using these skills she came to book art, which added the skills of working with words and with three-dimensional objects to her practice. She never collaborates and prefers to work alone. This has allowed her, in her own words, to become 'a printer, a haphazard typographer, a binder constantly amazed at the expertise needed, an unwilling box-maker, an occasional jeweller and maker of silver cages and pages, a sometime papermaker...'[3]

01. *Front cover. The rich ultramarine of leather, paper and silk binding radiates. A collage of prints drawing the eye to a distant horizon, from a textured foreground, is a precursor of the rich depth contained within this book.*

The book was handmade and published in 2018 in an edition of fifteen copies. By its nature, a book requires physical interaction to carry out its tasks of imparting information and stimulating thought. Such interaction is where an artist's book really comes into its own, by offering the reader or viewer (either term is appropriate in this context) a more intense, tactile experience than they might otherwise have with an 'ordinary' book or indeed viewing paintings or prints in a more traditional gallery environment.

STRUCTURE

Sea Air has the traditional structure of the codex – pages gathered and bound together in sequence – the standard format for Western book production, both for manuscripts and then printed books, since late antiquity. At the same time, Allix subtly makes us look afresh at many aspects of a conventional book, which as readers we usually take for granted, such as the materials from which it is made, the standard rectangular shape of its cover and pages, the way we move through it by automatically turning pages to follow the text, and the normally hierarchical connections between text and illustration.

The book is a substantial volume containing over 100 leaves. It is organised into 'eleven descriptive titles', preceded by an introduction; each of the titles evokes different, often contrasting, aspects of the sea and weather conditions, occasionally identifying different times of day: Sea and Land, Ocean, Calm, Evening, Mist, Storm, Night, Noon, Spray,

Depth, Wind. Each section is associated with a poem; Allix draws on the work of eight Romantic and Victorian poets, using two poems each in the case of Shelley, Rossetti and Arnold. Although the different poems refer to various localities (or none), the artist has described the prints as 'being observed and recorded on a stretch of English coastline'.

But the relationship between the chosen texts and the images associated with them is far from fixed or predictable. On the contrary, it changes constantly. The words precede or follow, juxtapose or even mingle with the images; they often vary font size and typeface (some words, for example the title of the second section 'Ocean', are printed in a specially designed typeface Allix herself has created, limited to the letters needed) and, in the tradition of concrete poetry, form different patterns, are jumbled or reversed or mirrored, or occasionally even turn into images themselves. Nor are the lines Allix quotes from the poems she has chosen always in the sequence in which they are found in the originals. The main set of images through the volume consists of twenty-two full-page intaglio prints depicting, with an extraordinary variety of technique, different effects of light and shadow and texture in their representations of sea and sky and shore. There are also woodcut blocks and linocuts. In addition, Allix continuously varies the consistency, texture and size of the paper she uses, cutting the pages into different shapes to evoke, for example, waves on a shore, or shaping windows through them so that part of the image on the next page can be glimpsed, or layering and interleaving different-sized leaves or strips of paper to suggest, for example, an approaching storm (Image 5). She also expressively balances the blank spaces on the pages of this large book with the vivid and rich colours she uses in the prints.

02. *The layout of lines from Byron, along with cutaway pages, gives the impression of eddying water washing over the page.*

03. *A pair of intaglio aquatints marks the passage of time. Lines from Wordsworth nestle between a cropped opening, its edges reddened, caught by the late afternoon light.*

04. *In crisscrossed pages the text appears reversed and jumbled until the half-page is turned.*

05. *The chaos of a storm is heightened by folds and contrasting papers that represent a departing cloud.*

The binding is a work of art in itself in its rich anticipation of the images, colours and techniques found inside; there are however no words indicating the book's content (Image 1). Laid on to ultramarine and navy-blue leather is a vertical assemblage, on both front and back boards, of strips of different materials (leather, paper, silk), variously coloured, textured and patterned, surmounted by richly coloured watercolours depicting sea, a distant shore and sky, a tripartite division echoed consistently throughout the book. The outer edges of the front and back boards are not straight as they normally are but gently scalloped like a wave rippling on the sand.

CONTENTS

The introduction is a good example of the subtle and playful sequences Allix constructs throughout the book whereby the normally mechanical gesture of turning the pages to advance through the book is slowed down and made meaningful (Image 7). It consists of a small plate with lines alongside in the original Latin from the Roman satirist Gaius Petronius Arbiter. The image and text are first shown blurred through a sheet of translucent paper naming Petronius and carrying the title Introduction, followed on turning the sheet over by a further differently textured half-sheet still obscuring the image and the left half of Petronius's verses. It is as if the reader is approaching the sea shortly after sunrise, with a low mist obscuring the view. When the half-sheet is turned, it reveals the image of a seascape on the left side by side with the lines of verse on the right: '*o litus vita mihi dulcius o mare...*'. This transforms what was, seen through the preliminary sheets, an 80 by 65 millimetres tonally grey rectangular image into a rich and vibrant intaglio aquatint where the tonal depth of the ultramarine sea is framed at the bottom by a cove with breaking surf and at the top by a headland emerging from the sea. Then the sequence is repeated (and reflected) on turning over the page: another slightly larger half-sheet obscures a translation of Petronius's lines, this time on the right – 'sea, sea shore, more precious to me than life' – with another intaglio aquatint of the same

a pleasure
PATHLESS WOODS,
a rapture on the
SHORE:
society where none intrudes
deep sea,
music in its roar.
NOT MAN THE LESS,
nature more
from these our
interviews

storm storm
storm
torm
torm
torm

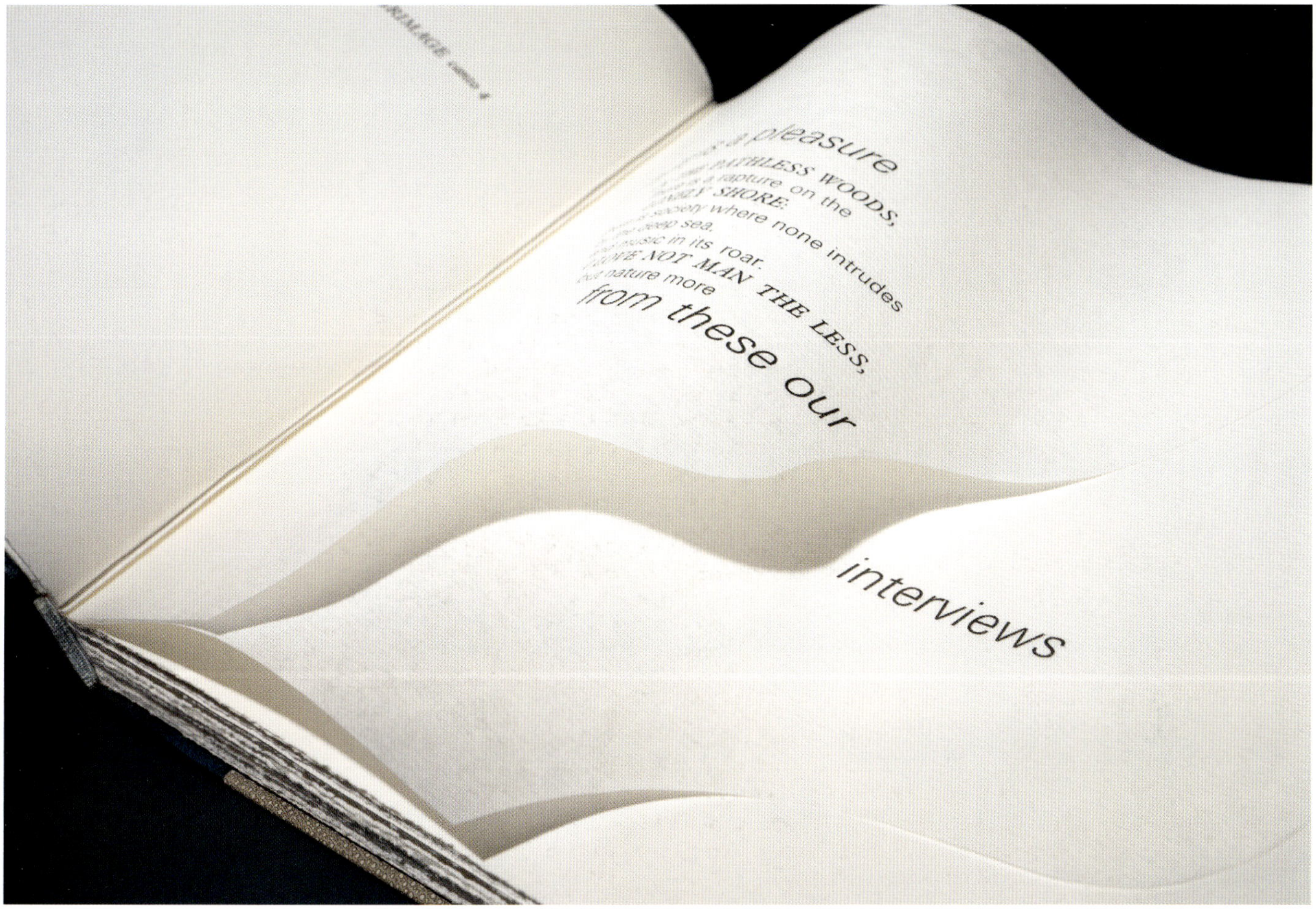

05.

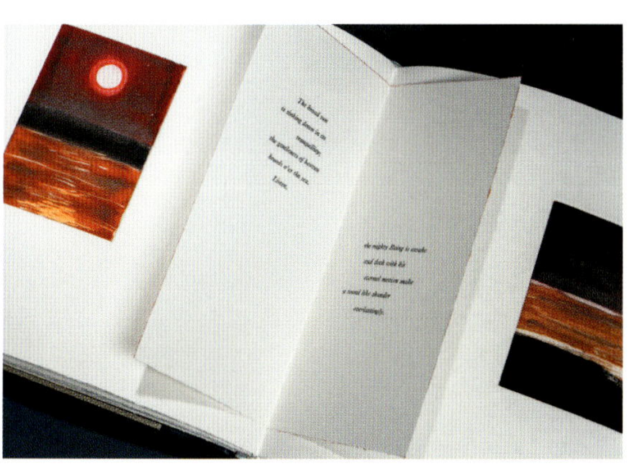

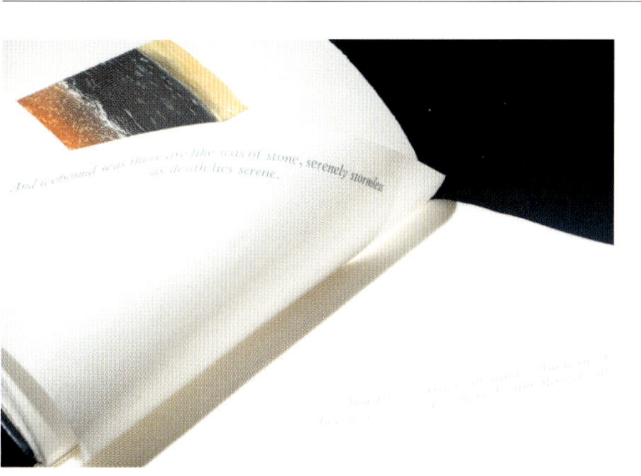

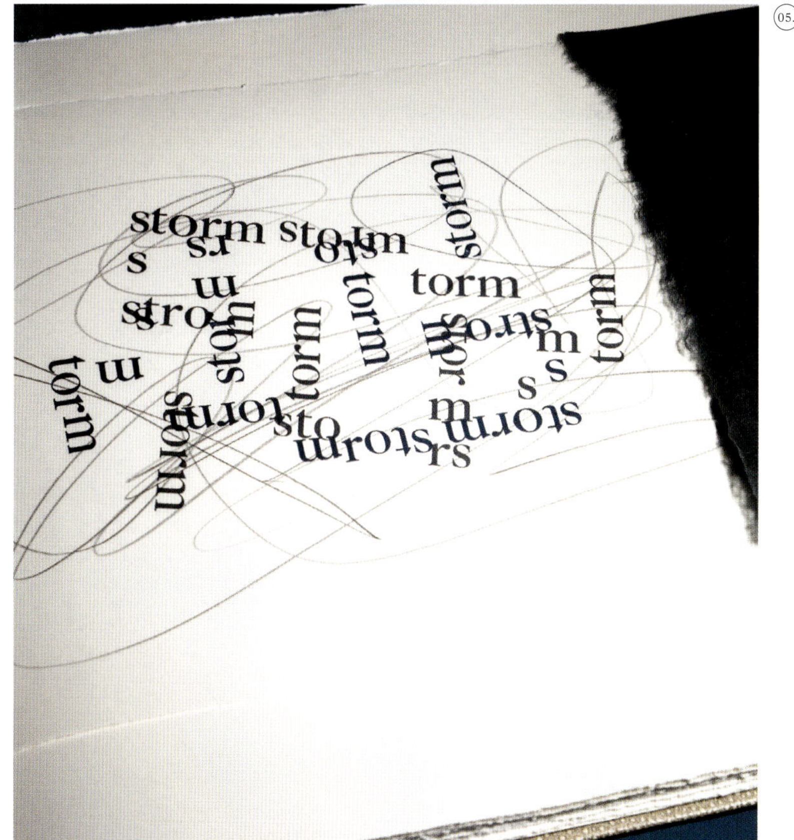

Samuel
Taylor
Coleridge
THE RIME
OF THE
ANCIENT MARINER
MIST
in all time: calm or convulsed, in
BREEZE
or gale or storm, icing the pole or in the torrid clime,
DARK-HEAVING, ENDLESS, BOUNDLESS
& SUBLIME.
OCEAN

06.

size on the left, showing a different scene but with the same three horizontal bands of shore, sea, sky.

The first section, entitled 'Sea and Land', focuses on a sonnet by Christina Rossetti and is a good example of Allix's inventiveness with the design of the text and the way text and image can overlap and interpenetrate (Image 8). The sonnet is shown as if the first eight lines or octave of the sonnet have been lifted by an incoming wave and thrown across the page, deposited on the shale as it withdraws. This effect of flotsam and jetsam is created by changing font, orientation and the size of letters within words. The text is printed over wavy lines which represent the shallows where sea, land and air meet. This concept is picked up on the opposite page in the image which highlights in bands the meeting points between the land and a three-tone ultramarine sea topped by sky mirroring the colours of the wavy lines used on the facing page. As the reader turns over the page, Rossetti's sonnet changes tone and Allix deploys a darker, more menacing palette to represent the words 'icebound seas there are like seas of stone'. The intaglio aquatint of deep stone grey is framed with rich rustic hues to emphasise the 'bright coloured' days that are behind us. Now the sea takes on a chill and the typographical arrangement of Rossetti's text – a couple of lines running from top left to bottom right printed on the reverse of a triangular semi-translucent sheet of paper which intersects a second triangular sheet below with the next two lines running from bottom right to top left – forms a giant X, like a stark cancellation of the movement expressed in the first eight lines, representing the ice and stone evoked in the poem. This arrangement produces a disorienting effect until the reader turns the first sheet over and the lines assemble themselves into the next four lines of the sonnet now both running in the same direction and mirroring each other across the opening (Image 4).

The section 'Mist', which uses words from Coleridge's *Rime of the Ancient Mariner* ('And now there came both mist and snow...'), is a fine example of how Allix accompanies or expands the reader's movement through the lines of verse, which here are typographically austere, as if reflecting the solemnity of the sight of the mist and snow lifting to reveal icebergs ('and ice, mast high, came floating by') with a sequence of almost entirely and similarly stern and solemn monochrome images. The single word MIST is printed, like the earlier chapter 'Ocean', in a typeface of Allix's own creation called Tin Lid, which is made up of only these five letters (Image 6). As the page is turned Allix uses paint and scoring on a transparency laid over two-tone striped black paper, echoing the vertical forms of the word MIST just seen on the previous page and evoking the uncanny superimposition of 'both mist and snow' in the poem. On the facing page a technique known as sugar-lift, which uses a sugar solution and a paintbrush to create painterly marks on the plate, is strikingly employed by Allix at various points in the prints and here imitates snow flurries as a huge iceberg looms out of the darkness. Alongside the print, the shape of the berg is indented or embossed on the thick handmade paper, adding, on both recto and verso of the page, another equivalent motif of the blankness of ice, in this case working both in terms of sight and touch.

In the next section, 'Storm', with lines from Kipling's poem *The Sea and the Hills*, the manner in which a storm is depicted is particularly ingenious. The letterpress appears randomised. The word 'Storm' has been overprinted in various directions over the page, with letters missing, reversed or knocked out of alignment; this scramble of words and letters is contained within a frantically scribbled pencil line. The page is folded back over a torn black sheet – only the approaching ragged line of the storm can be seen – concealing the destructive power which propelled the letterpress into such disarray (Image 5).

Matthew Arnold's 'Dover Beach' introduces 'Night'. A rich blue and green intaglio print sprinkled by hand with resin powder, a deep open bite or large

06. *Chapters open in a strong manner with the dynamic use of typography setting the theme and style of the forthcoming pages.*

Specification	*Scale*
SUSAN ALLIX, SEA AIR: PRINTS OF THE SEA WITH POETIC INTERLUDES AND INTERVENTIONS London: The Author, 2018 310 x 340 mm HS.74/2374, 7/15	

open area exposed to acid on the lower part of the plate and three sizes of holes drilled through the plate, all help to bring the opening stanza of Arnold's poem to life (Images 10 & 11). Here graduated aquatint captures the clear night sky. The image is framed between two folded half sheets with jagged black edges obscuring the outer edges of the print, perhaps in part a reference to an unquoted line in Arnold's poem 'Come to the window...'. When the two half sheets are opened they reveal the opening lines of the poem. The text continues on the following verso, with Allix again using a combination of differing sizes of letterpress and the use of upper case for emphasis, opposite a large print where again the use of sugar-lift subtly evokes 'the grating roar of pebbles'.

Perhaps the most striking example of contrast in the entire artfully constructed sequence in the volume follows 'Night'. We move directly to 'Noon' and also explicitly out of England since the poem is Shelley's 'Stanzas Written in Dejection near Naples' (Image 9). White space on the page and colour contrast represent reflections in water at the height of the day. In different hues of blue, echoing each other across their facing pages, words and image shimmer and dance. The following opening continues the theme with the order of image and text now reversed – a mirroring device Allix uses elsewhere as we have seen – and in the middle of the text at the top and bottom of the page (both beginning 'I see...') a series of horizontal lines broken up into differing lengths, as if the words themselves have intermittently disappeared, leaving only the trace of the lines of verse into which they were arranged, perhaps evoking Shelley's inner sense of vacancy before the enchanting sight of the Bay of Naples, while also reflecting the calm waves of the sea stretching out in front of him.

Another Arnold poem, 'The Forsaken Merman', accompanies the penultimate section entitled 'Depth'. 'Down down down down To the depths of the sea.' The repeated words tumble on to the page – one is printed upside down – indenting more deeply with each line. At the top right of the page a cutaway window frames what appears to show the depths of the sea, but on turning the page the perspective is changed and the viewer is located once more, as in Arnold's poem, on a rocky shore looking onto a view where the tide is far out.

To end the sequence of poems and images, Allix returns, in the section entitled 'Wind', to Christina Rossetti and her short eight-line poem 'The Wind Has Such A Rainy Sound', quoted in its entirety. After the complexity of some of the previous sections mentioned above, here we have a simple opening in which the text faces the final large intaglio print in the book, depicting once more and for the last time the triad of sky and sea and shore. Frantic etched lines tower in the sky over a narrow band of green/yellow sea reflecting a weak sun and balanced by an equally unsettling tangle of thick black lines blocking the shore. Once again there is no literal one-to-one connection between text and image, which are instead hauntingly parallel, the image expressing something of the unease – 'Will the ships go down?' – present in the nursery rhyme simplicity of Rossetti's poem.

CONCLUSION

Sea Air is a testament to the versatility of Susan Allix as an artist, printer and bookmaker, above all in the range of techniques she expertly employs to remarkable expressive effect. Continually playing with the connection between images and texts, the cumulative effect is to draw readers into a profound reflection on the coastline where sea, land and sky all meet. Allix's book is an accomplished example of the importance of design in the creation of form and its capacity to open up fresh perspectives on complex concepts.

07. *The introduction to* Sea Air *is presented over two openings with text in Latin and then in English.*

08. *The text mimics the flotsam and jetsam littering the foreground of the accompanying image.*

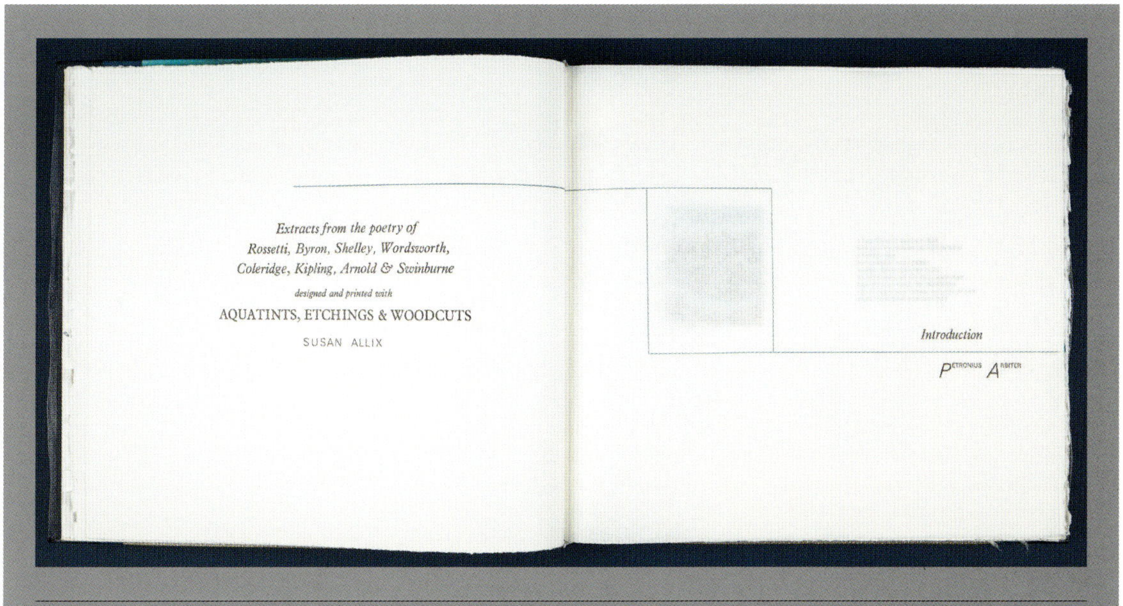
Extracts from the poetry of
Rossetti, Byron, Shelley, Wordsworth,
Coleridge, Kipling, Arnold & Swinburne
designed and printed with
AQUATINTS, ETCHINGS & WOODCUTS
SUSAN ALLIX
Introduction
PETRONIUS ARBITER

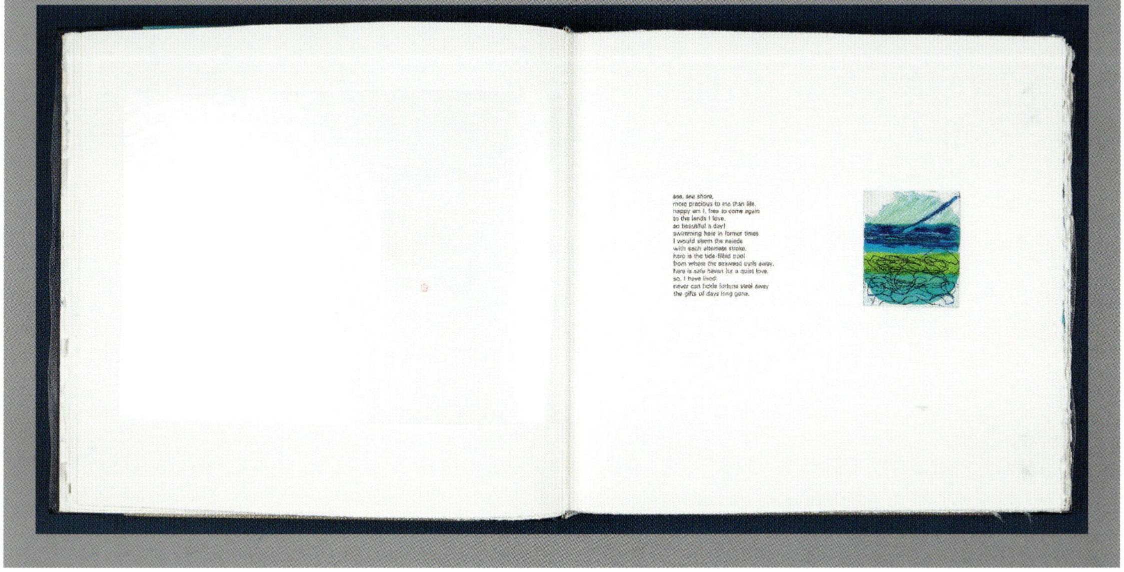
sea, sea shore,
more precious to me than life.
happy am I, free to come again
to the lands I love.
so beautiful a day!
swimming here in former times
I would alarm the naiads
with each alternate stroke.
here is the tide-filled pool
from where the seaweed curls away.
here is safe haven for a quiet love.
so, I have lived:
never can fickle fortune steal away
the gifts of days long gone.

07.

08.

Beyond the seas we know
stretch SEAs unknown,
BLUE
and
BriGht
COLOURED
for our dim and green.
Beyond the lands we see
stretch lands UNSEEN,
with
MANY
Tinted
Tangle
OVERgroWN.

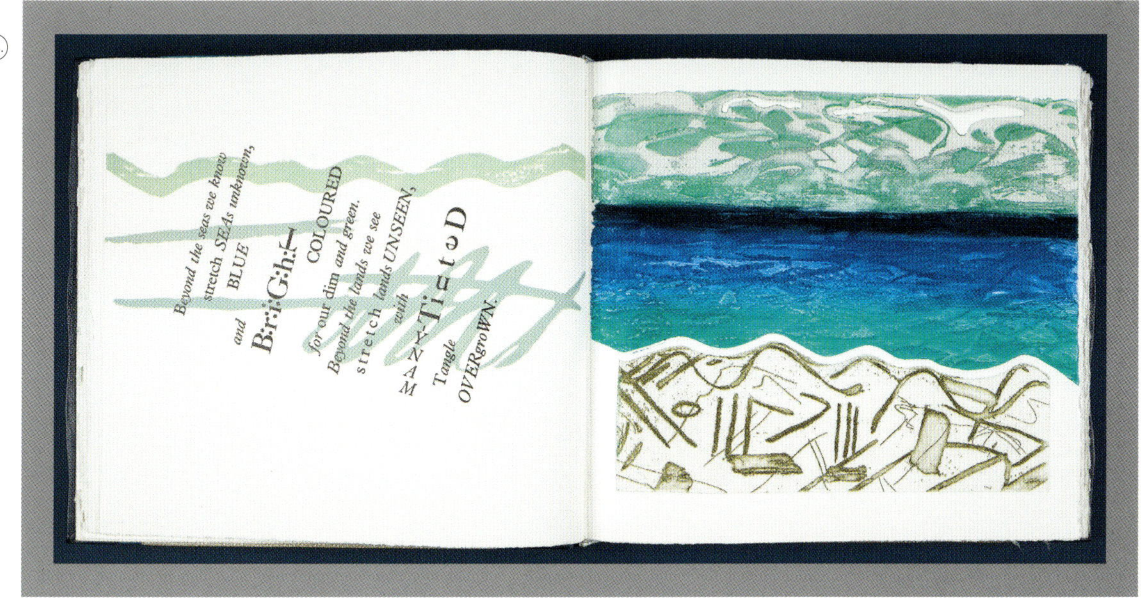

09. *Two openings capture the bright reflective qualities of a Mediterranean noon. Text and image give the impression of shimmering light; the text has fluidity.*

10. & 11. *A pair of images in the section 'Night' use a dense palette with sharp cuts to depict the frigid night. They open to reveal a portion of Arnold's 'Dover Beach'.*

(10.)

NIGHT

(11.)

The sea is calm tonight.
The tide is full, the moon
lies fair upon the straits.
On the French coast
the light
gleams and is gone.
The cliffs of England stand
glimmering and vast,
out in the tranquil bay.

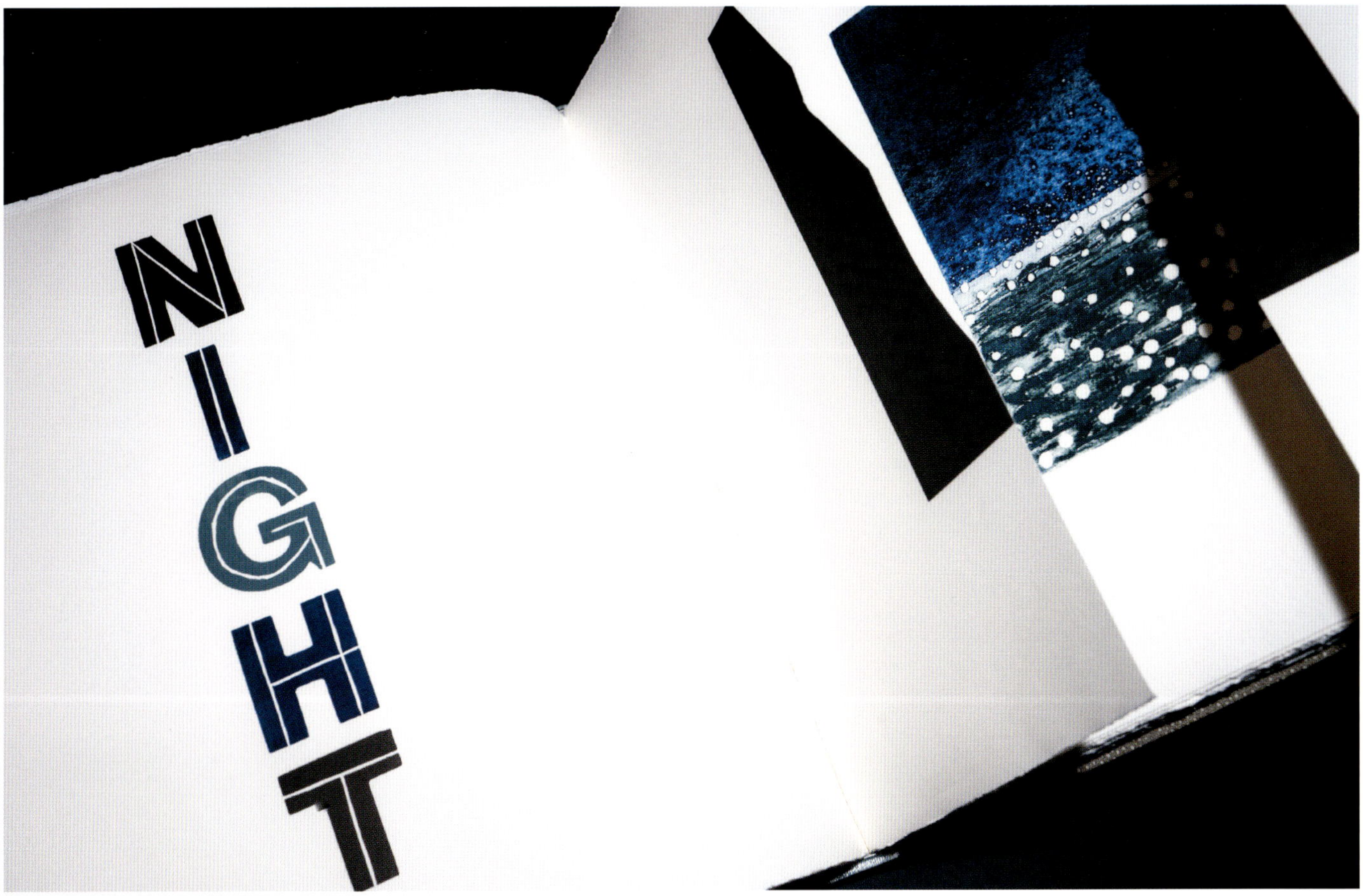

WOMEN PUBLISHERS AND DESIGNERS

ALEXANDRA PRINGLE

For many years the world of publishing was dominated by men, some of whom owned publishing houses which they named after themselves: André Deutsch, Hamish Hamilton, Secker & Warburg, Michael Joseph, Victor Gollancz and Weidenfeld & Nicolson. Women were secretaries or worked in publicity, and generally were neither seen nor heard.

When they were seen it was at such events as the Pergamon Press annual 'Miss Pergamon' contest where apart from beauty, women were judged for 'personality, poise, confidence and efficiency'. The winner got a weekend in Paris, a new wardrobe and a 'titled sash, cloak and crown' to wear at official company occasions.

But in the 1970s a revolution began as three new publishing houses appeared. The New York-based Feminist Press was created in 1970 by Florence Howe with a flickering flame for a logo. On the other side of the Atlantic, in 1973, the Virago Press was founded by Carmen Callil, Ursula Owen and Harriet Spicer; its logo an apple with a bite out of it. Then in 1977 the Women's Press was founded by Stephanie Dowrick; its logo an image of a clothes iron. The book spines sported black and white stripes to represent an iron's electric cord.

In 1978 I was the fourth person to join Virago. This was the same year that the first Virago Modern Classic was published. The mission of the Modern Classics was to demonstrate that there existed a canon of women's writing that had been disregarded by a male establishment. By so doing Virago shifted the idea of what made a 'classic'. The first Modern Classic was Antonia White's *Frost in May*, originally published in 1933. We went on to publish further neglected writers of the early twentieth century – Sylvia Townsend Warner, Rosamond Lehmann, Margaret Kennedy, Rose Macauley among them. We also published great American writers who were almost unknown in the UK including Willa Cather, Ellen Glasgow, Zora Neale Hurston and modernists Jane Bowles, Kay Boyle and Djuna Barnes.

I became Editorial Director of the series and held that post for nearly a decade. Carmen and I worked closely, choosing titles to reprint, commissioning new introductions and finding cover images. Our cover designs echoed the Penguin Modern Classics with their use of paintings contemporary to the novel, but the Modern Classics were larger in size and their designs were unified with spines and a top panel in dark green.

We realised that famous paintings rarely make good book jackets and decided to find the work of little-known artists. In our search we scoured the reserve collections of provincial art galleries for forgotten artists. I spent hours sourcing paintings at the Witt Library at the Courtauld Institute. Carmen and I pored over Sotheby's catalogues of early twentieth-century art, and for modern novels we'd go to the Summer Exhibition of the Royal Academy, touring the show at breakneck speed stopping only to look at work by women. As we hunted, our greatest pleasure was to find women artists such as Dod Proctor, Laura Knight, Dora Carrington, Gwen John, Romaine Brooks, Stella Bowen, Marie Laurencin, Vanessa Bell.

We also worked to uncover the history of women in art. Nancy Heller's *Women Artists: An Illustrated History* was a pioneering work originated by the Abbeville Press in the US and published by Virago in the UK in 1987; *Women Artists and the Pre-Raphaelite Movement* by Jan Marsh and Pamela Gerrish Nunn and *Women Engravers* by Patricia Jaffé added to our list and the understanding of British women in art history.

In 1990 I moved from Virago to Hamish Hamilton where I worked with a highly talented young designer called Suzanne Dean. She has been the Creative Director of Vintage Books since 2000 and is probably the most significant art director in publishing today. Responsible for the jackets of such writers as Julian Barnes and Ian McEwen, she has also overseen the creation of new visual identities for classic writers of the last 200 years, ranging

from Jane Austen through Virginia Woolf to Margaret Atwood.

Even today there are fewer women than men art directors. Loulou Clarke at Ebury, Jo Walker at Pushkin, Claire Ward at HarperCollins, Charlotte Abrams Simpson at Orion and Donna Payne at Apple Books are among them. Many talented women designers and illustrators leave publishing houses to work freelance. Two of these are Holly Ovenden and Emma Ewbank. Holly has created a famous new look for Agatha Christie and designed jackets for such writers as Elif Shafak and India Knight, and Emma designed the arresting cover of Peter Frankopan's ground-breaking *The Silk Road* and the cover of Maggie O'Farrell's *The Marriage Portrait*.

The publishing landscape has changed and it is hard to imagine today how three independent radical presses could spring up at the same time. The Women's Press has folded; the Feminist Press moved to the City University of New York Graduate Center campus in 1985; and in 1996 Virago was bought by Little Brown, which is part of Hachette. The Modern Classics series endures but has fewer titles. And while the presence of women in publishing is growing, it remains the case that women tend to get stuck in lower-level jobs and earn less. For a while it looked as though women had broken through the glass ceiling. Gail Rebuck was CEO of Random House, Helen Fraser managing director of Penguin, Annette Thomas CEO of Macmillan, Ursula Mackenzie of Little Brown and Victoria Barnsley of HarperCollins. But one by one they left publishing and have been replaced by men. You need only look at the structure of boards of publishing companies to see there is still a long way for women to go. It is true that in 2023 half the boards of the big houses are comprised of women, but they do not hold the most senior posts of group chief executive, group chief operating officer and group chief finance officer, positions where the real power lies. It is not until this shifts that there will be a significant change in the lives and careers of women in publishing.

01. *Rebecca West's* The Judge *reflects the distinctive design of the Virago Modern Classics, with green panel and a painting by Carrington. (x_908/43343)*

02. *The Women's Press edition of Kate Chopin's* The Awakening *includes their logo on the front cover. (x_958/21052)*

XXI.

EDITIONS AT PLAY

Interactive digital narratives that use mobile technology to enhance the structural and design elements of the book form

GIULIA CARLA ROSSI

INTRODUCTION

'... any book is a negotiation, a performance, a dynamic event that happens in the moment and is never the same twice.' (Amaranth Borsuk) As extensively discussed in Amaranth Borsuk's *The Book* (2018), our definition of 'book' can be more broad and complex than what we might think at first: it can refer to content, to the interface needed to access said content, to the object itself. For print books, the physical object is the book, often in its codex form. For digital books, the physical object we get to hold is the powered-up electronic device required to access the book. Digital books transform text into data: it is no longer confined within a single medium but becomes unbound and accessible via multiple interfaces. They can consist of just plain text; include images and illustrations; feature video and audio tracks; and sometimes even make use of uniquely technological features to deliver the narrative.

There's a significant challenge in trying to illustrate highly visual, responsive and interactive digital books using a fixed medium such as print. This chapter attempts to convey the dynamic nature of these books and the often personalised reading experience they offer through static images and descriptive text. The books discussed in this chapter are a selected sample of what the digital publishing landscape is offering at this moment in time – the rapid pace at which technology develops and decays makes design features ever changing and adaptive to new affordances.

Digital books, however, are hardly a new concept: ereaders, and the idea of portable digital devices that could grant users access to digital versions of print books, have been around since the late 1990s. E-ink and e-paper display technology were developed by the Massachusetts Institute of Technology (MIT) in 1997 and 1998 saw the launch of what can now be considered the first ereaders, the NuovoMedia Rocket eBook and the SoftBook.[1] The current ereader market offers a variety of devices with different interfaces to access content and different features. All of them, though, adapt print text to the digital environment by emulating the physical book structure: ebooks (be they PDF, EPUB, MOBI or HTML[2]) seem to be subordinate to print, their main purpose to make the reading experience as close to reading a print book as possible. At the same time, within this same publishing landscape we have also seen a rise in experimental and innovative digital books written specifically for the digital environment and its affordances.

These complex digital books are usually multimedia and make for highly interactive and often non-linear reading experiences. They are produced in a variety of formats, from web-based, to apps for tablets and smartphones, to bespoke and not-yet-standardised formats. For this reason, they are generally not meant to be read on ereaders, as these can only support standard ebook formats and have limits on interactivity. Their spread can be linked to the rise of portable devices that can connect to the Internet; in 2007, the same year that saw Amazon launch its first Kindle device, Apple introduced its first iPhone, followed two years later by the first iPad tablet.

Editions At Play is a publishing initiative dedicated to producing these kinds of complex digital books, and specifically 'books powered by the magic of the internet'.[3] Launched in 2016 as a collaboration between Google Creative Lab in Sydney, Australia and London-based creative agency Visual Editions, Editions At Play publishes books designed for mobile devices (for both iOS and Android systems)

01. Breathe *by Kate Pullinger, Editions At Play and Google Creative Lab, 2018.*

01.

Breathe
Welcome to the world of Flo.
She can talk to ghosts.
And she knows where you are.
Is your phone in your hand?
Yes. I'm ready.

Breathe
I talk to my mother at night, but she doesn't answer me. I listen for her, I wait for her, I do my best to let her in. I know she must be there, somewhere. But she does not speak to me.
1 / 105

Breathe
I'm here. Right here next to you.
Trying to get through to you.
Can you feel me?
3 / 105

Breathe
It is too late. It's too late for Flo, too late for you. It doesn't matter if it's 10am Thursday or 1am Friday — she's left it too long. So have you.
8 / 105

Seed
WRITTEN BY Joanna Walsh
ACKNOWLEDGEMENTS

(02.)

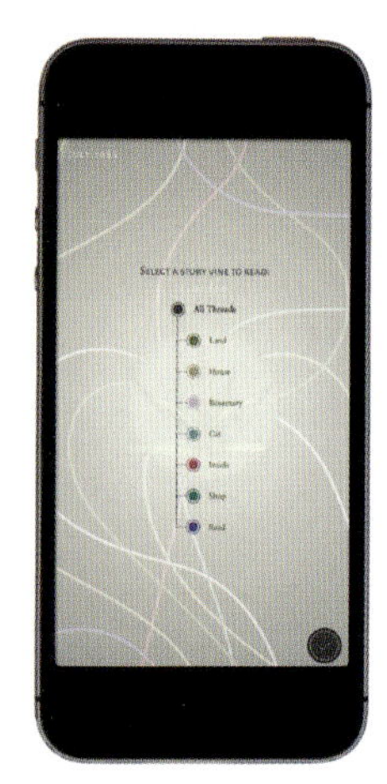

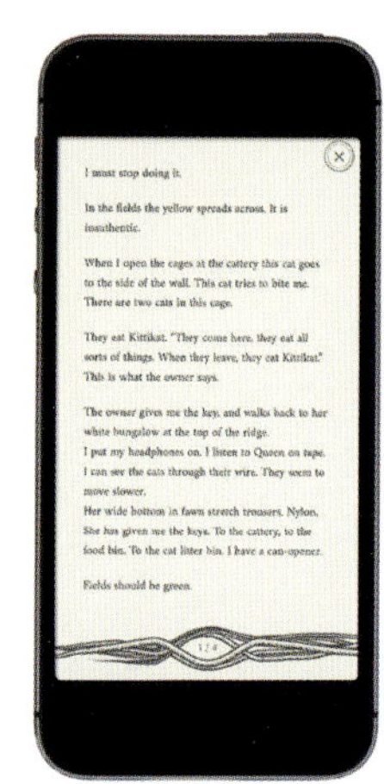
I must stop doing it.
In the fields the yellow spreads across. It is inauthentic.
When I open the cages at the cattery this cat goes to the side of the wall. This cat tries to bite me. There are two cats in this cage.
They eat Kittikat. "They come here, they eat all sorts of things. When they leave, they eat Kittikat." This is what the owner says.
The owner gives me the key, and walks back to her white bungalow at the top of the ridge.
I put my headphones on. I listen to Queen on tape. I can see the cats through their wire. They seem to move slower.
Her wide bottom in fawn stretch trousers. Nylon. She has given me the keys. To the cattery, to the food bin. To the cat litter bin. I have a can-opener.
Fields should be green.

and accessible for free through the web. Through collaboration with established authors, it has published seven books so far and contributed to two other interactive digital stories.

Its books vary in content, genre and length, but they all have one unique thing in common: they cannot be replicated in print. These are not merely digital versions of print books – they are books whose form and content complement and depend on each other. None of these titles can be fully recreated in print without affecting the meaning of the narrative, making the production technology and the access devices not just aesthetic choices, but integral to the experience and the meaning of the book. They include characteristics that don't directly transfer to print: they are digitally native, responsive, data-led, locative, adaptive, reliant on external technology, collaborative. The fact that they use mobile devices as the medium to deliver their narratives contributes to their accessibility, as it removes the need for a dedicated reading device and has the potential of reaching audiences that wouldn't necessarily see themselves as consumers of digital books. When viewed up close, however, it is clear that they still retain the structural and design elements that make us recognise them as books, enhanced by current technology and its affordances to provide us with a snapshot of innovative digital publishing at this moment in time.

MATERIAL AND INTERFACE

The fact that all Editions At Play books are designed to be read on mobile devices makes them virtually omnipresent: they follow us and can be accessed anywhere at any time – as long as one has battery life and an Internet connection.

Written by Kate Pullinger, *Breathe* (2018) is a ghost story 'that comes to you', populating the text with data about the reader and their surroundings (Image 1). In this case, the technological features already present in our phones are used to the full to deliver a narrative: the reader receives a tailored version of the story that uses data about their location, time of day, local weather and even the possibility of a personalised background through their phone camera. Based on this description, readers might expect this process to be very intrusive, but it is actually achieved in quite a subtle way. The story weaves in data from different Application Programming Interfaces (APIs) and integrates the reader's surrounding environment into the narrative in almost unnoticeable ways. It's at the access point that these books' digital interface becomes most visible: in the case of *Breathe*, the reader is immediately confronted with a request for access to their camera and location on the 'front page', making their active participation in the narrative apparent.

02. Seed *by Joanna Walsh, Editions At Play and Google Creative Lab, 2017.*

Another way in which interactive digital books make their interface visible is through the gestures we make in order to access them. Editions At Play books respond to specific gestural conventions that belong to the touch-screen devices used to access them: swiping, pinching, scrolling, tapping, tilting. These gestures become integral to the reading experience and knowledge of these conventions is necessary to access the content. The ghost's presence in *Breathe* becomes dependent on the reader's gestural summoning, as sections of the text spoken by the ghost can only be revealed by tilting the reading device or rubbing the screen.

PAGES AND BINDING

Editions At Play books retain a 'page' structure: the text is presented in sections and the reader needs to turn the page in some way in order to progress through the story. How that is achieved, and whether it needs to be sequential, is the experimental part of these narratives.

In a web-based story, 'pages' are 'bound' by the Internet, which is to say not bound at all. This opens up the possibility of non-linear narratives and of taking different paths through a story. *Seed* (2017) by Joanna Walsh is an online book whose pages are bound by the roots and vines of botanical illustrations that extend between chapters (Image 2). The reader can choose to follow all the vines and read all the text in the story, or they can select a specific 'branch' and read only parts of the story, which reveal different perspectives. Similarly, *The Truth About Cats & Dogs* (2016) is a book that asks the reader to take sides – described as 'a failed collaboration between novelist Joe Dunthorne and poet Sam Riviere' the book is presented as a series of journal entries by the two writers, which can be read in a non-sequential way (Image 3). The reader is allowed to switch between perspectives and decide which narrative to follow, and which side of the story to believe.

While most of these books have page numbers, they also contain attributes that are hard to track: multiple points of view, multiple narrators, multiple and often non-linear ways of accessing and reading these stories. On its website, Editions At Play suggests an alternative method to keep track of the length of these publications: read time. Each book in its collection has a 'Read time' specified for it, spanning from 30 to 300 minutes. These are not fixed values, as they are dependent on reading speed, but it's an interesting way of accounting for the variations in how much content a reader chooses to view or is capable of uncovering.

TEXT AND LAYOUT

Ebooks often prioritise accessibility over design and style, treating the text as reflowable[4] and making it as 'plain' as possible. This approach brings many benefits, as it increases compatibility, makes the content more resistant to software and hardware obsolescence, and opens up options for further accessibility, such as supporting text-to-speech programs.

All Editions At Play books use text to deliver their content, yet they also experiment with text as a design element. Many titles employ dynamic, responsive text and make it so the design and the content are subject to manipulation through the reader's interaction with the medium. *All This Rotting* (2016) by Alan Trotter is a prime example of this: it's a story about death and loss told from the perspective of a son and a father suffering from dementia. As the reader progresses through the story, the text starts trembling, the letters get jumbled and some words fade away (Image 4). If the reader decides to go back to a previous page, they'll notice that portions of the text have completely disappeared, an echo of the memory loss that one of the protagonists is experiencing. Following in the tradition of experimental print text such as concrete poetry, the text placement and layout are used as a way to reinforce the emotion that the text as content is conveying, using technology to affect the reading experience in a dynamic way that could not be re-created in print.

Another book that uses the placement of text to reflect and enhance the content of its narrative is *A Universe Explodes* (2017). Written by Tea Uglow, Creative Director at Google's Creative Lab, it's the first book that used blockchain as a distribution technology. It narrates the story of a parent whose world is gradually falling apart: there is only one copy of the original story, preserved as it was first written. That digital copy was passed on to new owners, who in turn donated it to other people – but not before editing the text. Each new owner had to add one word and delete two from each page in order to be able to pass on the book (Image 5). This was an exercise in keeping track of digital property via the blockchain – making the immutable digital copy become subject to the passing of time and of ownership, in the same way that a second-hand print book bears the marks of previous owners.

IMAGES AND COVER

While text can be considered the core of all Editions At Play titles, their appearance is very much dictated by their striking visual elements: vibrant full-colour illustrations, pictures and animations appear in many of the books, and in many instances they are integral to the delivery of the story. That's the case in *Seed*, for example, where the reader has to move from illustration to illustration on the digital canvas in order to unveil the story. Another example is Reif Larsen's book *Entrances & Exits* (2016), a modern 'Borgesian love story' that mixes a fictional account with real-life places through the use

03. The Truth About Cats & Dogs *by Sam Riviere and Joe Dunthorne, Editions At Play and Google Creative Lab, 2016.*

04. All This Rotting *by Alan Trotter, Editions At Play and Google Creative Lab, 2016.*

05. A Universe Explodes *by Tea Uglow, Editions At Play and Google Creative Lab, 2017.*

THE TRUTH ABOUT
CATS & DOGS
SAM RIVIERE & JOE DUNTHORNE
Published by Visual Editions

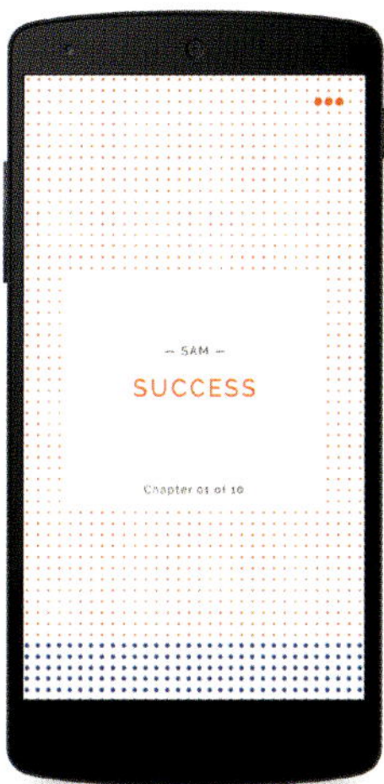

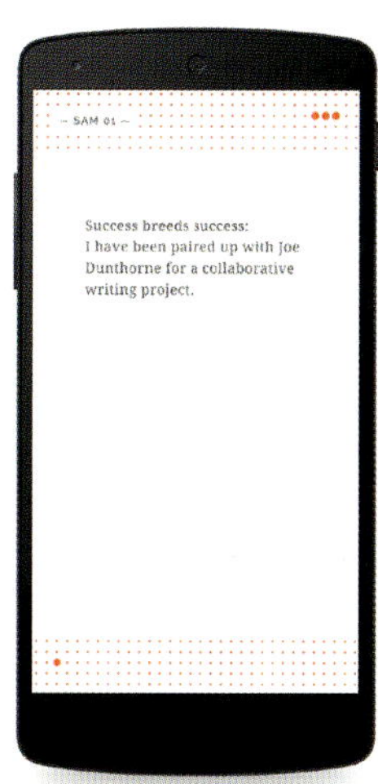

03.

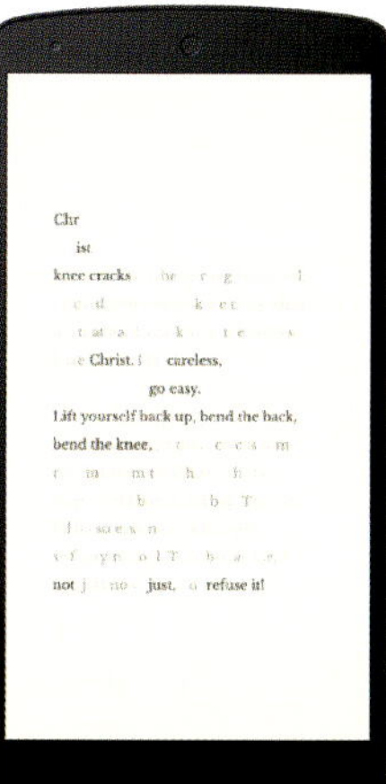

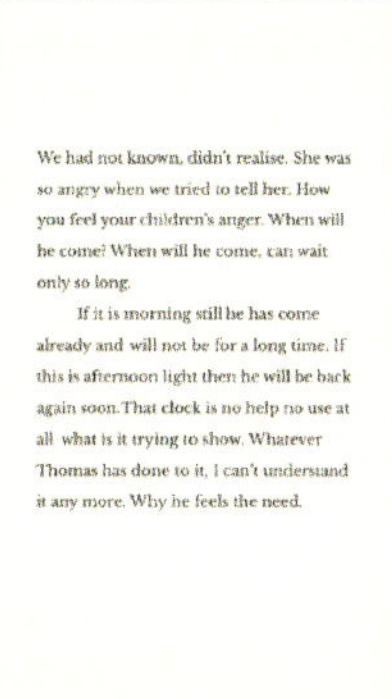

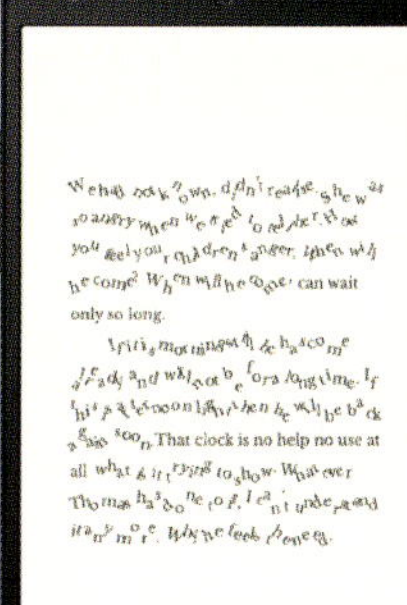

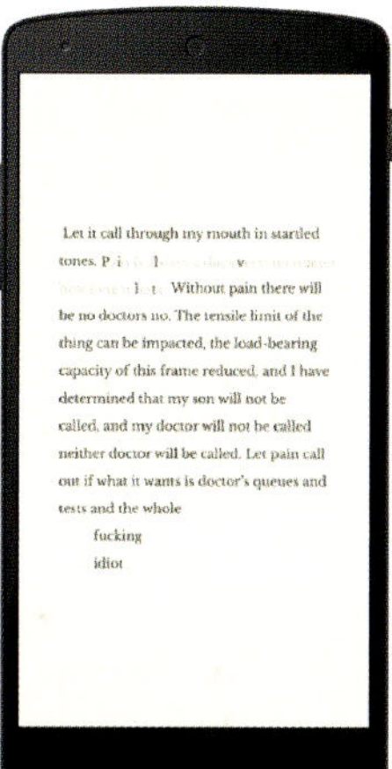

04.

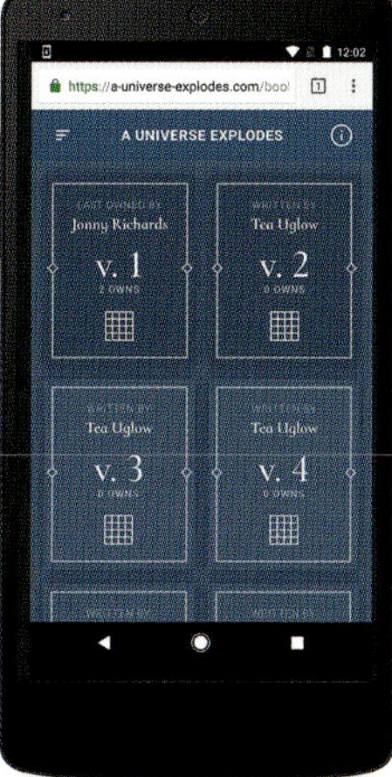

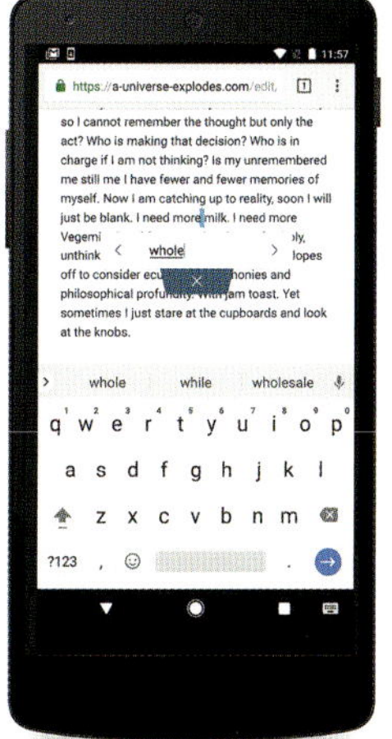

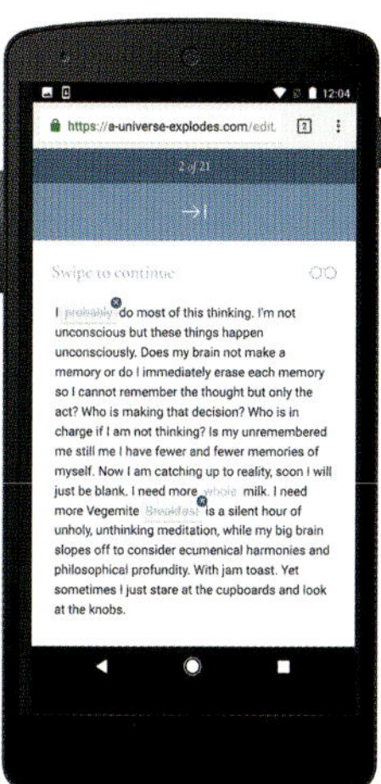

05.

of Google Street View. In this case the pictures are the only way to navigate the book, with the reader moving around virtual streets across the world in order to find a 'portal' into the next chapter (Image 6). This book employs a familiar feature of our smartphones, but takes it out of context and makes it into a narrative framing device, adding an explorative quality to the book that is distinctly digital.

Interactive visual elements can be extended to include cover design as well. Tea Uglow's *We Kiss the Screens* (2019) – written in collaboration with an AI called George – gives readers the option of a personalised cover and background. On the front page, the reader is asked to tap their device in order to select a colour gradient, which will follow them through the book as the pages' background colour (Image 7). If, after reading the digital version, they decide to order a Print On Demand (POD) edition of the book, their choices will follow them into the physical world, with the same colour gradient repeated across the print pages and used for the decorative element on the cover.[5]

PHYSICALITY AND PERSONALISATION

Recurring themes in the Editions At Play output are also concepts we might consider when reflecting on the idea of print vs. digital books: physicality and personalisation. Physicality is something that seems to be in direct contrast to the concept of digital text, yet there have been experiments in adding distinctly physical qualities to digital books. In *A Universe Explodes* the ability to lend and borrow copies, so characteristic of print works, is recreated through the use of blockchain technology. It also raises the question of ownership of digital goods, and how with digital books (but also music, movies, etc.) what we usually own is a licence to access the product, not the product itself.

We Kiss the Screens also returns to the concept of ownership, and of adding physical qualities to digital books. A retelling of the Galatea and Pygmalion myth from Ovid's *Metamorphoses*, the book presents eight perspectives of the same story, based on eight different social media hashtags. While readers can't fully own the digital version, they can own a POD unique edition of the book, which keeps track of the pages read online by printing them on a different colour paper than the pages left unread.

Personalisation plays a major role in all these books. *A Universe Explodes* gives a limited number of people the option of creating and distributing unique copies of the book, evoking oral traditions in which stories change as they are passed between people. *Breathe* takes interactivity into the realm of immersion, using mobile tech to personalise the story to each user. The idea that there is not one single truth, but that each of us might have a different reading of the same story, is explored in different ways in *Seed*, *The Truth About Cats & Dogs* and *We Kiss the Screens*. The latter in particular, with its echoes of 'fake news' and 'alternative facts', brings into focus the question of what is the one

06.

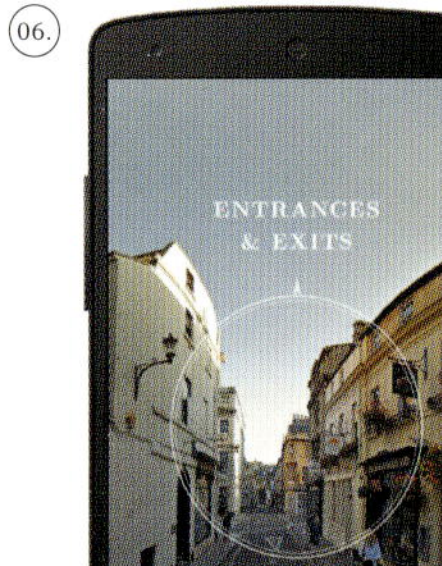

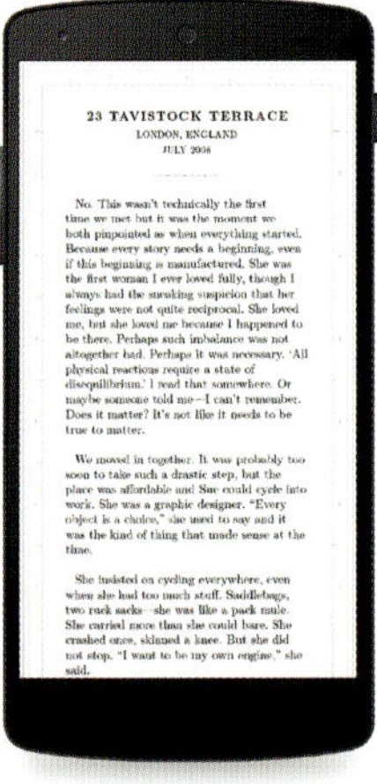

23 TAVISTOCK TERRACE
LONDON, ENGLAND
JULY 2006

No. This wasn't technically the first time we met but it was the moment we both pinpointed as when everything started. Because every story needs a beginning, even if this beginning is manufactured. She was the first woman I ever loved fully, though I always had the sneaking suspicion that her feelings were not quite reciprocal. She loved me, but she loved me because I happened to be there. Perhaps such imbalance was not altogether bad. Perhaps it was necessary. 'All physical reactions require a state of disequilibrium.' I read that somewhere. Or maybe someone told me—I can't remember. Does it matter? It's not like it needs to be true to matter.

We moved in together. It was probably too soon to take such a drastic step, but the place was affordable and Sue could cycle into work. She was a graphic designer. "Every object is a choice," she used to say and it was the kind of thing that made sense at the time.

She insisted on cycling everywhere, even when she had too much stuff. Saddlebags, two rack sacks—she was like a pack mule. She carried more than she could bare. She crashed once, skinned a knee. But she did not stop. "I want to be my own engine," she said.

07.

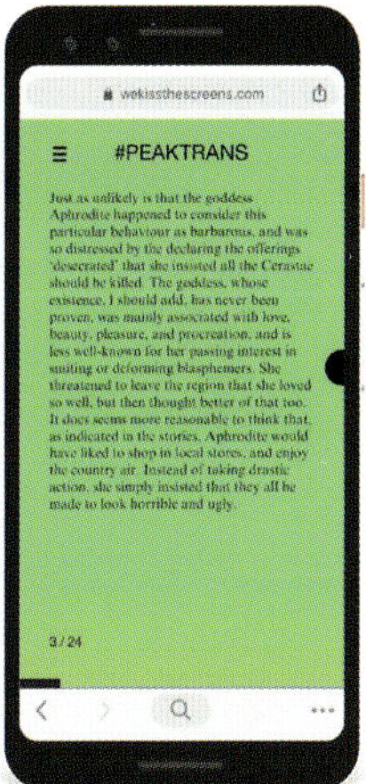

true story – and if such a thing exists. There's an emphasis on the value of the personal experience and the coexistence of multiple perspectives, often contradicting each other yet inhabiting the same space – it's up to the reader to determine which one to believe.

THE ROLE OF THE READER IN INTERACTIVE DIGITAL BOOKS

The user's interaction with the device, and, by association, the narrative itself, is one of the main points these digital books designed for mobile bring attention to – whether that's through gestures, like in the Editions At Play publications, or through new types of actions afforded by current technology, like voice activation, or even face recognition. This connects to the idea of the reader playing a role in the creation of the book. As exemplified by *A Universe Explodes* – where the chosen owners of the book are asked to take on an active role in shaping and distributing the book – interactivity and personalisation are becoming defining characteristics of digital literature, blurring the line between writing and reading.

Digital books and their access devices shape the way we read and write, as the fluidity of text, the preference for shorter sentences and the adoption of concepts like 'Read time' can testify. In turn, digital books are shaped by contemporary readers' needs and expectations – the affordances of what we now consider new technology allowing us to meet our requirements in terms of accessibility, portability, ubiquity and immediacy.

Digital books don't reinvent the book form, or turn it into something unrecognisable – they augment the traditional form through the affordances of technology. In this respect Editions At Play is at the forefront: by stripping the codex form to its bare components and enhancing them with technology, it interrogates our idea of what constitutes a book, while making us aware of those attributes (like order and sequentiality) that we might be taking for granted. Editions At Play offers a perspective on how new tools can serve us in actualising the potential of a form that's been around for centuries. In doing so it makes the medium visible and makes us aware of our role in relation to it.

Just as the print word only acquires meaning through reading, and our experience of a story is unfixed, personal and unique to each one of us, so is the digital book a result of the collaboration between writer, text and reader – its highly interactive, networked form making this connection even more apparent.

06. Entrances & Exits *by Reif Larsen, Editions At Play and Google Creative Lab, 2016.*

07. We Kiss the Screens *by Tea Uglow with George AI, Editions At Play and Google Creative Lab, 2019.*

BOOK DESIGN AS AN AGENT OF CONSERVATION

KATIE MCELVANNEY

The role of design as a means of conservation is most commonly associated with urban planning and environmental and sustainability projects. Yet it can also play an important function when applied to book production. One example of such an approach can be seen in the works created by the Ukrainian Cultural Centre (UKK) in Tallinn, Estonia; every design decision is rooted in a desire not only to highlight and preserve a particular culture or species in danger of disappearing, but also to showcase traditional bookmaking techniques.

The secular UKK is affiliated with Tallinn's Ukrainian Greek Catholic Church of the Virgin with Three Hands, which was founded in 1991 by Anatoli Ljutjuk, a Benedictine monk born in Western Ukraine who has lived in Estonia for many years. The Church's emphasis on the natural world around it has influenced the UKK's publishing projects: its first book series, *The Poetics of Endangered Species*, focused on vanishing plants and animals in Ukraine and Estonia. UKK created a small number of handmade books for this series as well as a few hundred facsimile copies, two of which are held by the British Library. Stemming from this project, Ljutjuk was keen to explore and document cultures and communities whose traditions are under threat. This led to the creation of *The Ark of Unique Cultures: The Hutsuls*, which celebrates the history and culture of the Hutsuls, an ethnic group from the Carpathian Mountains in Eastern Europe. Thirty-five handmade books were donated to national libraries around the world, including the British Library.

Each item was made almost entirely in the UKK's Labora design studio and workshop using raw materials. Inspired by monastic medieval book production, the studios employ a small group of printers, calligraphers and bookbinders who skilfully craft the books – and pass on these techniques. In the case of *The Ark of Unique Cultures*, plant specimens of significance to the communities and regions which the books seek to document were collected and embedded in the paper. Labora's handmade paper mill was the first to appear in the Baltic region in over a century.

The calligraphy is reminiscent of an illuminated manuscript, once again inspired by the medieval monasteries located along the Baltic shore before the Reformation. All of UKK's handmade books are distinctively bound in thick wooden boards and fastened with two wooden clasps and pegs. These design decisions emphasise the unique nature of the items and their connection with the natural world and ancient traditions; the clasps, for example, evoke the authority of medieval bindings with their precious texts, while also providing a practical means of keeping the boards together.

One of the most striking and important aspects of UKK's projects is the involvement of community-led design. For example, in addition to the plant specimens, each copy of *The Ark of Unique Cultures* contains postcards and bookmarks from community members with their comments and reflections on aspects of Hutsul life and culture, as well as a cycle of poems in the Hutsul dialect by the poet Mariya Korpanyuk. The postcards were distributed in Hutsul villages and the hundreds of responses, with their stamps and postmarks, were divided among the individual books, further adding to their unique composition and design.

The UKK's books can be read in various ways. While meaning is of course conveyed through the subject matter, the physical structure of the books and their components, such as the flowers incorporated into the paper and the tactile wooden bindings, present an experience which is greater than the sum of its parts. By combining natural materials, ancient craft techniques and community-led design, the books successfully document and preserve threatened cultures and aspects of our world for generations to come.

01. *Opening from* The Ark of Unique Cultures *featuring the poem 'The Potion'. (RF.2020.b.31)*

02. *The wooden bindings and clasps of* The Ark of Unique Cultures.

03. *Page from* The Poetics of Endangered Species: Ukraine. *(YF.2017.b.1282)*

THE POTION
And wasn't it I my dear
Who boiled the herbal potion,
And wasn't it I who fell
In love with you forever,
And wasn't it I who brought you
The rare arnika flower from the field,
And wasn't it I who heard
Your footsteps in the night.

01.

02.

Ліс, мов зрадник, відступає.
Сліди вовчі,
а пахне людиною.
РИСЬ
ЗВИЧАЙНА
LYNX
LYNX

03.

EPILOGUE

The Book by Design explores the many ingenious ways in which humans have responded to the concept of the book across a range of societies and 1,400 years. In part, it was inspired by the question of why the book in all its forms seemed as popular and pervading as ever in the third decade of the twenty-first century. In 2007, traditional publishers shuddered as commentators were happy to call time on the old-fashioned printed-paper book with the relentless growth in the sales of ebooks and the launch of Amazon's kindle ereader (joined by the Apple iPad in early 2010).

But the predicted extinction of the book did not come to pass. What happened instead was most intriguing. Sales of ebooks continued to grow in certain categories until they plateaued in the mid-2010s and have since either stabilised or seen a small decline. The ebook became just another book format alongside Allen Lane's paperbacks and the colossal growth in audiobooks as consumers accessed them through the headphones of their newly and widely adopted smart phones.

Yet the physical book has undergone a new lease of life almost as a counter-response to the digital revolution. Sales of physical books were on the increase even well before the pandemic boom and there has since been a steady growth in new bookshops opening in the UK. At the same time, and perhaps echoing William Morris's crafted publishing response to mass-manufacture in the 1890s, the perceived existential threat of ebook technology in the 2000s has actually brought about a significant increase in the physical production quality, design and material nature of the printed book. Paper stock is better. Jacket finishes are more ornate; more books carry specially commissioned artworks and publishers have reintroduced inventive and beautiful sprayed edges. Special editions proliferate. As with the objects featured throughout *The Book by Design*, these twenty-first-century books are for enjoyment, inspiration, information and indeed display, reminders of book obsessions on a bookshelf or as a signifier of taste on an Instagrammer's coffee table. Conversely, in the digital world our ebook and audiobook collections disappear the second we delete them or unsubscribe.

01. *Detail of a page from* The Works of Geoffrey Chaucer, *as published by the Kelmscott Press, 1896. (C.43.h.19)*

The consumption of book content by either physical means or in digital form has, in the last fifteen years, been a question of choosing the most suitable of a proliferating range of formats. Yet, as John B. Thompson has argued, the most profound change in the last two decades has not been the invention of the digital book but instead the actual data-driven, digital and physical infrastructure of how we discover, acquire and consume books across this variety of formats.[1]

However, as we go to press on this volume, media commentary has been dominated by discussion of the major opportunities, advantages and concerns raised by accessible Artificial Intelligence (AI) and Virtual Reality (VR) across the cultural and wider spheres. Will these be the developments that ultimately take humankind into a post-Gutenberg and post-Aldus world? And if so, how many decades will it take for such a change to happen? If we have learned anything from *The Book by Design*, it is that this change will be deeply creative, a development of previous traditions and dictated both by users and by the commercial and financial requirements of those leading the change. Most importantly, it will be highly surprising and very unlike what we are even able to conceive today.

01.

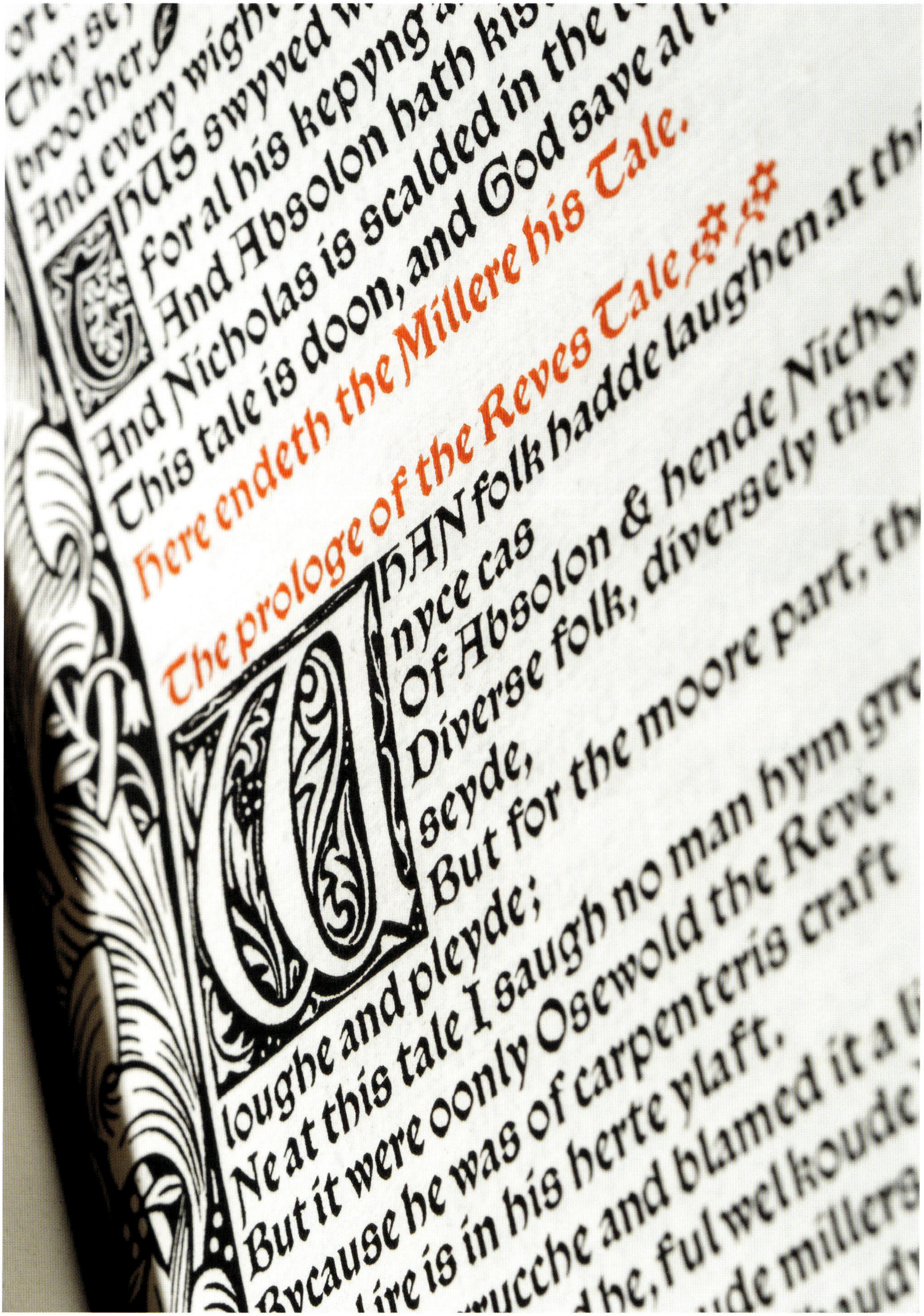
broother,
And every wight
THUS swyved was
For al his kepyng
And Absolon hath kis
And Nicholas is scalded in the
This tale is doon, and God save al
Here endeth the Millere his Tale.
The prologe of the Reves Tale.
WHAN folk hadde laughen at th
nyce cas
Of Absolon & hende Nichol
Diverse folk, diversely they
seyde,
But for the moore part, th
loughe and pleyde;
Ne at this tale I saugh no man hym gr
But it were oonly Osewold the Reve.
Bycause he was of carpenteris craft
ire is in his herte ylaft.
rucche and blamed it a li
d he, ful wel koude
ude millers

GLOSSARY

aquatint Term used to describe the intaglio process or the tonal print made with a special kind of etching ground composed of particles of resin.

bas-de-page Literally the bottom of the page, which may contain drawings and illumination.

bestiary A book of beasts, including descriptions of the characters and habits of animals, usually with allegorical interpretations and moral lessons.

black-letter font Typefaces that are inspired by the calligraphic letters of the Middle Ages.

blocking Decoration cut into a (brass) die, then heated and impressed onto a book cover and spine, with or without the application of gold leaf or colours.

carpet page An ornamental page filled entirely with decoration, usually used to preface religious texts.

casting off Approximating the number of pages for a published work by counting the number of words.

chapbook A small book or pamphlet that historically contained poems, ballads, stories or religious tracts.

chromolithography A method for making multicolour prints using separate stone or metal plates for each colour. A sheet of paper is placed on each stone or plate and overprinted in sequence.

codex/codices A book composed of folded sheets secured along one edge to form pages or folios, distinct from other formats of book such as the scroll or tablet.

colophon A statement typically found on the final page of an early hand-press book, or at the end of a manuscript text, which records information about its creation, such as the date and place of production, and the name of the printer and scribe.

compositor A person who studies a manuscript and the designer's layout, then recommends the appropriate combination of type, style, size and spacing.

copperplate engraving Engraving made on a 1- or 2-millimetre-thick metal plate, usually copper but sometimes iron, steel or zinc. Incisions are made and the plate then inked and wiped clean, so that when printed under pressure the ink is pulled from the grooves to create an image.

cul-de-lampe A typographic ornament used to mark the end of a text, usually a triangular shaped marking.

deckle A removable frame that rests on top of the mould used for making sheets of handmade paper.

deckle edge The irregular, rough edge of a sheet of handmade paper.

die-cutter A process by which paper is cut using a die.

double elephant format A large size of paper measuring 40 by 27 inches (100 by 68 centimetres).

double-page spread Two pages opposite each other that are viewed together.

doublures The ornamental linings on the inside covers of a binding.

electrotyping The process for making duplicate plates for printing by using a thin shell of metal (usually copper) in a mold (usually wax) of the usual type form and then backing the shell with metal.

erratum/errata A list of corrected errors included in a later printing or edition of a book.

flap book A book which contains flaps that cover certain information that is revealed when the reader lifts those flaps.

folio A sheet of writing material, from the Latin for 'leaf', one half of a bifolium, the larger sheet that is folded in two. The upper and lower surfaces of a folio are referred to as recto (r.) and verso (v.) respectively. In modern publishing, a printed page number.

folio format A book or pamphlet that is made up of folio sheets. On each sheet four pages of text are printed, two on each side, and then folded once to produce two leaves.

font The particular size, weight and style of a typeface.

format The size of a book as determined by the number of times the original sheet of paper has been folded to form the leaves, also known as trimmed page size (tps). The general appearance of a book, from binding to typeface and layout.

frontispiece An illustration or plate that is inserted immediately before the title page.

glassine Strong, thin, glazed semi-transparent paper used for book jackets.

Gospel harmony An attempt to demonstrate the concord (or harmony) across the four Gospels by compiling a single account.

gutter The space on the inside margins on two facing pages that is lost when the pages are bound.

hand press A printing press that is operated by hand.

headpiece A panel of decoration at the beginning of a chapter or piece of text.

historiated initial An enlarged, decorated letter at the beginning of a word, containing an identifiable scene or figures inside the body of the letter.

hot type machine A technology for typesetting text in letterpress printing.

illumination Embellishment of a manuscript with colours, from the Latin '*illuminare*' meaning 'to enlighten' or 'to illuminate'.

incipit page The opening of a page of text, often featuring decorated initial letters. The word '*incipit*' means 'it begins' in Latin.

incunabulum/incunabula An early printed book in Europe, especially one printed before 1501.

italic Letters or words that slope to the right.

leaf A standard physical unit of paper or parchment usually with writing on each side.

letterpress A printing technique in which raised type or letters are covered in ink and pressed onto paper by using a printing press.

linotype A nineteenth-century printing technique which printed an entire line at a time rather than individual characters.

lithography A method invented in the late eighteenth century to print text or images based on the fact that oil and water do not mix. The image to be printed is drawn using a greasy substance on a stone or metal plate with a smooth surface. This surface is treated and dampened with water so that when an oil-based ink is applied it will only stick to the greasy sections. Paper is then laid on the stone or metal plate and run through a printing press to transfer the text or image.

majuscule A large letter either capital or **uncial**, used in both printed work and manuscripts.

mezzotint A seventeenth-century method of engraving a copper or steel plate by scraping and burnishing the roughened surface.

micrography Extremely small writing, which forms the shape of a picture or design.

miniature In manuscripts, a painting not in an initial, from the Latin '*miniare*', referring to 'minium', the original red colour used to decorate manuscripts. In printing, a small book less than 7.5 centimetres in width, height or depth.

mise-en-page The layout of a page, including the arrangement of text, margins and images.

movable book A book with elements that can be manipulated by the reader; includes flap books.
movable type A printing system and technology which uses individual letters or characters that can be reorganised into different texts.

octavo format Full sheets of paper on which sixteen pages of text are printed, and then folded and cut to make up the individual leaves of a book.

offset lithography Also known as offset printing, a method often used in mass-production printing to produce particularly clear and detailed images. An image on a metal plate is transferred to an intermediate surface such as rubber blankets or rollers and printed from this surface.

pagination Page numbering in a book.

paratext The components of a book that are not part of the main text, such as **title page**, contents page, index, footnotes, etc.

parchment A broad term for any type of animal skin used for writing, printing or binding books. Often used synonymously with **vellum**.

photolithography Printing techniques which use light to produce patterned thin films.

plate Full page illustrations, pictures, photographs that are printed separately from the text of the book but are bound in during production. Any single printing surface, such as a lithographic plate.

pop-up book A book with three-dimensional pages that 'pop-up' upon opening the double-page spread.

press The act or process of printing.

print The act or process of publishing matter either in print or electronically; one of a number of copies of an image created by a printmaking process or a photograph.

Psalter A book containing the Psalms, but also other elements, such as a calendar, a litany of the saints and prayers.

punch-cutting The process of creating a single piece of **type** in the early printing days by punching a soft metal (such as copper) with a steel bar cut into the shape of the letter and filling it with type metal.

quarto format Full sheets of paper on which eight pages of text are printed, this is then folded twice and cut to form the individual leaves of a book.

quire A set of folded sheets that are gathered one inside another together to form a booklet. These are usually bound together with other quires to form the text block of a codex.

recto The upper surface of a folio.

roman Formal Latin type inspired by the stone-cut inscriptions on tombs and monuments in ancient Rome, as distinct from black letter and gothic type.

rubric A title or heading usually written in red ink.

sans serif Typeface without **serif**s.

scriptorium/scriptoria Room in a monastery for writing.

Septuagint A Greek version of 39 books of Jewish scripture, including the Torah, the Prophets and the Writings, known as the Septuagint, (seventy in Latin), as it was traditionally attributed to seventy or so scholars working in Alexandria for Ptolemy II Philasephus (308–246 BCE).

serif A small stroke that is added to the main stroke of a letter.

stereotyping A solid plate of type metal made from a mould of the original type.

text block The pages that make up the contents of a book, excluding the cover or final binding such as endpapers; the portion of each page with text.

title page The page at or near the front, containing the title of the book and usually the names of the author, publisher, place of publication and sometimes the date.

type The form of individual letters.

typeface A classification for the style of different scripts; a collection of various fonts that share an overall design.

typefoundry/typefounding A collection of a type of font.

uncial A type of rounded majuscule script commonly used in the fourth to eighth centuries.

vellum A type of **parchment**. Relates specifically to calfskin, which may be used for writing, printing or binding books, but can be used interchangeably with parchment by some experts.

verso The lower surface of a folio.

watermark A mark created by the maker of the paper in the wire mesh of the tray in which the paper is made to indicate the maker's identity and where the paper originated; it can be used to help date the paper.

NOTES

The Lindisfarne Gospels
No Notes. See Further Reading.

Ethiopia, African Scribes and the Illustrated Apocalypse

1 Due in part to the Library's exhibition of the Magdala collection and recent research. Eyob Derillo, 'Exhibiting The Maqdala Manuscripts: African Scribes: Manuscript Culture Of Ethiopia', in African Research & Documentation, suppl. Special Issue: Archives and Collections for/in Ethiopian Studies; London Iss. 135, (2019), 102–116.

The Diamond Sutra Printed in 868

1 Chiew Hui Ho, *Diamond Sutra Narratives: Textual Production and Lay Religiosity in Medieval China* (Leiden; Boston: Brill, 2019), 11.
2 In Buddhism, *bodhisattva*s are compassionate beings who have chosen to help others follow them on the path towards *buddha*hood.
3 Yongyou Shi, *The Diamond Sutra in Chinese* Culture (Los Angeles: Buddha's Light Publishing, 2010), 74–78.
4 Lionel Giles, *Descriptive Catalogue of the Chinese Manuscripts from Tunhuang in the British Museum* (London: British Museum, 1957).
5 These manuscripts are Or 8210/S 5644 and Or 8210/S 87 in the British Library's Stein collection.
6 Tsien Tsuen-Hsuin, *Written on Bamboo & Silk: The Beginnings of Chinese Books & Inscriptions*, 2nd edn. (Chicago; London: University of Chicago Press, 2004), 96–125.
7 Two such manuscripts, Or 8210/S 36 and Or 8210/S 513, are copies of the Diamond Sutra respectively dated to 672 and 676. They are part of the British Library's Stein collection. For a list of the manuscripts with tabulated colophons see Lionel, Giles, *Descriptive Catalogue of the Chinese Manuscripts from Tunhuang*, 1957.
8 Jean-Pierre Drège, (ed.), 'Les Codices', in *La Fabrique du Lisible: La Mise en Texte des Manuscrits de la Chine Ancienne et Médiévale* (Paris: Collège de France, Institut des Hautes Etudes Chinoises, 2014), 373–376.
9 This manuscript is Or 8210/S 5669. Other booklets by this anonymous devotee include British Library's items Or 8210/S 5534, Or 8210/S 5444, Or 8210/S 5965 and Or 8210/S 5451.
10 Tsien Tsuen-Hsuin and Joseph Needham, *Science and Civilisation in China*, vol. 5, *Chemistry and Chemical Technology*, Part 1: *Paper and Printing* (Cambridge: Cambridge University Press, 1985), 194–201.
11 Susan Whitfield and Ursula Sims-Williams (eds), *The Silk Road: Trade, Travel, War and Faith* (The British Library, 2004), 301.
12 This manuscript is Or 8210/P 11.
13 Jean-Pierre Drège, 'De l'icône à l'anecdote: Les frontispices imprimés en Chine à l'époque des Song (960–1278)' in *Arts Asiatiques* 54 (1999), 44–65.
14 Tsuen-Hsuin and Needham, op. cit., 201–222.
15 Frances Wood and Mark Barnard, *The Diamond Sutra: The Story of the World's Earliest Dated Printed Book* (The British Library, 2010), 82–101.
16 Conrad Walters and Joyce Morgan, *Journeys on the Silk Road: Desert Explorer, Buddha's Secret Library, and the Unearthing of the World's Oldest Printed Book* (Picador Australia: Picador, 2011), 203.

The Development of Paper

1 Arantza Dobbels, 'The Missal of Silos: A treasure of conservation', Blog post from the Institute of Conservation, 7 August 2019, /iconbpg.wordpress.com/2019/08/07/the-missal-of-silos-a-treasure-in-paper/ (accessed 31 March 2023)
2 Keith Houston, *The Book* (New York: W.W. Norton & Co., 2016), 128. 'The age of early printing 1450–1550' at *Encyclopaedia Britannica*. https://www.britannica.com/topic/publishing/The-age-of-early-printing-1450-1550 (accessed 23 April 2023)
3 ibid, Chapters 3 and 4.
4 Sylvia Rodgers Albro, *Fabriano: City of Medieval and Renaissance Papermaking* (New Castle, Delaware: Oak Knoll Press, 2016).
5 Tsien Tsuen-Hsuin and Joseph Needham, *Science and Civilisation in China*, vol. 5, *Chemistry and Chemical Technology*, Part 1: *Paper and Printing* (Cambridge: Cambridge University Press, 1985), 71.
6 Dard Hunter, *Papermaking: The History and Technique of an Ancient Craft*, 2nd edn. (London: Pleiades Books, 1947); Sarah Werner, *Studying Early Printed Books 1450–1800* (Hoboken; Chichester: Wiley Blackwell, 2019). See especially 27–31 and 42–53; Timothy Barrett, *European Hand Papermaking: Traditions, Tools & Techniques* (Ann Arbor, Michigan: The Legacy Press, 2018); T. Barrett et al, 'European papermaking techniques 1300–1800' in *Paper through Time: Nondestructive Analysis of 14th- through 19th-Century Papers*, University of Iowa, last modified 4 May 2022, paper.lib.uiowa.edu/index.php (accessed 1 April 2023).
7 Philip, Gaskell, *A New Introduction to Bibliography*, 2nd edn. (New Castle, Delaware: Oak Knoll Press, 1995), 66–75; 'Libelli portatiles, Aldus Manutius, a legacy more lasting than bronze', Grolier Club online exhibition grolierclub.omeka.net/exhibits/show/aldus-manutius/libelli-portatiles (accessed 23 April 2023); Mark Kurlansky, *Paper: Paging Through History* (New York; London: W.W. Norton & Company, 2016), 189.
8 Joshua Calhoun, *The Nature of the Page: Poetry, Papermaking and the Ecology of Texts in Renaissance England* (Philadelphia: University of Pennsylvania Press, 2020), see especially 30–40.
9 James Raven, 'The industrial revolution of the book' in Leslie Howsam (ed.), *The Cambridge Companion to the History of the Book* (Cambridge: Cambridge University Press, 2015), 143–161, 146.

The Arnstein Bible

1 Now Darmstadt, Hessische Landesbibliothek, MS 4128.
2 Jeffrey F. Hamburger, 'Hand of God and the Hand of the Scribe: Craft and Collaboration at Arnstein' in *Die Bibliothek des Mittelalters als dynamischer Prozess*, ed. by Michael Embach, Claudine Moulin and Andrea Rapp, *Trierer Beiträge zu den Historischen Kulturwissenschaften*, 3 (Wiesbaden: Reichert, 2012), 64.

King Henry VIII's Copy of the 'Great Bible'

1 Susan Doran (ed.), *Elizabeth & Mary: Royal Cousins, Rival Queens* (London: The British Library, 2021), 68.
2 Tatiana C. String, 'Henry VIII's Illuminated "Great Bible"' in *Journal of the Warburg and Courtauld Institutes*, vol. 59 (1996), 315, 319, 324.
3 Marler's inscription reads, 'This Booke is presented unto your moste excellent highnes by youre loving, faithfull, and obedient Subiect and daylye Oratour Anthonye – Marler of London haberdassher.'
4 String, op. cit., 323.
5 ibid, 319, 320.
6 Lucas Horenbout had worked for Henry VIII since 1526. See: String, op. cit., 324.

The Golden Haggadah

1 British Library Hebrew manuscript Add. MS 27210.
2 Jewish art form consisting of weaving of minute lettering into abstract, geometric and figurative patterns.
3 A handwritten manuscript made of quires stitched together. Oldest form of book.
4 Small illustrations used to decorate medieval illuminated manuscripts.
5 Known as the Old Testament; the first part of the Christian Bible comprising thirty-nine books.
6 Known as *piyutim* in Hebrew.
7 During the reigns of Ferdinand III, called the Saint, and James I the Conqueror.

The Queen Mary Psalter

1 See C. M. Kauffmann, *Biblical Imagery in Medieval England 700–1550* (London: Harvey Miller Publishers, 2003), 215.
2 Jacobus de Voragine, *The Golden Legend: Readings on the Saints*, trans. by William Granger Ryan, 2 vols (Princeton: Princeton University Press, 1993), II, 149.
3 George Warner, *Queen Mary's Psalter: Miniatures and Drawings by an English Artist of the 14th Century, Reproduced from Royal MS. 2 B. VII in the British Museum* (London: British Museum, 1912), 39.
4 Lucy Freeman Sandler, *Gothic Manuscripts 1285–1385* in J. J. G. Alexander, *Survey of Manuscripts Illuminated in the British Isles* (London: Harvey Miller Publishers, 1986), I, 18.

The Harmonies of Little Gidding

1 For example, *Joyce Ransome, The Web of Friendship: Nicholas Ferrar and Little Gidding*, Cambridge: James Clarke & Co., 2011); Paul Dyck, '"A New Kind of Printing": Cutting and Pasting a Book for a King at Little Gidding', *The Library* 9, no. 1 (2008), 306–30; Paul Dyck, '"So rare a use": Scissors, Reading, and Devotion at Little Gidding', *George Herbert Journal* 27, 1–2 (2003), 67–81; and J. E. Acland, *Little Gidding and its Inmates in the Time of King Charles I, with an Account of the Harmonies Designed and Constructed by Nicholas Ferrar* (London: SPCK, 1903), 35–64.
2 James I granted a charter to a group of individuals in 1606 to 'vouchsafe unto them our licence to make habitacion, plantacion and to deduce a colonie of sondrie of our people into that parte of America commonly called Virginia'. S. M. Bemiss (ed.), *The Three Charters of the Virginia Company of London* (Williamsburg: Virginia 350th Celebration Corporation, 1957), 1. Nicholas Ferrar became involved in the company in 1619; Dyck, 'A New Kind of Printing', 307. There is a large body of scholarship on the English colonisation of Virginia in the late sixteenth and early seventeenth centuries; for example, L. H. Roper, *The English Empire in America, 1602–1658: Beyond Jamestown* (London: Routledge, 2009); Karen Ordahl Kupperman, *The Jamestown Project* (Cambridge, Massachusetts; London: The Belknap Press, 2007); Andrew Fitzmaurice, *Humanism and America: An Intellectual History of English Colonisation, 1500–1625* (Cambridge University Press, 2003).
3 Dyck, 'A New Kind of Printing', 308.
4 Such as John Calvin, *A harmonie vpon the three Euangelists, Matthew, Mark and Luke, with the commentarie of M. Iohn Caluine: faithfullie translated out of Latine into English, by E.P. Whereunto is also added a commentarie vpon the Euangelist S. Iohn, by the same author* (London, 1584), C.126.e.5, 1005. c. 14–15; Johan Hiud, *The Storie of Stories* (London, 1632); Henry Garthwait, *Monotessaron The evangelicall harmonie, reducing the foure Evangelists into one continued context* (Cambridge, 1634); John Lightfoot, *The Harmony of the Foure Evangelists* (London, 1644–50).
5 Such as Willem van Branteghem's *Iesu Christi vita, iuxta quatuor Euangelistarū narrations* (Antwerp, 1537), C.69. ff.22.
6 Dyck, 'New Kind of Printing', 312–13; C. L. Craig, 'The Earliest Little Gidding Concordance', *Harvard Library Bulletin* 1 (1947), 318–20.
7 Adam Smyth, '"Shreds of Holinesse": George Herbert, Little Gidding, and Cutting Up Texts in Early Modern England [with Illustrations]', *English Literary Renaissance*, vol. 42, no. 3, 2012, 452–81.
8 Michael Cop, 'Compositions for a King: Little Gidding's Use of Henry Garthwait's Monotessaron', *Script & Print* 40:1 (2016), 29–44.
9 Margaret Aston, 'Moving Pictures: Foxe's Martyrs and Little Gidding' in Sabrina A. Baron, Eric N. Lindquist, and Eleanor F. Shevlin (eds), *Agent of Change: Print Culture Studies after Elizabeth L. Eisenstein* (Amherst: University of Massachusetts Press, 2007), 82–104.
10 He reconstructs the fragments in *The Print in Early Modern England* (New Haven and London, 2010), 275, and draws our attention to a panel painting sold at Bonhams in 2009 as 'Allegory of Death', c. 1600, from the collection of Severin Wunderman bonhams.com/auctions/17697/lot/202/ in 'The Little Gidding Concordances', *Print Quarterly*, xxxvii, 2020, 1, 98–101.
11 Cop, op. cit., 29.
12 British Museum Gg,6.6.2, Gg,6.6.3, Gg,6.6.8. See entry by Robert Gerard from Antony Griffiths, *The Print in Stuart Britain: 1603–1689* (London: British Museum, 1998), cat.84. He writes that the British Museum's copy of *Flora*: '...was published by Peter Stent, and first appears in his catalogue of 1653 as "Flora: 13 plates: Beasts, Birds

etc". But traces of an erasure are evident and there was clearly an earlier edition of which no copies have survived, engraved by Payne before his death *c.* 1639. The most likely first publisher was Compton Holland, though this is only an inference, arrived at largely through elimination (for this and the date of the set, see R. A. Gerard, "De Passe and early English natural history printmaking", *Print Quarterly*, XIV 1997, 174–9). One peculiarity that needs explanation is the second part of the title, "with their true colours lively described", for the prints themselves have no notes to aid the colourist. Presumably either the first edition had accompanying letterpress with instructions in the manner of the *Hortus Floridus*, or it was issued already coloured.' Michael Gaudio notes that 'the page from the polyglot harmony [in private hands] is rather unusual in that the Collets have added colour to the three largest flowers', Gaudio, 41.

The Mainz Psalter of 1457

1 British Library, *Incunabula Short Title Catalogue*, data.cerl.org/istc/ (accessed 17 May 2023).
2 Seymour de Ricci, *Catalogue raisonné des premières impressions de Mayence (1445–1467)* (Mainz: Gutenberg-Gesellschaft, 1911), 52. This source also establishes that Grenville acquired it from the London booksellers George and William Nicol.
3 British Museum, *Catalogue of Books Printed in the XVth Century now in the British Museum. Part 1: Xylographica and Books Printed with Types at Mainz, Strassburg, Bamberg and Cologne* (London: British Museum, 1908), 19.
4 The copy at the Austrian National Library also contains a Fust and Schöffer printer's mark or device immediately after the colophon, the first such mark ever to appear in a European printed book.
5 Russell Martineau, 'The Mainz Psalter of 1457', *Bibliographica: Papers on Books, their History and Art*, 1 (1895), 308.
6 British Museum, op. cit., 18.
7 The prevailing theories are described in Mayumi Ikeda, 'The Fust and Schöffer Office and the Printing of the Two-Colour Initials in the 1457 Mainz Psalter' in Ad Stijnman and Elizabeth Savage (eds), *Printing Colour 1400–1700* (Leiden: Brill, 2015), Ch. 5, 65–75.
8 Alan May, 'The Fust and Schöffer Psalter Initials', 2018. makerpress.co.uk/fust-and-schoffer-psalter/ (accessed 17 May 2023).
9 Ikeda, op. cit., 73.
10 The earliest surviving book to contain music notation printed from movable type is a *Gradual* produced in Konstanz or Augsburg in around 1473.
11 Three additional 'Alleluias' have been added to leaf 133v, for example. Close examination shows that there have also been erasures and corrections to the musical notation itself, as on leaf 3v.
12 British Museum, op. cit., 19, gives specific examples of both additions and corrections.
13 ibid.
14 Robert Cowtan, *Memories of the British Museum* (London: Richard Bentley and Son, 1872), 334.
15 Martineau, op. cit., 310.
16 Eric Marshall White, 'Printed for Performance: Ceremonial and Interactive Aspects of Books from Europe's First Presses' in *RBM: A Journal of Rare Books, Manuscripts, and Cultural Heritage* (2014), 15–30.

Hypnerotomachia Poliphili

1 Peter Burnhill, *Type spaces: In-house norms in the typography of Aldus Manutius* (London: Hyphen Press, 2003), 34 (and 10 for the Yciar quotation). Lodovico Guicciardini, *Descrittione ... di tutti I Paesi Bassi...*, 2nd edn. (Antwerp: appresso Christoforo Plantino, 1581), 312. I am grateful to Anna Giulia Cavagna for drawing my attention to the Guicciardini passage.
2 Neil Harris, 'Aldus and the Making of the Myth (or What Did Aldus Really Do?)' in *Aldo Manuzio: La costruzione del mito*, a cura di Mario Infelise (Venice: Marsilio, 2016), 346–385.
3 ibid, 370.
4 One indication of the success of the octavo format was that, within a year of publication in Venice, pirated imitation copies of the editions were being printed in Lyon in France, one of the most important centres of early European printing – and opportunely far removed from the reach of embryonic Venetian attempts at jurisdiction in the field of what today would be called intellectual property.
5 The identity of the unnamed artist(s) responsible for them has been long debated, with the consensus for the main contribution centring on the Paduan illuminator and cartographer Benedetto Bordon. See, for example, Lilian Armstrong, 'Benedetto Bordon, *Miniator*, and Cartography in Early Sixteenth-Century Venice' in *Imago Mundi: The International Journal for the History of Cartography*, vol. 48, 1996, 65–92.
6 Burnhill, op.cit., 102.

Bodoni's *Manuale Tipografico* and His Followers

No Notes. See Further Reading.

Akbar's *Khamsah* of Nizami

1 Ellen Smart, 'Akbar, illiterate genius' in Joanna Williams (ed.), *Kalādarśana: American Studies in the Art of India* (New Delhi: Oxford University Press and IBH Publishing Co.,1981), 99–107.
2 Ch. 34 of vol. 1 'On the arts of writing and painting' in Abu'l-Fazl's *A'in-i Akbari*, trans. H. Blochmann (Calcutta: Asiatic Society of Bengal, 1873), 103.
3 As seen in an inventory shown to the traveller Mandelslo in 1638, *The Voyages and Travels of J. Albert de Mandelslo* ..., trans. J. Davies, in A. Olearius, *The Voyages and Travels of the Ambassadors sent by Frederick Duke of Holstein...* (London: Thomas Dring and John Starkey, 1662), 48.
4 Bodleian MS Elliott 254.
5 Walters Ms. W. 624.
6 F. R. Martin, *The Miniature Painting and Painters of Persia, India and Turkey from the 8th to the 18th Century* (London: Bernard Quaritch, 1912), 81.
7 Peter J. Chelkowski, *Mirror of the Invisible World: Tales from the* Khamseh *of Nizami* (New York: Metropolitan Museum of Art, 1975), 1–10.
8 Keir collection K.1.2014.18, see B. W. Robinson, *Islamic Painting and the Arts of the Book* (London: Faber and Faber, 1976), 238–48.
9 Walters Ms. W.613 ff. 1–6 fit between Or 12208 ff. 72 and 73; W 613 ff. 7–36 between Or 12208 ff. 239 and 240; and W 613 ff. 37–9 follow directly from Or 12208 f. 323v, after

which there are further pages missing before Or 12208, f. 324.

10 *Makhzan al-asrar* f. 31r, undated; *Khusraw u Shirin* f. 109v, dated 20 Mihr, regnal year 38 (12 October 1593); *Layla u Majnun* f. 168r, dated 10 Isfandarmuz, regnal year 38 (1 March 1594); *Haft paykar* f. 230v, undated; *Iskandarnamah* f. 284v, dated Shahrivar, regnal year 40 (August/September 1595) and f. 325v, dated 24 Azar, regnal year 40 (15 December 1595).

11 M. A. Chaghatai, 'Abd-Al-Rahim "Anbarin-Qalam"' in *Encyclopædia Iranica* 1/2, 140–141.

12 Dated at the beginning of Bahman, regnal year 4, corresponding to 14 Shavval 1017 (21 January 1609).

13 Priscilla Soucek, 'Persian Artists in Mughal India: Influences and Transformations' in *Muqarnas* 4 (1987), 172; M. A. Chaghatai, 'The illustrated edition of the Razm Nama (Persian version of the Mahābhārata) at Akbar's court' in *Bulletin of the Deccan College Post-Graduate and Research Institute* 5 (1943/44), 287.

14 Bada'uni, *Muntakhab al-Tavarikh*, vol. 2, trans. W. H. Lowe (Calcutta: Asiatic Society of Bengal, 1884), 299.

15 Folio 82r.

16 U. Sims-Williams, 'Or 6810: The Afterlife of a Manuscript' in Barbara Brend, *Treasures from Herat: Two Manuscripts of the Khamsah of Nizami in the British Library* (London: Gingko Library, 2022), 218.

17 K.1.2014.18, ff. 73v, 157v.

18 Abu'l-Fazl, *A'in-i Akbari*; trans. H. Blochmann (Calcutta: Asiatic Society of Bengal, 1873), 107.

19 Variously written *Mādhū* or *Mādhava* and *Mādhū/Mādhava khānah-zād* who may in fact be two different artists.

20 On Islamic illumination see Marianna Shreve Simpson, 'Illumination (art)' at Brill Online, *Encyclopaedia of Islam, THREE* (2021) at dx.doi.org/10.1163/1573-3912_ei3_COM_35356.

21 Ornamental rosettes on folios 1r, 31v, 32r, 110r, 168v, 169r, 231r, 285r; headings on folios 1v, 32v, 110v, 169v, 231v, 285v.

22 Walters Ms. W.613, f. 42r and f. 174v.

23 Bodleian MS. Elliott 254, f. 21v.

24 John Seyller, 'Pearls of the Parrot of India: The Walters Art Museum "Khamsa" of Amīr Khusraw of Delhi' in *The Journal of the Walters Art Museum* 58 (2000), 123 and 138, fn. 9.

25 An example of a centrally placed imperial seal can be seen in the 'Shah Jahan Album' (Metropolitan Museum of Art 55.121.10.40).

26 Folio 32v.

27 Folio 169v.

28 Walters Ms. W 631, f. 42v.

29 Royal Asiatic Society 258, f. 3v.

30 John Seyller, ibid, 120.

31 For a study of Mughal marginal decoration see J. P. Losty, 'The "Bute Hafiz" and the Development of Border Decoration in the Manuscript Studio of the Mughals' in *The Burlington Magazine* 127, no. 993 (Dec. 1985), 855–856; 858–871.

32 On ff. 132r, 169v and 294v.

33 John Seyller, ibid, note 25, 139.

34 F. R. Martin, *The Miniature Painting and Painters of Persia, India and Turkey from the 8th to the 18th Century* (London: Bernard Quaritch, 1912), vol. 1, 81–2.

35 For a history of Dyson Perrins as a collector, see Laura Cleaver, 'Charles William Dyson Perrins as a Collector of Medieval and Renaissance Manuscripts *c.* 1900–1920' in *Perspectives médiévales*, 41 (2020), accessed online 24 April at journals.openedition.org/peme/19776.

The Shakespeare First Folio of 1623

1 Eric Rasmussen and Anthony James West (eds), *The Shakespeare First Folios: A Descriptive Catalogue* (Basingstoke, Hants: Palgrave Macmillan, 2012), xi.

2 Christie's, New York, 14 Oct. 2020. Hammer price US$8,400,000; price with buyer's premium US$9,978,000.

3 Peter W. M. Blayney, *The First Folio of Shakespeare* (Washington D.C.: Folger Shakespeare Library, 1991), 25–26.

4 Blayney, op. cit., 2.

5 Reed Reibstein, 'The Text Font of the First Folio of Shakespeare: History, Description, and Identification of the Font', 7. reedreibstein.com/assets/reibstein-first-folio.pdf (accessed 17 May 2023).

6 B. D. R. Higgins, 'Printing the First Folio' in Emma Smith (ed.), *The Cambridge Companion to Shakespeare's First Folio* (Cambridge: Cambridge University Press, 2016), 34–35.

7 Higgins, op. cit., 38.

8 Blayney, op. cit., 21.

9 The five copies in the British Library and their earlier owners are: C.7.c.14 (George III); C.21.e.16 (Clayton Mordaunt Cracherode); C.39.i.12 (Charles Burney); C.39.k.15 (Arthur William Clifford); and G.11631 (Thomas Grenville).

10 Gabriel Egan, 'The Provenance of the Folio Texts' in Emma Smith, op. cit., 68.

The Title Page and Other Paratexts

1 Seán Jennett, *The Making of Books*, 3rd edn. (London: Faber and Faber, 1964), 312.

2 *New Oxford Style Manual* (Oxford: Oxford University Press, 2003), 2 ('Preliminary matter'), 17 ('End matter').

Excerpts from The Tale of Genji

1 The years of her birth and death and even her name are unknown. Like most women at the Heian Court – and the majority of the characters in her novel – she is known to history only by a title.

2 Poetry written in Japanese is known as *waka* as opposed to poetry composed in classical Chinese which is called *kanshi*.

3 This is an interesting spin on the assumption of male *noms de plume* by later Western women writers including the Brontës and George Eliot.

4 The chrysanthemum has been closely associated with the Japanese Imperial House since at least the reign of Emperor Go-Toba (1180–1239, r. 1183–98), who chose it as his personal emblem.

5 Minister of the Right *(Udaijin)* was the most junior of the three Ministers of State after the *Daijō Daijin* (Chief Minister of State) and the *Sadaijin* (Minister of the Left). For more on Japan's traditional government see Richard J. Miller, *Japan's First Bureaucracy: A Study of Eighth-Century Government* (East Asia Papers, no. 19) (China-Japan Program: Cornell University, 1978).

6 See Tsuji Eiko, 'Dai-Ei Toshokan shozō "Genji monogatari kotoba" no honbun to kaisetsu' [*Genji monogatari kotoba* in The British Library: text and commentary] in *Zaigai Nihon jūyō emaki shūsei* [Important Japanese Picture

Scrolls in Overseas Collections] (Tokyo: Kasama Shoin, 2011) [in Japanese].

7 Much of Jokei's early life, including his parentage, is unclear. Like many Japanese artists, he used a variety of personal and artistic names over his career.

8 See Shimohara Miho, 'Sumiyoshi Jokei, Gukei ni yoru Yamato-e seisaku ni tsuite: gadai no keikō o chūshin ni' [The Production of Yamato-e by Sumiyoshi Jyokei and Gukei: Consideration of Motifs], *Kagoshima Daigaku Kyōiku Gakubu kenkyū kiyō: Jinbun shakai kagaku hen* [Bulletin of the Faculty of Education, Kagoshima University, Cultural and Social Science], 60 [2009], 237–253 [in Japanese]. See also core.ac.uk/download/pdf/144565388.pdf

9 See Tsuji Eiko, *Zaigai Nihon jūyō emaki shūsei* [Important Japanese Picture Scrolls in Overseas Collections] (Tokyo: Kasama Shoin, 2011) [in Japanese].

10 The majority of items collected during Siebold's first period in Japan were purchased by the Dutch government in 1837 and are today in Leiden University.

A Modern Meosamerican Codex

1 Enrique Chagoya, Prospectus for *Codex Espangliensis: From Columbus to the Border Patrol*, (Santa Cruz: Moving Parts Press, 1998).

2 Oral history interview with Enrique Chagoya, 25 July–6 August, 2001, Archives of American Art, Smithsonian Institution.

3 ibid.

William Leighton's *The Teares or Lamentacions of a Sorrowfull Soule*

1 Peter Holman, *Dowland: Lachrimae (1604)* (Cambridge: Cambridge University Press, 1999), 9.

2 Jacques Moderne (ed.), *Le paragon des chansons* (Lyon: Jacques Moderne, 1538).

3 National Library of Florence, Magl. XIX, 141. Dated post-1513. Alfred Einstein, *The Italian Madrigal*, trans. Alexander H. Krappe, Roger H. Sessions and Oliver Strunk (Princeton: Princeton University Press, 1971), vol. 1, 59; Bonnie J. Blackburn, 'Two "Carnival Songs" Unmasked: A Commentary on MS Florence Magl. XIX, 121' in *Musica Disciplina*, 35 (1981): 149. See also: Tessa Murray, *Thomas Morley: Elizabethan Music Publisher* (Woodbridge: The Boydell Press, 2014), 83.

4 Pierre Phalèse (ed.), *Hortus musarum* (Louvain: Pierre Phalèse, 1552), sig. Lr.

5 British Library, Add. MS 31390.

6 Richard Rastall, 'Spatial effects in English instrumental consort music, *c*. 1560–1605' in *Early Music* 25 (1997): 271; Warwick Edwards, 'Clement Woodcock' at Grove Music Online.

7 For the *First Booke*'s financial success: Peter Holman and Paul O'Dette, 'John Dowland' at Grove Music Online. Reissues of this edition are listed at RISM (Répertoire International des Sources Musicales) D3478–3482.

8 For Dowland's role in devising the format of the *First Booke*: Holman, *Dowland: Lachrimae*, 7.

9 The will of Leighton's father, also William Leighton, is preserved at: National Archives, PROB 11/111/525.

10 For an annotated presentation copy with handwritten message from composer to the dedicatee, Anne of Denmark: Tobias Hume, *Captain Hume's Poeticall Musicke* (London: John Windet, 1607), Sig. [A1v]. British Library, K.2.g.11. For a musical reward given to Thomas Vautor for presenting *The First Set Beeing Songs* to the Duke of Buckingham: David C. Price, *Patrons and Musicians of the English Renaissance* (Cambridge: Cambridge University Press, 1981), 185.

11 Folger Shakespeare Library STC 15434 and Royal College of Music D29.

12 See British Library C.47.i.12. for similar binding of Diego Ufano, *Artillerie* (1614).

13 Cecil Hill, *Sir William Leighton: the tears or lamentations of a sorrowful soul 1614* (University of St Andrews, 1966).

The Design of Human Atlases

No Notes. See Further Reading.

A Description of Three Hundred Animals

1 Seth Lerer, *Children's Literature: A Reader's History from Aesop to Harry Potter* (Chicago; London: University of Chicago Press, 2008), 1.

2 According to the *English Short Title Catalogue*, the census of books printed in English or in England between 1473 and 1800.

3 Co-published with Richard Ware and Thomas Game.

4 Arthur Adrian Lisney, *A Bibliography of British Lepidoptera* (London: The Chiswick Press, 1960), 86.

5 Thomas Bewick, *A Memoir of Thomas Bewick Written by Himself*, Iain Bain (ed.) (Oxford: Oxford University Press, 1979).

6 Usually produced in Germany or Italy, this decorated paper was meant to imitate the brocades of this period. It featured metal-leaf embossing over coloured or uncoloured paper. It is known as brocade paper, gilt paper or Dutch paper.

7 Daniel Hahn, *Oxford Companion to Children's Literature*, 2nd edn. (Oxford: Oxford University Press, 2015), 177.

8 Andrea Korda, 'Thinking with Pictures: Memory, Imagination and Colour Illustration in Victorian Teaching and Learning' in *Paedagogica Historica*, 2020, vol. 56, no. 3, 269–92.

9 Baxter was building on the work of Alois Senefelder (1771–1834) who had developed the process of lithography in Germany.

10 Charles Thomas Courtney Lewis, *The Story of Picture Printing in England during the Nineteenth Century* (London: Sampson Low & Co., 1928), 5.

11 Hahn, op. cit., 135.

12 Joyce Irene Whalley and Tessa Rose Chester, *A History of Children's Book Illustration* (London: John Murray, 1988), 109.

13 Mark Girouard, *Sweetness and Light: The 'Queen Anne' Movement, 1860–1900* (Oxford: Clarendon Press, 1977), 146.

14 M. H. Spielmann and G. S. Layard, *Kate Greenaway* (London: Adam and Charles Black, 1905), 172.

15 The term 'movable book' includes any book with three-dimensional elements including pop-ups, volvelles, flaps or tabs.

16 Whalley and Chester, op. cit., 99.

Miniature Books: Their Charm and Purpose

1 Louis W. Bondy, *Miniature Books: Their History from the Beginnings to the Present Day* (London: Sheppard Press, 1981), 1.

2 W. M. Stone, *Charm of Miniature Books* in *Newsletter of the LXIVmos* no. 13 (Dec. 15, 1928), 1.
3 Kristina Myrvold, Andreas Johansson, 'Miniature Qur'ans in the First World War: religious comforts for Indian Muslim soldiers' in *Miniature Books: The Format and Function of Tiny Religious Texts*, Kristina Myrvold and Dorina Miller Parmenter (eds), (Bristol, Connecticut: Equinox, 2019), 132–157.
4 For an account of the British Library archive of war despatches and Indian soldiers' correspondence with their families, see the accurate bibliography reported within Myrvold and Johansson 'Miniature Qur'ans in the First World War', 151–155, and Kristina Myrvold, 'Mite Qur'ans for Indian Markets: David Bryce in the Late Nineteenth and Early Twentieth Century' in *Postscripts: The Journal of Sacred Texts, Cultural Histories, and Contemporary* Contexts, vol. 9, no. 2–3 (2013). Special issue: Miniature iconic books.

A Qur'an from Aceh

1 Annabel Gallop, The, 'An Acehnese style of manuscript illumination' in *Archipel* (68), 2004.

Owen Jones's *The Grammar of Ornament*

1 Michael Twyman, 'The illustration revolution' in David McKitterick (ed.), *The Cambridge History of the Book in Britain: Volume VI 1830–1914* (2014), 136. See also Edmund M. B. King 'Electrotyping of books in mid-Victorian Britain', victorianbookbindings.blogspot.com/2018/04/ (accessed 15 Nov. 2020).
2 Another lavish production using chromolithography was *Dickinson's Comprehensive Pictures of the Great Exhibition of 1851* (1854), bl.uk/collection-items/dickinsons-comprehensive-pictures-of-the-great-exhibition-of-1851 (accessed 13 Nov. 2020).
3 Carol A. Hrvol Flores, *Owen Jones: Design, Ornament, Architecture, and Theory in an Age of Transition* (Rizzoli International, 2006). Appendix A lists fifty-four works: 'Authored, Edited, Designed... or Bindings (Covers) by Owen Jones' between 1842 and 1867.
4 For details of these contemporary advertisements relating to the book design work of Owen Jones, see Edmund M. B. King, 'Owen Jones Publishing Activities', victorianbookbindings.blogspot.com/2020/03/ (accessed 14 Nov. 2020).
5 Owen Jones article ODNB: '...the first three parts [were published] in 1836, but [he] did not complete the first volume (in ten parts) until 1842'.
6 Jones probably knew of Lord Kingsborough's *Antiquities of Mexico*... which began publication in 1830, the drawings lithographed by Augustine Aglio on stone, some hand-coloured.
7 Ruari McLean, *Victorian Book Design and Colour Printing*, 2nd edn. (University of California Press, 1972), 78: 'Volume published as a whole in 1842, cost £12 10s on small paper; the two volumes were published together at £36 10s.'
8 Owen Jones, 'An Attempt to describe the Principles which should regulate the Employment of Colour in the Decorative Arts. With a few Words on the Present Necessity of an Architectural Education on the Part of the Public', Lecture XX of *Lectures on the Results of the Great Exhibition of 1851*, (London: D. Bogue, 1853), 253–301. The lecture is dated 28 April 1852. Copy available at books.google.co.uk (accessed 4 Dec. 2020).
9 John Leighton published *Suggestions in Design* (London: David Bogue, 1853). The sub-title states its intended audience 'for the use of artists and art-workmen ... for workers in metal, wood, ivory, glass, and leather; the potter weaver, printer in colours, engraver, decorator, etc'. The designs were in monochrome only.
10 Advertisement in *The Staffordshire Sentinel* 22 March 1856, 9.
11 £19 10s in 1860 is the equivalent of £2,387 in 2020. www.in2013dollars.com/uk/inflation/1860?amount=19
12 'Just published, extra half bound, morocco, £19. 12s. ...3000 examples from various styles...' *North and South Shields Gazette*, 10 December 1857, 5.
13 For example, discounting for books designed by Jones in *Illustrated London News* 6 December 1862, 13: 'New Books at less than half the published prices. Victoria Psalter by Owen Jones, £4, pub. at £12 12s.'; *Aris's Birmingham Gazette* 22 December 1860, 2: 'Illustrated Christmas Books. – Cornish Brothers ... new Illustrated Christmas Books. Paradise and the Peri beautifully illuminated. Offered at £1.15.0; Published at £2.2.0.'
14 *The Devon and Wiltshire Gazette*, 24 December 1856, 1: 'The Book of Job; illustrated with 50 beautiful Engravings after drawings by John Gilbert – Small Quarto, 18s.'
15 British Library copy C.109.d.9. *Newcastle Daily Chronicle* 2 December 1859, 1: 'Books suitable for Christmas Presents, New Year's Gifts, and School Prizes. On sale by J. J. Lynch ... Moore's Lallah Rookh; an Oriental Romance, ... 4to., cloth richly gilt, antique, 15s. 1860.'
16 British Museum copy 1992,0406.231. *Sun* (London) 17 October 1860, 1: 'Moore's Lallah Rookh Illustrated by Tenniel. On the 30th inst., will be published, in One Volume, fcap., 4to, price 21s., in ornamental covers; or 36s. bound in morocco by Hayday.'
17 *Clayhanger*, Penguin edn., 1973, 194.
18 Ian Zaczek, 'Introduction' [to a re-issue of *The Grammar of Ornament*] (Princeton University Press, 2016), 12–17, see also assets.press.princeton.edu/chapters/i10788.pdf (accessed 11 Dec. 2020).
19 Fiona Melhuish, 'The Grammar of Ornament: Special Collections featured item for February 2009', 11–12, at collections.reading.ac.uk/special-collections/wp-content/uploads/sites/5/2020/02/Featured-Item_Grammar-of-Ornament-compressed-screen.pdf (accessed 28 Feb. 2023).
20 A scanned copy of the 1856 edition is at library.si.edu/digital-library/book/grammarornament00jone (accessed 31 March 2023).

American Publishers' Bindings, Nineteenth Century

1 Most of the designs in this feature, and many more, can be found in the British Library database of bookbindings at bl.uk/catalogues/bookbindings/ (accessed 30 Aug. 2020).
2 BL shelfmark C.188.a.396. bl.uk/catalogues/bookbindings/LargeImage.aspx?RecordId=020-000027468&ImageId=ImageId=62697&Copyright=BL (accessed 30 Aug. 2020); Richard Minsky, *American Publishers' Bindings 1886–1926 and The Amelia E. Barr Collection: a catalog of books for sale*, 2016, 7.
3 BL shelfmark C.188.a.395. bl.uk/catalogues/bookbindings/LargeImage.aspx?RecordId=020-000027466&ImageId=ImageId=62696&Copyright=BL (accessed 30 Aug. 2020); Minsky, op. cit., 8. Minsky cites Rome K. Richardson as cover designer.

The Buddha's Last Birth Tale
No Notes. See Further Reading.

A Material Identity in Oceania Book Design

1 Arthur Philip, *The Voyage of Governor Philip to Botany Bay* (London, 1789). Copy at shelfmark C.47.i.10. bound in kangaroo skin.
2 John Murray, *An account of the Phormium Tenax; or New-Zealand Flax. Printed on paper made from its leaves with a postscript on paper* (London: Henry Renshaw, 1836). Shelfmark 7034.b.27.
3 A book bound in kangaroo skin by Alderson and Sons of Sydney was recorded later at the Melbourne Exhibition in 1880, but the use of kangaroo skin was otherwise largely confined to the binding of more prosaic material such as government ledgers and reports. Carol Mills, 'Australian Bookbinders and Bookbinding in the 19th century' in *Collaboration and Connections: Postprints of the AICCM Paper, Books and Photographic Materials Special Interest Group Symposium*, Sydney 1–3 April 2004, 67–77.
4 Te Papa Tongarewa – Museum of New Zealand, 'Harakeke – New Zealand flax' at https://collections.tepapa.govt.nz/topic/3623 (accessed 19 May 2023).

Audubon's *The Birds of America*

1 See Julie Melby, 'Audubon's Copperplates for *Birds of America*', *Print Quarterly*, XXXVII, 2020, 3, 283–293 for a recent account.
2 Havell's father, Robert Havell Snr, was also briefly employed on the project.
3 There is no mention of their contributions as artists on the prints, but he does acknowledge most in his *Ornithological Biography* – for example, for white-crowned pigeon: 'I procured a large bough, from which the drawing was made, with the assistance of Mr Lehman' (vol. II, 448). The extent of Joseph Mason's contribution is still disputed. He claimed to have made between 150 and 200 plant and flower drawings for Audubon but complained about his lack of attribution on the drawings and plates, perhaps as retaliation he is not mentioned. Some birds are silently borrowed from Alexander Wilson, at least one background from a 1784 engraving by John Webber. He also employed copyists like Joseph Kidd. See Theodore E. Stebbins, 'Audubon's Drawings of American Birds, 1805–38', 3–26 in *John James Audubon, The Watercolors for THE BIRDS OF AMERICA, The New York Historical Society*, 1993.
4 'For he that engraves figures from his own drawings after nature, may always be supposed rather to correct the errors of such drawings of his own plates, than to fall short of their perfections, which is not the case when drawings are given to common engravers to be copied; for, though they may give them a softer finish in the copper, yet they generally fall short of the spirit of the originals: so that it is always a great advantage, an any work of Natural History, when the author can perform both the drawing and engraving parts with his own hand', George Edwards, *Gleanings of Natural History*, part 2, 1760, xi–xii.
5 Letter of 4 March 1836 to George Ord, Charles Waterton, *Essays on Natural History Edited with a Life of the Author,* 1871.
6 Will 14 Nov. 1831, with probate, 7 Apr. 1835, The National Archives, PROB 11/1845/350. More on Hardwicke: Turner, I. M. (2015). 'Thomas Hardwicke (1756–1835): botanical drawings and manuscripts from the Hardwicke Bequest in the British Library.' Archives of Natural History. 42 (2): 236–244. doi:10.3366/anh.2015.0308. ISSN 0260-9541.
7 Baber's note to the Trustees of 11 April 1835, minute 3854. Thanks to Francesca Hillier at the Museum and Hannah Graves at the Library for help sourcing archival material.
8 Minute 3967, 11 April 1835.
9 See *The history of the collections contained in the Natural history departments of the British Museum, London: Printed by order of the Trustees*, 1904–12, 37–38 for an outline of the 4,528 drawings transferred to the Natural History Museum – thanks to Andrea Hart for this source. Add. MSS. 10974–10984, 10986–11004, 11007 and 11009 were transferred to the then Department of Zoology in 1883. On these, and on Hardwicke's career, see W. R. Dawson, 'On the History of Gray and Hardwicke's "Illustrations of Indian Zoology" and some Biographical Notes on General Hardwicke', *Journal of the Society for the Bibliography of Natural History*, ii, 1946, 55–69. 11808 was also transferred to the Natural History Museum. The British Library also later acquired 96 drawings of Indian birds as part of the India Office Library, purchased by the IO in 1891 and identified as Hardwicke's by Mildred Archer (NHD39). Archer was aware that the Natural History Museum holdings were not representative of the whole, but assumed the reason was that 'he was continually giving drawings to his friends'. She identifies other works in Marquis Wellesley's collection as acquired from Hardwicke (Natural History Drawings in the India Office Library, London, 1962, 8–10, 79).
10 Evidence to Select Committee, 7 June 1836, 4971.
11 Credits, legends, part numbers and plate numbers vary in first ten prints. Lizars produced only about fifty prints each of the first ten images and some portion of these was retrieved from the subscribers. Prints that are 'wholly the work of Lizars have naturally become extremely rare'. Francis Hobart Herrick, *Audubon the Naturalist: A History of His Life and Time*, 2nd edn., 1938, 199.
12 Hardwicke's drawings presented in a similar manner, laid down to larger sheets and bound.
13 On 10 Dec. 1826 he noted: 'The little drawings in the center of those beautiful large sheets have a fine effect and an air of richness and wealth.' John James Audubon, Alice Ford, Henry Bradley Martin, *The 1826 Journal of John James Audubon*, 1967, 346.
14 Melby, op. cit., 283.
15 Maria Audubon, *Audubon and His Journals*, vol. I, 190. Minutes of a committee 9 July 1831, 3383.
16 Such as Sir William Jardine, who cancelled in March or April 1832. Christine E. Jackson and Peter Davis, *Sir William Jardine: A Life in Natural History* (London; New York: Leicester University Press, 2001), 82. Jardine and Selby cite using Hardwicke's drawings in *Illustrations of Ornithology*, vol. 2, 1826–35, 104, and thank Hardwicke, 110.
17 This was not an isolated case – Robert McCraken Peck notes, 17: 'Because of their prominence in scientific and/or social circles at the time, John Gould (1804–1881), Thomas Campbell Eyton (1809–1880), Edward Smith Stanley (later the 13th Earl of Derby) (1799-1869) and the Marchioness of Hertford (1759–1834) were figures whose names Audubon was particularly pleased to count among owners of his work. Little did he know that the magnifi-

cent 39½ x 26½ inch plates he sold them would soon be snipped apart and the birds they contained removed from their carefully constructed settings to serve the disparate purposes of their various owners.'

18 Neville Wood, *The Ornithologist's Text-book* (London, 1836), 89–90.
19 Maria Audubon, op.cit., 85.
20 Correspondence with Dr Alex Bond, December 2020.
21 Mullens and Swann, *A Bibliography of British Ornithology* (London: Witherby & Co., 1919), 218.
22 Audubon and Havell did sell some as bound volumes towards the end of the project, using the binder Hering of Newman Street.
23 Evidence to the Select Committee, 7 June 1836, 4810.
24 Melby, op. cit., 286.

'An Error of Taste': Smithers, Beardsley and *The Savoy*

1 The title refers to a criticism of Beardsley's frontispiece to *Plays* by John Davidson, in *The Daily Chronicle,* wherein Beardsley had caricatured Oscar Wilde and Sir Augustus Harris. In response, Beardsley wrote to the editor: 'Sir, – in your review of Mr. Davidson's plays, I find myself convicted of an error of taste, for having introduced portraits into my frontispiece to that book. I cannot help feeling that your reviewer is unduly severe. One of the gentlemen who forms part of my decoration is surely beautiful enough to stand the test even of portraiture, the other owes me half a crown. I am, yours truly, AUBREY BEARDSLEY.'
2 *Portsmouth Evening News*, Saturday, 6 April 1895, page 3, col. 2. This same copy appears in the 6 April edition of the *Glasgow Evening Post*, *Dundee Evening Telegraph*, *Yorkshire Post* and *Leeds Intelligencer*, *Yarmouth Independent*, and other provincial newspapers.
3 Eccles 1085. *The Yellow Book: an illustrated quarterly* (London: Elkin Mathews & John Lane; Boston: Copeland & Day, 1894–1897).
4 H. M. Hyde claimed, 'Actually, the book in question was *Aphrodite,* a novel of Wilde's friend Pierre Louÿs, and it happened to have a yellow cover' (*The Trials of Oscar Wilde,* (London, 1948, 61). However, this theory seems unlikely because *Aphrodite* was not published until late March 1896 – a full year after Wilde's arrest. (As noted by H. P. Clive, 'Pierre Louÿs and Oscar Wilde: A chronicle of their friendship' in *Revue de Littérature Comparée*, (1969), 43(3), 382.)
5 Merlin Holland, *Oscar Wilde: A Life in Letters*, (2006), 271.
6 This attitude can be observed in the notation across L. Smithers, *Catalogue of Rare Books*, Ten Issues, (1895–1897).
7 General Reference Collection C.193.b.56. *Catalogue of Rare Books*. Ten Issues (London: Leonard C. Smithers; Leeds: Fred R. Spark and Son; London: Chiswick Press, H. S. Nichols, 1895–1897).
8 Eccles 1040. *The Savoy: an illustrated quarterly*, edited by Arthur Symons. (London : Leonard Smithers, 1896).
9 A. Symons, 'Editorial Note' in *The Savoy*, no.1.
10 Discussions on paper can be found in R. A. Walker (ed.), *Letters from Aubrey Beardsley to Leonard Smithers* (London: The First Editions Club, 1937). These discussions even extend to the 'contentious question' of wallpaper. See Letter LXXXV, G.83 H.I.47.
11 J. G. Nelson, *Publisher to the Decadents: Leonard Smithers in the Careers of Beardsley, Wilde, and Dowson* (Penn State University Press, 2000), 5.
12 M. D. Stetz, 'Sex, Lies, and Printed Cloth: Bookselling at the Bodley Head in the Eighteen-Nineties' in *Victorian Studies*, Autumn 1991, vol. 35, no. 1, 74.
13 In 1896 alone, Beardsley produced thirty drawings for *The Savoy,* illustrated *The Rape of the Lock*, *Lysistrata* and *The Pierrot of the Minute*. He also began three unfinished works, *Ali Baba*, *Table Talk* and a translation of the *Sixth Satire* of Juvenal, all including illustrations. Between these commitments, he continued writing his unfinished opus, *Venus and Tannhäuser*.
14 'Prospectus', *The Savoy: an Illustrated Quarterly Prospectus* (London, 1895). BL Shelfmark: K.T.C.35.a.14a.
15 *The Academy*, vol. 69, no. 1761 (3 Feb. 1906).
16 Letter CLXXXV, G.180.H.II.83 in Walker (ed.), op. cit.

The Works of Geoffrey Chaucer

1 *A Note by William Morris on his aims in founding the Kelmscott Press, together with a short description of the press by S. C. Cockerell, & an annotated list of the books printed thereat* (Hammersmith: Printed at the Kelmscott Press; sold by the Trustees of the late William Morris at the Kelmscott Press, 1898), 44.
2 *Pall Mall Gazette*, Thursday, 14 April 1898, 3: 'The Kelmscott Press. -1. A Retrospect', by Sir James Knowles, architect and editor of the *Nineteenth Century*.
3 *The Poetical works of Geoffrey Chaucer etc.* (London; New York: Routledge, Warne & Routledge, 1864), Preface, i.
4 Letter from Morris to the Secretary of the Clarendon Press, 9 August 1894, held in Oxford University Archives (DUP/PUB/11/23). Quoted in William S. Peterson, *A Bibliography of the Kelmscott* Press (Oxford: Clarendon Press, 1984), 109.
5 A Note by William Morris, op. cit., 47.
6 William Morris, *News from Nowhere; or, An Epoch of Rest, Being Some Chapters from a Utopian Romance* (Hammersmith: Printed at the Kelmscott Press; sold by Reeves & Turner, 1892).
7. *Arts and Crafts Essays by Members of the Arts and Crafts Exhibition Society* (London; Bombay: Longmans Green & Co., 1899), 133.
8 *The Ideal Book: A Paper by William Morris Read before the Bibliographical Society, London, 19th June, 1893.* (London: L.C.C. Central School of Arts & Crafts, 1907, finished February 1908), 12–13.
9 *The Complete works of Geoffrey Chaucer edited from numerous manuscripts by the Rev. Walter W. Skeat* (Oxford: Clarendon Press, 1894–97).
10 Quoted in William S. Peterson, *A Bibliography of the Kelmscott Press* (Oxford: Clarendon Press, 1984), 106.
11 *The Ideal Book*, op. cit., 5: 'Next, if you want a legible book, the white should be clear & the black black.'
12 ibid., 11: 'Our ideal book must, I think, be printed on handmade paper as good as it can be made; penury here will make a poor book of it.'
13 ibid., 10.
14 The four special bindings were to have been executed by Cobden-Sanderson at the Doves Press and by Messrs. J. and J. Leighton. These are described in the Kelmscott Publications list of 22 January 1896 as a full white tooled pigskin binding at £13, and a half pigskin and oak boards, £9 at the Doves Press, and a full pigskin with different tooling at £9, and a half pigskin and oak boards for 5 Guineas by Messrs. J. and J. Leighton. Morris's death

in October 1896 meant that only the design for the full pigskin binding at the Doves Press Bindery could be completed.

15 CPI (Consumer Price Index) Inflation Calculator £20 in 1896 equivalent to £3,404.12 in 2023 | UK Inflation Calculator (in2013dollars.com).

16 Inscription by May Morris in the volume at BL shelfmark C.43.h.17 reads: 'Owing to the difficulties of printing on vellum, it was necessary, in order to secure the full number of perfect copies, to print one more of each sheet than was required ... The majority of these are quite satisfactory but in some cases the vellum may be too thick or the inking defective or there may be stains or other blemishes.' This volume contains 182 of these extra leaves that demonstrate the difficulties Morris faced when printing on vellum.

17 CPI (Consumer Price Index) Inflation Calculator £126 in 1896 equivalent to £21,445.96 in 2023 | UK Inflation Calculator (in2013dollars.com).

18 Letter from Edward Burne-Jones to Charles Eliot Norton, 8 December 1894. Quoted in *Paul Needham, William Morris and the Art of the Book* (New York: Pierpont Morgan Library; London: Oxford University Press, 1976), 139.

19 *St. James's Gazette,* 5 October 1896, 15, 'The Arts and Crafts Exhibition, New Gallery'.

20 *Athenaeum*, 3 October 1896, 444–5.

21 *The Globe*, Saturday, 18 August 1894, 6: 'Literary Gossip'; *Pall Mall Gazette*, 14 April 1898, 3.

22 A. L. Bowley, *Wages in the United Kingdom in the Nineteenth Century* (Cambridge: Cambridge University Press, 1900), 52.

23 CPI (Consumer Price Index) Inflation Calculator £30 in 1896 equivalent to £4,988.80 in 2023 | UK Inflation Calculator (in2013dollars.com).

24 *The Daily Chronicle*, Wednesday, 22 February 1893, 3: 'Master Printer Morris: A visit to the Kelmscott Press'.

25 John Carter, *Printing and the Mind of Man*, compiled and edited by John Carter & Percy H. Muir, assisted by Nicolas Barker, H. A. Feisenberger, Howard Nixon and S. H. Steinberg (London: Cassell, 1967), 223.

26 Quoted in *You are Invited to View an Exhibition of Finely-printed Books Since William Morris, of which this is the Catalogue, at the Lakeside Press Galleries, September, October, and November, 1932* (Chicago: R. R. Donnelley & Sons Co., 1932), 19.

27 ibid, 71.

28 Will Ransom, *Private Presses and Their Books* (New York: R. R. Bowker, 1929), 35.

Twentieth-Century Typefaces

No Notes. See Further Reading.

***Sadok Sudei* and Other Futurist Books from Russia**

1 V. Mayakovski, 'A few words about my mamma', trans. Patricia Blake. RuVerses: ruverses.com/vladimir-mayakovsky/a-few-words-about-my-mom/1465/ (accessed 23 Jan. 2023).

2 David Burliuk, *Fragmenty iz vospominanii futurista. Pis'ma. Stikhotvoreniia* (St Petersburg: Pushkin fond, 1994), ebook. Here and below the translations are mine, unless stated otherwise.

3 O. Matiushina, 'Vospominaniia' in *Zvezda*, 3, 1973, 141–144.

4 Aage A Hansen-Löve, *Intermedial'nost' v russkoi kul'ture: ot simvolizma k avangardu* (Moscow: RGGU, 2016), 55.

5 Torben Jelsbak, 'Visual language: The Graphic Signifier in Avant-Garde Literature' in *Acta Linguistica Hafniensia*, 42:S1, 2010, 177–188, DOI:10.1080/03740463.2010.482330, 183.

6 ibid, 183.

7 V. Kamenskii, *Ego-moia biografiia velikogo futurista* (Moscow: Kitovras, 1918), 132.

8 Jelsbak, op. cit., 186.

9 ibid.

10 V. Poliakov, *Knigi russkogo kubofuturizma* (Moscow, 1998), 11.

Cartonera Books and Publishers

1 Information on the cartonera collective's website, dulcineiacatadora.com.br

2 See the resources on the website of the AHRC-funded research project Cartonera Publishing, cartonerapublishing.com/wp-content/uploads/2019/08/wind-and-mirrors-final.pdf

3 *Akademia cartonera: a primer of Latin American cartonera publishers = un abc de las editoriales cartoneras en América Latina*, edited by Ksenija Bilbija, Paloma Celis Carbajal, Lauren Pagel and Djurdja Trajković (Madison, Wisconsin: Parallel Press, University of Wisconsin-Madison Libraries, 2009) [Shelfmark: EMD.2020.b.2].

4 Lucy Bell, 'Recycling Materials, Recycling Lives: Cardboard Publishers in Latin America' in Johns-Putra A., Parham J., Squire L. (eds), Literature and Sustainability: Concept, Text and Culture (Manchester: Manchester University Press, 2017), 76–96. [Shelfmark: YC.2018.a.14443].

5 Ksenija Bilbija, *Cultural Shape-Shifters:* Cartonera *Publishers* (Buffalo, New York: The Poetry Collection of the University Libraries, University at Buffalo, The State University of New York, 2019) [Shelfmark RF.2020.a.20].

6 Alex Flynn and Lucy Bell, 'Returning to form: anthropology, art and a trans-formal methodological approach' in *Anthrovision* [online], vol. 7.1 (2019), (accessed 1 March 2022). journals.openedition.org/anthrovision/5001

Century

1 Although the first phototypeset publication was created in 1945, it was not until 1957 that the first complete book, *Private Angelo* by Eric Linklater, was set using the Fotosetter. This first generation of phototypesetting machines was relatively inflexible, without the ability to include multiple typefaces and sizes in a single page setting. This only became possible with second-generation phototypesetters such as the Photon, introduced in 1949. S. H. Steinberg, *Five Hundred Years of Printing* (The British Library, 1996), 221.

2 Phaidon in its Vienna phase was an early pioneer of integrating images and text, helped by the concentration of high-quality printing houses in Germany and Austria. The survival of Phaidon was greatly assisted by Stanley Unwin, who purchased his entire stock of books in Horovitz's Vienna warehouse to protect it from confiscation by the Nazis. Horovitz was not the only refugee from Nazi persecution to establish a successful illustrated publishing venture: Walter Neurath, the founder of Thames & Hudson, also fled to Britain, working first for an agency producing the King Penguin series for Penguin and then

in 1949 setting up his own company (which took its name from the rivers running through London and New York, and which acted as the distributor in the UK of titles from the Metropolitan Museum of Art). Andrew Nash, Claire Squires and I. R. Willison (eds), *The Cambridge History of the Book in Britain: Volume VII The Twentieth Century and Beyond* (Cambridge: Cambridge University Press, 2019), 448–449.

Penguin Books and the Paperback Revolution

No Notes. See Further Reading.

Sea Air

1 Drucker, Joanna, 'Artist's book' at Grove Art (oxfordartonline.com), doi.org/10.1093/gao/9781884446054.article.T2220480 (accessed 12 Jul. 2022); Stephen Bury, *Artists' Books: The Book as a Work of Art, 1963–1995*, (Aldershot: Scolar Press, 1995), 1.

2 *Sea Air* Prospectus (London: Fine Press Artists Books, 2018).

3 Susan Allix, in correspondence with the author, 10 Dec. 2018.

Women Publishers and Designers

No Notes. See Further Reading.

Editions At Play

1 High price was a barrier to devices becoming popular in these early experiments and it wasn't until the late 2000s, with the launch of Amazon's first Kindle, that ereaders properly entered the book market and started to proliferate.

2 Portable Document Format (PDF), Electronic Publication (EPUB), Mobipocket (MOBI) and HyperText Markup Language (HTML).

3 All direct quotes in the main body of the text are taken from the Editions At Play's website: editionsatplay.withgoogle.com/

4 In this context reflowable means that the text can be easily adapted to fit different output devices.

5 Although the book has interactive elements with multiple routes through the text, the division of the story into numbered pages allows for a reasonably straightforward transition into print.

Book Design as an Agent of Conservation

No Notes. See Further Reading.

Epilogue

1 John B. Thompson, *Book Wars: The Digital Revolution in Publishing* (Cambridge: Polity Press, 2021), 474–487.

FURTHER READING

The Lindisfarne Gospels

Backhouse, Janet, *The Lindisfarne Gospels* (Oxford: Phaidon, 1981).

Breay, Claire and Story, Joanna (eds), *Anglo-Saxon Kingdoms: Art, Word, War* (London: The British Library, 2018).

Brown, Michelle P., *Painted Labyrinth: The World of the Lindisfarne Gospels* (London: The British Library, 2003).

Brown, Michelle P., *The Lindisfarne Gospels: Society, Spirituality and the Scribe* (London: The British Library, 2003).

Gameson, Richard, *From Holy Island to Durham: The Contexts and Meanings of the Lindisfarne Gospels* (London: Profile, 2013).

Gameson, Richard (ed.), *The Lindisfarne Gospels: New Perspectives* (Leiden: Brill, 2017).

Henderson, George, *From Durrow to Kells: The Insular Gospel-books 650–800* (London: Thames & Hudson, 1987).

Jackson, Eleanor, *The Lindisfarne Gospels: Art, History & Inspiration* (London: The British Library, 2022).

Kendrick, T.D., and others, *Evangeliorum Quattuor Codex Lindisfarnensis: Musei Britannici Codex Cottonianus Nero D.IV*, 2 vols (1956–60).

Ethiopia, African Scribes and the Illustrated Apocalypse

Cowley, R., *The Traditional Interpretation of the Apocalypse of St John in the Ethiopian Orthodox Church* (Cambridge: Cambridge University Press, 1983).

Heldman, M., Grierson, R., and Munro-Hay, S. C., *African Zion: The Sacred Art of Ethiopia* (New Haven, Conn.; London: Yale University Press in association with InterCultura Fort Worth, Walters Art Gallery Baltimore, Institute of Ethiopian Studies Addis Ababa, 1993).

Keene, Bryan C., *Toward a Global Middle Ages: Encountering the World through Illuminated Manuscripts* (Los Angeles: Getty Publications, 2019).

McEwan, R., *Picturing Apocalypse at Gondär: A Study of the Two Known Sets of Ethiopian Illuminations of the Revelation of St. John and the Life and Death of John* (Turin: Nino Aragno, 2006).

The Diamond Sutra Printed in 868

Ho, Chiew Hui, *Diamond Sutra Narratives: Textual Production and Lay Religiosity in Medieval China* (Leiden, Boston: Brill, 2019).

Drège, Jean-Pierre, 'De l'icône à l'anecdote: Les frontispices imprimés en Chine à l'époque des Song (960–1278)' in *Arts Asiatiques* 54 (1999), 44–65.

Drège, Jean-Pierre (ed.), 'Les Codices' in *La Fabrique du Lisible: La Mise en Texte des Manuscrits de la Chine Ancienne et Médiévale* (Paris: Collège de France, Institut des Hautes Etudes Chinoises, 2014), 373–376.

Shi, Yongyou, *The Diamond Sutra in Chinese Culture* (Los Angeles: Buddha's Light Publishing, 2010).

Tsien, Tsuen-Hsuin, *Written on Bamboo & Silk: The Beginnings of Chinese Books & Inscriptions*, 2nd edn. (Chicago; London: University of Chicago Press, 2004).

Tsien, Tsuen-Hsuin, and Needham, Joseph, *Science and Civilisation in China*, vol. 5, *Chemistry and Chemical Technology, Part 1: Paper and Printing* (Cambridge: Cambridge University Press, 1985).

Walters, Conrad and Morgan, Joyce, *Journeys on the Silk Road: Desert Explorer, Buddha's Secret Library, and the Unearthing of the World's Oldest Printed Book* (Picador Australia: Picador, 2011).

Whitfield, Susan and Sims-Williams, Ursula (eds), *The Silk Road: Trade, Travel, War and Faith* (London: The British Library, 2004).

Wood, Frances and Barnard, Mark, *The Diamond Sutra: The Story of the World's Earliest Dated Printed Book* (London: The British Library, 2010).

The Development of Paper

Albro, Sylvia Rodgers, *Fabriano: City of Medieval and Renaissance Papermaking* (New Castle, Delaware: Oak Knoll Press, 2016).

Barrett, Timothy, *European Hand Papermaking: Traditions, Tools & Techniques* (Ann Arbor, Michigan: The Legacy Press, 2018).

Calhoun, Joshua, *The Nature of the Page: Poetry, Papermaking and the Ecology of Texts in Renaissance England* (Philadelphia: University of Pennsylvania Press, 2020).

Houston, Keith, *The Book* (New York: W.W. Norton & Co., 2016).

Werner, Sarah, *Studying Early Printed Books 1450–1800: A Practical Guide* (Hoboken, New Jersey; Chichester, West Sussex: Wiley Blackwell, 2019).

The Arnstein Bible

Cahn, Walter, *Romanesque Bible Illumination* (Ithaca, NY: Cornell University Press, 1982), 26, 230, 253 no. 8, pls 157, 162.

Hamburger, Jeffrey F., 'The Hand of God and the Hand of the Scribe: Craft and Collaboration at Arnstein' in *Die Bibliothek des Mittelalters als dynamischer Prozess*, by Michael Embach, Claudine Moulin and Andrea Rapp (eds), *Trierer Beiträge zu den Historischen Kulturwissenschaften*, 3 (Wiesbaden: Reichert, 2012), 53–78 (62, fig. 22, colour plate 17).

McKendrick, Scot and Doyle, Kathleen, *The Art of the Bible: Illuminated Manuscripts from the Medieval World* (London: Thames & Hudson and The British Library, 2016, reprinted in reduced format), no. 23.

King Henry VIII's Copy of the 'Great Bible'

Daniell, David, *The Bible in English* (New Haven, Conn.; London: Yale University Press, 2003).

Doran, Susan, 'Henry VIII and the Reformation' at Discovering Sacred Texts, British Library, 2019, bl.uk/sacred-texts/articles/henry-viii-and-the-reformation.

Poleg, Eyal, *A Material History of the Bible, England 1200–1553* (Oxford: Oxford University Press, 2020).

String, Tatiana, *Art and Communication in the Reign of Henry VIII* (Aldershot: Ashgate, 2008).

The Golden Haggadah

Avrin, Leila, *Scribes, Script, and Books: The Book Arts from Antiquity to the Renaissance* (Chicago: American Library Association, 1991, reprinted 2010), especially Ch. 5 'The Hebrew Book', 101–138.

Beit-Arie, Malachi, *The Makings of the Medieval Hebrew Book: Studies in Palaeography and Codicology* (Jerusalem: Magnes Press, c. 1993).

Epstein, Marc Michael, *The Medieval Haggadah: Art, Narrative, and Religious Imagination* (New Haven, Conn.: Yale University Press, 2011), 129–200.

Harris, Julie, 'Polemical Images in the Golden Haggadah (British Library Add. MS 27210)' in *Medieval Encounters*, vol. 8 (2002), 105–122.

Kogman-Appel, Katrin, 'Hebrew Manuscript Painting in Late Medieval Spain: Signs of a Culture in Transition' in *The Art Bulletin*, 84, no. 2 (June 2002), 246–272.

Kogman-Appel, Katrin, *Illuminated Haggadot from Medieval Spain: Biblical Imagery and the Passover Holiday* (University Park: Pennsylvania State University Press, 2006), 47–88.

Kogman-Appel, Katrin, 'Jewish Art and Non-Jewish Culture: The Dynamics of Artistic Borrowing in Medieval Hebrew Manuscript Illumination' in *Jewish History*, vol. 15, no. 3 (2001), 187–223.

Mann, Vivian B. (ed.), 'Jews and Altarpieces in Medieval Spain' in *An Uneasy Communion: Jews, Christians, and the Altarpieces of Medieval Spain* (London: Giles, 2010), 112–115.

Narkiss, Bezalel, *The Golden Haggadah: A Fourteenth-century Illuminated Hebrew Manuscript in the British Museum* (London: British Museum, 1970) [facsimile].

Reeve, John (ed.), *Sacred: Books of the Three Faiths: Judaism, Christianity, Islam* (London: The British Library, 2007), p. 172 [exhibition catalogue].

Tahan, Ilana, *Hebrew Manuscripts: The Power of Script and Image* (London: The British Library, 2007), 94–97.

The British Library, bl.uk/hebrew-manuscripts/articles/passover-in-14th-century-ce-catalonia, 'Passover in 14th-century CE Catalonia' by Katrin Kogman-Appel.

The Polonsky Foundation Catalogue of Digitised Hebrew Manuscripts, British Library, 2016, bl.uk/hebrew-manuscripts.

The Queen Mary Psalter

McKendrick, Scot and Doyle, Kathleen, *The Art of the Bible: Illuminated Manuscripts from the Medieval World* (London: Thames & Hudson, 2016; reprinted in reduced format, 2023), no. 30.

Sandler, Lucy Freeman, *Gothic Manuscripts 1285–1385, Survey of Manuscripts Illuminated in the British Isles* (London: Harvey Miller 1986), no. 56, 16–19, 25, 30–34, 38.

Smith, Kathryn A., 'History, Typology and Homily: The Joseph Cycle in the Queen Mary Psalter' in *Gesta*, 32 (1993), 147–59 (figs 1, 5–8).

Stanton, Anne Rudloff, 'The Queen Mary Psalter: A Study of Affect and Audience' in *Transactions of the American Philosophical Society*, New Series, 91 (2001), 1–287.

Warner, George, *Queen Mary's Psalter: Miniatures and Drawings by an English Artist of the 14th Century, Reproduced from Royal MS. 2 B. VII in the British Museum* (London: British Museum, 1912).

The Harmonies of Little Gidding

Acland, J. E., *Little Gidding and its Inmates in the Time of King Charles I, with an Account of the Harmonies Designed and Constructed by Nicholas Ferrar* (London: SPCK, 1903).

Dyck, Paul, '"So rare a use": Scissors, Reading, and Devotion at Little Gidding', *George Herbert Journal* 27, 1–2 (2003), 67–81.

Dyck, Paul, '"A New Kind of Printing": Cutting and Pasting a Book for a King at Little Gidding', *The Library* 9, no. 1 (2008), 306–30.

Ransome, Joyce, *The Web of Friendship: Nicholas Ferrar and Little Gidding* (Cambridge: James Clarke, 2011).

The Mainz Psalter of 1457

British Museum, *Catalogue of Books Printed in the XVth Century now in the British Museum (BMC). Part 1: Xylographica and Books Printed with Types at Mainz, Strassburg, Bamberg and Cologne* (London: British Museum, 1908), 18–9.

Ikeda, Mayumi, 'The Fust and Schöffer Office and the Printing of the Two-Colour Initials in the 1457 Mainz Psalter' in Ad Stijnman and Elizabeth Savage (eds), *Printing Colour 1400–1700* (Leiden: Brill, 2015), Ch. 5, 65–75.

Martineau, Russell, 'The Mainz Psalter of 1457' in *Bibliographica: Papers on Books, their History and Art*, 1 (1895), 308–23.

Masson, Irvine, *The Mainz Psalters and Canon Missae 1457–1459* (London: Bibliographical Society, 1954).

May, Alan, 'The Fust and Schöffer Psalter Initials', 2018, makerpress.co.uk/fust-and-schoffer-psalter (accessed 17 May 2023).

White, Eric Marshall, 'Printed for Performance: Ceremonial and Interactive Aspects of Books from Europe's First Presses' in *RBM: A Journal of Rare Books, Manuscripts, and Cultural Heritage* (2014), 15–30.

Hypnerotomachia Poliphili

Barolini, Helen, *Aldus and His Dream Book* (New York: Italica Press, 1992).

Burnhill, Peter, *Type spaces: In-house norms in the typography of Aldus Manutius* (London: Hyphen Press, 2003).

Davies, Martin, *Aldus Manutius: Printer and Publisher of Renaissance Venice* (London: The British Library, 1995).

Lowry, Martin, *The World of Aldus Manutius: Business and Scholarship in Renaissance Venice* (Oxford: Basil Blackwell, 1979).

Bodoni's *Manuale Tipografico* and His Followers

Alberto Tallone, *Manuale Tipografico Dedicato Ai Frontespizi E Ai Tipi Maiuscoli Tondi & Corsivi* (Alpignano: Alberto Tallone Editore, 2005).

Bodoni, Giovanni Battista, *Manuale Tipografico, 1788. Facsimile a cura di Giovanni Mardersteig* (Verona: Officina Bodoni, 1968).

Brooks, Hugh Cecil, *Compendiosa Bibliografia di Edizioni Bodoniane* (Florence: Tipografia Barbèra, 1927).

De Pasquale, Andrea and Dradi, Massimo, *B Come Bodoni: i Caratteri di Bodoni a Brera e nella Grafica Contemporanea* (Milan: Silvana Editoriale, 2013).

Franco Maria Ricci, *Bodoni, 1740–1813* (Parma, 2013).

Mardersteig, Giovanni, and Schmoller, Hans (ed. and trans.), *The Officina Bodoni: An Account of the Work of a Hand Press 1923–1977* (Verona: Edizioni Valdonega, 1980).

Akbar's *Khamsah* of Nizami

Brend, Barbara, *The Emperor Akbar's Khamsa of Nizami* (London: The British Library, 1995).

Brown, T. J., Meredith-Owens, G. M. and Turner, D. H., 'Manuscripts from the Dyson Perrins Collection' in *The British Museum Quarterly* 23/2 (Jan. 1961), 27–38.

Cleaver, Laura, 'Charles William Dyson Perrins as a Collector of Medieval and Renaissance Manuscripts c. 1900–1920' in *Perspectives médiévales*, 41 (2020), accessed online 24 April at journals.openedition.org/peme/19776.

Losty, Jeremiah P., *The Art of the Book in India* (London: The British Library, 1982), 90–91.

Losty, J. P. and Roy, Malini, *Mughal India: Art, Culture and Empire* (London: The British Library, 1912), 48–55.

Martin, Fredrik Robert, *The Miniature Painting and Painters of Persia, India and Turkey from the 8th to the 18th Century [With Five Plates in Colour, 271 Other Plates, and Illustrations in the Text]* (London: Bernard Quaritch, 1912).

Minissale, Gregory, 'Painting Awareness: A Study into the Use of Exotic Cultural Traditions by the Artists of the Emperor Akbar's *Khamsa* of Nizāmī', Thesis submitted for Doctor of Philosophy, School of Oriental and African Studies, University of London, 2000.

Seyller, John, 'Pearls of the Parrot of India: The Walters Art Museum "Khamsa" of Amīr Khusraw of Delhi' in *The Journal of the Walters Art Museum* 58 (2000), 5–176.

The Shakespeare First Folio of 1623

Blayney, Peter W. M., *The First Folio of Shakespeare* (Washington D.C.: Folger Shakespeare Library, 1991).

Hinman, Charlton, *The Printing and Proof-reading of the First Folio of Shakespeare* (Oxford: Clarendon Press, 1963).

Rasmussen, Eric, and West, Anthony James (eds), *The Shakespeare First Folios: A Descriptive Catalogue* (Basingstoke, Hants.: Palgrave Macmillan, 2012).

Smith, Emma (ed.), *The Cambridge Companion to Shakespeare's First Folio* (Cambridge: Cambridge University Press, 2016).

West, Anthony James, *The Shakespeare First Folio: The History of the Book* (Oxford: Oxford University Press, 2001–3).

The Title Page and Other Paratexts

Fowler, Alastair, *The Mind of the Book: Pictorial Title Pages* (Oxford: Oxford University Press, 2017).

Genette, Gérard, *Paratexts: Thresholds of Interpretation* (Cambridge: Cambridge University Press, 1997).

Smith, Margaret M., *The Title-Page: Its Early Development 1460–1510* (London and New Castle, Delaware: The British Library and Oak Knoll Press, 2000).

Excerpts from The Tale of Genji

Miller, Richard J., *Japan's First Bureaucracy: A Study of Eighth-Century Government* (East Asia Papers, no. 19) (China-Japan Program: Cornell University, 1978), hdl.handle.net/1813/57643.

Shimohara Miho, 'Sumiyoshi Jokei, Gukei ni yoru Yamato-e seisaku ni tsuite: gadai no keikō o chūshin ni' [The Production of Yamato-e by Sumiyoshi Jokei and Gukei: Consideration of Motifs] in *Kagoshima Daigaku Kyōiku Gakubu kenkyū kiyō: Jinbun shakai kagaku hen* [Bulletin of the Faculty of Education, Kagoshima University, Cultural and Social Science], 60 [2009], 237–253, core.ac.uk/download/pdf/144565388.pdf.

Tsuji Eiko, 'Dai-Ei Toshokan shozō "Genji monogatari kotoba" no honbun to kaisetsu' [*Genji monogatari kotoba* in British Library: text and commentary] in *Zaigai Nihon jūyō emaki shūsei* [Important Japanese Picture Scrolls in Overseas Collections] (Tokyo: Kasama Shoin, 2011) [in Japanese].

A Modern Mesoamerican Codex

Austin, Kat, Montiel, Carlos-Urani and Furio, Victoria J. (trans.), '*Codex Espangliensis*: Neo-Baroque Art of Resistance' in *Latin American Perspectives*, vol. 39, no. 3, 88–105.

Chagoya, Enrique, Gómez-Peña, Guillermo and Rice, Felicia, *Codex Espangliensis: From Columbus to the Border Patrol* (Santa Cruz: Moving Parts Press, 1998).

González, Jennifer A., 'Review of *Codex Espangliensis: From Columbus to the Border Patrol* by Guillermo Gómez-Peña, Enrique Chagoya and Felicia Rice' in *Aztlán: A Journal of Chicano Studies*, 24, no. 1 (spring 1999), 211–215.

Hanley, Sarah Kirk, 'Visual Culture of the Nacirema: Enrique Chagoya's Printed Codices' in *Art in Print*, vol. 1, no. 6 (March–April 2012), 3–15.

William Leighton's *The Teares or Lamentacions of a Sorrowfull Soule*

Dimsdale, Verna, 'English sacred music with broken consort' in *Lute Society Journal*, 16, 1974, 39–64.

Hill, Cecil, *Sir William Leighton: the tears or lamentations of a sorrowful soul 1614* (Doctoral dissertation: University of St Andrews, 1966).

Hill, Cecil (ed.), 'William Leighton: The Tears or Lamentations of a Sorrowful Soul' in *Early English Church Music*, 11 (London: Stainer & Bell, 1970).

Holman, Peter, *Dowland: Lachrimae (1604)* (Cambridge: Cambridge University Press, 1999).

Morehen, John, Rastall, Richard and Murphy, Emilie, 'Table-book' at Grove Music Online, retrieved 12 Dec. 2022, from oxfordmusiconline.com/grovemusic/view/10.1093/gmo/9781561592630.001.0001/omo-9781561592630-e-0000027341.

Rastall, Richard, 'Instructions for performing in Sir William Leighton's The Teares or Lamentacions of a Sorrowfull Soule (1614)' in *Early Music Performer*, 21, Nov. 2007, 2–12.

Rastall, Richard, 'Spatial effects in English instrumental consort music, *c.* 1560–1605' in *Early Music*, XXV/2, May 1997, 269–290.

The Design of Human Atlases

Aldersey-Williams, Hugh, *Anatomies: The Human Body, Its Parts and the Stories They Tell* (London: Viking, 2013).

Brown, Meg, 'Flip, Flap, and Crack: The Conservation and Exhibition of 400+ Years of Flap Anatomies', presented at the Book and Paper Group Session, AIC's 41st Annual Meeting, 29 May–1 June 2013, Indianapolis, Indiana, The Book and Paper Group Annual 32 (2013), 6, cool.culturalheritage.org/coolaic/sg/bpg/annual/v32/bpga32-02.pdf.

Carlino, Andrea, *Paper Bodies: A Catalogue of Anatomical Fugitive Sheets, 1538–1687*, trans. by Noga Arikha (London: Wellcome Trust, 1999).

d'Agoty, Jacques Gautier, *Myologie complette en couleur et grandeur naturelle, composée de l'essai et de la suite de l'essai d'anatomie, en tableaux imprimés, etc.* (Paris: Gautier, Quillau, Lamesle, 1746).

Moore, Rosemary, 'Paper Cuts: The Early Modern Fugitive Print', discovery.ucl.ac.uk/id/eprint/1472891/1/08%20 object%2017%20-%20Rosemary%20Moore.pdf.

Vesalius, Andrea, *Andreae Vesalii de humani corporis fabrica libri septem* (Basileæ: ex officina Joannis Oporini, 1543).

Witkowski, Gustave-Joseph, *Anatomie iconoclastique. Atlas complémentaire de tous les ouvrages traitant de l'anatomie et de la physiologie humaines composé de planches ... coloriées et superposées, etc.* (Paris: H. Lauwereyns, 1875–1878).

A Description of Three Hundred Animals

Hahn, Daniel, *Oxford Companion to Children's Literature* (Oxford: Oxford University Press, 2015).

Grenby, M. O., *The Child Reader, 1700–1840* (Cambridge: Cambridge University Press, 2011).

Salisbury, Martin with Morag Styles, *Children's Picture Books: The Art of Visual Storytelling* (London: Laurence King, 2020).

Shefrin, Jill (ed.), *One Hundred Books Famous in Children's Literature* (New York: Grolier Club, 2014).

Whalley, Joyce Irene and Chester, Tessa Rose, *A History of Children's Book Illustration* (London: Murray, 1988).

Miniature Books: Their Charm and Purpose

Benson, A. C. and Weaver, Sir Lawrence (eds), *The Book of the Queen's Doll's House*, Volume I, and Lucas, E. V. (ed.), *The Book of the Queen's Doll's House*, Volume II (London: Methuen & Co, 1924).

Bromer, Anne C., Edison, Julian I., *Miniature Books: 4,000 Years of Tiny Treasures* (New York: Abrams, 2007).

Thomas, Peter and Donna, *More Making Books by Hand: Exploring Miniature Books, Alternative Structures, and Found Objects* (Hove: Apple Press, 2004).

Welsh, Doris V., *The History of Miniature Books* (Albany, New York: Fort Orange Press, 1987).

A Qur'an from Aceh

Bennett, James (ed.), *Crescent Moon: Islamic Art & Civilisation in Southeast Asia* (Adelaide: Art Gallery of South Australia, 2005).

Gallop, Annabel The, 'An Acehnese style of manuscript illumination' in *Archipel* (68), 2004, 193–240.

Kumar, Ann and McGlynn, John H. (eds), *Illuminations: The Writing Traditions of Indonesia* (Jakarta: Lontar, 1996).

Owen Jones's *The Grammar of Ornament*

Ball, Douglas, *Victorian Publisher's Bindings* (London: The Library Association, 1985).

Cooke, Simon, '"A Clever Man": Joseph Swain as an Engraver and Interpreter' at victorianweb.org/graphics/swain/cooke.html.

Cooke, Simon, *Illustrated Periodicals of the 1860: Context & Collaborations* (London: The British Library, 2010).

Cooke, Simon, 'Owen Jones as a Book Cover Designer' at victorianweb.org/art/design/books/cooke18.htm.

Dalziel, George and Edward, *The Brothers Dalziel: A Record of Fifty Year's Work, 1840–1880* (London: Methuen 1901 & 1978).

Goldman, Paul, *Victorian Illustrated Books 1850–1870: The Heyday of Wood-engraving, Selections from The Robin de Beaumont Collection in the British Museum* (London: British Museum, 1994) Ch. 4 – Readership.

Kooistra, Lorraine Janzen, *Poetry, Pictures, and Popular Publishing: The Illustrated Gift Book and Victorian Visual Culture, 1855–1875* (Athens, Ohio: Ohio University Press, 2011)

McLean, Ruari, *Victorian Book Design and Colour Printing*, 2nd edn. (University of California Press, 1972).

Twyman, Michael, *A history of chromolithography: printed colour for all* (London: The British Library, 2013).

American Publishers' Bindings, Nineteenth Century

Allen, Sue and Gullans, Charles, *Decorated Cloth in America: Publishers' Bindings, 1840–1910.* (Los Angeles: University of California, 1994).

Henry Altemus Company, Vademecum Series, at henryaltemus.com/series/series179.htm (accessed 15 Aug. 2022).

Minsky, Richard, *The Art of American Book Covers 1875–1930* (New York: George Braziller, Inc., 2010).

Morris, Ellen K. and Levin, Edward S., *The Art of Publishers' Bookbindings 1815–1915: An Exhibition held at the Grolier Club, New York, 17 May–19 July 2000* (Los Angeles: William Daley Rare Books Ltd, 2000).

University of Alabama, Publisher's Bindings Online, 1815–1930: The Art of Books. bindings.lib.ua.edu (accessed 30 Aug. 2020).

University of Rochester, Rare Books & Special Collections, Beauty of Commerce: Publishers' Bindings 1830–1910, rbscp.lib.rochester.edu/3352 (accessed 30 Aug. 2020).

The Buddha's Last Birth Tale

Dāsa, Jagannātha Prasāda, *Chitra-pothi: Illustrated Palm-leaf Manuscripts from Orissa* (New Delhi: Arnold-Heinemann, 1985).

Dāsa, Jagannātha Prasāda and Williams, Joanna, *Palm-leaf Miniatures: The Art of Raghunath Prusti of Orissa* (New Delhi: Abhinav Publications, 1991).

Guy, John, *Palm-leaf and Paper: Illustrated Manuscripts of India and Southeast Asia*, with an essay by O.P. Agrawal (Melbourne: National Gallery of Victoria, 1982).

Hinzler, H. I. R., 'Balinese palm leaf manuscripts: manufacture, manipulation and magic: writing materials, writing and scribes' in Royal Institute of Linguistics and Anthropology (Leiden, 1992).

Igunma, Jana, 'The beautiful art of Tai palm leaf manuscripts' in *Southeast Asia Library Group Newsletter* (December 2014), 35–50, sealg.org/pdf/newsletter2014.pdf.

Igunma, Jana, *A Thai royal edition of Pannasa Jataka* (ปัญญาส ชาดก) (5 June 2020), blogs.bl.uk/asian-and-african/2020/06/a-thai-royal-edition-of-pannasa-jataka.html

Jacobs, David, 'Workshop Notes on the Conservation and Stabilization of Palm Leaf Manuscripts' in *Southeast Asia Library Group Newsletter* (December 2010), 22–31, sealg.org/pdf/newsletter2010.pdf.

Kumar, D. Udaya, Sreekumar G.V. and Athvankar, U. A., 'Traditional writing system in Southern India – Palm leaf manuscripts' in *Design Thoughts* (July 2009), 2–7, idc.iitb.ac.in/resources/dt-july-2009/Palm.pdf

Patnaik, Durga Prasad, *Palm Leaf Etchings of Orissa* (New Delhi: Abhinav Publications, 1989).

Vijayan, K. (ed.), *Rāmāyana in Palm Leaf Pictures: Citrarāmāyana* (Trivandrum: Oriental Research Institute &

Manuscripts Library, University of Kerala, 1997).
Gunawardana, Sirancee, *Palm Leaf Manuscripts of Sri Lanka* (Ratmalana: Sarvodaya Vishva Lekha, 1997).

A Material Identity in Oceania Book Design

Ellis, Markham, 'That singular and wonderful quadruped: the kangaroo as historical and intangible natural heritage in the eighteenth century' in Dorfman, Eric (ed.) *Intangible Natural Heritage: New Perspectives on Natural Objects* (London: Routledge, 2012).

Jackson, Simon, 'Sacred Objects—Australian Design and National Celebrations' in *Journal of Design History*, vol. 19, Issue 3, Autumn 2006, 249–255, doi.org/10.1093/jdh/epl019.
Mills, Carol, 'Australian Bookbinders and Bookbinding in the 19th Century' in *Collaboration and Connections: Postprints of the AICCM Paper, Books and Photographic Materials Special Interest Group Symposium*, Sydney, 1–3 April 2004, 67–77.
Murray, John, *An account of the Phormium Tenax; or New-Zealand Flax. Printed on paper made from its leaves with a postscript on paper* (London: Henry Renshaw, 1836).
Philip, Arthur, *The Voyage of Governor Philip to Botany Bay* (London, 1789).

Audubon's *The Birds of America*

Audubon, John James, *Ornithological Biography* (Philadelphia: Judah Dobson, 1832).
Blaugrund, Annette and Stebbins, Theodore E., Jr (eds), *John James Audubon: The Watercolors for The Birds of America* (New York: The New York Historical Society, 1993).
McCraken Peck, Robert, 'Cutting up Audubon for Science and Art' in *The Linnean, Newsletter and Proceedings of the Linnean Society of London*, vol. 21, (1), January 2005, 16–29.
Melby, Julie, 'Audubon's Copperplates for *Birds of America*' in *Print Quarterly*, XXXVII, 2020, 3, 283–293.

'An Error of Taste': Smithers, Beardsley and *The Savoy*

Nelson J. G., *Publisher to the Decadents: Leonard Smithers in the Careers of Beardsley, Wilde, and Dowson* (Penn State University Press, 2000).
Walker, R. A. (ed.), *Letters from Aubrey Beardsley to Leonard Smithers* (London: The First Editions Club, 1937).
Symons, A., *Aubrey Beardsley* (London: At the Sign of the Unicorn, 1898).

The Works of Geoffrey Chaucer

Blewitt, John (ed.), The William Morris Society, *William Morris & John Ruskin: A New Road on Which the World Should Travel* (Exeter: University of Exeter Press, 2019).
Mackail, J. W., *The Life of William Morris ... with an introduction by Sir Sydney Cockerell* (London: Oxford University Press, 1950).
Parry, Linda (ed.), *William Morris* (London: Philip Wilson Publishers in association with The Victoria and Albert Museum, 1996).
Peterson, William S., *The Kelmscott Press: A History of William Morris's Typographical Adventure* (Oxford: Clarendon Press, 1991).
Tidcombe, Marianne, *The Doves Press* (London: The British Library, 2002).
Waggoner, Diane (ed.), *The Beauty of Life: William Morris & the Art of Design* (London: Thames & Hudson, 2003).

Twentieth-Century Typefaces

Blackwell, Lewis, *Twentieth Century Type* (London: Laurence King, 1992).
Gill, Eric, *An Essay on Typography* (London: Sheed & Ward, 1931).
Loxley, Simon, *Type is Beautiful: The Story of 50 Remarkable Fonts* (Oxford: The Bodleian Library, 2004).
Stirton, Paul, *Jan Tschichold and the New Typography: Graphic Design between the World Wars* (New Haven, Conn.: Yale University Press, 2019).
Loxley, Simon, *Type: The Secret History of Letters* (London: I.B.Tauris, 2004).

***Sadok Sudei* and Other Futurist Books from Russia**

Bury, Stephen, *Breaking the Rules: The Printed Face of the European Avant Garde, 1900–1937* (London: The British Library, 2008).
Compton, Susan (ed.), *The World Backwards: Russian Futurist Books 1912–1916* (London, The British Library, 1978).
Compton, Susan. *Russian Avant-garde Books 1917–1934* (London: The British Library, 1992).
Gratchev, Slav N. (ed.), *The Poetics of the Avant-garde in Literature, Arts, and Philosophy* (Lanham, Maryland: Lexington Books, 2020).
Gray, Camilla, *The Great Experiment: Russian Art 1863–1922* (New York: Harry N. Abrams, Inc., 1962).
Hellyer, Peter (ed.), *A Catalogue of Russian Avant-Garde Books, 1912–1934 and 1969–2003*, 2nd edn. (London: The British Library, 2006).
Ioffe, Dennis G. and White, Frederick H. (eds), *The Russian Avant-Garde and Radical Modernism: An Introductory Reader* (Boston: Academic Studies Press, 2012).
Janecek, Gerald, *The Look of Russian Literature: Avant-Garde Visual Experiments, 1900–1930* (Princeton: Princeton University Press, 2019).
Perloff, Nancy, *Explodity: Sound, Image, and Word in Russian Futurist Book Art* (Los Angeles: Getty Publications, 2016).
Rowell M. and Wye D., *The Russian Avant-garde Book 1910–1934* (New York: Museum of Modern Art, 2002).

Cartonera Books and Publishers

Bilbija, Ksenija, Carbajal, Paloma Celis, Pagel, Lauren and Trajković, Djurdja (eds), *Akademia cartonera: a primer of Latin American cartonera publishers = un abc de las editoriales cartoneras en América Latina* (Madison, Wisconsin: Parallel Press, University of Wisconsin-Madison Libraries, 2009).
Bell, L. and O'Hare, P., 'Latin American politics underground: Networks, rhizomes and resistance in cartonera publishing' in *International Journal of Cultural Studies*, vol. 23, Issue 1, 2020, 20–41. doi.org/10.1177/1367877919880331
Bell, L., Flynn, A. U. and O'Hare, P. *Taking Form, Making Worlds: Cartonera Publishers in Latin America* (New York: University of Texas Press, 2022).
Brand, Isadora, *Cartoneras* (Documentary, 2018), cartonerapublishing.com/cartonera-new-documentary-on-the-cartonera-movement-by-isa-brandt/ (acessed 18 April 2023).

Century

Clair, Colin, *A Chronology of Printing* (London: Cassell, 1969).

Stevenson, Iain, *Bookmakers: British Publishing in the Twentieth Century* (London: The British Library, 2010).
Nash, Andrew, Squires, Claire and Willison, I.R. (eds), *The Cambridge History of the Book in Britain, Volume VII The Twentieth Century and Beyond* (Cambridge: Cambridge University Press, 2019).
Bhaskar, Michael and Phillips, Michael (eds), *The Oxford Handbook of Publishing* (Oxford: Oxford University Press, 2019).
Bartram, Alan, *Making Books: Design in British publishing since 1945* (New Castle, Delaware: Oak Knoll Press, 1999).
Bernard, Bruce and McNamee, Terence, *Century: One Hundred Years of Human Progress, Regression, Suffering and Hope* (London: Phaidon, 1999).
Clark, Giles and Phillips, Angus, *Inside Book Publishing*, 4th edn. (London: Routledge, 2008).
Overy, Richard (ed.), *The Times Complete History of the World*, 9th edn. (London: HarperCollins Publishers, 2015).

Penguin Books and the Paperback Revolution

Baines, Phil, *Penguin by Design: A Cover Story 1935–2005* (London: Allen Lane, 2005).
Doubleday, Richard B.,*Jan Tschichold, Designer: The Penguin Years* (London: Lund Humphries, 2006).
Hare, Steve, *Penguin Portrait: Allen Lane and the Penguin Editors 1935–1970* (London: Penguin, 1995).
Lewis, Jeremy, *Penguin Special: The Life and Times of Allen Lane* (London: Penguin, 2006).
Williams, William Emrys, *The Penguin Story* (London: Penguin, 1956).

Sea Air

Allix, Susan, *Susan Allix: A Catalogue of Fine Press Artists Books* (London: Susan Allix, 2023).
Allix, Susan, *Space Time & the Book* (London: Susan Allix [2003]).
Athanasiu, Eva, 'Belonging: Artists' Books and Readers in the Library' in *Art Documentation*, 2015, vol. 34, no. 2.
Bodman, Sarah, *Creating Artists' Books* (London: A&C Black, 2005).
Bury, Stephen, *Artists' Books: The Book as a Work of Art* (Aldershot: Scolar Press, 1995).
Drucker, Joanna, 'Artist's book' at Grove Art (oxfordartonline.com), doi.org/10.1093/gao/9781884446054.article.T2220480 (accessed 12 Jul. 2022).
Kulp, Louise, 'Artists' books in Libraries: A Review of the Literature' in *Art Documentation*, 2005, vol. 24, no. 1.
Reed, Josie, 'The Complete Book Artist' in *Printmaking Today*, vol. 31, Autumn 2022, Issue 123.
Worthy, Hugo, 'God is in the Detail' in *Rare Book Review*, 2004, July/August.

Women Publishers and Designers

Owen, Ursula, *Single Journey Only: A Memoir* (Norwich: Salt, 2019).
Goodings, Lennie, *A Bite of the Apple: A Life with Books, Writers and Virago* (Oxford: Oxford University Press: 2020).
Massey, Anne, *Women in Design* (London: Thames & Hudson, 2022).

Editions At Play

Borsuk, Amaranth, *The Book* (Cambridge, Massachusetts: MIT Press, 2018).
Larsen, Reif, *Entrances & Exits* (Editions At Play, 2016), entrances-exits.com
Pullinger, Kate, *Breathe* (Editions At Play, 2018), breathe-story.com.
Riviere, Sam and Dunthorne, Joe, *The Truth About Cats & Dogs* (Editions At Play, 2016), truthaboutcatsanddogs.com.
Trotter, Alan, *All This Rotting* (Editions At Play, 2016), allthisrotting.com
Uglow, Tea, *A Universe Explodes* (Editions At Play, 2017), a-universe-explodes.com.
Uglow, Tea with George AI, *We Kiss the Screens* (Editions At Play, 2019), wekissthescreens.com.
Walsh, Joanna, *Seed* (Editions At Play, 2017), seed-story.com.

Book Design as an Agent of Conservation

Amato, Anthony J., *The Carpathians, the Hutsuls, and Ukraine: An Environmental History* (Lanham, Maryland: Lexington Books, 2020).
Magocsi, Paul Robert, *With Their Backs to the Mountains: A History of Carpathian Rus' and Carpatho-Rusyns* (Budapest: Central European University Press, 2015).
The Ark of Unique Cultures: The Hutsuls (Tallinn: Ukrainian Cultural Centre, 2014).
The Poetics of Endangered Species: Ukraine (Kyiv; Tallinn: Ukrainian Cultural Centre, 2007).

INDEX

Bold page numbers refer to main illustrated entries; *italic* page numbers indicate other illustrations

A
'Abd al-Rahim *98*, 101
About Britain series (Rainbird and McLean) 231
Aceh culture: illumination/calligraphy style **158–67**
Acts and Life of St Takla Haymanot, The (Ethiopian manuscript) *27*
Adobe: PostScript 215
advertising
books 117, 168, 174, 177
industry 214, 228
AI (Artificial Intelligence) 256, *257*
Aidan of Lindisfarne, St 16, 19
Akbar, emperor (Mughal empire) 97, 98–105, *105*
Aldine Press 38, *90*
'portable octavos' (*libri portatiles*) 38, 85, 87–90, *87*, 93, 117
Alighieri, Dante, *Le terze rime* 90, *90*
Allix, Susan 12
Sea Air **239–46**
almanacs 12, 36, 155–57, *157*
Almanzi, Joseph (Giuseppe) 57
anatomy, human *see* atlases, human
Anderson, Sue 191
antisemitism 57
Aotearoa New Zealand: traditional binding materials of 191, *191*
Apple
iPhone/iPad 250
software development 215
Apple Books 249
aquatints 192, *192*, *194*, *196*, *199*, 239, 240–44, *240*
Arabic script 158, 161
Arial (typeface) 215
Ark of Unique Cultures, The (UKK) 258, *258*
Arnold, Matthew 243–44, *246*
Arnstein Bible, the **40–46**
Art Nouveau 178, 214
Art of Angling, The 178, *178*
artefacts, books as 11, 12, 15, 85, 86, 87, 227, 258
artists' books 191, 227, **239–46**; *see also* cartoneras
Arts and Crafts movement 177, 178, 205, 209–11, 212, 214
Ashbee, Charles Robert 212
Aspley, William 109, 114
Asukai Masaaki 126
atlases (geographic) *231*, 232–33
atlases, human **143–45**
Audubon, John James, *Birds of America, The* 12, **192–99**
Australia: traditional binding materials of 191, *191*

B
Banks, Joseph, *Voyage of Governor Philip to Botany Bay, The* 191
Baskerville, John 94
Baxter, George 151–52
Beardsley, Aubrey **202–3**
Beilby, Ralph 148
Bembo, Pietro 90
Beowulf 20
Bernard Shaw, George, *Intelligent Woman's Guide to Socialism, Capitalism, Sovietism & Fascism* 236, *237*
Berry, Mary, *Hamlyn All Colour Cook Book* 231
Bewick, Thomas 148
Bibles 16, 71, 106
bindings of 12
canon tables 46, *46*
early printed 38, 74, 77, *77*
Hebrew 40, 51–52, 56
illustrations in 20–22, *20*, *40*, 42–45, *45*
miniature ('Thumb') 155, *155*
outsize ('Giant Bibles') 40–46, 48–49, *49*, 117; *see also* Arnstein Bible, the
translations of 40–42
see also Gospel Books; Latin Psalters
bindings 12–15
cloth *122*, 125, *129*, *158*, 167, *177*, 178, 202
decorative/illustrated 27, *27*, *102*, 105, *105*, 155, *158*, 178, *178*
folding *119*, 122, 130, *131*
harakeke (New Zealand flax) 191, *191*
kangaroo skin 191, *191*
lacquered *102*, 105, *105*, 187
leather 12, 27, 157, 191, *191*, *239*, 240
medieval 12, 40, 258
paper/cardboard 12, *15*, 178, 227, *227*
personalised 12–15, 109, 192, 220
silk 77, 239
stationery 12
tooled 27, *27*, *51*, *132*, 141, 195, *209*
vellum 109, *132*, 141
velvet 77
wooden 27, *27*, 258, *258*
see also book cover designs; book covers; manuscripts: storage/protection of
Biscop, Benedict 19
blockchain technology 254, 256
Blount, Edward 106, 109, 114
bodhisattvas (Buddhist deities) *29*, 32, *35*, 36, 37, 183
Bodoni, Giovanni Battista 94, 117
Manuale Tipografico 94–95, *95*
'Bodonian' (typeface) 94
Bolzanio, Urbano, *Institutiones Graecae grammatices* 87, *87*
book cover designs 117
artworks 239, *239*, 248, *248*
and branding 228, 236, *237*
collage/appliqué, use of *158*, 167
digital 256, *257*
highly decorated 105, *105*, 174, *174*, *177*, 178, *178*, 202, *203*
as sales tools 12, 178, *178*
typographic *228*, 233, 236, *237*
book covers
cardboard 15, 227, *227*
gilding, use of 178, *178*, 202, *203*
lacquered 188, *188*
paper 151, *151*, 178, *178*, 191; *see also* wallpaper, books printed on
sackcloth 219, *219*, 220, 221
textiles (Japanese *orihon*) *122*, 125, *129*
wooden *102*, 180, *182*
see also bindings; book cover designs; wrappers (protective)
Book of Job, The (Nisbet) 174, *174*
book packagers 232
Booke of In nomines and other solfege songs, A 135, *135*
booklets (Chinese, 9th/10th c.) 35, 36–37
Boreman, Thomas **147–51**, *151*
Curiosities in the Tower of London 151
Description of Three Hundred Animals, A 117, 147–48, *147*, *148*
Gigantick Histories 148–51, *151*
Bote Cartonero, Jalisco, Mexico 227
branding/brand identity 15, 228, 231, 236–37, *237*
Bronzino, *Portrait of a Young Man 87*
Browning, Robert, *Pied Piper of Hamelin* 152, *152*
Bryce, David 155
Buddha, the
Gotama (Southeast Asia) 180–82, *180*, 183, 187
Shakyamuni (China/Japan/Korea) 29, *29*, 32, 36, 37

Buddhism
and artworks/illustrations 29, *29*, *35*, 36–37, 180, 182, 183–88
Mahāyāna 29
and use of the *orihon* 122
sacred texts 29–32, *33*, 35, 180–88, *180*, *182*; *see also* Diamond Sutra; Vessantara Jataka ('Birth Tale')
Theravada 180
Burliuk, David 216
Sadok Sudei (*Trap for Judges*) 216–19, *216*, *220*, 221
Slap in the Face of Public Taste, A 219–21, *219*
Tango with Cows 221–24, *221*
Burliuk, Vladimir
Sadok Sudei (*Trap for Judges*) 216–19, *216*, *220*, 221
Tango with Cows 221–24, *221*
Burma (Myanmar): Buddhist manuscripts 187, *187*, *188*
Burne-Jones, Edward 206, *206*, 209, *209*, 211, 212
Burns, Robert, *Tam O'Shanter* 178, *178*

C
Cabinet of Lilliput, The 151
Cai Lun 33, 38
Caldecott, Randolph 152
calendars, religious 65, *65*, 74; *see also* Judaism: Passover
calligraphers 15
Aceh 167
Chinese 35
European 77, 258
Japanese 119, 125, *125*, 126, *126*, 129
Mughal court 97, 101
calligraphy 45, 77, 78–81, 214
Acehnese 167
Buddhist sacred texts 188
Islamic texts 164, *164*, 167
Japanese 119, 125, *125*, 126, *126*, 129
modern 258, *258*
see also illumination
Callil, Carmen 248
capital letters, large 15, 20
coloured 77, 78–81, *78*
historiated (manuscripts) *40*, 42–46, *42*, *45*, 65, 69, *69*
ornamented 19, 23, 42, 65, 77–78, *78*, *168*
cartography *231*, 232–33
cartoneras 12, *15*, **227**
casting off (pre-press) 109, 113
Catadora, Dulcinéia 227
cataloguing, methods of 198
Catholicism
and antisemitism 57
and manuscript design traditions 77
Caves of the Thousand Buddhas *see* Mogao Caves (Caves of the Thousand Buddhas), Dunhuang
Century *228*, 233–34, *234*
Chagoya, Enrique, *Codex Espangliensis* **130–31**
chapbooks 147
chapter headings 15
Charles I, King of England 70, 71, 138–40, 141
'Chaucer' (typeface) 206
Chaucer, Geoffrey, *Canterbury Tales* 205, 206; *see also* Morris, William: *Works of Geoffrey Chaucer*
Child, Theodore, *Summer Holidays* 178, *178*
children's books **147–52**, 155, 236
China
book formats used 33–5, 122; *see also* scrolls: Chinese
and Buddhism 29–32, *29*, 35, *35*, 36–37
papermaking *12*, 33, 38
printing, development of 29, 35–37, *36*, 74
see also Mogao Caves (Caves of the Thousand Buddhas), Dunhuang
Chiswick Press 202
choirbooks 132, *135*
Chopin, Kate, *Awakening, The* *249*
Christianity 16, 19, 20, 23
in Africa 27
and Judaism 56–57
see also Bibles; Catholicism
chromolithography *143*, 145, 168, *168*, 171, 174, 199
Cinderella 151, *152*
Cobden-Sanderson, Thomas James 206, 212
Codex Espangliensis (Chagoya, E., Gómez-Peña, G., Rice, F.) **130–31**
codices 131, 239, 250
medieval biblical 51, 52, 55
Mesoamerican 130–31
Coleridge, Samuel Taylor 243, *243*
collage 131, *131*, 224, 227, *227*, *239*; *see also* artists' books; harmonies
Collier, Price, *America and the Americans* 178, *178*
colophons 77, *77*, *90*, *98*, 101, 116; *see also shamsah*)
compositors 90, 109, 113, 206
Condell, Henry 109, 110
content, organization of 15, 78, 87, 93
use of decorative/graphical devices 46, 158–67
use of illustrations/decorated pages 15, 20–22, 158–67
use of large capital letters 15, 20, 78, 81
contents pages 110, *110*, 116
copyright law (British) 199; *see also* rights, publishing
Countdown (typeface) 214
Coverdale, Miles 48
Cranmer, Thomas, Archbishop of Canterbury 48
Cromwell, Thomas 48
cultural conservation 258
Curiosities in the Tower of London (Boreman) *151*

D
Dawlat *98*, 101, 102
Dean, Suzanne 248
decorative styles
Gothic 55–56, 206
Islamic 168–71, *171*, 174, *174*
medieval 168, *168*, 205, 206
Neoclassical *171*
Persian 174, *177*
Defence of Guenevere, The (Kelmscott Press) 206
Dent, Joseph Malaby 236
Description of Three Hundred Animals, A (Boreman) 117, 147–48, *147*, *148*
desktop publishing 215, 231, 234
devices (trade marks), publishers' *90*, 117; *see also* branding/brand identity
Diamond Sutra **29–37**, 38
digital books 12, **250–57**
and accessibility 254
atlases 233
reading experience 12, 250–57
digital technology
book design software 215, 231, 234
e-ink and e-paper 250
see also digital books
Dorling Kindersley (DK) 232, 234
Doves Press 212
Dowland, John, *First Booke of Songes or Ayres* 135, *135*
Dowrick, Stephanie 248
Dowson, E. *Pierrot of the Minute, The* *203*
Dream of John Ball and a King's Lesson, A (Kelmscott Press) *206*, 209
Droeshout, Martin: portrait of William Shakespeare 106, *106*, *109*, 110
Dunhuang, China
early printing industry in 35, 36
Mogao Caves (Caves of the Thousand Buddhas) 29, 32, 33, 35, 36
Dunthorne, Joe, *Truth About Cats & Dogs, The* 254, *254*, 256
dust jackets *see* cover designs
Dyson Perrins *Khamsah*, the 97, **98–105**

E
Eadfrith, bishop of Lindisfarne 16, 20, 23
ebooks 12, 250, 254; *see also* digital books
Ebury 249
Eckmann (typeface) 214
Editions At Play 250–57, *250*, *253*, *254*, *257*

education 55, 145, 147, 148, 155, 171, 177, 232, 236
Edwards, George 194, *194*
Edwards, George Wharton 178, *178*
Ellis, Edward Sylvester, *From Tent to White House* 178, *178*
Eloísa Cartonera 227
enchiridia (Aldine octavos) 38, 85, 87–90, *87*, 93, 117
endmatter 116, 117; *see also* indexing
endpapers, decorated *122*, 125, *129*
England
early printed books 48–49, *49*, 106–14, *106*, *109*, *110*, *113*, *114*
flapbooks 145
and illustrated book publishing (20th c.) 228–34, *228*, *231*, *234*
medieval manuscript production in 16–23, *16*, *19*, *20*, *23*, 56, 60–69, *60*, *64*, *65*, *69*
miniature books 155–57, *155*, *157*
tablebooks 135–41, *135*, *138*
and typography design 205, 206, 212
see also harmonies
English bijou almanac, The 155–57, *157*
engravings 71, 94, 117, 174, 237
copperplate 110, 147, *147*, *148*, 151
wood 148, 151, 168, 174, 211–12, 228; *see also* illustrations: woodcut
ereaders 12, 250
errata lists 87
Essex House Press, The 212
Ethiopia: manuscript production **26–27**
Eusebius, Father, bishop of Caesarea (Palestine) 46
Evans, Edmund 152
Everyman Library 236
Ewbank, Emma 249

F
Feely, John 178, *178*
Feminist Press 248, 249
Ferrar family, Little Gidding: King's Concordance, the **70–71**
flap books 12, *15*, **143–45**
folding formats
Japanese (*orijō*) *119*, 122–25
palm leaf books 180, *187*, 188
paper (Southeast Asia) 180, 188
pre-Hispanic codices 130, *131*
folio (print format) 12, 106, 114
fonts 113, *113*, **214–15**
formats (print)
folio 12, 106, 114
octavo 38, 85, 87–90, *87*, 93, 109, 117, 199
quarto 12, 106–9, 110, 209
quire 106
see also bindings; miniature books; music notation; outsized books

Fournier, Pierre-Simon 94
France
anatomical atlases 145
Hebrew manuscript painting 52, 56
frontispieces 116
illustrated/decorative *29*, 36–37, 117, 147
see also title pages
Frutiger (typeface) 215
Fust Master, the 78
Fust, Johann 74–77, 81
Futura (typeface) 214
Futurism 214
Italian 221, 228
Russian **216–24**

G
Gallico, Joav 57
Garthwait, Henry, *Monotessaron, The Evangelicall Harmony* 71
Gautier d'Agoty, Jacques Fabien 145, *145*
Genette, Gérard 114
Genji monogatari see Murasaki Shikibu, *Tale of Genji, The*
Germany
early printed books 38, 74–81, *74*, *77*, *78*, *81*
Hebrew manuscript painting 51–52
monastic manuscript production 40–46, *40*, *42*, *45*, *46*
and typeface design 214, 228, 236–37
Gigantick Histories (Boreman) 148–51, *151*
Gill Sans (typeface) 214
Gill, Eric 214
Gleniffer Press 157, *157*
Go-Mizuno-o, Emperor of Japan 125–27
gold leaf/gilding *11*, 45, 46, *51*, 64, 65, 77, 183, 184,187; *see also* tooling: gold
Golden Haggadah, the **51–57**
'Golden' (typeface) 206
Gombrich, Ernst, *Story of Art, The* 234
Gómez-Peña, Guillermo, *Codex Espangliensis* **130–31**
Goncharova, Natalia, *Mirskontsa* 224, *224*
Google Creative Lab 250–54, *250*, *253*, *254*, *257*
Google Street View 256
Gospel Books 16, 22
Ethiopian 27
Lindisfarne Gospels 12, **16–23**, 38
see also Bibles; harmonies
Gospels, the 16, 22, 27, 45–46
canon tables 46, *46*
Evangelist portraits 20–22, *20*, *40*, 42–45, *45*
see also Arnstein Bible, the; Gospel Books; harmonies

Gotama Buddha (Southeast Asia) 180–82, *180*, 183, 187
Goudy, Frederic William 214
Alphabet and Elements of Lettering *215*
'Great Bible' (Henry VIII's copy of) **48–49**, 117
Great Exhibition, The (London, 1851) 171
Greenaway, Kate 152, *152*
guinea books 174–77
Gutenberg Bible, the 38, 74, 77, *77*
Gutenberg, Johann 38, 74, 78, 81, 157

H
haggadot 55, *55*, 56–57
Golden Haggadah, the **51–57**
half title pages 116, 168, *168*
Hamish Hamilton 248
Hamlyn (publisher) 231, 232
Hamlyn, Paul 231
handmade books 12, *15*, 227, *227*, 258, *258*; *see also* artist's books; palm leaf books; Russia: Futurist books
Hardwicke, Thomas, Major-General: collection of 194–95, 198
harmonies **70–71**
HarperCollins 234, 249
Harris, John 151
Harrison, Gwen 191
Hart's Rules (later *New Hart's Rules*) 116
Hassell, John (illustrator), *London Characters* 157, *157*
Havell, Robert 192, 195, *196*, 198, 199
Helvetica (typeface) 214
Heminges, John 109, 110
Hemingway, Ernest, *Farewell to Arms, A* 236, *237*
Henry Altemus Company of Philadelphia 178, *178*
Henry VIII, King of England
'Great Bible' **48–49**, 117
Hiromichi, Tosa *see* Sumiyoshi Jokie
Hitchcock, Mary Evelyn, *Two Women of the Klondike* 178, *178*
Horenbout, Lucas 48
Howe, Florence 248
Husayn *101*, 102
Hutsuls 258
Hypnerotomachia Poliphili *85*, *87*, 90–93, *93*

I
illumination
manuscripts 15, 22, 51, 55–56, 65–69, *101*, 102–5, 158–67, *161*, *164*, *167*; *see also* illustrations, manuscript
palm leaf books 180, *180*, 182–83, *187*, 188, *188*
printed books 48–49, *49*, 77, *168*
see also ornamentation/decora-

tive devices; scripts, decorative (medieval)
illustrated book publishing (20th c.) **228–34**
illustrations 116, 168
children's books **147–52**
integrated with text 228, 231–32, *231*, 232–33
painted *97*, 98, *98*, 101–5, *105*, 122, 125, *125*, 129, *180*, 183, 187; *see also* artists' books
woodcut 48, *49*, 93, *93*, 117, *138*, 147, 148, 151, *151*
see also aquatints; chromolithography; engravings; illustrations, manuscript; illustrated book publishing (20th c.); portraits
illustrations, manuscript 15, *16*
animal interlace designs 19–20, 22–23
Buddhist 180, *180*, 182, 183–88, *184*, *187*
carpet pages 22–23, *23*, 51
and decorative letter forms *16*, 19, *19*, 20, 23, 42–46, *42*, 51
Evangelist portraits 20–22, *20*, *40*, 42–45, *45*
graphic devices, use of 19, 20, 42–45
Hebrew 51, *51*, 55–56, *57*
incipit pages 23, *23*, 117, *184*
marginalia/marginal ornaments 15, 69, 167, *167*
Persian (Mughal court) *97*, 98, *98*, 101–2
used to mark text divisions 20–22
see also scripts, decorative (medieval)
Impediment Press 191, *191*
In the Tideway 178, *178*
indexing 87, 93, 116
India, Mughal
manuscript centres of 97
and Persian painting *97*, 98, *98*, 101–2
see also Nizami: *Khamsah*
Indonesia *see* Aceh culture
Infant's Library, The 151, *151*, *152*
inks
for calligraphy 125, 161, 167, *167*
coloured 15, 46, 60, 77, *77*, 78–81, *78*, 125, 130, 131, *131*, 164, *164*, 184, *184*, 209, 221
e-ink 250
used for printing 74, 77, 78–81, *78*, 147, 157, 209
see also printing: colour
Intertype Fotosetter, the 228
iPad (Apple) 250
iPhone (Apple) 250
Ireland, manuscript traditions of (5th–8th c.) 19, 20, 23
Islamic art 51, *52*, 171; *see also* manuscripts: Islamic
Italy
early printed books 85–86; *see also* Manutius, Aldus
and Futurism 221, 228
Hebrew manuscript painting/illustration 52, *55*
late antique books 19, 20
and typography design 94–95
Iwakura Tomoaki 129
Iyasu I, King of Ethiopia 27

J
Jaggard, Isaac 106, 109, 114
Jaggard, William 109, 114
Japan
and Buddhism 29, 36, 119, 125
calligraphy 122, 125, *125*, 126, *126*
and Chinese culture, influence of 119–22
collaborative albums 199, 122, 125, 126–29
literature *see* Murasaki, *Tale of Genji, The*
orihon format 122
orijō (folding album) format *119*, 122–25
women writers 119–22
yoriaigaki 119
Jennett, Seán, *Making of Books, The* 116
Jerome, St 40
Jokei, Sumiyoshi *see* Sumiyoshi Jokie
Jones, Owen 168–71
Grammar of Ornament, The **168–77**
Plans, Elevations, Sections and Details of the Alhambra 171
Jonson, Ben 109, *109*, 110
Workes (Folio) 106, 109, *109*, 114
Judaism 51
Hebrew manuscripts 40, **51–57**
Passover 52–55, 56, *57*

K
Kamenskii, Vasilii
Sadok Sudei (*Trap for Judges*) 216–19, *216*, *220*, 221
Tango with Cows 221–24, *221*
Keller, Friedrich Gottlob 39
Kelmscott Press **205–12**
Khlebnikov, Velimir 216, 219, 224
Sadok Sudei (*Trap for Judges*) 216–19, *216*, *220*, 221
Slap in the Face of Public Taste, A 219–21, *219*
Khvajah Jan *101*, 105
Ki no Tsurayuki, *Tosa Diary, The* 122
Kindle (Amazon) 250
King's Concordance, the (Little Gidding community) **70–71**
Kipling, Rudyard *240*, 243
Korea
Buddhism 29, 36
early printing (movable type) 74
Korpanyuk, Mariya 258
Kruchenykh, Aleksei 219, 224
Slap in the Face of Public Taste, A 219–21, *219*

L
lacquer
use in palm leaf books 184, *184*, 187–88, *188*
manuscript bindings/covers *102*, 105, *105*, *182*, 187, 188
Landon, Letitia Elizabeth (L.E.L.) 157, *157*
Lane, Allen 236, 237
Lane, John 202
Lanston Monotype Corporation *215*
Larsen, Reif, *Entrances & Exits* 254–56, *257*
Lascaris, Constantinus, *Erotemata* 87, *87*
Latin Psalters 56, 60, 65, 77
Mainz Psalter, the 38, **74–81**
Queen Mary Psalter, the *11*, **60–69**
legibility
and text/type design 15, 20, 23, 81, 87
and typefaces 15
see also readability; reading, experience of
Leighton, William, *Teares or Lamentacions of a Sorrowfull Soule, The* *132*, *135*, **138–41**
letterpress printing 93, 130, 131, *131*, 168, 243, 244
'Library Cave' *see* Mogao Caves (Caves of the Thousand Buddhas), Dunhuang
Lindisfarne Gospels 12, **16–23**, 38
Linotype 214, *215*, 228
lithography *12*, 224, *224*
offset 157, *157*, 231
see also chromolithography
Lizars, William 192, 195
Ljutjuk, Anatoli 258
Lombard capitals 78
Longman (publisher): *Lallah Rookh* (Moore) 174–77, *177*
Ludwig III, count of Arnstein 40
Lunandus 40, 42, 45
luxury books 109–10, 151, 171, 174–77, 192–99, 211–12
medieval codices 42, 55
see also production costs; Latin Psalters

M
MacGillivray, William 199
Magdala collection, the (British Library) 27
Mainz Psalter, the 38, **74–81**
manuscripts
bindings of 12, 19, 27, *102*, 105, *105*
Christian 17–23, 27

Hebrew 40, **51–57**
Islamic 38, 51, 155, *155*, **158–67**
monastic production of 11, *12*, 16–20, 27, 40, 46, 77, 111, 232; *see also* Arnstein Bible, the; Lindisfarne Gospels
Mughal **97–105**
storage/protection of 12, *158*, *161*, 167, 180, 187, *187*, 188, *188*
see also illustrations, manuscript; scribes; scripts, decorative (medieval); *and under individual entries*
Manutius, Aldus **85–93**
Hypnerotomachia Poliphili 85, 90–93, *93*
Mardersteig, Hans ('Giovanni') 94–95
Marinetti, Filippo Tommaso 228
Manifeste technique de la literature futuriste 221
Marler, Anthony 48
Marshall Cavendish 232
Marshall, John 151, *151*, *152*
Masorah (Hebrew script/writing system) 52
mass production 117, 205, 216, 221; *see also* movable type
Matiushin, Vladimir 216, 219
Matthews, Harry B. 178, *178*
Mayakovski, Vladimir 216, 221
Slap in the Face of Public Taste, A 219–21, *219*
McKenzie-Kerr, Ian 231
McLean, Ruari, *About Britain* (series) 231
McLeod, Tara 191
Merrymount Press, The 212
Mesoamerica *see Codex Espangliensis*
mezzotint process 145
micrography 51
Million Pagoda Dharani *35*, 36
Milton, John, 'Thou God of might' (Leighton's *Teares*) *135*, 140
miniature books 12, 148–51, *151*, **155–57**; *see also* 'portable books'
Mite, The 157, *157*
mobile devices 250–53, *250*, *253*, *254*, *257*
Modern Classics (Virago Press) 248, 249, *249*
Moderne, Jacques, *Le paragon des chansons* 135
Mogao Caves (Caves of the Thousand Buddhas), Dunhuang 29, 32, 33, 35, 36
monasteries, Buddhist 183
monasteries, medieval: and manuscript illustration *12*, 16–20, 27, 40, 46, 77, 111, 232; *see also* Arnstein Bible, the; Lindisfarne Gospels
Moore, Thomas, *Lallah Rookh* 174–77, *177*
Morris, William 117, 177, *209*, 214, 216
and Kelmscott Press **205–12**
News from Nowhere 206, 209
Works of Geoffrey Chaucer 205, *205*, **206–12**
Morse, Alice Cordelia 178, *178*
movable type 15, 93, 157, 214
Chinese (9th c.) 29, 37, 74
German innovations in (Mainz, 15th c.) 49, 74, 78, 81, 157
Korean (13th c.) 74
metal blocks/type 74, 78, 109, 110
see also letterpress printing; typography
Moving Parts Press 130, 131
Murasaki Shikibu (Lady Murasaki), *Tale of Genji, The* **119–29**
Murdoch, Rupert 232, 234
Murray, John, *Account of the Phormium Tenax or New Zealand Flax, The* 191
music notation
manuscript 74, 81, *81*, 132
printed **132–41**, 168
Myanmar (previously Burma): Buddhist manuscripts 187, *187*, *188*

N
New Hart's Rules see Hart's Rules
New Zealand *see* Aotearoa New Zealand
News International 234
newspapers, advertisements in 168, 174, 177
Nijō Yasumichi *125*, 126, 129
Nisbet (publisher)
Book of Job, The 174, *174*
Nizami 97–98, *97*
Khamsah **97–105**
North America
influence of William Morris on printers in 212
19th c. book binding designs in 178, *178*
see also Audubon, John James, *Birds of America, The*

O
Oceania: book design *see* Aotearoa New Zealand; Australia
octavo (print format) 12, 90, 109
Aldine *libri portatiles* 38, 85, 87–90, *87*, 93, 117
Audubon's *Birds of America, The* 199
Old King Cole 157, *157*
orihon 122; *see also orijō*
orijō 119, 122–25, *119*, *122*, *125*, *129*
Orion 249
ornamentation/decorative devices
gilding, use of 45–46, 78, 102
letter forms/typography *16*, 19, *19*, 20, 23, 42–46, *42*, 51, 65, 77–78, *78*, 81, *168*, 224
marginal/borders 15, 69, 158–67, 167, *167*, 206–9, *206*, 211, *211*
in printed books 113, *113*, *114*, 206–9, *206*, *209*, 206–12
see also illustrations, manuscript
outsized books 12, 48–49, *49*, 117, 192, 196–98; *see also* Arnstein Bible
Ovenden, Holly 249
Owen, Ursula 248

P
pagination 87, 93, 113, 254
Pali language 180, 182, 184, *184*
palm leaf books **180–88**
paper 12, **38–39**
amate 130
and appliqué *158*, 167
artistic use of 240, *240*, 243
book covers 151, *151*, 178, *178*, 191
coloured 38, 243
e-paper 250
and early printing, use in 77, 90, 106–9, 114
handmade *12*, 38, 39, 125, 209, 258
harakeke (New Zealand flax) 191, *191*
scrolls 32–35, *32*
watermarks 38
see also collage; flap books; *orijo*; palm leaf books; production costs: paper; wallpaper, books printed on
paperbacks **236–37**
papermaking *12*, 33, **38–39**
paratexts 87, **116–17**; *see also* illustrations; ornamentation/decorative devices
parchment 12, 19, 27, 38, 52, 191
partbooks 132, 141
parts, books issued in 171, 174, 198; *see also* subscription publishing
Payne, John, *Flora: flowers fruicts beastes birds and flies exactly drawne* 71, *71*
Pear Tree Press, The 191, *191*
Peignot (typeface) 214
Pelican (Penguin brand) 236, *237*
Penguin 232, 234, **236–37**, 248
Pepys, Samuel 12, 71
Pergamon Press 248
personalisation
in bindings 12–15, 109, 192, 220
in digital books 250–54, 256–57
Phaidon 231, 234
Century 228, 233–34, *234*
Phalèse, Pierre, the Elder, *Hortus musarum* 135
photocomposition process 214–15, 231, 232
phototypesetting 214–15, 228
plays **106–114**
Poetics of Endangered Species, The (UKK) 258, *258*
poetry 109, 110, 138, 157, *157*, 174,

239, 240
'concrete' 221, 224, 240, 254
Japanese **119–29**
performance 131
Persian **97–105**
Russian Futurist 219, 221–24, *221*
see also artists' books; cartoneras
pop-up books 12, 143
Pope, Jessie, *London Characters* 157, *157*
'portable books'
Aldine octavos 38, 85, 87–90, *87*, 93, 117
Penguin paperbacks **236–37**, 248
see also mobile devices
portraits
of authors (printed books) 106, *106*, 109, *109*, 110, 117
Evangelist (manuscript) 20–22, *20*, *40*, 42–45, *45*
of patrons (Persian/Mughal manuscripts) 105, *105*
prefaces 86, 90, 116, 171
prelims 116; *see also* contents pages; frontispieces; prefaces; title pages
presentation copies 70, *132*, 140–41
Print On Demand (POD) 256
printing
colour 74, 77–81, *78*, 145, *145*, 151–52, *152*, 231, *231*, 232–33; *see also* chromolithography
early development of 35–37, 86–87, 116, 117, 214
hand-press 12, *12*, 116, 205–6, 212
handwritten/calligraphic additions to 77, 78–81, *81*, 151, 167
palm leaf books 180
see also formats (print); letterpress printing; movable type; printing presses; woodblock printing
printing presses 12, 15, 74, 90, 109, 110, 180, 205, 214; *see also* chromolithography; movable type
production costs
and use of colour 151, 171, 231
and illustrations 114, 151–52, 171, 174, 194, 199, 231
manuscripts 19
paper 114, 202, 205, 212, 228
scrolls 52
see also luxury books
Psalms, book of 56, 60, 64, 65–69, 74
translations of 40–42, *42*
see also Latin Psalters
publishing
industry development 116, 117, 228–34
and mass production techniques 117, 205
Puffin (Penguin brand) 236
Pullinger, Kate, *Breathe* *250*, 253, 256
punctuation 15, 23, 87
per cola et commata 19, 20
Pushkin 249

Q
quarto (print format) 12, 106–9, 110, 209
'Queen Mary Master', the 60
Queen Mary Psalter, the *11*, **60–69**
Qur'an, the
from Aceh 38, **158–67**
miniature 155, *155*

R
Rainbird, George, *About Britain* (series) 231
readability 15, 16, 20, 87; *see also* content, organization of; legibility; reading, experience of
reading, experience of 12, 16, 81, 258
aloud 32, 40, 55, 81, 97
interactivity of 250–57
non-linear 250, 253–54
Renner, Paul 214
Revelation of St John, The (Ethiopian manuscript) *27*
Rice, Felicia, *Codex Espangliensis* **130–31**
rights, publishing 110, 114; *see also* copyright law (British)
Riverside Press 212
Riviere, Sam, *Truth About Cats & Dogs, The* 254, *254*, 256
Rogers, Bruce 212
rosettes (Mughal decorative devices) *see shamsah*
Rossetti, Christina 243, 244, *244*
Routledge (publisher) 152
Lallah Rookh (Moore) 174–77, *177*
Rozanova, Olga 224
rubrics 15, 42, 46
running titles/headings 15, 113
Russia: Futurist books **216–24**

S
Sabon (typeface) 214
Sadok Sudei (*Trap for Judges*) 216–19, *216*, *220*, 221
Savoy, The **202–3**
Schöffer, Peter 74–77, 81
scribes (manuscript) *12*, 15, 16, 19, 27, 183, 184
scriptoria 27, 111
scripts, decorative (medieval)
Hebrew 51–52, *52*, 56
Insular 20, 22
Insular half-uncial *19*, 20
uncial 19, 20
zoomorphic 51–52, *52*, 56
see also calligraphy; capital letters, large; micrography; rubrics
scrolls
Chinese 29–37, *29*, *33*, *35*, 38
Hebrew Bible 52
palm leaf (South Asia) 184
Selby, Prideaux John, *Illustrations of British Ornithology* 198
series, books issued in 87; *see also* subscription publishing
Shakespeare, William
First Folio **106–114**
portrait of 106, *106*, *109*, 110
Shakyamuni Buddha (China/Japan/Korea) 29, *29*, 32, 36, 37
shamsah *101*, 102
Sharif, Muhammad 101
Shelley, Percy Bysshe 244, *246*
Shepherd's Historical Atlas 232
Siddhattha, Prince (later Gotama Buddha) 182
Sidonia the Sorceress (Kelmscott Press) 206
Siebold collection, the (British Library) 129
Slap in the Face of Public Taste, A (Burliuk, D., Kruchenykh, Mayakovski, Khlebnikov) 219–21, *219*
smartphones 250–53, *250*, *253*, *254*, 256, *257*
Smethwick, John 109
Smithers, Leonard **202–3**
South America *see* cartoneras
Spain
and the Americas 130–31
and antisemitism 57
haggadot 55, *55*, 56–57
Spicer, Harriet 248
Sri Lanka: palm leaf books 180, 184, *187*
Stansby, William 140
Stein collection, the (British Library) 36
Stein, Marc Aurel 29, 32, 36
Stoppard, Miriam, *Complete Child and Babycare* 232
Subhūti *29*, 36, 37
subscription publishing 196, 211
Sumatra *see* Aceh culture
Sumiyoshi Jokei (Tosa Hiromichi) 125, *125*, *126*
sutras 35
Gem Hip Sutras *33*
Perfection of Wisdom 29–32
see also Diamond Sutra

T
tablebooks **132–41**
tablets 250–53
Tallone, Alberto and Enrico 95
Taschen 231
Te li le 224, *224*
Tewodros II, King of Ethiopia 27
textura quadrata (type style) 78, 81
Thailand: Buddhist manuscript production in 180, *180*, 182–83, *182*, *188*
Thames & Hudson 231–32, 234
Thoughts of Marcus Aurelius, The 178, *178*

Times Atlas of World History, The *231*, 232–33
Times New Roman (typeface) 214
title pages *55*, 57, 77, *90*, 94, *113*, 116, 117
illustrated/decorative 48, *49*, 109, *109*, 110, 117, 138–40, *138*, 147, *147*
Tommy Thumb's Pretty Song Book 151
tooling
blind (bindings) 27
gold *51*, 55, *57*, *122*, 125, 141, 178, *209*
Torah, the 52–55
Torresani, Andrea 86
Tosa School of painting 125, 129
Town and Country 178, *178*
Trotter, Alan, *All This Rotting* 254, *254*
'Troy' (typeface) 206
Tschichold, Jan 214, 228, 236–37
'Tuscan' linguistic model 90
typefaces 15
digital 215, 231, 254
and early printing 15, 74, 78, *78*, 85, 94–95, *95*, 113
gothic 77, *77*, 78, 81, 206
italic 87, 113, *113*
roman 87, 93, 113, *113*, 206
20th c. 15, **214–15**
see also typography
typography 94
artistic treatments of 239, 243–44, *243*, *244*
and Arts and Crafts movement 205, 212
and commercial identity 15, 228, 236–37, *237*
and Futurism 221, 224, 228
and legibility 15, 81, 94
20th/21st c. 214–15, 228, 231, 236–37, *237*
see also movable type

U
Uglow, Tea
Universe Explodes, A 254, *254*, 256, 257
We Kiss the Screens 256–57, *257*
Ukrainian Cultural Centre (UKK) 258, *258*
Ultimate La Tène 19, 23
Univers (typeface) 215
Updike, Daniel Berkeley 212

V
Vajra (Buddhist deities) 32, *35*, 37
vellum
as a binding 109, *132*, 141
printing on 48, 49, 74, 77, 202, 211
versals *see* capital letters, large
Vesalius, Andreas 143
Vessantara Jataka ('Birth Tale') (South-east Asia) 180–83, *180*, *182*, *184*
Vintage Books 248
Virago Press 248, 249, *249*
volumes, books published in 87–88, **106–114**
Vulgate Bible 40

W
Walker, Emery 206, 212
wallpaper, books printed on 216–19, *216*, *220*, 221, *221*
Walsh, Joanna, *Seed* 253–54, *253*, 256
Wang Jie 32, 35
watermarks 38
Weißenburg Abbey, Alsace 77
Well at World's End, The (Kelmscott Press) 209, *209*
West, Rebecca, *Judge, The* *249*
Whittingham, Charles 205
Wilde, Oscar 202
Wilfrid of Ripon, St 19
Witkowski, Gustave Joseph, *Anatomie iconoclastique* *15*, *143*, 145
women in publishing **248–49**
Women's Press, The 248, 249, *249*
woodblock printing 29, 35–37, *36*, 138–40, 141
and colour 151
wrappers (protective) 12, 33, *158*, *161*, 167, 180, 188, *188*

X
xylography *see* woodblock printing

Y
Yellow Book, The 202
yoriaigaki 119
Young, Edward 236

Z
zaum 224

CREDITS

All the contributors express their thanks to John Lee, P. J. M. Marks, Stephen Parkin, Alison Moss, Sally Nicholls, Jonathan Vines and Chris Westhorp. In addition: Kathleen Doyle would like to thank Scot McKendrick and Claire Breay for reviewing drafts of The Arnstein Bible and The Queen Mary Psalter; Adrian S. Edwards would like to acknowledge the assistance provided by Ewan Clayton, calligrapher and Professor of Design at the University of Sunderland, for the chapter on the Mainz Psalter of 1457; Chris Scobie would like to thank Rupert Ridgewell for his help and advice on William Leighton's *The Teares or Lamentacions of a Sorrowfull Soule*; Lucy Rowland would like to thank Impediment Press and The Pear Tree Press for generously providing information about their creative processes for A Material Identity in Oceania Book Design; Felicity Myrone would like to thank Andrea Hart and Alex Bond at the Natural History Museum, Francesca Hillier at the British Museum, and Hannah Graves at the British Library for the chapter on Aububon's *The Birds of America*; Giulia Carla Rossi would like to thank Google Creative Lab (Sydney), Editions At Play and especially Anna Gerber for their support and their help sourcing the images for her chapter; Katie McElvanney would like to thank the Ukranian Cultural Centre (ukk.ee) for allowing us to feature their work in Book Design as an Agent of Conservation.

QR CODES

The following principal volumes from the chapters of the book are fully digitised and can be viewed by scanning the codes below. A few of the links will take you direct to the pages. If the link takes you to a Digitised Manuscripts page, please scroll down and click on 'View: bindings'. If the link takes you to Catalogue of Illuminated Manuscripts, scroll down to the images at the bottom of the screen.

Other manuscripts and books featured in the current volume are available online in full at
bl.uk/manuscripts
explore.bl.uk

Selected images for manuscripts can be found at
bl.uk/catalogues/illuminatedmanuscripts/welcome.htm

The Lindisfarne Gospels
(Cotton MS Nero D IV)

The Arnstein Bible
(Harley 2798 (Vol. 1))

The Arnstein Bible
(Harley 2799 (Vol. 2))

The Golden Haggadah
(Add MS 27210)

The Queen Mary Psalter
(Royal MS 2 B. vii)

Akbar's *Khamsah* of Nizami
(Or 12208)

The Shakespeare First Folio of 1623
(C.39.k.15)

Excerpts from The Tale of Genji
(Or 1287)

A Description of Three Hundred Animals
(976.c.14)

A Qur'an from Aceh
(Or 16915)

Owen Jones's *The Grammar of Ornament*
(RB.31.c.200)
Note that the digitised copy is for the Bernard Quaritch edition of 1868

The Buddha's Last Birth Tale
(Or 1245)

The Buddha's Last Birth Tale
(Or 1245b)